D0871753

AMERICAN PROPERTY

AMERICAN PROPERTY

A History of How, Why, and What We Own

———◆——

STUART BANNER

HARVARD UNIVERSITY PRESS
Cambridge, Massachusetts
London, England
2011

Library of Congress Cataloging-in-Publication Data

Banner, Stuart, 1963–
American property : a history of how, why, and what we own / Stuart Banner.
p. cm.
Includes bibliographical references and index.
ISBN 978-0-674-05805-7 (alk. paper)
1. Property—United States—History.
2. Right of property—United States–History.   I. Title.
KF562.B36 2011
330.1'7—dc22   2010039752

Contents

AMERICAN PROPERTY

Introduction

WHEN Richard Newman died in Los Angeles in 1997, his body was taken to the county coroner's office for a routine autopsy. Two years later, Newman's father learned that during the autopsy the coroner had removed his son's corneas without asking the family's permission. At the time, this was the office's normal practice. It was the product of both high and low motives. There was a desperate shortage of corneas for transplant, and corneas must be transplanted very soon after death, often too soon to obtain the consent of the next of kin. On the other hand, this same shortage made corneas a valuable commodity, and the coroner's office earned $250 per pair by selling them to an eye bank. Newman's father sued the coroner's office for damages. The basis for the suit was that the coroner had violated the constitutional rights of Newman and his father by depriving them of property without due process of law. But were Newman's corneas a kind of property? And if they were, who was their owner once Richard Newman was dead?[1]

Many American Indian tribes are unhappy with the way aspects of their culture have been used by others, from the commercialization of traditional art forms and medicines to the use of stereotyped figures as the mascots of sports teams. These grievances are increasingly taking the form of property claims, arguments that the heritage of indigenous groups is something that belongs solely to them. Can something as amorphous as culture or heritage be a kind of property? If it can, who owns it?[2]

New technologies allow consumers to copy music and video and do all sorts of things they could never have done before. They can give copies to friends or to millions of strangers, they can listen or watch at times and places different from the ones the producers intend, and they can even use a copy as the raw material for creative works of their own. When do such activities infringe the property rights of others? How far does the ownership of a song or a film extend?[3]

These current controversies, and many others one could add, all raise a basic question: what is property? To decide whether a dead man's cornea or an indigenous culture or a digital representation of a song is a kind of property, one has to develop, at least implicitly, some idea of what property means and some method of distinguishing what should count as property from what should not. To do that, in turn, requires some thought (again, at least implicitly) about the nature of property itself. How does it originate? What purposes does it serve? What are its outer limits?

This book is about the ways in which the answers to questions like these have changed over time. Property is, of course, an institution at the root of our political and economic life. The Constitution is just one of the many sources of law that protect the rights of property, and a market economy could scarcely exist without some kind of property. "There is nothing which so generally strikes the imagination, and engages the affections of mankind, as the right of property," the English judge William Blackstone wrote in the mid-eighteenth century, and his words are just as true today.[4] But the concept of property Blackstone and his contemporaries had in mind was in many respects very different from the one we hold today. We still rely heavily on the idea of property, but it is an idea whose content has constantly been changing.

One approach to understanding these changes is to look closely at the historical emergence of new forms of property in response to technological and cultural change. Several of the chapters in this book are about such episodes; they examine, for example, the development of property in news in the late nineteenth and early twentieth centuries, the emergence of property in fame in the early twentieth century, and the rise of property in sound, also in the early twentieth century. As with today's controversies over property rights in body parts and living organisms, these earlier battles were occasions for the elaboration of ideas about the nature of property more generally.

Another approach is to scrutinize changing ideas about the limits of appropriate government regulation of property. When, and how, may the government interfere with the use of property? When does the use of public power unconstitutionally infringe the rights of property owners? As with the issue of what should count as property, one cannot form an opinion about the proper limits of the regulation of property without having, at least implicitly, some conception of the nature of property itself. What exactly *is* property? Is it a natural right or one created by law? Which of its attributes are essential and which are subject to alteration to advance some public goal? Some of the chapters in this book thus examine the rise of new kinds of regulation and the development of new ideas about the Constitution's protection of property rights.

The basic message of the book is that our ideas about property have always been contested and have always been in flux. Property is a human institution that exists to serve a broad set of purposes. These purposes have changed over time, and as they have, so too has the conventional wisdom about what property is really like. As new coalitions have formed around particular goals, they have pushed conventional understandings of property in one direction or another.

In focusing on our changing ideas about the nature of property, this book will have little to say about several topics that might loom larger in a history of property with a different emphasis. It does not address the acquisition of land from American Indians and the disposition of the public domain to settlers, or the methods by which property has been conveyed from one generation to the next, or the surveying of land and the recording of title, or mortgages, or the expansion over time of the property rights of women and African-Americans, or, no doubt, many other equally important subjects.[5] The omission of such topics is not meant to imply their insignificance. The full history of property is so broad that it cannot be encompassed in a single book. There is plenty of room for more.

1

Lost Property

IT HAD been "a complete revolution," one lawyer recalled in 1829, a transformation producing "a substantial improvement" in the lives of Americans. "What abundant reason have we to be satisfied with our condition," another exclaimed the following year, now that Americans had been "disencumbered from most of the burthensome and intricate legal regulations" that had fettered them in the past.[1] This was the language of July 4 speeches in the early republic, but these lawyers were not celebrating the Declaration of Independence or the successful outcome of the war. They were talking about the law of property.

American lawyers marveled at how quickly so many of the old rules had been cast aside. In Virginia, reported St. George Tucker, there had been "almost total change in the system of laws relative to property." William Blackstone's four-volume *Commentaries*, first published in the 1760s, had become the standard legal reference on both sides of the Atlantic, but forty years later the portions of the *Commentaries* about property were already out of date in the United States. "That celebrated work could only be safely relied on," Tucker counseled, "in apprizing the student of what the *law had been;* to know *what it now is,* he must resort to very different sources of information."[2] Entire categories of property familiar to English lawyers had ceased to exist in the United States. American judges and legislators were constantly replacing ancient doctrines with new ones. Few areas of the law, if any, were changing more rapidly than property.

Into Oblivion

The most basic change concerned the nature of land ownership itself. "The grand and fundamental maxim" of English real property law, Blackstone had explained, was that "all lands were originally granted out by the sovereign, and are therefore holden, either mediately or immediately, of the crown." In principle, no one in England except the king owned land outright. Land could be held by a variety of tenures, but all of them implied some form of obligation to someone else higher up the ladder. In the United States, by contrast, "the title of our lands is free, clear and absolute," the Connecticut judge Jesse Root declared. "Every proprietor of land is a prince in his own domains." American landowners still obtained their land from the sovereign—the federal or state government—but without any ongoing duties to render service or pay money. English property lawyers were accustomed to parsing the fine distinctions between different sorts of land tenure, but to American lawyers even their names sounded exotic. Words like *escuage, burgage, knight service, frankalmoin*—it was almost like a foreign language. The whole subject of land tenure was purely of historical interest, St. George Tucker remarked, the legal equivalent of "viewing the majestic ruins of Rome or Athens." Generations of English lawyers had learned the different tenures by studying the treatises of authors like Edward Coke and Thomas Littleton, but only the most historically minded of Americans ever would. Those "immense stores of learning," noted the New York judge James Kent, had "become obsolete."[3]

On paper the change had come shortly after independence, but in practice it had come long before. English land tenure was formally transplanted to North America in the colonial charters. It remained a feature of colonial law thereafter, but the enforcement of tenure obligations, uneven right from the start, generally declined over time. In colonial Connecticut, explained the congressman and future judge Zephaniah Swift, land was nominally held in a form of tenure called socage, but few ever had any occasion to notice. In practice, landowners were free of any of the obligations associated with socage. In the 1790s Connecticut passed a statute vesting absolute title in property owners—in effect abolishing socage—but the statute only brought the law into conformance with actual practice. The same was true in most of the other states, which enacted similar statutes shortly after independence, statutes killing on paper what for most landowners had long been dead in everyday life. By the mid-nineteenth century, the old system survived only on the great manors of New York's Hudson River valley, where the resentment of the thousands of people still subject to archaic tenure obligations fueled decades of conflict and sporadic violence.[4]

No one lamented the loss of English land tenure, which was widely understood as a feudal relic unsuitable for the modern world. Swift was grateful Connecticut was not "embarrassed with the slavish principles of the system of feuds." James Sullivan, the attorney general and later the governor of Massachusetts, was relieved that his state's land had been "stripped of the clogs and incumbrances" characterizing land in England. American law still retained some of the vocabulary of the English system of tenures, Timothy Walker pointed out. There were still *tenants,* who might inhabit *tenements,* and Americans still spoke of *landlords,* even when there was nothing especially lordly about them. But Walker, a law professor in Cincinnati, was adamant that such words had lost their original meanings. One who studies the history of property, he instructed his students, "cannot fail to be thoroughly disgusted with the narrow, arbitrary, and mystifying spirit which dictated all the early doctrines; nor to be equally gratified with the bold, liberal and determined spirit which has since been manifested, to substitute new ones in their place." With the abandonment of English land tenure, Walker had "no doubt that the law of realty in Ohio, could be written in one-third of the space which would be required for the law of realty in England."[5] The old conceptual structure of land ownership had vanished.

Many of the forms of intangible property familiar to English lawyers had vanished as well, and many more were in the process of disappearing. These were what English lawyers called *incorporeal hereditaments*—nonphysical things connected, sometimes tenuously, with interests in land. "In England they make a very important part of real property," Timothy Walker told his students, but in the United States they scarcely existed, "and we are thus relieved from a great variety of perplexing questions." Blackstone had devoted an entire chapter to the incorporeal hereditaments, so aspiring American lawyers continued to read about them for decades, but, as one lawyer admitted in the early 1840s, "this subject is rather one of curiosity than practical utility."[6] An entire category of property was almost gone.

Some of these forms of intangible property had never caught on in the colonies. An *advowson* was the right to appoint a minister to a church. In England wealthy individuals owned advowsons and could pass them to others upon death, just like any other kind of property. A colonist from England might bring an advowson with him: Isaac Johnson, the richest of the early settlers of Boston, died with a large estate including substantial landholdings and an advowson attached to a church back in England. In his will he left the advowson to two fellow settlers. American churches, however, tended to be built and managed by congregations rather than individuals, so there was little occasion for individuals to have the power to select ministers. There was an advowson for Trinity Church in New York, for example, but it was not owned by any person; rather, it was vested in the church as a corporate body. By the early nineteenth century, neither St. George Tucker nor James Kent, perhaps the most learned lawyers in Virginia and New York respectively, could remember any instances of advowsons in their states.[7]

Differences in the financing of English and American churches caused other forms of intangible property to disappear as well. In England, the clergy had an inheritable property right in *tithes*, or one-tenth of the annual produce of the land within the parish. There had never been any such thing in Virginia, Tucker assured his readers. "The most litigious cases in the Exchequer Reports, are those relating to tithes," Kent observed; "and it is a great relief to the labours of the student, and a greater one to duties of the courts, and infinitely more so to the agricultural interests of the country, that the doctrine of tithes is unknown to our law." Some states still had established churches in the early republic, but even those states lacked tithes, and once they disestablished their churches there would never be any occasion for instituting them. "Here there are no benefices," declared Thomas Duncan of the Pennsylvania Supreme Court, "no church establishments of the state, no tithes." Nor were there any *corodies*. A corody was the right to receive food or money from a religious institution. Under English law corodies were yet another familiar form of nonphysical property, but, as an early American legal treatise put it, "the subject may be considered as entirely obsolete with us."[8]

If American lawyers were dismissive of the intangible property unique to the English church, they could grow positively indignant about *dignities,* a kind of property rooted in England's social structure. A dignity, a property right in a noble title, "is of great importance in the English law," Kent explained, "though unknown to us." In a nation without titles of nobility, insisted Tucker, there could be no dignities, because no one could inherit special privileges. Thomas Bartley, chief justice of the Ohio Supreme Court, was even more emphatic. "The theory and foundation of the British government is essentially different from ours," he argued. "The sovereignty there, is said to be in the King instead of the people." The king, "as the original *source* or *proprietor* of honor," could grant "titles of nobility in such manner as to create vested rights of property in them. This, however, is upon the principle, that government is instituted for the benefit of the RULERS rather than the GOVERNED."[9]

Advowsons, tithes, corodies, dignities—these were forms of intangible property that never took root in the United States. There were others that were in the process of disappearing in the early republic, forms of intangible property that *had* been transplanted during the colonial period but began to fade away with independence.

In England, public office was a kind of property. There was a long tradition, in England as in much of Europe, of acquiring office by purchase. Sometimes the buyer just got the right to exercise the office (and collect the fees that went along with it) for a term of years, Blackstone explained, but sometimes he got that right for life, and sometimes he got it in perpetuity, so he could pass it along to an heir. Blackstone noted that statutes and court decisions had curtailed some of the powers of the owner of an office. Certain offices couldn't be sold to others, for example, and some offices weren't allowed to be granted for periods exceeding the life of the holder. It was nevertheless clear that English law counted offices as incorporeal hereditaments, intangible property that for most purposes was treated just like any other kind of property.[10]

Offices in the United States could not be acquired by purchase. But did American officeholders have a property right in their offices? Some distinguished American lawyers believed they did. "Let it not be said that an office is a mere trust for public benefit, and excludes the idea of a property or a vested interest in the individual," cautioned Alexander Hamilton. "Every office combines the two ingredients." Treating an office as property, even property that could be owned in perpetuity, provided the right incentives, in Hamilton's view. "The idea of a vested interest holden even by a permanent tenure," he reasoned, "so far from being incompatible with the principle that the primary and essential end of every office is the public good, may be conducive to that very end by promoting a diligent, faithful, energetic, and independent execution of the office."[11] Hamilton, writing in early 1802, was criticizing the recent repeal of the Judiciary Act of 1801. The Judiciary Act had created new federal judgeships; its repeal abolished those judgeships, thus taking offices away from their holders. The judgeships were a form of property, Hamilton argued, and so the repeal amounted to an unconstitutional taking of property.

Hamilton had a political motive for classifying public office as a kind of property, because the judges deprived of office in 1802 were his political allies. But the issue also arose in many contexts less influenced by partisan politics, where it could be considered on its own merits. The most thorough statement of the pro-property position was authored by Thomas Ruffin, the long-serving chief justice of the North Carolina Supreme Court, in an opinion resolving a dispute between two men who both claimed to be the rightful clerk of the same county court. Lawson Henderson had been appointed as clerk in 1807, when North Carolina clerks had life tenure. In 1832 a new law made the position elective rather than appointive, and John Hoke won the election. But had the 1832 law deprived Henderson of property? The answer turned on whether a public office was a kind of property. Property was "whatever a person can possess and enjoy by right," Ruffin reasoned, and on that definition, an office was property. That didn't necessarily mean people could do with offices whatever they did with other sorts of property, he cautioned. One couldn't sell an office, or let it lie idle, the way one could with land. "But with these limitations," Ruffin concluded, "a public office is the subject of property, as every other thing corporeal or incorporeal, from which men can earn a livelihood and make gain." A man's office was his property "as much as the land which he tills, or the horse he rides or the debt which is owing to him." Lawson Henderson's position as clerk was his property, and the law that took it away from him was therefore invalid.[12]

By the 1830s, however, many lawyers found incongruous the notion that a public office could be a form of private property. "In a republic," the senator (and future Supreme Court justice) Levi Woodbury insisted, "office-holders have no property in their offices." Indeed, "liability to removal tends to increase industry and fidelity." In his *Commentaries,*

James Kent acknowledged that in England offices were a type of property, but he explained that the American practice was different, because "it would not be consistent with our manners and usages, to grant a private trust" in a public office. "*Property* in an office," agreed Francis Hilliard, "is for the most part inconsistent with republican constitutions and principles." By the 1840s and 1850s, American courts were unanimous in holding that public office was not a type of property.[13] Another kind of property had disappeared.

One very important form of property in rural England was the right of *common*, the right to use land belonging to another for certain defined purposes. Blackstone distinguished four different sorts of common: common of pasture, the right to feed one's animals on another's land; common of piscary, the right to fish in another's water; common of turbary, the right to cut turf on another's land; and common of estovers, the liberty of taking wood from the land of another. The land involved typically belonged to the wealthy, while the possessors of rights of common were often poor farmers who depended on them for subsistence. The steady enclosure of the English countryside meant the gradual disappearance of rights of common, but in the late eighteenth century, rights of common were still a vital part of the English rural economy.[14]

There was much more land per person in North America than in England, so American farmers had much less need of rights of common. St. George Tucker had never heard of any examples in Virginia. The right "does not exist in Virginia," he concluded, and "if it does, it can only be in a few cases." In Pennsylvania, remarked William Tilghman, the state's chief justice, "I know of very few instances of rights of common." "All these rights of common were originally intended for the benefit of agriculture, and for the support of the families and cattle of the cultivators of the soil," summarized one New York judge. "There is much learning in the books relative to the creation, apportionment, suspension and extinguishment of these rights, which fortunately in this country we have but little occasion to explain."[15] In the United States, rights of common were uncommon.

They did exist, particularly in the manors of New York, where grants of common from the colonial period lingered on and gave rise to litigation throughout the early nineteenth century. Occasional cases raising issues of common popped up in older towns in other northern states as well, like Marshfield, Massachusetts, where a 1645 grant had included rights of pasture that were still being argued over in 1830. By then they were curiosities, of interest to historically minded lawyers precisely because of their rarity. "The change of manners and property, and the condition of society in this country, is so great," James Kent observed, "that the whole of this law of commonage is descending fast into oblivion, together with the memory of all the talent and learning which were bestowed upon it by the ancient lawyers." Related property rights lasted longer. Americans still had land they called "commons," often in the form of public squares in the center of towns, and many commons in this sense of the word still exist today. In the South, for much of the nineteenth century, the owners of animals had the right to pasture them on unfenced land owned by others, an echo of the old common of pasture.[16] But the right of common in Blackstone's and Kent's sense all but disappeared before the Civil War.

Meanwhile another kind of property was vanishing as well. In the eighteenth century, the labor of other people was understood as a kind of property. This was most obviously true of slavery and indentured servitude, both of which existed all over North America, but it was also true of labor in general. Blackstone referred to "the property that every man has in the service of his domestics; acquired by the contract of hiring, and purchased by giving them wages," and the idea was equally accepted on both sides of the Atlantic. Slavery and indentured servitude were thus less different from other forms of labor than they seem today. In legal contemplation, an employer owned his employee's labor just as much as a planter owned the labor of his slave.[17]

The labor of children, by the same token, was understood as the property of their father. "The child hath no property in his father or guardian; as they have in him," Blackstone explained. Fathers often bound their children out to other adults as apprentices in exchange for compensation to the father rather than to the child, transactions that could not have taken place had fathers not owned their children's labor. A father, like an employer, was a property owner.[18]

This whole complex of thought gradually crumbled away in the early republic. The northern states abolished slavery. Changing economic conditions caused indentured servitude to decline into insignificance. Ordinary employment relations were reconceived as voluntary transactions between juridical equals rather than the ownership by one person of another's labor. New ideas about the nature of the family made American lawyers recoil at the classification of children or their labor as property. The Maryland law professor David Hoffman scoffed at the "fancied property given to the parent in his offspring." Kent thought the doctrine "barbarous and unfit for a free and civilized people." The lawyer and historian Edward Deering Mansfield acknowledged that "the services of a minor child belong to the parent. Legally they belong to the father." But he wasn't happy about it. "This is one of the lamest parts of the English and American law," he declared. "It is barbarian."[19]

In the South, slavery of course lasted longer. Defenders of slavery often analogized it to other forms of labor. "The person of the slave is not property," insisted the Mississippi educator E. N. Elliott; "but the right to his labor is property, and may be transferred like any other property, or as the right to the services of a minor or an apprentice may be transferred." Slaves "cannot be owned," agreed Albert Bledsoe of the University of Virginia. The buying and selling of slaves was *merely the transfer of a right to labor,* no different from a father's binding out of his child as an apprentice. Arguments like these might have sounded more persuasive a century earlier, when slavery had been just one end of a continuum of property-based employment relationships. By the mid-nineteenth century, however, slavery appeared more and more anomalous, because it was the only such relationship left. Analogies to other forms of labor seemed absurd. "You can scarcely look into a southern secular newspaper without being met by advertisements for the sale of slaves of almost every age, character, and sex," jeered one abolitionist minister. "Do they propose to sell the 'right of property' in the time and labor of slaves, to the exclusion of or apart from the *identical persons of the slaves?*" It was clear enough that the slaves themselves were the property, not the slaves' labor.[20] At the conclusion of the Civil War, this last remnant of property rights in other people came to an end.

If an American lawyer had been asked in 1760 for a catalog of all the kinds of property he knew, many of the entries on that list would have ceased to exist a century later. The feudal land tenures had been abolished. All sorts of intangible property, from historical relics like advowsons to once-important rights in offices and commons, had faded into obscurity. Lawyers no longer spoke of children or employees as a form of property. Between the middle of the eighteenth century and the middle of the nineteenth, Americans had lost a great deal of property.

Some historians have argued that property in the eighteenth century was generally understood as dominion over physical things, in contrast to a nineteenth- and twentieth-century conception of property as encompassing intangible rights in assets that themselves often lacked any physical existence.[21] But this picture of the eighteenth century is not quite right.[22] Much of eighteenth-century property consisted of nonphysical assets like labor or offices. Even the possession of land, the most physical thing a person might own, was carved up into bundles of intangible privileges and obligations. When an English lawyer tried to argue in 1762 that property required tangibility—"It should be something that may be seen, felt, given, delivered, lost, or stolen, in order to constitute the subject of property," the lawyer asserted—Lord Mansfield dismissed the claim as absurd. "How would you steal an option, or the next turn of an advowson?" he quipped.[23] Lawyers of the eighteenth century could not have known of the array of intangible property rights the future would bring, but they were not in the grip of any physical conception of property, because they would have been familiar with a different set of intangible property rights. The transition would not be from physical property to nonphysical property, but rather from one group of nonphysical property rights to another.

A Distinct and Independent System

Many important rules of property law changed dramatically as well. When an English landowner died without a will, his land descended to his oldest son rather than being divided equally among his children. This doctrine, called *primogeniture,* originated in an era when land could not be transferred by a will, and when the oldest son was the one most likely to be able to perform feudal obligations of military service. By the eighteenth century neither of those conditions had been true for some time, and primogeniture instead served to keep estates intact from generation to generation. Primogeniture crossed the Atlantic to New York, Rhode Island, and the southern colonies, while the remaining colonies rejected it in favor of a more equal division of land among children. New York and the southern colonies were politically dominated by large landowners who shared the English aristocracy's interest in preserving their estates.[24]

Shortly after independence, all seven states with primogeniture abandoned it. Many writers of the 1780s and 1790s shared Noah

Webster's opinion that "an equal distribution of landed property, is a singular advantage, as being the foundation of republican governments and the security of freedom." There seemed something aristocratic— "an old fragment of monarchy," as the minister Peres Fobes put it— about a policy that encouraged some to engross huge estates and others to possess no land at all. "The nature and character of aristocracy shews itself to us in this law," Thomas Paine declared. "It is a law against every law of nature, and nature herself calls for its destruction." The physician Benjamin Rush counted the abolition of primogeniture along with "the universal practice of inoculation for the small-pox, and the absence of the plague" as among the blessings enjoyed by the new nation.[25] There must still have been some support for primogeniture among large landowners, but they could keep their holdings together simply by drafting wills leaving their land to one child rather than all, so there was no need to stick one's neck out for an unpopular cause. By the 1790s primogeniture had disappeared.

Out with primogeniture went the *fee tail* (or *entail*, as it was sometimes called). Land held in fee tail would remain in a family forever, passing down to each new generation of descendants, for as long as the family continued to produce offspring. A substantial amount of land in the colonies was held in fee tail—on one estimate, as much as 78 percent of some counties in Virginia. "Entails," St. George Tucker remembered, "were formerly greatly favoured in Virginia." With independence, however, the fee tail came under sharp criticism on several grounds. Like primogeniture, the fee tail seemed unrepublican and even aristocratic, a form of land tenure conducive to maintaining landed dynasties and skewing the distribution of political power. "In the earlier times," Thomas Jefferson recalled toward the end of his career, "some provident individuals secured large grants; and, desirous of founding great families for themselves, settled them on their descendants in fee tail. The transmission of this property from generation to generation, in the same name, raised up a distinct set of families, who, being privileged by law in the perpetuation of their wealth, were thus formed into a Patrician order." James Sullivan agreed that the fee tail "was much less fitted for our country than for England." The poet and diplomat Joel Barlow predicted, for this reason, that "the simple destruction of these two laws, of *entailment* and *primogeniture*, if you add to it the *freedom of the press*, will ensure the continuance of liberty in any country."[26]

There were also pragmatic reasons to dislike the fee tail. With land assured to remain in the family, many feared, successive generations would become lazy, as their initiative was sapped by a guaranteed estate. The result, Kent lamented, would be "to leave an accumulated mass of property in the hands of the idle and the vicious." Just as bad, land held in fee tail could not be sold, or even alienated at all for a period longer than the life of the current possessor, without first undertaking an expensive legal procedure, because the current owner had no power to curtail the right of his son to take possession after he died. The fee tail was thus a clog on the real estate market. With the abolition of the fee tail, Zephaniah Swift exulted, "we have the pleasure to observe that the transfer of our lands, is not fettered and burdened by the restrictions and incumbrances, with which they are perplexed and embarrassed in England." These two concerns were related. As property escaped the clutches of established families and came onto the real estate market, it would flow to those who could best afford to buy it—the most enterprising and talented of each generation. The result would be an aristocracy of merit rather than one of inherited wealth.[27]

As a result, the fee tail vanished shortly after independence. "*Entailments* are nearly done away in this country," Francis Hilliard explained in his summary of American law. "The *subject itself*, therefore, has become obsolete,—it has been struck out from the jurisprudence of the United States."[28] Existing fee tails were generally converted into fee simple titles (that is, into the ordinary form of land tenure), capable of being transferred to anyone at the pleasure of the owner. It was no longer possible to guarantee that land would remain in the family.

A related change took place soon after. The primary methods by which two or more people could co-own property were called *tenancy in common* and *joint tenancy*. With tenancy in common, each owner could leave his share in a will to whomever he chose. With joint tenancy, the share of the first to die would be divided among his surviving co-owners; if only one survivor remained, he would become the sole owner. English law favored joint tenancy, so that ambiguous cases were resolved in favor of deeming the owners joint tenants. Like primogeniture and entail, this presumption served the goal of keeping landholdings together, by preventing the fractionation of estates unless it was clear that fractionation was what the parties wanted.

In the United States, preserving concentrated land ownership was a much less attractive goal. There was little reason to favor joint tenancy. On the other hand, as Chief Justice William Tilghman of the Pennsylvania Supreme Court observed, "the right of survivorship between joint-tenants is frequently unknown to the parties, and bears hard on the heirs of the one who dies first." American judges accordingly switched the presumption to favor tenancy in common. Where two people "have joined fortunes, to take up or purchase lands, in order to advance their fortunes in life," declared Tilghman's colleague Jasper Yeates, "I should require strong proof to satisfy my mind, that they meditated survivorship in their transactions, and gambled their lives respectively against each other." Tenancy in common, agreed Hugh Henry Brackenridge, a third member of the court, was "more congenial with the spirit of our laws." The Ohio Supreme Court even announced that "estates in joint tenancy do not exist under the laws of Ohio," because joint tenancy "is adverse to the understandings, habits, and feelings of the people." Most states did not go that far; they kept joint tenancy, but only where landowners had made it clear that they wanted it. In ambiguous cases, the courts would presume tenancy in common. By the 1820s, the Philadelphia lawyer Peter du Ponceau listed this presumption along with the abolition of feudal tenures, primogeniture, and the fee tail as the most important improvements in American law.[29]

Meanwhile other property doctrines were changing as well. Under the English and early American doctrine of *ancient lights,* once sunlight had reached a landowner's window for a long enough period (usually said to be twenty years), the landowner's neighbor could no longer construct a building so tall that it would block the sun from reaching the window. "The peace and repose of the community," explained Joseph Angell in his treatise on the subject, "require, that some definite and precise time should be fixed upon, beyond which a person shall not be seriously incommoded in that which he has long and exclusively enjoyed, and which directly appertains to the comfort and convenience of the house he lives in." On this point "the common law is very clear," declared the South Carolina judge John Belton O'Neall. The doctrine was "too well settled to require discussion," as one New York judge put it. Sunlight was a valuable asset at a time long before the invention of electric light. After twenty years of sun, a homeowner had earned the right to expect that he or she would continue to enjoy it. In a contest between the settled expectations of one landowner and the rudeness of another in blocking the sun, the law chose in favor of the former. "It would seem unreasonable, that in those places where land is cheap, and the country thinly settled, a party, after being permitted to build his house and place his windows on the side adjoining the open fields of another man, and especially after so long a possession as to presume a grant for that purpose, should have them obstructed by the erection of a wall or another building," a New Jersey judge reasoned, "when perhaps a little accommodation, by placing the new building a few feet further off, might work no injury to any body." The judge acknowledged that things might be different in a crowded city, "where land is very valuable, and it is the constant practice to place buildings side by side."[30] But the United States was a distinctly nonurban country in the early nineteenth century. In most of it there was plenty of room to build houses that did not block the neighbors' ancient lights.

On the other hand, many lawyers and judges complained, the doctrine deterred real estate development. "The value of vacant lots, and of lots with old and low buildings upon them, would be destroyed," James Kent worried, "if substantial buildings could not be erected on them, lest they obstruct the light and prospect of the side lights of some building on an adjoining lot." The New York judge Greene Bronson thought the doctrine "may do well enough in *England*," but was utterly unsuited for the United States, where new and bigger buildings were going up all the time. Ancient lights "cannot be applied in the growing cities and villages of this country," he concluded, "without working the most mischievous consequences." "It is against the spirit of our people to incumber their lands with privileges in favor of other, though adjoining lands," agreed another New York judge. "They are proverbially distinguished for looking to the future, and as they expect future greatness to their country from the course of years, so they are confident that the future will add to the value of their lands, and create the expediency and necessity of improving them by more extensive buildings."[31]

Arguments like this came to dominate court opinions on the subject. In South Carolina, one judge fretted over "how seriously improvements might be here hindered" if the court were to recognize the doctrine of ancient lights. The Illinois Supreme Court doubted the doctrine's applicability "to a country in the infancy of its improvements, containing hundreds of embryo cities and villages and thousands of vacant lots, waiting the demands of future population." In Texas, reasoned that state's supreme court, the earliest buildings in any new town were usually "low and inferior houses." Allowing such houses a perpetual right to sunlight "might render useless and waste the most valuable lots for business purposes or residences in our growing towns and cities. A doctrine fraught with such consequences cannot be the common law of this country." In the conflict between the stability of existing land uses and the possibility of improvement, stability had once been the winner, but as time went on improvement gained the upper hand. By the middle of the century, when Emory Washburn wrote his treatise on American property law, the doctrine of ancient lights was no longer a part of it. "It seems to be now settled," Washburn concluded, "that the English doctrine does not prevail, being inapplicable to the condition of a rapidly growing and changing country like America."[32] Americans could build ever newer and taller buildings without worrying about their neighbors' light.

The desire not to deter development led to other changes in property law in the early nineteenth century. Under the traditional rule, structures built by tenants were considered part of the land itself. When the tenancy expired and the tenant moved away, the structures remained with the land and became the property of the land's owner. But that soon changed. "I confess, I never could perceive the reason, justice or equity of the old cases, which gave to the landlord such kind of erections as were merely for the use and convenience of the tenant," the New York judge Ambrose Spencer admitted. "The rule anciently was very rigid; but I think it has yielded materially to the more just and liberal notions of modern times." The purpose of the change, explained Justice Joseph Story, was to encourage tenants to build. "The country was a wilderness, and the universal policy was to procure its cultivation and improvement," Story recalled. "Yet, in the comparative poverty of the country, what tenant could afford to erect fixtures of much expense or value, if he was to lose his whole interest therein by the very act of erection?"[33]

Under English law, a tenant could not chop down trees and clear land for farming without his landlord's permission. The trees belonged to the landlord, so a tenant who cut them down would be liable to the landlord for *waste*. In the early United States, where clearing land was perceived as an unalloyed good, this doctrine did not last long. "The situation of our country is so very different, in the point of agriculture, from what they are in Europe, that we hardly know to apply the precedents there to our cases," James Sullivan observed. "With us, the course of husbandry and improvements allows the changing of mowing into tillage, and tillage into mowing; and there can be no charge of Waste for doing it." The Pennsylvania Supreme Court agreed. "It would be an outrage on common sense to suppose, that what would be deemed waste in *England,* could receive that appellation here," the court held. "Lands in general with us are enhanced by being cleared." By the 1820s, the Massachusetts lawyer Nathan Dane could report that the American law of waste had diverged considerably from the English law. "England is an old country where trees are raised even for fuel by planting and industry, almost as much as corn or grain is," he explained. "This is a new country, where, except in some parts, of late years, the great object has been to destroy trees, to clear up the land, and to bring the wilderness or natural forests into cleared lands for cultivation or pasturing."[34] To accommodate that goal, judges had changed the law of waste.

By the middle of the nineteenth century, many of the basic doctrines of American property law looked nothing like they had a few decades before. "We have been gradually departing," one American lawyer remarked in the late 1830s, "from the principles on which the English law of real property is founded." Americans were developing "a distinct and independent system of American" property law.[35]

New Species of Property

There was no mystery about why all these changes were taking place. The kinds of property in existence at any given time, and the rules that would govern that property, were not written in stone. They changed along with the times—indeed, it was the responsibility of legislators and judges to make them change when events warranted. "The immense variety of human affairs, and their incessant fluctuation," reflected one lawyer, would inevitably produce "new species of property, and new rights." Justice Nathan Weston of the Maine Supreme Court expected that "new kinds of property" would "spring into existence, in the progress of society."[36] Americans had little doubt that they were living in an era of rapid social and economic change. It was hardly surprising that property should be changing too.

St. George Tucker, for example, traced many of the changes, including the abolition of primogeniture and entail, and the preference for tenancy in common over joint tenancy, to "a desire to conform to the newly adopted principles of republican government." These were aspects of the law that had made it easier for families to maintain large estates over several generations, but once the political system was premised on widespread land ownership rather than the persistence of aristocratic families, these doctrines were ripe for change. Tucker might have added to his list the demise of assets like advowsons and corodies, and had he written a generation later he might have added property in offices and in the labor of other people, as these were forms of property that to many likewise seemed inconsistent with republican principles. "Why should a young Republic be ruled by laws framed for the particular purpose of a monarchical government"? wondered Benjamin Austin. "We may as well adopt the laws of the Medes and Persians."[37] Lawyers expected that property law would change to suit the new political world.

They also recognized that property would adapt to changing economic conditions. Land in England was scarce and valuable, so the English system of land tenures sliced it up into complex pieces. In the United States land was more plentiful and less expensive. The intricacies of English tenure were not worth the cost of keeping. The old rules and forms of property had originated when land was primarily a marker of class status and a source of military power. These functions had not completely disappeared, but they had weakened considerably. Land had become, to a great extent, just another commodity to be bought and sold. "Lands in this country," remarked the lawyer Henry Dwight Sedgwick, "are nearly as much the subject of traffic, as the public stocks."[38] Many of the old doctrines, from rights of common to ancient lights, slowed that traffic down in order to advance other goals, and these too were ripe for change.

None of these changes happened by themselves, of course. *People* made them happen. In an era when property law was mostly made by judges while deciding cases, judges may have played the biggest role, but much of the work was also done by the lawyers who formulated arguments encouraging judges to make these changes, the clients who stood to benefit from the changes, the legislators who enacted statutes altering the common law, and the various people who expected some gain from these statutes and so urged their legislatures in that direction. In later years the task of pressuring government officials to change the law would often be undertaken by more or less organized interest groups, whose efforts are easy to see. There were some groups like that in the early republic—the antislavery movement is an example—but not nearly as many. There was no centrally organized campaign to abolish feudal land tenures, or to reclassify public office as something other than property, or to abandon the doctrine of ancient lights. Efforts at reform were scattered and sporadic, arising case by case, whenever and wherever someone perceived some benefit from legal change. But when there were enough people in that position, battering enough judges or legislators with arguments for changing the law, the law would eventually change.

These changes were usually accompanied by rhetoric suggesting that they were universally beneficial, that everyone would come out better under a rule that more closely reflected prevailing material and cultural circumstances, but this is quite unlikely to have been true. There were winners from all these changes, and there must have been many losers as well—the landowners no longer entitled to feudal obligations, the officeholders whose jobs were no longer their property, the homeowners stripped of the protection of the doctrine of ancient lights whose windows were now darkened by the taller building next door. Some litigant lost every single court case mentioned in this chapter. The judges and legislators ultimately responsible believed that the overall gains from these changes exceeded the overall losses, but that must have been small consolation to the losers.

Whether the gains actually did exceed the losses is impossible to know for sure. Some were measurable, at least in principle, but many were not. Even if we could figure out how much real estate appreciated in value from the abolition of the fee tail, for example, that would not be a full accounting of the gain, which was as much ideological as economic. Some of the most ardent proponents of abolishing the fee tail, if we believe their public statements, probably derived more utility from the knowledge that an aristocratic remnant of English law had been banished than from any rise in the value of their real estate holdings. How would we place a value on that? On the other side of the ledger, how would we assess the psychological losses suffered by the landowners who could no longer entail their land and so now had to worry that their improvident sons would dissipate the family estate, an estate that was probably worth more out of entail than in? Virtually any legal change had winners and losers, but for many it is impossible to tally it all up.

The one thing we *can* say is that Americans in the early nineteenth century, especially lawyers, expected property to change over time. Old forms of property would cease to exist, new forms would be created, particular rules would come and go—all in response to changing material and intellectual conditions. Some of these changes would not take place very often; the country was unlikely, for example, to switch from republicanism to some other form of government any time in the near future. But some kinds of change could be expected to recur. As the population grew, land would become more valuable. Technological change might yield new kinds of assets or new ways of establishing property rights in familiar commodities. Property was a human institution that could be expected to change along with the changing human environment. Americans had already seen it happen in their own lives.

2

The Rise of Intellectual Property

IN HIS *New and General System of Physic,* published in 1769, the London physician William Smith reported the results of several medical experiments carried out by others, but scarcely any that he performed himself. "We are grieved at his extreme reservedness," one reviewer despaired. "What a niggard this Doctor is of his own, and how profuse he is of other people's intellectual property!"[1]

As this quotation suggests, people were speaking of intellectual property at least as early as the middle of the eighteenth century, but the term had a slightly different meaning. Today it connotes legally enforceable rights in products of the mind, such as patents, copyrights, and trademarks. In the eighteenth century, the phrase meant something closer to the sum of knowledge possessed by a person or a society. Thus the minister John Clayton urged his parishioners to visit one another and talk, so that they might learn from one another, "for intellectual property is improved by circulation." Judith Sargent Murray was an early advocate for the education of women in part because of the permanence of knowledge. "Literary acquisitions cannot, unless the faculties of the mind are deranged, be lost," she argued, "and while the goods of fortune may be whelmed beneath the contingencies of revolving time, intellectual property still remains." This sense of the term lasted into the early nineteenth century. The study of painting, one promoter declared in 1818, would "produce a more general acquaintance with the uses, and a juster conception of the value, of intellectual property." A few years later, a proponent of literary societies encouraged Americans to follow the ancient Greeks, among whom "the works of their greatest writers immediately became the intellectual property of the nation," and a supporter of schools urged "the enlargement and preservation of the intellectual property of the public."[2]

By then, however, this sense of intellectual property was already being eclipsed by its current meaning. The scientist Samuel Mitchill, who represented New York in Congress between 1801 and 1813, was put in charge of a committee to amend the patent laws. His report, never implemented, referred to the "revision of all the acts now in force relative to intellectual property." In 1811 the New York surgeon John Francis vowed that "the intellectual property of an individual is as sacred as the wealth he may have acquired."[3] These were references to patents and scientific knowledge, but copyrights and creative work—already widely called "literary property"—were soon subsumed within the broader category of intellectual property as well, first in England and then in the United States.[4] Gulian Verplanck introduced in Congress the legislation that became the Copyright Act of 1831. At a dinner in his honor held by authors and artists in New York, Verplanck was toasted for "assuring to intellectual property the same protection which the laws afford to other property." Discussions of the rights of authors included a claim of "the natural inviolability of intellectual property" and even a whole chapter titled simply *Intellectual Property*. By 1845, when Supreme Court justice Levi Woodbury described patents as intellectual property, the phrase had long been familiar to American lawyers. By 1855, when Lysander Spooner published a book about the rights of authors and inventors, he could call it *The Law of Intellectual Property* without pausing to explain why.[5]

Patents and Copyrights

Patents and copyrights were established features of the English legal system long before the independence of the United States.[6] Both originated as ad hoc discretionary monopoly grants from the Crown: in the case of patents, the sole right to practice a trade, and in the case of copyrights, the sole right to print copies of a book. By the late eighteenth century, copyrights had mostly shed their discretionary character. After the Revolution all the states but Delaware enacted general copyright laws protecting all applicants who met certain minimal criteria. Connecticut's statute of 1783, for example—captioned "An Act for the Encouragement of Literature and Genius"—conferred upon all authors the exclusive right to print, publish, and sell their books for a term of fourteen years.[7] Patents remained discretionary a bit longer. None of the newly independent states passed general patent laws. Rather, state legislatures granted or denied patents on a case-by-case basis, to one applicant at a time.

This divide between an automatic copyright and a discretionary patent was briefly replicated when the federal government assumed responsibility for patents and copyrights in 1790. The Constitution authorized Congress "to promote the progress of science and useful arts, by securing, for limited times, to authors and inventors, the exclusive right to their respective writings and discoveries." The copyright act passed by the first Congress provided a fourteen-year initial term and an additional fourteen-year renewal term for all authors of maps, charts, and books who complied with the registration requirements. The first patent act, by contrast, established a three-person committee, consisting of the attorney general and the secretaries of state and war, to review applications from inventors and grant patents "if they shall deem the invention or discovery sufficiently useful and important."[8] Unlike copyrights, patents were not a matter of right.

This discretionary patent system did not last long, because the number of patent applications quickly overwhelmed the three cabinet members, who already had full-time jobs. The Patent Act of 1793 solved this problem by making patents available to all applicants, just like copyrights. This procedure created a different problem: with no review of applications to ensure that a claimed invention was genuinely new, patents were granted to too many spurious inventions. Eventually, in 1836, Congress settled on the intermediate solution still in place today, in which the Patent Office scrutinizes applications to determine whether a claimed invention is truly "new and useful" and must grant patents to all that are.[9]

By the early nineteenth century, then, there was no longer anything discretionary about copyrights or patents. When authors or inventors satisfied certain criteria, they were entitled to a copyright or patent as a matter of right. Copyrights and patents had become kinds of property. "If the right can be distinctly traced to original possession and invention," reasoned the Boston lawyer George Ticknor Curtis in his treatise on the law of copyright, "and if the exercise of the right involves the general attributes which belong to property, there is no reason why it should not be placed among the rights of property." A copyright was property "as clearly distinguishable as houses and lands, or gold and silver coin," insisted another writer. "When the author, after great study and research, has produced a book, by the joint labors of his mind and hands, he is justly entitled, and is entitled by law to regard it as his property." Patents were property too. "An inventor holds a property in his invention," Levi Woodbury declared, "by as good a title as the farmer holds his farm and flock." While a patent was in effect, agreed Justice Joseph Story, an inventor has "a property in his inventions; a property which is often of very great value, and of which the law intended to give him the absolute enjoyment and possession."[10] Copyrights and patents were not just monopoly privileges to use a new tool or to print a new book; they were property rights in information. They were intangible, and they were limited in duration, but there was no doubt that they were property.

The economic importance of patents and copyrights increased over time. The annual number of new patents per capita roughly quadrupled between 1840 and 1860, and nearly tripled again between 1860 and 1890. Patents became valuable articles of commerce in their own right; by the 1870s, the annual number of patents licensed or assigned to someone else was nearly 70 percent of the number of new patents granted. "It is interesting to observe how closely the grant of patents and the prosperity of the country are related," *Scientific American* noted at the end of the nineteenth century. "The past fifty years represents an epoch of invention and progress unique in the history of the world. . . . It is probably safe to say that fully nine-tenths of all the material riches and physical comforts of to-day have grown into existence in the past fifty years."[11]

The growth of copyright was even easier to see. The original copyright act applied just to books, maps, and charts, but coverage expanded to include prints in 1802, musical compositions in 1831, plays in 1856, photographs in 1865, and paintings, drawings, and sculpture in 1870. The inclusion of photography was a product of technological change, but the other expansions were not. They were new applications of copyright to old forms of expression. The substantive content of copyright expanded at the same time. Originally a copyright only prohibited others from literally copying a work. Anything short of actual copying, such as publishing an abridgment or a translation of a copyrighted work, did not constitute infringement. When Harriet Beecher Stowe, for example, sued over an unauthorized German translation of *Uncle Tom's Cabin*, Justice Robert Grier had little trouble dismissing the suit. "To make a good translation of a work often requires more learning, talent and judgment, than was required to write the original," Grier reasoned. "To call the translations of an author's ideas and conceptions into another language, a copy of his book, would be an abuse of terms." By the end of the century, however, a copyright had come to include the exclusive right to publish such modifications of works—what lawyers would later call *derivative works*—as well as the underlying works themselves.[12]

Perhaps the most important expansion of copyright in the nineteenth century, and certainly the one that got the most attention, was its extension to foreigners. Patents were available to anyone, but for a long time only American citizens and residents could obtain a copyright in the United States. Books by foreign (especially English) authors could be copied freely and often were, in the form of unauthorized inexpensive American editions. In an era when the United States was a net literary importer, the politics of the issue favored the domestic reading public over foreign authors and publishers. The issue was repeatedly before Congress all through the nineteenth century, spurred in part by foreign publishers and in part by American authors who found themselves undercut by low-priced competition and who were harmed abroad by other countries' retaliation. "The mischievous effects upon our own literature is by far the most profound cause for regret," lamented one American proponent of international copyright. "The American publisher, governed by a sense of interest, had rather print an edition of an English work which has received the stamp of foreign favor, and whose author is of sufficient celebrity to ensure its success, than to critically examine an American manuscript, judge of its merit, pay for it, publish it, and take the hazard of losing his time and investment."[13] As the American publishing industry grew over the course of the century, the balance of trade in copyrighted work started to even out. Finally, in 1891, Congress extended copyright protection to foreign authors.

In the twentieth century, patents and copyrights continued to expand. The term of a patent lengthened from fourteen years to twenty, while the term of a copyright ballooned from fourteen years (with a possible renewal for another fourteen years) to the life of the author plus another seventy years, or ninety-five years in the case of a corporate author. With new technologies came a greater scope for both. Patents were extended to things like new kinds of plants and computer programs, while copyright was applied to sound recordings and movies. The force behind these changes has of course been the firms that have benefited from them. Any losses consumers suffered, in the form of higher prices for patented or copyrighted items, were spread so thinly that few would notice. This steady expansion was also likely due in part to the conception of patents and copyrights as a kind of property. Proponents of longer or stronger protection could cast themselves as upholders of property rights, and they could depict unauthorized users as pirates or thieves. When legislators are asked to choose between property owners and thieves, the thieves will very rarely win.

Trademarks and Goodwill

Manufacturers have been placing words and symbols on their goods for thousands of years, sometimes simply to denote ownership, but also sometimes to signify to customers the source, and thus the quality, of their products. In any sort of long-distance trade where the buyer has no personal acquaintance with the seller and the quality of what is being sold cannot easily be judged just by looking, the reputation associated with a producer's mark has long been an important indicator of the worth of a product. Counterfeit marks have been a problem for just as long. Efforts to prohibit counterfeit marks go back at least to medieval Europe. A mark placed on goods "is what ascertains the Property or Goodness thereof," explained the English lawyer Giles Jacob in his early eighteenth-century legal dictionary. "And if one Man shall use the *Mark* of another, to the Intent to do him Damage, Action upon the Case lieth."[14]

Colonial Americans imported many things from Europe, so they had reason to pay attention to the names and symbols associated with what they bought. The apothecary Zabdiel Boylston advertised in 1711 that visitors to his Boston shop could find "the true and famous Lockyer's Pills." Two decades later his Philadelphia counterpart Peter Sonmens stocked a much larger selection of branded medicine, including "Squire's Grand Elixir, Bateman's Pectoral Drops, Easton's Stiptick,

Lockhart's and Matthew's Pills, Daffie's Elixir, Bateman's and Blagrave's plain & golden Spirit of Scurvey Grass, Owner's Lozenges, Clifton's and Banister's golden Spirit of Venice Treacle, [and] Turner's Drops and Pills for curing Convulsions, Epilepsies, and Falling-Sicknesses." Some colonial Americans were exporters, particularly of agricultural commodities, and they used marks too. Local governments sometimes kept registries of these marks. In 1772, for example, when George Washington began producing and exporting flour on a large scale, he registered the mark *G:Washington* with the Fairfax County Court and then placed the mark on sacks of his flour.[15]

There were occasional calls in the late eighteenth century for state or even federal trademark legislation. "There is no greater check to this laudable spirit of enterprise," declared one correspondent to a Philadelphia paper, "than that of imposters fraudulently counterfeiting of marks, and imposing & selling bad & spurious articles for good, real and genuine." He accordingly urged state legislatures to pass laws punishing forged marks. In 1791, when the Boston sailmaker Samuel Breck petitioned Congress for a law protecting his mark against infringement, Thomas Jefferson took the opportunity to argue for a federal trademark law that would "secure to every Manufactory an exclusive Right to some Mark . . . rendering it penal in others to put the same Mark to any other Wares."[16] But nothing ever came of these early proposals. The law governing trademarks would remain judge-made common law for some time.

Names and symbols used in trade had long been called *marks*, but they were not conventionally called *trade marks* until well into the nineteenth century. The term's first use in print was in an 1838 English case, which Lord Chancellor Cottenham was reported to have described as "very different from the cases of this kind which usually occur, where there has been a fraudulent use, by one person, of the trade marks or names used by another." Cottenham did not find any further explanation necessary, so it seems a fair inference, not only that suits about counterfeit marks were already common, but that lawyers were already calling them "trade marks." The term in any event quickly began popping up in print all over. An 1840 article in an English lawyers' magazine was titled "Trade Marks," and the article was republished under the same title in an American lawyers' magazine the following year. The barrister Charles Drewry used the term, without pausing to explain its meaning, in his 1841 treatise on injunctions. By 1844, when the English thread maker John Taylor, producer of the well-known Taylor's Persian Thread, had to file simultaneous suits in Boston and New York against an American infringer, the lawyers and judges referred to the name of the thread as a trade mark.[17]

By the middle of the century, *trade mark* was the conventional term in the commercial world as well. Advertisements for products began to call the products' names "trade marks." An 1847 ad for Joseph Gillott's Steel Pens, for example, warned purchasers not to be fooled by competing pens bearing the "trade marks of Mr. Gillott." Gillott had recently secured a court order prohibiting the competitor from using his marks, but some of the spurious pens were still in shops, awaiting incautious purchasers. An 1852 advertisement for Dr. J. S. Houghton's Pepsin—a "great cure for dyspepsia!"—noted that every bottle bore Houghton's trade mark. The term began to assume its colloquial popular meaning, that of a characteristic trait, soon after. In 1859, when the lawyer Francis Wharton published a treatise that attempted to prove the existence of God, he cited as support the fact that natural laws were the same throughout the universe. "Here we find a singular evidence of the *unity* of the Divine Machinist," Wharton concluded. "The *trade-mark*, if I may use the expression, is always the same." A decade later, recounting his struggles with Old Master paintings in *The Innocents Abroad*, Mark Twain could assume his readers already knew the expression. "When we see a monk going about with a lion and looking tranquilly up to heaven," he explained, "we know that that is St. Mark. When we see a monk with a book and a pen, looking tranquilly up to heaven, trying to think of a word, we know that that is St. Matthew. . . . When we see other monks looking tranquilly up to heaven, but having no trade-mark, we always ask who those parties are."[18]

The amount of American trademark law, in the form of statutes and published court opinions, grew quickly in the middle decades of the nineteenth century, in response to what contemporaries considered an epidemic of counterfeit marks. "The evil," a House of Representatives committee concluded, "is one of growing magnitude and injurious consequences to society, requiring a legislative remedy." In 1845, New York became the first state to enact a statute prohibiting counterfeit trademarks, and similar laws were passed by many other states soon after, including all the leading commercial states. (Congress also passed a trademark law in 1870, but the Supreme Court found it unconstitutional, so significant federal regulation would have to await the twentieth century.) These statutes added remedies to what was already an expanding body of case law that likewise prohibited the false use of someone else's mark.[19] As many judges noted, trademark law, from whatever source, served two related policy goals. It protected purchasers from being defrauded by false indications of the quality of products, and it protected honest merchants from having their customers diverted to the dishonest.[20] In the typical case, where one manufacturer falsely used a competitor's mark, there was no tension between these goals. Both led to the same result.

In the early cases, trademarks were not classified as a form of property. "A party cannot acquire, strictly speaking, any exclusive title to a particular trade mark," Charles Drewry explained in his treatise. Courts enjoined infringement not because the infringer was taking any property but in order to prevent a kind of fraud. The long-serving federal judge Samuel Betts agreed that trademark suits "are not maintained upon the ground that the plaintiff has a right of property in the trademark." Rather, "the relief is given because the mark is a sign or representation" of the source of the article being purchased, and infringers were attempting to "delude purchasers by vending inferior articles, or diminish the owner's business by acquiring sales to themselves under color of his reputation."[21] A trademark was understood as an assertion that a particular good came from a particular source. Counterfeiting a trademark was just one species of fraud, like making any other false claim about something one was trying to sell.

As trademark litigation became routine, however, judges began to speak of the trademark itself as a form of property in its own right. There is "an exclusive property in trade marks," the New York judge John Duer declared in 1849. When the public was misled by the use of another's mark, a court would intervene "for the plain reason that when a right of property has thus been acquired, it must be protected." Such statements soon became common. "The law of trademarks," another New York judge explained, "may be comprehended in the proposition that a dealer 'has a property in his trademark.'" When the Philadelphia pistol maker Henry Derringer sued a San Francisco competitor who stamped the name "Derringer" on his guns, the California Supreme Court allowed the suit to proceed, despite the fact that Henry

Derringer had not complied with the registration requirements of California's trademark statute. "The trade mark is property," the court concluded, "and the owner's right of property in it is as complete as that which he possesses in the goods to which he attaches it." By the late 1860s at the latest, it was clear that trademarks were property—"as undeniable property as any other possession," *Scientific American* explained to its readers.[22]

Thinking of trademarks as property gave rise to some tricky questions. In the 1850s the well-known watchmaker James Brindle sold to Morris Samuel the right to stamp Brindle's name on watches manufactured by Samuel. Samuel then brought suit, for trademark infringement, against merchants selling Brindle watches made by Brindle himself. By purchasing Brindle's trademark, had Samuel acquired the right to suppress competition from Brindle's own watches? Samuel's suit could not be allowed to proceed, a judge insisted; if successful, the suit would drive the genuine article from the marketplace, to be replaced by a simulation. A trademark was evidently not property in the same sense as a physical object: it could not be bought and sold on its own, separated from the product it was meant to designate. Thoughtful lawyers and judges quickly recognized that trademarks, although property, were a special kind of property. "The right of property in trade marks does not partake in any degree of the nature and character of a patent or copyright, to which it has sometimes been referred," cautioned the New York lawyer Francis Upton in his 1860 *Treatise on the Law of Trade Marks,* the first book devoted to the subject. A trademark "is a property, not in the words, letters, designs or symbols, as things—as signs of thought—as productions of mind—but, simply and solely, as a means of designating things." Upton accordingly explained that "this property has no existence apart from the thing designated—or separable from its actual use." The owner of a trademark did not own a word; he owned only the right to use that word to designate a particular product. Upton's nuanced definition of property in a trademark soon became standard.[23]

Even with this more sophisticated understanding of trademarks, difficult questions continued to arise regarding the scope of a trademark holder's property right. When a glassmaker in Galen, New York, sold "Galen glass," did the word "Galen" denote a *kind* of glass (the sort made in Galen) or did it indicate a *producer* of glass (a resident of Galen named Stokes)? What about "Merrimack prints"—were they a particular style of print, or were they prints produced by the Merrimack Manufacturing Company? All agreed that names indicating a manufacturer could be protected as trademarks, but that the actual generic names of goods could not. No one could have the exclusive right to sell a product called "glass," or "prints," or, as one New York case held, "dessicated codfish." The hard cases were somewhere in the middle. Did the producer of a new perfumed liquid soap called "Balm of Thousand Flowers" have a property right in the name, as applied to the commodity known as soap? Or had he invented a new kind of commodity called "Balm of Thousand Flowers," in which case the phrase, like "soap," could be used by anyone? What about "Ferro-Phosphorated Elixir of Calisaya Bark"—was that a new *brand name* for medicine, or was it a new *kind* of medicine? And what if it was both at once?[24] Trademark cases kept raising hard questions about how words were being used to designate products.

At first it made little difference whether or not trademarks were thought of as property. Cases would come out the same either way. But trademarks continued to grow in importance over time, as businesses grew larger and sold branded products in ever-bigger markets. "How much is this trade-mark worth?" wondered one admirer of the Collins Company of Hartford County, Connecticut, manufacturers of axes used throughout the Western Hemisphere by the 1870s. "It would be hard to say without seeming extravagant." The Collins mark was known everywhere. "In the West Indies and in South America it is almost impossible to sell an axe or a machete bearing any other; those tropical people are suspicious of Americans, but think themselves quite safe when they see the familiar stamp." Even if some other company could make better tools, "forty years, at least, of hard work would be required to build up a business of equal extent." The more valuable trademarks became, the more incentive trademark owners had to protect their investments. They began to urge courts and legislatures to expand trademark law to cover forms of competition it had not previously covered. These arguments began to prevail in the early twentieth century, and their acceptance was facilitated by the conception of trademarks as property.[25]

For example, one of the twin purposes of trademark law had always been to prevent the deception of consumers. But if a trademark was a kind of property, wasn't it wrongfully appropriated by a competitor who used it, even if no consumers were confused? In 1900 a federal court of appeals decided that it was. The genuine user of a trademark "comes into a court of equity in such cases for the protection of his property rights," reasoned William Day, who would soon be promoted to the Supreme Court. "The private action is given, not for the benefit of the public, although that may be its incidental effect, but because of the invasion by the defendant of that which is the exclusive property of complainant." After several similar cases, trademark experts concluded that "in trade-mark law, confusion of source is irrelevant" where the marks were very similar. The basis of a trademark suit was "that there is 'property' in a trademark," regardless of whether any customers had been deceived.[26]

The conception of a trademark as property facilitated a second and probably more far-reaching change as well. Throughout the nineteenth century, trademarks functioned to designate the source of a particular good. Indeed, judges in some of the early cases applied this rule so strictly that they refused to acknowledge the validity of marks that were not actually the names of the people or firms that produced them. "Meen Fun" was not a proper trademark for skin powder, one New York judge concluded, because "it can hardly be pretended that the words 'Meen Fun' indicate the manufacturer." Such strictness did not last long; courts soon began to recognize that "fancy names" (or what we would today call fanciful or made-up names) could function equally well as trademarks, so long as consumers associated them with the products of a particular manufacturer. But a trademark had to go along with a product; one could not own the right to a word in all commercial settings or even as applied to other products. The owners of the trademark "Amoskeag" as applied to *unprinted* cloth, to pick one extreme example, had no right to prevent another firm from using the name "Amoskeag" on *printed* cloth. "The doctrine of trademarks must not be extended beyond its just limits," the judge declared, "or, in a country like ours, filled as it is with enterprise, capital, skill, inventive genius, and with men possessed of progressive ideas, it will in the end be productive of greater injury than good." A merchant could not be permitted to lock up all commercial uses of a word, or else there might not be enough words left. As a result, the lawyer William Henry Browne observed in the 1870s, "it is not uncommon for the same mark to be placed upon different classes [of products] by different owners. The word

'MAGNOLIA' may properly serve to indicate a certain manufacture of *gin* for one proprietor, and a certain brand of *whiskey* for another; for although both contain a large proportion of alcohol, the fluids cannot be said to belong to the same class."[27]

But this view started to change as well in the early twentieth century. Courts prohibited the use of "Aunt Jemima" for pancake syrup upon the complaint of the owner of "Aunt Jemima" for flour, the use of "Vogue" for hats upon the complaint of the owner of "Vogue" for magazines, and—the biggest stretch—the use of "Rolls-Royce" for radio tubes upon the complaint of the car company. "The right to a trademark, though strictly appurtenant to the trade, becomes a property right as soon as it identifies the trade," the court explained in the Aunt Jemima case, and once it was property it could be protected against any use that might reduce the mark's value. No one could confuse cars and radios, conceded the Rolls-Royce court, "but that is not the test and gist of this case." If a customer bought an unsatisfactory Rolls-Royce radio tube, "it would sow in his mind at once an undermining and distrust of the excellence of product which the words 'Rolls-Royce' had hitherto stood for." Trademarks, as property in their own right, were coming to be protected against *any* commercial conduct that might make them less valuable, with respect to any product. In the past, "a trademark indicated either the origin or ownership of the goods to which it was affixed," observed the New York trademark lawyer Frank Schechter. "To what extent does the trademark of today really function as either? Actually, not in the least!" Trademarks had become valuable for their selling power, and that value could be whittled away by *any* use that reduced the distinctiveness of a name.[28]

These expansions of the rights of a trademark holder had their critics, who argued that they flowed from a too-simple understanding of a trademark as property. "The word 'property' as applied to trademarks," Oliver Wendell Holmes suggested, was nothing more than "an unanalyzed expression of certain secondary consequences of the primary fact that the law makes some rudimentary requirements of good faith." For the law professor Felix Cohen, the expansion of trademark law was a prime example of the "transcendental nonsense" of legal argument, "the divorce of legal reasoning from questions of social fact." Judges called a trademark *property* because it was valuable, but the only reason it had value in the first place was that the law considered it property. "The circularity of legal reasoning in the whole field," he insisted, "is veiled by the 'thingification' of *property*."[29]

But this sort of criticism had little effect. Trademarks continued to grow more valuable. In 1998 the Tax Court appraised the trademark "DHL," the name of an air courier company, at $100 million. Many other marks are worth a lot more. In 2008 *Business Week* valued the name "Coca-Cola," the leader of its "100 Best Global Brands," at more than $66 billion, with "IBM" and "Microsoft" not far behind. (These are values just for the names, not for the corporations that make the products those names denote.) DHL did not make the list; even the hundredth-most valuable name, "Visa," was worth more than $3 billion. "If this business were to be split up," the chairman of Quaker Oats has said, "I would be glad to take the brands, trademarks and goodwill and you could have all the bricks and mortar—and I would fare better than you."[30] The more valuable trademarks became, the more resources were poured into lobbying and litigation intended to entrench them even more firmly as property. By the late twentieth century, trademarks were protected by federal statute and many state statutes against "dilution," roughly any commercial use of a word that could diminish the word's distinctiveness as a trademark.

Occasional critics charged that "propertizing trademarks comes at a rather significant cost to society," in the form of suppressed expression and higher prices for trademarked products, but warnings like these were no more effective at the end of the century than in the days of Holmes and Cohen. In the 1990s alone, explained the law professor Mark Lemley,

> trademark laws have been used to preclude artists from painting in the same style as another, to prevent an author from using the term "Godzilla" in the title of his book about Godzilla, to prevent a comic book from featuring a character known as Hell's Angel, to prevent a satirical political advertisement from using the "Michelob" trademark to help make its point, to prevent a tractor manufacturer from making fun of its competitor's logo in an advertisement, to prevent a movie about a Minnesota beauty pageant from using the title "Dairy Queens," to prevent a political satire of the O. J. Simpson case called "The Cat NOT in the Hat!", to prevent individuals from setting up web pages critical of a company or product, and to prevent a theme bar from calling itself "The Velvet Elvis."[31]

The protection afforded trademarks had grown to a degree that could scarcely have been anticipated a century earlier. Perhaps all of this would have happened even if trademarks had not been understood as a form of property, but it seems unlikely. The more a trademark was thought of as property, the more sense it made for the legal system to guard against potential reductions in its value.

Goodwill followed a similar trajectory: it was not classified as property in the early nineteenth century but by the middle of the century there was little doubt that it was a kind of property. Goodwill was a familiar commercial concept long before Joseph Story provided its canonical American definition in his 1841 treatise on partnerships.[32] "This good-will," Story explained, "may be properly enough described to be the advantage or benefit, which is acquired by an establishment, beyond the mere value of the capital, stock, funds, or property employed therein, in consequence of the general public patronage and encouragement, which it receives from constant or habitual customers." A successful business was worth more than an unsuccessful one, even if both possessed the exact same assets, and the value of the difference "is commonly called the good-will of the establishment."[33] Goodwill could become important whenever a business was transferred from one owner or group of owners to another—for example, when one partner in a partnership died, or when the partnership was dissolved for some other reason.

Was goodwill itself a kind of property? Goodwill "is often treated as in some sort a part of the partnership property," Story acknowledged, but it was not, "strictly speaking, a part of the partnership effects" that could be divided among the partners when a partnership was dissolved. "It is certainly not a visible, tangible interest, or a commodity" that could be apportioned among multiple people. If an entire business were sold, "then the good-will will accompany such sale, and may create a speculative value in the mind of the purchaser, of which each partner will be entitled to a share of the benefit." But while goodwill could enhance the value of *other* property, Story seems to have thought, it was not a kind of property in its own right.[34]

The question arose in two cases in the first half of the nineteenth century, and in both the judges agreed with Story that goodwill, although very much like property, was not itself a kind of property. In a tavern owner's suit to prevent the diversion of a road (which would

cause him to lose business), the Virginia Supreme Court explained that
his investment in the tavern in reliance on the road's location "gave him
rights, which, although not amounting to absolute property, were in the
nature of property, (as the good-will of a trade)." The distinction made a
difference: had the tavern owner truly lost any property, he would have
been entitled to prevent the diversion of the road for any purpose, but
because his losses were merely "in the nature of property," he could prevent the diversion of the road only if the diversion was intended to benefit another private property owner rather than to benefit the public as a
whole. A few years later, the creditors of a partnership that owned a
newspaper sought to recover the value of the newspaper's goodwill from
the person to whom the partners assigned the newspaper when the
partnership became insolvent. "This question," the court observed, "turns
chiefly upon the nature of that, which the parties have denominated
the good will of the paper." The creditors were entitled to any property
that had belonged to the partnership, so if goodwill was property, it
would belong to the creditors. The partners had labeled the goodwill as
"property" in their partnership agreement, which declared the paper's
goodwill to be "the common property of the firm." But this label was in
fact inaccurate, the court held. Goodwill was an incident of a successful
newspaper, but it was not a kind of property in its own right. The creditors "have already had the benefit of all the *property* of their debtors," the
court held, and they could recover no more.[35]

While goodwill was not a kind of property in the first half of the
century, it was nevertheless a valuable item, as a steady stream of partnership cases kept bringing to mind. When a business that leased its location changed hands, "the good will of course enters into the value of
the lease, and enhances the purchase money," one judge observed in
1839. "In truth, in a lease of a trading establishment it constitutes a large
part of the value." Another judge agreed that goodwill "is an important
and valuable interest, which the law recognizes and will protect."[36]
Goodwill was valuable, it was bought and sold, the law protected it—
goodwill may not have been considered a form of property in the first
half of the century, but it had nearly all of the attributes of property. To
the lawyers and judges who negotiated transactions and decided cases
involving goodwill, it must have felt an awful lot like property.

In the second half of the century, courts accordingly began classifying goodwill as property in its own right. "The valuable part of the

partnership property consists in the goodwill," one New York judge declared in 1859. "This value is partnership property, as much as the furniture of the office." Judges and lawyers in other states began making similar assertions. "Goodwill, though intangible, is property, and often valuable property," explained a court in Ohio. "It is the very atmosphere that envelops and pervades a business and that gives it the breath of life." In the first extended academic treatment of goodwill, the Philadelphia lawyer Arthur Biddle determined that it was "a species of incorporeal personalty"—that is, intangible personal property— "subject with but few exceptions to the general laws which regulate that kind of property."[37] By the turn of the century there was a consensus among commentators that goodwill was property.[38]

Once trademarks had been accepted as property, there was little reason not to accord the same treatment to goodwill. Lawyers thought of them as falling within the same category. Both were intangible, and the value of both was inextricably attached to the operation of an ongoing business. "The character and value of good-will is very similar, in many respects, to that of a trademark," one lawyer noted in 1870. "It serves as an assurance to the customers, or purchasers, that they are being dealt with fairly, or are obtaining the goods they desire. And Courts of Equity protect the property in both much upon the same principle."[39] Indeed, one could think of a trademark as a repository or a sign of goodwill; they would grow in value together as an enterprise gained customers.

Classifying trademarks as property had given rise to some tricky questions, and so too did the conception of goodwill as property. When a person died, all his property was supposed to become part of his estate, and the administrator of an estate had to comply with strict standards in accounting for that property. But when the dead person owned a business, what about the goodwill that went along with it? Did its value have to be accounted for, apart from the value of the business itself? People often used their property as security for loans; could goodwill be used this way too? If the debtor could not repay the loan, could the creditor foreclose on the goodwill? States and local governments imposed property taxes, often according to statutes that told them to tax "all property" within the jurisdiction. Could they tax goodwill?[40] In some situations, classifying goodwill as property threatened to allow double counting of goodwill's value. If a business was worth a certain amount, part of that amount was the value of goodwill, so it made little sense to require an administrator to account for goodwill separately, or to allow creditors to foreclose on goodwill apart from the underlying business, or to permit states to tax goodwill along with the value of the business itself. Goodwill might be property, but like trademarks it was property that needed some special rules of its own, because unlike other kinds of property it had no value by itself. It derived all its value from the existence of *other* property, the assets of an ongoing business.

On the other hand, there were times when treating goodwill differently from other kinds of property threatened to confer a windfall on its owner. The Adams Express Company, for example, delivered letters and packages throughout the country. It had tangible assets in many states, each of which taxed the portion of the company's property within state boundaries. Adams Express owned roughly $4 million in horses, wagons, and the like, but the market value of the company was $16 million, which meant that 75 percent of it was goodwill. The company argued that Ohio could tax only the value of its tangible property located in Ohio—$23,430—because its goodwill was not physically present in the state. But the Supreme Court had little patience for the argument. "Considered as distinct objects of taxation, a horse is, indeed a horse; a wagon, a wagon; a safe, a safe; a pouch, a pouch," conceded Chief Justice Melville Fuller. "But how is it that $23,430 of horses, wagons, safes, and pouches produces $275,446 in a single year?" The answer was that the primary asset of the Adams Express Company was not a tangible item; it was the company's goodwill. "In the complex civilization of today, a large portion of the wealth of a community consists in intangible property, and there is nothing in the nature of things or in the limitations of the federal constitution which restrains a state from taxing at its real value such intangible property," Justice David Brewer concluded. "To ignore this intangible property, or to hold that it is not subject to taxation at its accepted value, is to eliminate from the reach of a taxing power a large portion of the wealth of the country." If the company was worth $16 million, it had to be taxed at that value, even if the sum total of its physical assets was only a quarter of that amount. "Businessmen do not pay cash for property in moonshine or dreamland," Brewer scoffed. "The value which property bears in the market, the amount for which its stock can be bought and sold, is the real value."[41] Goodwill was like older forms of property in some ways, but unlike it in other ways, and it would not be a simple matter to figure out which was which.

Trade Secrets

Trade secrets became property at approximately the same time. Like trademarks and goodwill, trade secrets were already familiar in the early nineteenth century. "A person may lawfully sell a secret in his trade or business," Joseph Story explained in 1836, "and restrain himself from using that secret." That same year, for example, the Massachusetts chocolatier Jonas Welch sold his factory, along with his "secret manner of making chocolate," to John Vickery. Welch then claimed that he had the right to tell others how he made chocolate—while he had indeed divulged his recipe to Vickery, he contended, he had never promised that Vickery would be the only one. The Massachusetts Supreme Court had little trouble dismissing Welch's argument. The purpose of the contract had obviously been for Vickery to take up Welch's business, and that would have been impossible if Welch's secret became common knowledge. A few years later a New York court enforced a contract for the sale of a secret for converting cast iron into malleable iron.[42] American lawyers were familiar with earlier English cases that said much the same thing. Courts had the power to prohibit and punish the disclosure of trade secrets.

But trade secrets were not understood as a form of property. A *patent* on an invention was a kind of property, the lawyer Willard Phillips explained in the 1830s. Without a patent, one could try to prevent others from copying an invention by keeping it secret. "But then it would not be a *property*," Phillips concluded; "it would, after all, be only his *secret*." For industrial knowledge to be a kind of property one needed a patent, because "an inventor cannot assert a right of property in an invention independently of the patent law."[43]

This view did not survive the nineteenth century. John Norfolk was a machinist employed at midcentury by Joseph Peabody, who had built machines and devised a new process for producing gunny cloth, a coarse material used for making sacks. In his contract, Norfolk explicitly promised not to disclose any information about the process. After a couple of years, Norfolk left Peabody and went to work for a different gunny cloth manufacturer. The Massachusetts Supreme Court prohibited

Norfolk from communicating any information to his new employer about Peabody's machines or his method for making gunny cloth. "It is settled," the court held, "that a secret art is a legal subject of property." Similar statements soon began popping up everywhere. "A secret of trade is fully recognized in equity as property," declared a court in New York, in a case involving the secret formula for a kind of makeup called "Champlin's Liquid Pearl." "One who invents or discovers and keeps a secret process of manufacture," agreed a New Jersey court, "has a property therein which this court will protect." Any sort of property could be held in a trust, explained the author of a treatise on the subject; that included land and other tangible items, but it also included trade secrets, which were a kind of property as well. Thoughtful writers recognized that a trade secret differed in one important respect from other types of property. It would cease to exist if it were ever revealed in a legitimate way—if the owner disclosed it voluntarily, for example, or if it were reverse-engineered by a competitor. But trade secrets were nevertheless property.[44]

As with trademarks, the conception of trade secrets as property facilitated expanded legal protection for them. In the typical case, where an employer sought to prevent a former employee from revealing a secret to a new employer, the secret was characterized as "the property of the employer." Earlier in the century, the opinions barring the disclosure of trade secrets had relied on the existence of an explicit contract in which the employee had promised not to divulge the secret. Once trade secrets became property, however, the existence of such a contract no longer made any difference. With or without a contract, it was wrong to take someone else's property. Courts accordingly began barring employees from revealing secrets even where the employees had never made any promises not to do so.[45]

In 1887, for example, a Cincinnati trial court heard the case of John Dodds, the former foreman for the Blymyer Manufacturing Company, a producer of copper and tin bells. When the company was sold, Dodds left and went into business for himself, using the bell-making knowledge he had acquired over the years. His contract with Blymyer had said nothing about trade secrets, and no one had ever told him not to use his knowledge or communicate it to others. Did that mean Dodds could make his own bells? The case came before a brand-new thirty-year-old trial judge named William Howard Taft, who held that it made no difference what Dodds had been told. "I am inclined to think that his obligation to preserve such secret as the property of his employer must be implied, even though nothing was said to him on the subject," Taft reasoned.[46] Property was property, regardless of the form it took.

In the twentieth century, the conception of trade secrets as property gave rise to another form of increased legal protection. In 1972, in response to growing concern about the environmental effects of pesticides, Congress required pesticide manufacturers to disclose the chemical composition of their products. The Supreme Court, in a suit brought by Monsanto, held that to the extent the law required the publication of trade secrets, it amounted to a taking of property without just compensation, in violation of the Fifth Amendment. After all, trade secrets were property, just like land or anything else the government might press into public service.[47]

Property in Reputation?

The New Jersey judge Francis Swayze delivered Yale Law School's commencement address in 1915. His topic, "The Growing Law," was broad enough for him to pad his speech with a catalog of recent legal changes, ranging from workers' compensation to the growing movement to prohibit alcoholic beverages, but one change Swayze emphasized was the growth of "new kinds of property of great value," including patents, copyrights, trademarks, goodwill, and trade secrets. Other commentators noticed the same development and wondered what sorts of new property the future would bring. "Many intangible rights" once "considered incapable of vindication by legal remedy, have been dignified with the name of property," one writer pointed out. What would be next? Recent cases held out tantalizing possibilities. Maybe the right to use the mail was a kind of property. Or maybe the promise of a tax exemption.[48] The way the law was developing, anything of value seemed likely to be classified as a form of property.

Homer Plessy's lawyers thought so too. At the end of the nineteenth century Plessy was challenging a Louisiana law requiring railroads to provide segregated cars. He lost, of course, in an opinion best remembered for the proposition that separate but equal facilities would satisfy the Constitution's guarantee of equal protection. But equal protection was not Plessy's only argument. His lawyers also contended that Plessy had light enough skin to pass as white, and that seating him in the "colored" car deprived him of property, because his reputation as a white person was a kind of intellectual property. Looking back, this may seem like a stretch, especially in light of our knowledge that the separate-but-equal aspect of Plessy's case would be overruled a half century later in *Brown v. Board of Education*. In the 1890s, however, it would have been hard to judge which was the stronger argument. The category of property was steadily expanding, to include all sorts of intangible assets. Homer Plessy's lawyers can hardly be faulted for hoping that a reputation for being white would be next. Such a reputation was certainly valuable at the time. It was, for a person, sort of like what a trademark was for a business—a sign of a certain credibility or status, a form of goodwill. Indeed, the Supreme Court was willing to concede that Plessy's reputation as white was a form of property; it held only that the state law at issue did not deprive him of it.[49]

That this was a plausible legal strategy suggests how much had changed in the nineteenth century and how wide open the future seemed. Within the memory of the oldest members of the bar, intellectual property had become an important part of the law, and the types of intellectual property had multiplied to include not just patents and copyrights but also trade secrets and trademarks with their associated goodwill. All were ways of owning information, a commodity that would grow ever more valuable, and would be the subject of even newer kinds of property, in the twentieth century.

3

A Bundle of Rights

LAWYERS speak of property as "a bundle of rights." As the best-selling introduction to the subject explains, "property is an abstraction. It refers not to things, material or otherwise, but to rights or relationships among people with respect to things. And the abstraction we call property is multi- not monolithic. It consists of a number of disparate rights, a 'bundle' of them: the right to possess, the right to use, the right to exclude, the right to transfer," and so on.[1] This conception of property is conventionally traced to the progressives and Legal Realists of the early twentieth century, and it is conventionally understood as a conception that facilitated the greater regulation of property, and the correspondingly reduced constitutional protection for property, characteristic of that period.[2]

The idea that property is a bundle of rights is actually considerably older than that, however, and when it first became widely held, it had a political significance exactly the opposite of the one ascribed to it in the conventional story. Property was first understood as a bundle of rights in the second half of the nineteenth century in order to argue for *greater* constitutional protection for property rights, and thus less regulation. In order to see the relationship between the changing constitutional law of the nineteenth century and the origin of the conception of property as a bundle of rights, we have to start at the beginning, with the ways in which property was treated as a constitutional matter in the early nineteenth century.

The Advantages of the Social Condition

In the early republic there was no doubt as to the importance of property. "Government is instituted to protect property of every sort," James
Madison declared. "That alone is a *just* government, which *impartially*
secures to every man, whatever is his *own*." The constitutions of each of
the states accordingly included broadly worded clauses sheltering property from government interference, and so too did the federal constitution. "Where is the security, where the inviolability of property," asked
the early Supreme Court justice William Paterson, "if the legislature . . .
can take land from one citizen, who acquired it legally, and vest it in
another?"[3] One of the primary purposes of having a constitution was
to prevent exactly that.

On the other hand, there was also no doubt that a properly functioning government sometimes had to enact laws and take other actions
that would limit the use of property and reduce its value.[4] Towns and
states regulated building materials and methods, to prevent fires and
other disasters. They banned from thickly populated areas activities that
were useful but bothersome to neighbors, like tanneries, breweries, and
gunpowder factories. They set licensing and inspection requirements for
food and other products, and sometimes set prices as well. They built
roads, wharves, and canals. Government actions like these often imposed substantial burdens on the owners of property, who might find
themselves, for example, required to relocate their businesses or to employ their property for something other than its most profitable use.

This tension between governing effectively and protecting property has been one of the central problems of American constitutional
law since the beginning. When, exactly, does the government overstep
its boundaries and infringe the rights of a property owner? How Americans have gone about trying to answer that question has changed considerably over time.

Constitutional law in the early nineteenth century offered several
alternatives to a property owner aggrieved by something the government had done. There remained a lingering tradition of natural law, for
example, according to which written constitutions were not the only
limits on government power. "An *act* of the Legislature (for I cannot call
it a law) contrary to the great first principles of the social compact, cannot be considered a rightful exercise of legislative authority," insisted

Supreme Court justice Samuel Chase, who offered as an example "a law that takes property from A and gives it to B." Even if nothing in the constitution prohibited such a law, "it is against all reason and justice, for a people to entrust a Legislature with *such* powers," Chase reasoned, "and, therefore, it cannot be presumed that they have done it."[5] This natural law tradition slowly faded away, however, and by midcentury there was something close to a consensus within the profession that the only bounds to government power were those written down in a constitution.

That still left property owners with a few options. The federal constitution, for instance, barred states from impairing the obligations of contracts and, more ambiguously, from interfering unduly with interstate commerce. These restrictions would form the basis of much of the constitutional law of the nineteenth century. But property owners found their most explicit protections in the two constitutional clauses that mentioned property by name. The federal constitution and nearly all state constitutions barred the government from taking property for public use without just compensation and from depriving a person of property without due process. Because these clauses appeared in the federal constitution only as limits on the power of the federal government, and because most property owners were affected much more by actions of their state government, state constitutional law was far more important than federal. To challenge regulation or other government activity as an unconstitutional infringement of property, a property owner relied primarily on the takings clause or the due process clause of the state constitution. To win, he would have to show that his property was either *taken* without compensation or that he had been *deprived* of it without due process.

Neither was easy to do in the first half of the century. As to takings, the dominant—although not universal—rule was that property owners could not recover when government action merely reduced the value of their property. While there was considerable disagreement on the issue, compensation was generally available only when property was actually physically taken. The word *taken* was interpreted according to its "obvious and popular meaning, so as to be restrained to property taken away," explained John Bannister Gibson, chief judge of the Pennsylvania Supreme Court. The word could not be "extended to property injured by an act which did not amount to an assumption of the possession."[6]

This rule was sometimes justified by a strict literal interpretation of the constitution's text. For instance, the owners of a mill in Charlestown, Massachusetts, suffered when the construction of a new railroad partially blocked the flow of water, which prevented the mill from working as well as it had before. The mill's owners lost nearly three thousand dollars in the value of their property. The Massachusetts Supreme Court decided against them, however, on the ground that the state's decision to allow the railroad to be built "was a mere regulation . . . and not a taking of private property." In a similar case the Supreme Court of Maine held that the state constitution's takings clause "was not designed, and it cannot operate to prevent legislation, which should authorize acts, operating directly and injuriously, as well as indirectly upon private property, when no attempt is made to appropriate it." Taking, the court concluded, literally meant taking. "The design appears to have been simply to declare, that private property shall not be changed to public property, or transferred from the owner to others, for public use, without compensation." A property owner whose property was damaged or reduced in value by government action was nevertheless still its owner. The property might be worth less than before, but it had not been *taken*.[7]

Sometimes the rule was justified as a necessary accommodation to the realities of governance. If everyone could recover whenever government caused them harm, worried William Tilghman of the Pennsylvania Supreme Court, "there would be no end to damages for *injuries*, considered in the most extensive sense of the word." A new dam, for example, might cause losses to people accustomed to fishing downstream, and to those who formerly used boats to move their produce to market, and maybe even to everyone in the surrounding area one way or another. "Where, then, are we to stop?" Tilghman wondered. "No one can calculate the mischiefs which would ensue" from a rule requiring the government to compensate everyone whose property it damaged, agreed Greene Bronson of New York's Court of Appeals.

> The opening of a new thoroughfare may often result in advancing the interest of one man or a class of men, and even one town, at the expense of another. The construction of the Erie Canal destroyed the business of hundreds of tavern-keepers and common carriers between Albany and Buffalo, and greatly depreciated the value of their property, and yet they got no compensation. And new villages sprung up on the

line of the canal, at the expense of old ones on the former line of travel and transportation. Railroads destroy the business of stage proprietors, and yet no one has ever thought a railroad charter unconstitutional, because it gave no damages to stage owners. The Hudson river railroad will soon drive many fine steamboats from the river; but no one will think the charter void because it does not provide for the payment of damages to the boat owners. A fort, jail, workshop, fever hospital, or lunatic asylum, erected by the government, may have the effect of reducing the value of a dwelling house in the immediate neighborhood; and yet no provision for compensating the owner of the house has ever been made in such a case.

The government simply did too many things that affected the value of private property to compensate everyone who suffered a loss. "Public works come too near some, and too remote from others," a resigned Vermont Supreme Court concluded. "They benefit many, and injure some. It is not possible to equalize the advantages and disadvantages. It is so with everything, and always will be."[8]

Sometimes the no-compensation rule was justified on the ground that all property owners expected, or at least should have expected, the risk that the government would do something to make their property less valuable. In the leading case of *Callender v. Marsh,* the regrading of a Boston street substantially lowered the ground level next to the plaintiff's house, which exposed the house's foundation. The plaintiff had to go to great expense to build new walls to make sure his house didn't collapse. The Massachusetts Supreme Court had little sympathy for him. "Those who purchase house lots bordering upon streets are supposed to calculate the chance of such elevations and reductions as the increasing population of a city may require," lectured Chief Justice Isaac Parker. "As their purchase is always voluntary, they may indemnify themselves in the price of the lot which they buy, or take the chance of future improvements, as they see fit." The opening of Hamilton Avenue in Brooklyn was the death knell of the Brooklyn and Gowanus Toll Bridge Company, because few would pay to use a bridge when they could use Hamilton Avenue for free. "If individuals suffer," the New York Supreme Court explained, "it is in consequence of a risk which all proprietors and patentees encounter, of the establishment of works of a public character, and they should make their calculations as to the prospective value of proposed new institutions accordingly." To build a house, or a bridge, or a mill, or indeed anything, was to assume the risk that the government might later reduce its value.[9]

The no-compensation rule was also sometimes justified, finally, with reference to what would much later come to be called the average reciprocity of advantage. In any given case, a government action that helped most people, like the construction of a dam or a road, might reduce the value of one person's property. But that person, over the course of his lifetime, would be the beneficiary of countless other government actions that would have the same pattern of general gains and concentrated losses. If one took the long view, everyone was a winner. When Trenton, New Jersey, passed an ordinance requiring the owner of every lot to build a brick sidewalk in front of his house, at his own expense, one homeowner alleged that the ordinance was a taking of his property. The New Jersey Supreme Court replied that he had already been amply compensated, "by his enjoyment of the like foot ways every where else, in which he freely participates without contributing to their expense," as well as "in regulated markets, a vigilant police, and the innumerable pleasures, conveniences, benefits and security of an orderly city." Occasional government-inflicted harm to private property, a New York judge held, "is to be borne as a part of the price to be paid for the advantages of the social condition." In such cases "private interest must yield to public accommodation," as the U.S. Supreme Court put it, in rebuffing a challenge to the regrading of K Street in Georgetown. "One cannot build his house on the top of a hill in the midst of a city, and require the grade of the street to conform to his convenience, at the expense of that of the public." The plaintiff would enjoy the benefit of graded streets throughout the rest of the city, so it was hardly unfair to require her to submit to the regrading of her own.[10]

The general, though not universal, rule in the first half of the nineteenth century, then, was that the takings clauses of state constitutions imposed no obligation on government to compensate property owners for actions that reduced the value of their property. Compensation was due only when property was actually taken in the literal sense of the word. This was a rule that sometimes yielded harsh results to individual property owners, however, and for that reason it was often criticized. Joseph Story, for one, didn't like it. "With all possible respect for the opinions of others," he explained, "I confess myself to be among those who never could comprehend the law" denying compensation.

James Kent didn't like it either. Just before he died in 1847 he inserted a new footnote in the sixth edition of his *Commentaries* blasting the leading cases as wrongly decided. The issue came before the Pennsylvania Supreme Court when the regrading of some streets in Pittsburgh so weakened the foundations of the city's Roman Catholic cathedral that it had to be torn down and rebuilt. "We have had this cause reargued in order to discover, if possible, some way to relieve the plaintiff consistently with law, but I grieve to say we have discovered none," apologized Chief Justice John Bannister Gibson. "The constitutional provision for the case of private property *taken* for public use, extends not to the case of property *injured* or *destroyed*." This sort of criticism never went away. Government sometimes conferred diffuse gains on many by imposing concentrated losses on a few, and in such cases, critics found it unjust not to require compensation. "But considerations of this kind have been silenced," the lawyer Theodore Sedgwick lamented, "by the universal demand for works tending to develop the internal resources of the country; a general disposition has been felt not to cramp these enterprises by a too sweeping or extensive compensation."[11]

But Sedgwick told only one side of the story. By the middle of the century, opposition to the no-compensation rule manifested itself in a few different forms. Some judges interpreted the rule as narrowly as they could. When the diversion of a stream threatened to ruin a farm by depriving it of water, for example, James Kent, as New York's chancellor, required compensation—not for the damage to the farmer's land but for the loss of the water itself, which he classified as a form of property in its own right, "as sacred as a right to the soil over which it flows." The land had only declined in value, but the water had actually been taken away. In other cases, where only part of a person's land was physically taken, even a very small part, judges required compensation for damage to the rest of the land that had not been taken, an outcome that was hard to reconcile with the general no-compensation rule but that allowed courts to avoid some of the rule's most unpleasant consequences.[12]

The clearest expressions of opposition to the no-compensation rule, however, were in the occasional cases in which judges simply disregarded it. John Barron's wharf became less valuable when sand and dirt, dislodged by street construction in Baltimore in the 1820s, landed in the harbor and made it too shallow for many vessels to reach him. Barron's property had not actually been *taken* from him, the trial judge conceded, but "there has certainly been what is equivalent to it. The plaintiff has his land, it is true, but he has been deprived of the profits growing out of its tenure." The judge accordingly ordered the city to compensate Barron.[13] In an 1841 Connecticut case, a state-built canal flooded the plaintiff's land with water. When the water receded his land was worth much less than before, but he still owned as much land as ever; the state had not literally taken any from him. Nevertheless the Connecticut Supreme Court, by a 3–2 vote, required compensation, over the objection of a dissenting judge who listed many of the cases establishing the no-compensation rule. The Ohio courts interpreted their own constitution to require compensation for government-inflicted reductions in the value of property, a practice, the state's supreme court recognized, that was "in direct conflict with the English and American cases." Thus while the general rule in the first half of the century was that compensation was unavailable in such circumstances, the rule was not universally applied. "The cases are not in perfect accord with each other," Theodore Sedgwick admitted.[14] A rule that made sense to most lawyers and judges when stated abstractly could yield harsh results in particular cases, so there was always some sentiment for interpreting the takings clause to require compensation for damage to property as well as literal takings.

If property owners in the first half of the century could expect little from the courts when they filed suits based on the takings clause, they could expect even less when they filed suits based on the due process clause. When property lost value because of something the government had done, had the owner been deprived of property without due process? The answer, even more emphatically, was no.

"Due process of law," or, as some state constitutions put it, "the law of the land" (the two phrases were treated as synonyms), was an infrequent basis for litigation in the first half of the nineteenth century, but there was nevertheless a rough consensus as to what the words meant. "After volumes spoken and written with a view to their exposition, the good sense of mankind has at length settled down to this," U.S. Supreme Court justice William Johnson explained in 1819. "They were intended to secure the individual from the arbitrary exercise of the powers of government, unrestrained by the established principles of private rights and distributive justice." The requirement of due process was understood as a way of preventing the government from playing favorites, by requiring that laws affecting life, liberty, and property apply to all. Without such a restriction on government power, the Tennessee Supreme Court feared, "an edict in the form of a legislative enactment, taking the property of A, and giving it to B, might be regarded as the *'law of the land,'* and not forbidden by the constitution; but such a proposition is too absurd to find a single advocate." This was not just a procedural hurdle the legislature had to surmount; it was a substantive limit on what the legislature could enact. "The terms 'law of the land' do not mean merely an act of the General Assembly," observed Thomas Ruffin of North Carolina's Supreme Court. "If they did, every restriction upon the legislative authority would be at once abrogated." No matter how impeccable the procedure a legislature followed, "a legislative act which deprives one person of a right and vests it in another, is not a 'law of the land' within the meaning of the Bill of Rights." If the phrase meant only that the legislature had to follow certain procedures, agreed the New York judge Greene Bronson, "that construction would render the restriction absolutely nugatory, and turn this part of the constitution into mere nonsense."[15] The constitutional guarantee of due process was thus generally understood to bar the government from transferring one person's property to another.

But this was more a theoretical possibility than an actual danger, because government rarely, if ever, simply transferred property straight from one person to another. Most government actions redistributed property only indirectly, by increasing some people's wealth and decreasing others'. A law requiring farmers to fence their cattle, for example, might impose significant costs on farmers who owned cattle, while conferring benefits on other farmers who no longer had to worry that roaming cattle would eat their crops. A law requiring railroads to construct cattle guards near the tracks might impose costs on the railroads, while conferring benefits on those who owned cattle. To mount a successful due process challenge to such laws, one would have to persuade a court that the due process clause barred not only outright transfers of property but this sort of indirect redistribution, brought about by the reduction of value suffered by the property owners most harmed.

In the first half of the nineteenth century, there appear to have been no cases in which any property owner, anywhere in the United States, succeeded on such a claim. Although property was protected by the constitution, James Kent explained in his widely read *Commentaries*, "the lawgiver has a right to prescribe the mode and manner of using it, so far as may be necessary to prevent the abuse of the right, to the injury or annoyance of others, or of the public." When property rights clashed with public aims, "private interest must be made subservient to the general interest of the community." In 1829, for example, the city of Boston filled in a creek adjoining Edmund Baker's land, cutting off access to the sea. Baker's tenant stopped paying rent and threatened to move out, because the land had become much less valuable than before. Baker had clearly been harmed by what the city government had done. But Boston had every right to fill in the creek, the Massachusetts Supreme Court held. The local sewers had emptied into it for so long that the water had become smelly and unhealthy. "The measure was a mere health law or regulation, and every citizen holds his property subject to such regulations," the court explained. "Regulations to direct the use of private property so as to prevent its proving pernicious to the citizens at large, are not void, although they may in some measure interfere with private rights." Government could scarcely go on at all, if all the laws that limited the use of property were to be declared void on that account. "A large portion of the duty of the lawgiver, in every civilized community, consists in regulating the conduct of individuals, in different matters, for the public welfare," the Ohio Supreme Court declared. Such laws were "justified by the obvious principle, that although a man's rights to his own are absolute and indefeasible, yet these rights must be so used as not to infringe the rights of others, and may be so regulated as to promote the general good."[16]

The government's undoubted authority to regulate in the service of public goals, even if that regulation happened to reduce the value of some people's property, soon came to be called the *police power*. "What are the police powers of a State?" asked Chief Justice Roger Taney, in the course of upholding three states' systems of licensing liquor retailers. He answered his own question, in words that would be quoted many times over the following century. "They are nothing more or less than the powers of government inherent in every sovereignty . . . , the power to govern men and things within the limit of its dominion." The definition offered by the Vermont Supreme Court was typical: "the police power of the state," the court explained, "extends to the protection of the lives, limbs, health, comfort, and quiet of all persons, and the protection of all property within the state." If regulation fell within the police power, it could not be in violation of the law of the land, regardless of its effects on property. "It is in the just exercise of this power," lectured the Illinois Supreme Court,

> that individuals have been required to fence their lands, or forfeit the right to recover damages for trespasses committed by stock, of other persons. So of quarantine regulations, to protect communities against the introduction, and spread of contagious diseases. And in prohibiting the exercise of noxious and unhealthy trades and manufactures, and in requiring the fencing of saltpetre caves, and growing castor beans. In prohibiting the sale of unwholesome provisions, and stock from running at large affected with contagious or infectious distempers. From the sale of obscene books and prints, cards and gaming implements. The law has imposed all of these and many other duties and prohibitions upon individuals, for the protection of citizens, their morals and property; and notwithstanding it may appear in some degree to abridge individuals, of a portion of their rights, yet we are not aware that their constitutionality has ever been challenged.

A railroad, then, could hardly complain about a state law requiring it to build fences to keep livestock off the tracks. The railroad lost money in complying, but that did not make the law unconstitutional. Bakers in Mobile, Alabama, could hardly complain about a city ordinance setting the price and weight of bread. The bakers lost money, but they were in the same position as all the other property owners whose rights were limited by laws aimed at advancing the public good. Fixing prices was perhaps an unwise method of assuring an adequate bread supply, the Alabama Supreme Court admitted, but it was well within the police powers of the government of Mobile.[17]

Like the no-compensation rule under the takings clause, this expansive understanding of the police power was sometimes justified on the ground that all property owners expected, or should have expected, that their property might one day be regulated to their disadvantage. "Every right, from an absolute ownership in property, down to a mere easement, is purchased and holden subject to the restriction, that it shall be so exercised as not to injure others," reasoned the New York Supreme Court. "Though, at the time, it be remote and inoffensive, the purchaser is bound to know, at his peril, that it may become otherwise by the residence of many people in its vicinity." The city of New York could thus force Trinity Church to stop burying its dead in the churchyard, even though the church owned the land and had been using it as a cemetery for more than a century. Lemuel Shaw, the chief justice of the Massachusetts Supreme Court, provided one of the most well-known discussions of the police power in an 1851 opinion rebuffing a challenge to Boston's authority to restrict the size of wharves. "Every holder of property, however absolute and unqualified may be his title, holds it under the implied liability that his use of it may be so regulated, that it shall not be injurious to the equal enjoyment of others having an equal right to the enjoyment of their property, nor injurious to the rights of the commonwealth," Shaw held. "Rights of property, like all other social and conventional rights, are subject to such reasonable limitations in their enjoyment, as shall prevent them from being injurious."[18]

And like the no-compensation rule under the takings clause, this deference to government regulation of property was sometimes justified on the ground that while any given property owner might suffer from one instance of regulation, he was simultaneously, as a member of the public, the beneficiary of many other instances. Bangor, Maine, like many cities, banned wooden buildings in densely populated neighborhoods to prevent fires. A man named Wadleigh, fined for violating the law, claimed the law unconstitutionally infringed his property rights, but the Maine Supreme Court disagreed. "Police regulations may forbid such a use, and such modifications, of private property, as would prove injurious to the citizens generally," the court explained. "This is one of the benefits which men derive from associating in communities. It may sometimes occasion an inconvenience to an individual; but he has a compensation, in participating in the general advantage." Wadleigh could live more safely because other property owners were equally unable to build wooden houses, so it was hardly unfair to subject his own property to the same restriction.[19]

The constitutional law of the first half of the nineteenth century thus offered scant protection for property rights against laws that reduced the value of property or restricted the ways in which it could be used. When property was literally taken by government, the owner would be compensated under the takings clause, and all agreed that the due process clause would be violated in the hypothetical case in which the government took property from one person and simply gave it to another. But so long as property was not literally taken from its owner, the constitution offered little redress.

A Bundle of Rights

What exactly was the "property" that the constitution protected? Judges and lawyers rarely defined the word explicitly in the first half of the nineteenth century, but it seems clear enough that they had an implicit understanding of property as an asset capable of being owned by someone. Land was a kind of property, shares of corporations were property, copyrights were property—tangibility or physical existence was not a necessary feature of property, but property was nevertheless a *thing*. This understanding of property was no different from the way nonlawyers used the term. A farmer called his land property, a miller called his mill property, and an investor in railroad shares called them property too. Just like the lawyers, they were thinking of property as a thing, physical or not, that someone owned.

Among lawyers, this understanding of property gradually came under attack in the nineteenth century. "In a loose and vulgar acceptation," the English law professor John Austin pointed out in the 1830s, "a horse or piece of land is called my property," but that was not the most accurate meaning of the word. Property was not a thing a person owned; rather, property was the assemblage of rights a person had over a thing. A person might have "the power of using indefinitely the subject of the right," for example, and "a power of excluding others" from using the same subject, and it was this collection of powers, not the subject itself, that constituted property. Strictly speaking, land was not property. Property was the right to use land, the right to exclude others from using land, and so on.[20]

This view of property was not completely new, either in Britain or in the United States. Back in the 1790s, James Wilson, one of the original justices of the U.S. Supreme Court, had referred to property as encompassing "a right to possess, to use, and to dispose of a thing" rather than the thing itself. The Pennsylvania judge William Tilghman likewise defined property, in 1813, as "the *right* or *interest* which one has in land or chattels." And all educated lawyers knew that the English judge Edward Coke had made nearly the same point in his widely read *Institutes,* first published in the early seventeenth century, when he asked the rhetorical question "what is the land but the profits thereof."[21]

But while Austin was not the first person to think of property as a collection of rights, his view was nevertheless extremely influential.

Austin's *Lectures on Jurisprudence* were first published in the 1860s. British lawyers soon began defining property with a standard phrase. "Proprietorship is a bundle of rights," the barrister George Sweet declared in 1873. In his 1881 treatise on commercial law, Robert Campbell explained that property "consists in fact of a great number of rights, and may be conceived of as a bundle of rights."[22] By the century's end, the idea that property was a bundle of rights had been repeated so often that it had been firmly planted in British lawyers' minds.[23] Property had once tended to be conceptualized as a thing; now, at least among lawyers, it tended to be conceptualized as rights in a thing. "Most persons, when they hear the word Property, think of some material things, such as lands, houses, money, corn, cattle, &c.," the lawyer and economist Henry Dunning Macleod told students in his 1881 economics textbook. "But that is not the true and original meaning of the word Property. Property in its true and original meaning is not any material substance, but the absolute right to something."[24]

It was not long before American lawyers also began thinking of property as a bundle of rights. "The owner of a lot of land does not, strictly speaking, own the ground," one Ohio attorney argued in the early 1880s. "His proprietorship consists of a bundle of rights." Property meant rights rather than things, agreed Lewis Bisbee and John Simonds, quoting Austin, in their treatise on the law governing the Chicago Board of Trade. By 1888 the lawyer John Lewis could scoff that even "the dullest individual among the *people* knows and understands that his *property* in anything is a bundle of rights." He acknowledged, following Austin, that "all men speak loosely of *things as property.*" Lewis insisted, however, that "practically all men understand that property consists of certain *rights in things* which are secured by law."[25] As in Britain, by the end of the century this definition had been repeated so often that American lawyers thought of property as a bundle of rights.[26]

For most of the nineteenth century, property had primarily been understood as a thing, but in the second half of the century it increasingly came to be understood as a bundle of rights in a thing. The language of the state and federal constitutions had not changed: they still required compensation when "property" was taken for public use, and they still prohibited the deprivation of "property" without due process. The words were the same, but within the legal profession the meaning of one important word was changing. That shift would have profound implications for how judges would interpret the takings and due process clauses.

Visible Manifestations of Invisible Rights

The no-compensation rule under the takings clause for property damaged, but not literally taken, was already beginning to weaken in the 1850s and 1860s, as a few state courts explicitly rejected it in cases involving serious flooding damage to land. The proposed demolition of a dam in New Jersey, for example, threatened to submerge John Glover's meadow. He would still own it, but it would be practically worthless. If that were to happen, the state's court of chancery held, Glover would have to be compensated. "The value of the meadow is destroyed," the court reasoned, "and thus may be said, with propriety, to be taken from the owners. A partial destruction, the diminution of their value, is the taking of private property." In Indiana, the state authorized the construction of a railroad embankment that likewise forced water onto a farmer's land, damaging his crops, while in Illinois, the regrading of a street caused water and mud to flow onto a homeowner's grounds, ruining the business he conducted out of his house. The supreme courts of both states, after considering and disagreeing with out-of-state precedents, held that the takings clause required compensation. A person who causes water "to overflow an ancient mill, 'takes' that mill and privilege from the owner as directly and effectually as though he entered upon the premises and demolished the building," the Maine Supreme Court determined. "The truth of it is self-evident."[27]

The no-compensation rule then took two major blows in the early 1870s, hits from which it would never recover. The first was an 1871 U.S. Supreme Court case, *Pumpelly v. Green Bay Company*, in which the Court, interpreting the constitution of Wisconsin, unanimously agreed that flooding land with water amounted to a taking of the land. "It would be a very curious and unsatisfactory result," Justice Samuel Miller argued, if the government could destroy the value of land without compensating the owner, merely because "in the narrowest sense of that word, it is not *taken* for the public use. Such a construction would pervert the constitutional provision," he concluded, "and make it an authority for invasion of private right under the pretext of the public good." Miller acknowledged that the Court's decision was contrary to

the decades of state court precedent that had established the no-
compensation principle in cases where property was not literally taken.
"But we are of opinion," he concluded, "that the decisions referred to
have gone to the uttermost limit of sound judicial construction in favor
of this principle, and, in some cases, beyond it." The Supreme Court
thus joined the emerging trend of requiring compensation in cases of
serious flooding damage.[28]

The second blow was struck the following year. In *Eaton v. Boston,
Concord, and Montreal Railroad,* yet another flooding case, in a lengthy
and thoroughly researched opinion, the New Hampshire Supreme Court
became the first court in the nation to decide a takings clause case according to the emerging conception of property as a bundle of rights.[29]
The court began by criticizing the conventional doctrine that compensation was required only where property was actually physically taken.
"These views seem to us to be founded on a misconception of the
meaning of the term 'property,' " the court reasoned. "In a strict legal
sense, land is not 'property,' but the subject of property. The term 'property,' although in common parlance frequently applied to a tract of land
or a chattel, in its legal signification means only the rights of the owner
in relation to it." The crux of a takings claim was thus not that the government had taken *land,* but rather that the government had taken a
right pertaining to land. "If property in land consists in certain essential
rights, and a physical interference with the land substantially subverts
one of those rights, such interference 'takes,' *pro tanto,* the owner's 'property,' " the court explained. Any government limitation on what an
owner could do with his land could be a taking of property, even if the
owner was left with just as much land as before, because the property
that had been taken was not the land itself but rather the ability to use
the land. In such a case, the owner might have the same quantity of land,
but "he has not the same property that he formerly had."

The New Hampshire Supreme Court then turned to a functional
defense of this conclusion. "Restricting A's unlimited right of using one
hundred acres of land to a limited right of using the same land, may
work a far greater injury to A than to take from him the title in fee simple
of one acre, leaving him the unrestricted right of using the remaining
ninety-nine acres," the court reasoned. "Nobody doubts that the latter
transaction would constitute a 'taking of property.' Why not the former?" If value resided not in land itself but in the right to do things with

land, regulation of the use of land should require compensation at least as much as physical confiscation of the land. A conception of property as a bundle of rights thus comported with intuitive justice, in the court's view. A law that restricted an owner's ability to use his land was a taking, just as surely as if the state had taken the land itself.

The court was well aware that it was bucking the conventional wisdom, so it was careful to rebut some of the standard justifications for not requiring compensation in such situations. Sometimes great public benefits would flow from limiting what a person could do with his land, the court conceded, but that was not a reason to deny the landowner compensation. "If the work is of great public benefit," the court declared, "the public can afford to pay for it." A compensation requirement might lead to a proliferation of claims whenever the government took any action, the court conceded, but that was no ground for denying compensation to plaintiffs who had sustained a substantial injury. If property meant the right to use land, the government took property when it curtailed that right.

Eaton and *Pumpelly*—especially *Eaton*—were enormously influential. One commentator praised *Eaton* as a "learned opinion" that deserved to be "usefully consulted" by other courts. Another called it "a grateful and refreshing recognition of the rights of private owners of property." *Eaton* was "the most satisfactory and best considered case which can be found in the books upon this subject," exclaimed Chief Justice Isaac Christiancy of the Michigan Supreme Court. Michigan accordingly followed New Hampshire in awarding compensation where land had been overflowed by water but not physically taken. Courts in many other states followed suit over the next two decades, some in cases also involving flooding, and others in cases involving different kinds of government interference with the right to use land.[30]

Within a few years of *Eaton* and *Pumpelly*, legal treatises were already explaining that the new takings clause cases had eclipsed the old. "The term 'taking' cannot be limited to the absolute conversion of real property to the uses of the public," explained Henry Mills in his 1879 treatise on the law of eminent domain. Any "encumbrance on property, or exclusion of the owner from its enjoyment, or substantial injury to the land . . . is a taking within the meaning of the constitution." To trigger the constitutional requirement of compensation, agreed the law professor Christopher Tiedeman in his widely read constitutional law treatise, "it is not necessary that there should be an actual or physical taking of the land. Whenever the use of the land is restricted in any way, . . . it constitutes as much a taking as if the land itself had been appropriated." By the 1890s, statements like these were commonplace.[31]

Defenders of the old view of the takings clause did not go down without a fight. Only seven years after its own opinion in *Pumpelly*, the U.S. Supreme Court described *Pumpelly* and *Eaton* as "the extremest qualification of the doctrine," still a sound one, that "acts done in the proper exercise of governmental powers, and not directly encroaching upon private property, though their consequences may impair its use, . . . do not entitle the owner of such property to compensation from the State." These words were written by Justice William Strong, who had been a member of the unanimous *Pumpelly* Court, and they were joined by all his colleagues, including Samuel Miller, the author of *Pumpelly*. Perhaps the justices were worried that lower courts were taking *Pumpelly* too far. Maryland stuck with the old view, that property "*injured* is not in the constitutional sense *taken* for public use."[32] In the last three decades of the nineteenth century, however, such expressions of support for the old no-compensation rule were far outnumbered.

Some argued that even if the Austinian definition of property as a bundle of rights was technically accurate, it was not the definition in the minds of those who had drafted the constitutional provisions being interpreted. The framers of the state and federal constitutions "must be supposed to have used the word in its ordinary and popular signification, as representing something that can be owned and possessed and taken from one and transferred to another," insisted Justice Robert Earl of the New York Court of Appeals. "If the word is to have the broad meaning given to it by Austin," Earl worried, then the takings clause would require compensation for "every interference with and injury or damage to land by which its use and enjoyment become less convenient or valuable. Such a sense has never been given to it." (Earl was fighting a losing battle; he was dissenting from a decision of his court awarding compensation to New Yorkers whose houses would soon be thrown into shadow when the city built an elevated railroad line above their street.) "At the time of the Constitution," agreed the lawyers Charles Haight and Arthur Marsh, "the idea of property as a 'bundle of rights' was not as exact" as it would become a century later. Property in the constitutional sense thus meant the thing being possessed, critics contended, "its common, comprehensive, and general meaning," its "common-law conception," not some refined technical meaning known only to specialists.[33]

But most commentators recognized that the redefinition of property as a bundle of rights had irrevocably changed the way the profession interpreted the takings clause. "The recent tendency of adjudication has been toward a more liberal construction of the constitutional guarantee," the *New York Times* explained in an editorial approving the recent elevated railroad decision. "It has been contended that property included whatever gave value to possession, such as convenience of location, ease of access, and free access of light and air, and that it carried with it the right of undivided use by the owner." When one of these rights or conveniences was abridged by the government, "the property is to that extent 'taken' for public use." As Supreme Court justice David Brewer declared in a speech at Yale Law School's graduation in 1891, "whether the thing be taken or its use stopped, the individual loses, he is deprived of his property."[34]

The two most thorough analyses of the way a reconception of property as a bundle of rights had changed the outcomes of takings cases were both written in the 1880s. The first was an article in the *North American Review,* a well-known literary magazine not limited to lawyers but intended for a general readership. The author was the New York lawyer Arthur Sedgwick, who used the controversy over New York's elevated railroads as an occasion to explain to nonlawyers how and why property rights were receiving more protection under the takings clause than ever before. "The meaning of the word 'property' seems to be undergoing a modification," Sedgwick began. Once it had meant land or some other thing capable of being owned, but now it was coming to be understood as a collection of rights. "Property is, in other words, the right to possess, use, enjoy, dispose of, rent, sell, give away, [or] devise the thing owned," he explained, "and anything which interferes with the beneficial enjoyment of all these rights substantially diminishes them, and consequently involves a 'taking,' *pro tanto,* of the property." Sedgwick identified *Eaton* and *Pumpelly* as the key cases effecting this transition. He concluded by predicting, correctly, that under the new conception of property, landowners abutting the elevated railroad would be awarded compensation, even though, under the old conception, the landowners would have lost their case.[35]

The other detailed discussion of the issue appeared in John Lewis's 1888 treatise on eminent domain, in which Lewis devoted an entire chapter to the question. Like Sedgwick, Lewis emphasized that once property was understood as rights rather than things, "it follows that, when a person is deprived of any of those rights, he is to that extent deprived of his property, and, hence, that his property may be taken, in the constitutional sense, though his title and possession remain undisturbed." This conclusion would not have been accurate two or three decades before, Lewis acknowledged, but "the law as to what constitutes a taking has been undergoing radical change in the last few years."[36]

Meanwhile many states were amending their constitutions to make this transformation more explicit. Between 1870 and 1890, seventeen states adopted newly worded takings clauses, to require compensation when property was taken *or damaged.*[37] These new provisions, which subjected governments to a broad range of new liabilities when public works caused incidental harm to neighbors, were evidence of a widespread sense that the old rule had been unfair to landowners.[38]

In the last three decades of the nineteenth century, government actions that caused damage to property, or that restricted the owner's ability to use property, were thus reclassified as takings requiring compensation under the constitution. This shift, in turn, opened up a new and even more difficult question. Many traditional government activities, from forbidding nuisances to regulating marketplaces, had the effect of limiting what an owner could do with his land. Such activities clearly could not *all* require compensation, because no government could contend with the volume of litigation or the level of compensation such a rule would require. Limitations on the height of buildings, for example, were obvious restrictions on the use of land, but the Supreme Court allowed them in 1909 despite the lack of compensation for landowners. In 1921 the Court upheld the constitutionality of rent control against a similar attack. "If to answer one need the legislature may limit height," Justice Oliver Wendell Holmes reasoned, "to answer another it may limit rent."[39] Some government restrictions evidently required compensation and others did not. Where, then, was a court to draw the line?

The Supreme Court first squarely addressed the question in *Pennsylvania Coal Company v. Mahon,* the 1922 case that would set the terms of debate on this issue for the rest of the century.[40] Due to a Pennsylvania law that prohibited coal mining in areas where excavation might causes houses to subside, the Pennsylvania Coal Company was forced to leave much of its coal in the ground. Under the law that prevailed before the 1870s, the company would have had little chance of succeeding on a claim under the takings clause, because the state had not literally taken any of its coal. According to the views of the most enthusiastic proponents of the new bundle-of-rights conception of property, on the other hand, the company's lawsuit was a clear winner. The "property" that had been taken was not the coal itself but the right to mine the coal, the most valuable part of the bundle. Justice Holmes struggled to find a middle ground. "Government hardly could go on if to some extent values incident to property could not be diminished without paying for every such change in the general law," he acknowledged. The state had to have some regulatory power it could wield for free. But when that power "reaches a certain magnitude," he cautioned, "in most if not all cases there must be an exercise of eminent domain and compensation to sustain the act." Not all regulatory power was costless; some would violate the takings clause unless the government made affected property owners whole. "The general rule," Holmes concluded, "is that while property may be regulated to a certain extent, if regulation goes too far, it will be recognized as a taking."

This was not the most useful guidance, as several subsequent generations of commentators would have ample opportunity to complain. The outcome of *Mahon* was that Pennsylvania's regulation had gone too far, and that the state accordingly had to compensate the coal company for its losses. But what about other factual circumstances, and other forms of government action? The new understanding of property as a bundle of rights had strengthened the protection of property under the takings clause, but all through the twentieth century lawyers would debate the question of exactly how much.

The reconception of property as a bundle of rights led to a similar, if similarly ambiguous, strengthening of the protection for property under the due process clause. At the center of the government's police power had always been the protection of public health and morality. In the nineteenth century, one increasingly popular way to advance both goals was to prohibit the sale of liquor. Thirteen states, including New York, went dry between 1851 and 1855. When New York's law was challenged by a Buffalo saloonkeeper named Wynehamer as a deprivation of property without due process, a majority of the state's Court of

Appeals agreed. The property that Wynehamer lost was not the liquor itself, explained Chief Judge George Comstock, but rather "his absolute power to sell and dispose of" the liquor. "As property consists in the artificial impression of these qualities upon material things," Comstock reasoned, "whatever removes the impression destroys the notion of property, although the things themselves may remain physically untouched." Even if Wynehamer could keep his liquor bottles in his own house, New York's prohibition law "sweeps them from the commerce of the state, and thus annihilates the quality of sale, which makes them valuable to the owner. This is destructive of the notion of property." Comstock was calling "qualities" what most commentators called "rights," but his point was the same: the right to sell liquor was a form of property, which the state could not take from him any more than it could confiscate the liquor itself.[41]

Judge T. A. Johnson dissented, in large part because he adhered to the older conception of property as a thing capable of being possessed. "We are asked to determine, that the legal property is not the article itself, but consists in some of its qualities or incidents," Johnson scoffed. In his view, such a definition of property was "more appropriate to the schools than the courts. Constitutions and general laws are not founded in any such subtleties. . . . If we permit ourselves to depart from the obvious, general fact, that the thing is property," he feared, the court would be led to "the grave absurdity of holding that a statute which forbids a person selling an article . . . really takes it away from him." Such a nonsensical conclusion could follow only from "the fallacy that the exchangeable value of the chattel is legal property, and that this is what the constitution was designed to protect."[42]

But Comstock's view prevailed, and the New York courts accordingly began interpreting the due process clause to protect against deprivations, not just of things, but of rights to use things in particular ways. A statute declaring certain bonds unnegotiable was "plainly unconstitutional," the Court of Appeals held. The law did not take away the bonds themselves, but "depriving an owner of property of one of its essential attributes is depriving him of property within the constitutional provision." A law prohibiting the manufacture of cigars in tenement houses was likewise a denial of due process, the court declared. The state had not taken any cigars or any houses, but the due process clause could "be violated without the physical taking of property" by a law which "takes away any of its essential attributes."[43] If property consisted of rights rather than things, regulation would be scrutinized much more closely.

Courts in other states were initially reluctant to follow New York's lead. "We must dissent," one Delaware court insisted, from the New York view "that the prohibition to sell an article of merchandise destroys its character as property." If that were true, the court worried, "the sovereignty of the State would be robbed of nearly all its police power." For the moment, property in Delaware still consisted of things. "The vendible quality of a thing is not of the substance of the thing in such sense that they may not be lawfully separated," the court held, "and the right to have or own a thing does not oblige the State to furnish a market for its sale." The Rhode Island Supreme Court disagreed as well. States had to have the power to place limits on what property owners could do with their property: "no one dreams that he can use his pick for burglary, or his sword for murder, merely because they are his."[44]

Eventually, though, the new conception of property took over. The Michigan judge Thomas Cooley's influential 1868 constitutional law treatise quoted extensively from *Wynehamer* in the course of arguing that the due process clause could be invoked whenever the government "interferes with the title to one's property, or with his independent enjoyment of it." Over the next few decades, courts found unconstitutional deprivations of property in an ordinance barring the sale of reserved seats in a theater once the show had started, a law requiring mining companies to pay miners in real money rather than scrip, a statute setting forth filing requirements for opening a bank, an ordinance requiring insane asylums to have fireproof buildings, an ordinance requiring houses to be a certain distance from the street, a law specifying maximum working hours for female employees, and many other comparable regulations.[45] None of these laws deprived anyone of property in the old sense of the word. All they did was regulate the use of property, but once property was a bundle of rights rather than a thing, the loss of a right was the deprivation of property. The constitution protected "the right to use, buy, and sell property," the West Virginia Supreme Court explained in the mining case. A bank could not be forced to file informational statements, the South Dakota Supreme Court reasoned, because such a requirement, if ignored by the bank's proprietor, "deprives him of his property employed in the business. The vaults, safes, and bank furniture of the banker may become comparatively valueless for other purposes. Yet, whatever that loss by diminution in value may be, it is property taken from him without 'due process of law.' " St. Louis, the city that tried to impose setback requirements for houses on its major boulevards, tried to argue that its ordinance did not deprive anyone of any property. The city was mistaken, the Missouri Supreme Court concluded. St. Louis had not deprived anyone of any *land,* but land and other physical things were not property. They were merely "the indicia, the visible manifestations, of invisible rights." Property was those invisible rights—"to wit, the unrestricted right of use, enjoyment, and disposal." It followed that "anything which destroys or subverts any of the essential elements aforesaid is a taking or destruction pro tanto of property, though the possession and power of disposal of the land remain undisturbed, and though there be no actual or physical invasion of the locus in quo."[46] By the end of the century, the new understanding of property had changed the way courts interpreted the due process clause just as it had changed the way they interpreted the takings clause.

The 1868 ratification of the Fourteenth Amendment to the federal constitution added a new due process clause limiting the power of state governments and enforceable in federal court. It was not long before the federal courts, including the Supreme Court, confronted the same due process claims as the state courts. "The docket of this court is crowded with cases in which we are asked to hold that State courts and State legislatures have deprived their own citizens of life, liberty, or property without due process of law," Justice Samuel Miller complained in 1877. It seemed that the Fourteenth Amendment's due process clause "is looked upon as a means of bringing to the test of the decision of this court the abstract opinions of every unsuccessful litigant in a State court."[47] Many of these cases, as in the state courts, involved claims that a state had deprived someone of liberty rather than property, because liberty too was increasingly being interpreted more broadly than before, to include the freedom to choose the sorts of contracts into which one would enter. But many of the cases concerned property, and so by the end of the century the Supreme Court was confronted with the same question that had been percolating through the state courts. Was a property owner deprived of property by a law that merely restricted its use?

The justices disagreed for many years. In the *Slaughter-House Cases* of 1872 the Court upheld the constitutionality of a state law restricting the slaughtering business of New Orleans to a single state-licensed firm, over the complaint of competing butchers. The vote was five to four, and the dissenting justices argued that the law had deprived the butchers of a form of property in the right to sell their labor without interference. "Property is everything which has an exchangeable value," Justice Noah Swayne insisted, "and the right of property includes the power to dispose of it according to the will of the owner." The same divide was evident four years later in *Munn v. Illinois,* when the Court upheld state price caps for grain storage. The dissenters again argued that the state had taken away property—not the grain warehouses themselves, but the right to use the warehouses in a particular way, to sell storage space at a market price.[48]

By the 1890s, however, the Court had committed itself to the conception of property as a bundle of rights, and to an interpretation of the due process clause that proscribed interference with those rights.[49] The regulation of railroad rates, the Court held, would deprive a railroad of due process if the rates were unreasonably low. "If the company is deprived of the power of charging reasonable rates for the use of its property," Justice Samuel Blatchford explained, "it is deprived of the lawful use of its property, and thus, in substance and effect, of the property itself, without due process of law." Property was not just the railroad line; it was also the right to use the railroad line to earn an adequate profit. Within a short time the Court found itself regularly reviewing the balance sheets of railroads to determine whether allowed rates were high enough to escape censure as deprivations of property without due process.[50]

A Change of Sentiment

The idea that property was a bundle of rights thus facilitated stronger constitutional protections for property. Of course, judges were motivated by much more than their conceptions of property. The bundle-of-rights metaphor was surely a less important cause of the shift than the fear—one that judges were not shy about expressing—that the nation would slide into socialism unless something was done to reinforce the constitutional right of property. "It cannot be denied that there has lately come a change of sentiment in certain of our people, by whom the right of private property is not now as highly regarded as formerly," William Howard Taft warned in 1894. "Events are happening each day which make a thoughtful man fear that if the tendency, indicated by them, is to grow in popular weight and intensity, our boasted constitutional guaranties of property rights will not be worth the parchment upon which they were originally written." Taft emphasized the importance of a vigilant judiciary in protecting what he viewed as the newly unpopular institution of private property.[51]

Taft was hardly the only judge who was worried. "At present, the tendency . . . is all toward socialism and paternalism," the Minnesota Supreme Court declared. But "the present constitution was not framed on any such lines." "Who can foretell the next subject of agitation?" asked the Pennsylvania Supreme Court. "Labor and capital are in strife. Agriculture wars on transportation. Communism, internationalism, and other forms of agitation excite the world." In 1895, when the U.S. Supreme Court held the income tax unconstitutional, Justice Stephen Field took the opportunity to predict that "the present assault upon capital is but the beginning. It will be but the stepping-stone to others, larger and more sweeping, till our political contests will become a war of the poor against the rich,—a war constantly growing in intensity and bitterness."[52] Many judges saw the constitution as the last defense against a rising attack on property. Any method of interpreting the constitution to provide stronger rights of property would look attractive in this climate. If thinking of property as a bundle of rights would help make it safer from the vandals at the gates, that was a powerful incentive to think of property as a bundle of rights.

This is not to say that the judges who took this view were creating legal doctrine out of whole cloth to suit their political preferences. There is by now a very large literature demonstrating that judges were engaged in what Howard Gillman has called "a serious, principled effort to maintain one of the central distinctions in nineteenth-century constitutional law—the distinction between valid economic regulation, on the one hand, and invalid 'class' legislation, on the other—during a period of unprecedented class conflict." But there can be little doubt that constitutional law actually did change during the period, in the direction of affording more protection to property rights than they had received earlier, and that some judges, at least, had explicitly political reasons for supporting the change.[53]

The bundle-of-rights metaphor did not *cause* these changes in constitutional law, but it made them easier to implement. The political context surrounding these decisions, meanwhile, helps explain why the idea of property as a bundle of rights first caught on in the late nineteenth century, rather than, say, in the late eighteenth or the late twentieth. The idea was not so clever that it couldn't have been hit upon much sooner. Indeed, scattered individuals were writing definitions of property very much like the bundle of rights a century before the metaphor became popular. And lawyers to this day speak of property as a bundle of rights, so there was nothing in the nature of property itself that made it more bundle-like in the late nineteenth century than it had been before or would be later. Why, then, did Austin's account of property as a collection of rights spread so quickly in the late nineteenth century?

Contrary to the views of some historians, it was most likely *not* because of the then-recent rise of new forms of intangible property, like patents, copyrights, trademarks, goodwill, and the like.[54] There had been a variety of earlier forms of intangible property, such as labor, public office, and all the incorporeal hereditaments, forms no less conducive to a conception of property as a bundle of rights, and yet that conception had to wait until the late nineteenth century before becoming part of conventional legal thought. Even more to the point, whether property is conceived of as a thing or as a bundle of rights bears no relation to its tangibility. One can have a bundle of rights in tangible things just as much as in intangible things—indeed, the asset described most often by the bundle-of-rights conception was land, which was as tangible as anything could be. Before property was widely understood as a bundle of rights, meanwhile, lawyers conceived of property as a thing whether that thing was tangible, like land, or intangible, like a copyright or a share in a corporation. Even if property was becoming less tangible in the nineteenth century (an uncertain proposition, given all the earlier forms of intangible property), that development likely had little to do with the spread of the conception of property as a bundle of rights.

The important thing was not the rise of new forms of intangible property but rather the surrounding political climate. In the late nineteenth century the idea of property as a bundle of rights was a distinctly antiregulatory idea, one that served the specific purpose of justifying constitutional doctrines that would limit the power of legislatures to regulate in ways that would reduce the value of property. At the time, there were many people, many of them judges, who wanted to achieve that goal. The idea of property as a bundle of rights had been in the air for some time, but before the late nineteenth century there had never been any particularly pressing reason to espouse it.

This political slant to the bundle of rights in the late nineteenth century is easy to miss today, when the best-remembered discussions of property as a bundle of rights are in the writings of the Progressive pro-regulatory legal writers of the early twentieth century like Wesley Hohfeld and Arthur Corbin. If one erroneously credits such writers with the development and popularization of the conception of property as a bundle of rights, it would be natural to think of that conception as one intended to reduce the constitutional protection for property.[55] Hohfeld and others would indeed think new thoughts about property in the early twentieth century, with an eye toward breaking down resistance to regulation that affected the use and value of property, but the notion of property as a bundle of rights was not one of them. It was an old thought, one that had grown popular a generation earlier, when it was put to use for precisely the opposite purpose.

4

Owning the News

MOST of the news in an early American newspaper was copied from other newspapers. The four-page *Connecticut Courant,* published weekly in Hartford, was a typical paper of the era. Of the twenty-two stories in its issue of May 21, 1822, fifteen bore notations that they had previously been published elsewhere. None of the other seven was about Connecticut—one was from as far away as Delaware—so some or even all of these might have been copied as well. No one would have thought the *Courant* was doing anything wrong. The news was "common property," one New Jersey editor explained.[1] No one owned the news.

Mightier Than the Pen

In fact, the federal government deliberately subsidized the copying of news by allowing printers to exchange newspapers with one another through the mail for free. The postal service carried an enormous volume of newspapers—by 1832, as much as 95 percent of the mail by weight. Each day, editors received dozens of papers, which provided most of the raw material for the next issue.[2]

Copying the news caused little harm in the early nineteenth century. Most newspapers published only weekly or even less frequently, so a story copied from another paper might not appear for several days or more. They included scarcely any local news, which would already have been widely known by the time it could be published in the newspaper. The news was almost entirely from other cities and countries. There were no reporters in the modern sense; news that was not copied from other papers usually came in letters received in the mail (which is why reporters at a distance are still sometimes called "correspondents") well after the events they described. The news was not very new by the time it reached readers. As papers in different cities were not competitors with one another, they had nothing to lose, and much to gain, from a norm allowing copying. Papers in the same city *were* competitors, but the long delay inherent in copying meant that the first paper to print a story was not harmed very much when another paper later published the same news.

Newspapers changed dramatically over the nineteenth century. Information began to travel much faster, first through improvements in transportation and later with the invention of the telegraph. More and more papers began to publish daily rather than weekly. Readers came to want their news new, so publishers began competing to report the news first.[3] A newspaper now had an incentive to prevent competitors in the same city from copying its news. That incentive was weakened, however, by several circumstances. It was still useful for a newspaper to be able to reprint stories originally published in papers in other cities, papers that were not competitors and so would suffer no harm. No paper could have correspondents everywhere, so even the paper with the freshest news in any given city would have had much to lose from rejecting the norm permitting copying.

When local competitors tried to pirate the news, moreover, a publisher had another weapon in his arsenal that could be more powerful than the law. Papers sometimes deliberately planted errors in their stories to expose copying. In one oft-repeated anecdote from the memoirs of Melville Stone, publisher of the *Chicago Daily News* in the 1870s, the *News* suspected that the *Chicago Post and Mail*, published by the McMullen brothers, was pirating its stories. The *News* retaliated by printing an account of a famine in Serbia, in which the local mayor was quoted as saying (ostensibly in Serbian) "Er us siht la Etsll iws nel lum cmeht." When the afternoon edition of the *Post and Mail* duly reproduced the quote, Stone ran to all the other Chicago papers to reveal the hoax: read backward, the supposed quote said "The McMullens will steal this sure." According to Stone, the *Post and Mail* never recovered from the embarrassment, and the *Daily News* was able to buy it for a pittance less than two years later. Biographies of nineteenth- and early twentieth-century journalists are full of similar stories.[4] In a local market for newspapers, this sort of gamesmanship was a partial substitute for a legally enforceable property right in news.

Local competitors, in any event, were not always harmed by copying. "All the evening journals copy from us and we rather like it," declared Horace Greeley, editor of the *New York Tribune.* In Greeley's view, the customers knew which paper printed the news first, and they would buy that one instead of its later competitors.[5] For all these reasons, the transformation in the nature of American newspapers in the nineteenth century did not, by itself, create much pressure for a property right in news.

The key development was rather the formation of the wire services, networks of papers that took advantage of the economies of scale offered by the telegraph. The first and the biggest was the Associated Press, established by the major New York papers in 1846. By 1880 the Associated Press had 355 subscribing members from every region of the country. More than a third of American newspapers were members.[6] The AP had a series of smaller and shorter-lived competitors, rival networks of newspapers that were also in the business of sharing the news by telegraph.

When the newspaper industry comprised, not thousands of scattered small local newspapers, but a handful of large national organizations, copying the news became a much more serious issue. If a paper that was a member of the Associated Press published a story in city A, within minutes it could be telegraphed to a nonmember paper in city B, which could then publish it contemporaneously with the Associated Press paper in city B. The news was common property when competition was local and copying caused little harm, but by the later nineteenth century competition was national, and copying the news could have major commercial consequences.

As the largest and best established of the wire services, the AP was the most frequent complainant. "Day after day," an AP official alleged about the American Press Association, briefly a competitor in the 1870s, "have dispatches been made up almost exclusively of what they would filch from our reports." The United Press was a rival through the 1880s and 1890s. "I have very good reason to believe that the United Press . . . is receiving regularly a copy of the news gathered by the Associated Press, and that it uses the same" in writing its own dispatches, asserted Frank O'Neil, the editor of the St. Louis *Missouri Republican,* one of the

AP papers. "If this be true," O'Neil worried, "it very seriously affects the value of our Assd. Press franchises."[7] The AP's managers repeatedly sent circulars to the publishers of its member papers, alerting them to the danger that competitors might bribe their employees in order to obtain a peek at the news.[8] The members of the Associated Press had made major investments in gathering and transmitting the news, but those investments would be worthless if competing wire services could copy the AP's news.

The AP and the leading newspaper publishers accordingly spent many years in the late nineteenth and early twentieth centuries trying to secure copyright protection for news. Under existing law, the news itself—the chronicle of facts and figures reported in each day's paper—was not copyrightable. The Constitution authorized Congress to enact a copyright law "to promote the progress of science and the useful arts," Supreme Court justice Smith Thompson had pointed out back in the 1820s, "and it would certainly be a pretty extraordinary view of the sciences to consider a daily or weekly publication of the state of the market as falling within any class of them." *Science* had a broader meaning than it does today; it also included what we would be more likely to call literary or creative merit. Even so, it connoted something durable, something that would have value well into the future. It could not, Thompson concluded, "with any propriety, be applied to a work of so fluctuating and fugitive a form as that of a newspaper." And if the *substance* of copyright did not seem to fit a newspaper, he added, copyright *procedures* were an even worse fit. To secure a copyright, one needed to deposit a copy of one's work in a district court and with the secretary of state in Washington. "It is so improbable that any publisher of a newspaper would go through this form for every paper," Thompson reasoned, that "it cannot be presumed that congress intended to include newspapers" in the copyright law. By the later part of the century it was well established that a newspaper itself could not be copyrighted.[9]

Particular material *in* a newspaper, on the other hand, could be copyrightable. "There can be no logical reason why literary matter in which property may exist, should lose that literary character from being first published in a newspaper," explained the New York lawyer James Appleton Morgan. In one 1886 case, for example, a federal judge accepted that a print published in *Harper's Weekly* could be copyrighted, just like a print published in any other way, and the judge's reasoning applied equally to a piece of writing that went beyond a bare recitation of the facts. The news itself was not protected by copyright, but the way the news was expressed could be. By the turn of the century, contrary to Smith Thompson's prediction, newspapers routinely mailed copies of every issue to the Copyright Office (which had succeeded the state department and the district courts as the repository for such things), in the expectation that they were thereby copyrighting whatever matter in the paper happened to be copyrightable.[10]

This sort of copyright was not useful to the Associated Press. AP telegraphers cabled shorthand versions of the news to the member papers, which each expanded the basic facts into the published story, the particular expression of which might differ from paper to paper. It was easy enough for a nonmember paper to do the same—to rewrite the story in different words—and thus to evade whatever copyright protection the original published story might have. "The art of 'expanding' despatches," the *Nation* explained, "supplies a ready means to the newspaper thief of stealing, and at the same time of covering his track completely."[11] The AP needed protection for the news itself, for the set of facts it transmitted to its members. It was piracy of the facts that harmed the AP, not piracy of the form of expression in which those facts were conveyed.

In 1884 the Associated Press sent Henry Watterson, the well-connected editor of the *Louisville Courier-Journal* (an AP member), to Washington, to lobby for copyright in news. Watterson managed to get a bill introduced in the Senate that would have prohibited copying the news for a period of eight hours after the newspaper went to press. Eight hours of protection would have been long enough to give morning editions of AP papers an edge over morning editions of rivals, and evening editions of AP papers an edge over evening editions of rivals, but eight hours would have been short enough to allow evening editions of rivals to copy morning editions of AP papers, and morning editions of rivals to copy AP papers from the previous evening. "Nobody can oppose" the bill, declared the *New York Times* (another AP member), "except a person who purposes to profit by the practice" of copying. But such people were more numerous than Watterson or the *Times* expected. Memorials against the bill poured in from small-town and rural newspapers all over the country, from papers in places like Manchester, New Hampshire, and Newark, Ohio, and Huron, Dakota—papers that relied for much of their news on the ability to copy from AP members. (Rural editors, the *Times* sneered, were "men with whom the scissors are mightier than the pen.") The publishers of nonmember papers, who already resented the AP's practice of granting membership to only one daily in all but the largest cities, feared that an eight-hour copyright law would drive them out of business. One evening Watterson had dinner with the recently retired Senator James Blaine, who predicted "you won't get a vote in either House." Blaine was right: the bill never made it out of committee. The AP tried again in 1899, but with no more success.[12]

Meanwhile other English-speaking jurisdictions were granting precisely this sort of short-term protection to certain kinds of news. New Zealand prohibited the copying of overseas news received by telegraph for a period of eighteen hours after first publication. Ceylon and Natal did the same, for forty-eight and seventy-two hours respectively. After some of the Australian states had granted protection to news, Australia as a whole did so in 1905, giving a twenty-four-hour copyright in telegraphic news from outside Australia. In Britain, the issue of a short-term copyright in foreign news was before Parliament for several years around the turn of the century.[13] In all of these places, the telegraph had worked the same changes in the news market as it had in the United States.

The Associated Press and its member newspapers must have been heartened, then, when the Copyright Office organized a series of conferences in 1905 to plan for the overhaul of American copyright law, an effort that would culminate in the Copyright Act of 1909. This time their representative was Don Seitz, the longtime business manager of the *New York World,* another AP paper. "In the very modern and up-to-date communities such as Tasmania and the Cape of Good Hope they have a system of copyrighting news which apparently works," Seitz testified. He pleaded for the government to "take up the law as it prevails in the Antipodes and give us a chance—forty hours, thirty-six hours, or even twenty-four hours would suffice." Without some such protection, he complained, "the type is not cool before the man across the street prints your telegram." Again, though, the idea of a copyright in news could not make it through Congress.[14]

The Associated Press was a net loser from the lack of property rights in news—certainly its managers thought so, and they were in the best position to know. But it was hardly a loser every time. The AP, like its competitors, copied when it could, sometimes to the detriment of its own members. In 1900, for example, the *Chicago Tribune* sued the AP for copying material from the *Times* of London, which had granted the *Tribune* the exclusive right to publish *Times* stories in the United States. The *Tribune* happened to be an AP paper; it discovered the copying when it received the same AP cables as the other members. The biggest cities had multiple AP papers; they were competitors with one another, and so had incentives to copy from one another on occasion. In 1909, for example, the *New York Times* purchased from Robert Peary the exclusive right to publish Peary's accounts of his expedition to the North Pole. The *Times* complied with the formalities of the copyright law, and even printed, on the front page of the paper, a large box warning other newspapers not to copy Peary's news. The story was promptly copied by newspapers in a few cities, including the *New York World* and the *New York Sun*, both, like the *Times*, members of the Associated Press. The *Times* filed suits against newspapers in New York, Chicago, and Toronto, but the damage had already been done.[15]

If the Associated Press and its members were sometimes copiers themselves, they nevertheless stood to gain more than they would lose from the establishment of a property right in news. When they failed in their efforts to persuade Congress to give them such a right, the only alternative was to seek it in the courts. But they weren't the first. There was another field besides journalism in which a special kind of news had value if one could be the first to use it, and other organizations besides the Associated Press with some experience in trying to keep news out of the hands of their competitors.

Quotations Are Property

Soon after the first American stock exchanges were established in the early nineteenth century, their members confronted a dilemma. How, and when, should stock prices be communicated to the public? On one hand, knowledge of the latest prices gave members an advantage over nonmembers, an edge that would be lost when the prices became generally known. On the other hand, a great deal of trading took place outside the exchange, so if the exchange kept its prices perpetually secret, they could become market prices, if at all, only after protracted trading between members and nonmembers. Information about prices was valuable only if it could be shared with the public, but it could be released to the public only after a delay that was long enough to allow members to exploit their superior knowledge. The exchanges tinkered with various solutions to this problem before eventually settling on the practice of publishing prices daily in newspapers, a rule that whittled members' time advantage down to the hours between the close of a trading session and the publication of the results.[16]

The invention of the stock ticker in 1867 raised a new version of the problem. The ticker was a great convenience to exchange members, because it enabled them to receive telegraphed price information in their own offices nearly in real time, almost anywhere in the country. It proved impossible, however, to prevent nonmembers from receiving the same information. Within a few years there were tickers in hotels, in restaurants, in saloons—anywhere people were interested in stock or commodity prices. The exchanges tried sporadically to pressure the telegraph companies to refuse service to nonmembers, but without much success, because the business was simply too lucrative for the telegraph companies to turn down. Even when nonmembers could not obtain ticker service legitimately, they could often get it on the sly by tapping telegraph lines or bribing telegraphers. The ticker was too useful not to use, but it caused the exchanges to lose their monopoly on price information.[17]

From the perspective of exchange members, the most grievous consequence of the loss of their control over information was the mushrooming of "bucket shops," or pseudo-brokerages, in which customers could in effect place wagers on price movements without ever actually buying or selling anything. By the last two decades of the nineteenth century there were bucket shops in towns all over the country. Some falsely held themselves out as genuine brokers; some offered honest gambles without engaging in any pretense of membership in an exchange; some were swindles with fake prices that inevitably moved in the house's favor. The bucket shops allowed smaller margins than the real exchanges and often permitted trading in fractional shares, which opened the market to customers who would have been unable to afford the real thing.[18]

For many wealthier customers, the bucket shops were a more convenient and less costly alternative to the exchanges, so they took commissions away from legitimate brokers. The bucket shops also harmed exchange members in less direct ways. Victims of swindlers sometimes could not distinguish bucket shops from genuine brokerages. Real brokers came into disrepute, a committee of the New York Stock Exchange complained, because "the ignorant people who have been robbed by a bucket-shop feel that they have been robbed by the Stock Exchange." In a real exchange, if there were more people wanting to buy than to sell, the price would rise, and if there were more willing to sell than buy, the price would decline. Bucket shops exerted the opposite effect, at least in the short run. The ersatz transactions themselves had no influence on the price at the Exchange. But a bucket shop operator was taking the opposite side of the bet cumulatively placed by his customers. If he received more orders to buy than to sell, he had a strong interest in seeing the price decline enough to wipe out his customers' margins, which might be as little as 2 percent. Consortia of bucket shop operators, the Stock Exchange despaired, "are constantly entering the stock markets and using this tremendous financial force to depress prices by every available means." Optimism about the price of stock or agricultural commodities could thus cause prices to drop temporarily. Even if they eventually rose again, whatever the bucket shops lost from short selling on the exchanges could well be swamped by the profits to be had from the bucket shops' customers. Indeed, the Exchange worried, the bucket shops might not lose anything at all: the price might stay depressed long enough for their operators to get out, because the market had been "deprived of its natural support, namely, that of the very men whose money the bucket-shops are using."[19]

The exchanges spent decades trying to stamp out the bucket shops. They persuaded several state legislatures to make bucket shops illegal, but in the end "even the best of these laws are not enforced and never can be enforced under existing conditions," the New York Stock Exchange concluded. The bucket shops were simply too popular and too well connected to local politicians. The exchanges turned instead to a different tactic. As the Stock Exchange explained, "the bucket-shops cannot exist without our quotations." A bucket shop without current price information had nothing to offer its customers. The exchanges could accordingly "put them out of business by depriving them of those quotations."[20] The telegraph companies had been uncooperative toward this end, but could the exchanges use the legal system instead? Could they establish that price information was a kind of property that bucket shops had no right to use?

The earliest American court opinion addressing the question was written by a New York trial judge in 1876, just as the bucket shops were getting off the ground. The suit was not brought by an exchange but rather by the Gold and Stock Telegraph Company, a subsidiary of Western Union, after the company discovered that a rival, the Manhattan Quotation Telegraph Company, was copying its news of European stock prices and interest rates and selling that news to customers. "It would be an atrocious doctrine," the judge concluded, "to hold that dispatches, the result of the diligence and expenditure of one man, could with impunity be pilfered and published by another." The Manhattan company argued that European prices were public knowledge in Europe, and that no one could claim to own such knowledge solely by collecting it and telegraphing it to the United States, but the argument failed to persuade the judge, who took a decidedly Lockean point of view. "A man may impress upon materials, which are open to all the world, a right of property," the judge held, "when he has, as the result of his own efforts and expenditure, collected and reduced to a form serviceable to the public such material." The Manhattan company also argued that the Gold and Stock company had abandoned any property rights in the information by transmitting it to its customers, but again the judge disagreed. Performing a play, or delivering a lecture, didn't constitute a forfeiture of rights in the play or the lecture, he reasoned. Property in financial news might be abandoned by publication to the world at large, but not by publication only to a select group of customers. The Manhattan company accordingly had no right to copy and sell the Gold and Stock company's financial news.[21]

The frequency of this sort of litigation increased markedly around the turn of the century, as the exchanges mounted their campaign against unauthorized users of their price information. By then there was little doubt that "market news is a species of property," as the Illinois Supreme Court put it. News about prices was not copyrightable, the Chicago judge Peter Grosscup acknowledged, but it was property nevertheless. "Property, even as distinguished from property in intellectual production, is not, in its modern sense, confined to that which may be touched by the hand, or seen by the eye," Grosscup declared.

Tangible property "has come to be, in most great enterprises, but the embodiment, physically, of an underlying life—a life that, in its contribution to success, is immeasurably more effective than the mere physical embodiment." Without some kind of property protection for news, he recognized, there would be less news produced, and while the world might not be much worse off for lack of news about stock prices, it *would* be worse off for lack of news about more important events. "Is the enterprise of the great news agencies, or the independent enterprise of the great newspapers, or of the great telegraph and cable lines, to be denied appeal to the courts, against the inroads of the parasite?" Grosscup asked. When the question was framed that way, the answer was obvious.[22]

Prices were property. But had the exchanges or the telegraph companies abandoned that property by transmitting it to members or to customers? Again the answer was clear by the turn of the century: revealing news about prices to customers was different from publishing prices to the general public. And again the reasoning of the court opinions relied on the need for incentives to gather the information in the first place. Most of the value of knowing prices (at least if one was not a speculator) was in the ability to sell that knowledge to others, so to say that prices were property only before they were sold was to say they were scarcely property at all.[23]

The exchanges got their biggest victory in 1905, when the U.S. Supreme Court affirmed their ability to prevent bucket shops from using their price information. The Chicago Board of Trade's collection of price quotations "is entitled to the protection of the law," Justice Oliver Wendell Holmes held. "It stands like a trade secret. The plaintiff has the right to keep the work which it has done, or paid for doing, to itself." And the Board of Trade could release that information selectively without being deemed to have abandoned its rights. "The plaintiff does not lose its rights by communicating the results to persons, even if many, in confidential relations to itself, under a contract not to make it public," Holmes concluded. Two years later, in a similar case involving the New York Cotton Exchange, the Court repeated that price "quotations are property and are entitled to the protection of the law."[24]

The bucket shops survived for another decade or so, but the exchanges had won the legal war. The lesson of the "ticker cases" was that news about prices was a form of property. The leaders of the Associated

Press were paying close attention. "It is foolish to think that in this day of cheap telegraphy we can absolutely stifle competition," reasoned AP president Victor Lawson. "The next best thing, and the practical thing, is to in a large degree control it."[25] If news about prices was property, what about news of world events, the sort of news the AP gathered and transmitted to its members? Wasn't that a kind of property too?

Property in News

After the Associated Press failed in its effort to get copyright for news into the Copyright Act of 1909, it waited several years before suing a competing wire service for copying its news. The delay is hard to understand as a commercial matter, so the likely explanation is simply that the AP was waiting to catch a rival red-handed, an event that finally happened in 1916. The competitor was the International News Service, founded in 1909 by William Randolph Hearst to supply news to the many papers owned by Hearst. (The INS would last until 1958, when it merged with the AP's other primary rival, the United Press, to form United Press International.) In November 1916 the British and French governments barred the INS from using telegraph lines in Britain and France, after the INS had published several stories about the world war containing information that had not been approved by British censors. Some of the news was unduly sympathetic to Germany, in the view of the censors, and some of it was utterly fraudulent: it had not been cabled by European correspondents at all but had been made up by INS employees in the United States. After it was denied the use of European telegraph lines, the INS nevertheless continued to supply its papers with a regular flow of European war news, a feat that raised eyebrows at the AP, as it was hard to imagine how an organization unable to send cables from Europe could report European news without copying the AP's own dispatches.

Meanwhile a telegrapher named Fred Agnew, the manager of the INS's Cleveland office, was growing bitter. When he was denied a pay raise, and then demoted for failing to report a story, Agnew swore to get even with his employer. He contacted Kent Cooper, the AP's general manager, and revealed how the INS was obtaining its news about the war: it was bribing the telegraph man at the *Cleveland News* (an AP paper) to leak the telegrams the AP was sending out to its members. In fact, the AP discovered, the *Cleveland News* was furnishing the INS with highlights of the AP's local and national dispatches as well. The AP at last had its case.[26]

By the time the case got to court the AP had found out about even more copying. The INS was getting leaks from AP newspapers in other cities besides Cleveland. It was also copying news from early editions of AP papers in eastern cities and transmitting it to INS papers in the midwest and the west, in time for the INS papers to publish the news simultaneously with the local AP papers. By free riding on the AP's newsgathering efforts, the AP alleged in its complaint, the INS was able to provide news at less cost than the AP could. The AP accordingly asked for a preliminary injunction barring the INS from copying its news.[27]

The suit landed before Augustus Hand, who would become one of the more distinguished federal judges of the first half of the twentieth century (although he would never be as prominent as his slightly younger cousin Learned Hand, with whom he served for many years). Augustus Hand was at first skeptical of the AP's claim to own the news even after it had been published in the newspaper. "I don't get your point," Hand told Frederic Jennings, the AP's lawyer. "I don't see anything immoral at all, when a thing has been put out on a bulletin board . . . in copying it and giving to anyone else." After all, Hand reasoned, wasn't the whole purpose of journalism to find information and then print it? The AP itself hired reporters to speak with people and publish what they found. Wasn't that just what the INS was doing? By the time he reached a decision two months later, Hand had been persuaded that a newsgatherer should be entitled to prevent rivals from copying the news even after publication, but his lingering doubts were strong enough that he granted only half the remedy the AP requested. He ordered the INS to stop copying the news it obtained by prepublication leaks of AP telegrams, but he refused to grant a preliminary injunction ordering the INS to stop copying the news from published newspapers. On that point he preferred to await a full trial.[28]

Both sides appealed. Henry Ward, the judge who wrote the majority opinion for a three-judge panel of the Court of Appeals, shared none of Hand's uncertainty. He was sure the Associated Press owned its news. "There is no doubt," Ward declared, "that there is a property right in news capable of and entitled to legal protection. Property . . . covers everything that has an exchangeable value," and news obviously possessed that quality, because the AP exchanged it for money every day. If financial news was a kind of property, he reasoned, then so too was news about the war or anything else. "There is no distinction entailing a legal difference, between news of the prices of corporate securities . . . and news of current political, social or national events. Both require labor and expense in acquisition, transmission, and dissemination, both have exchangeable values, and all alike lose by exposure the quality of news." Ward accordingly concluded that the AP "should have a property right in its news until the reasonable reward of each member is received, and that means (with due allowance for the earth's rotation) until plaintiff's most Western member has enjoyed his reward, which is, not to have his local competitor supplied in time for competition with what he has paid for." The court ordered the INS not to copy the AP's news so long as the news still had commercial value.[29]

The INS asked the U.S. Supreme Court to hear the case. Normally the winning party in the Court of Appeals tries to persuade the Supreme Court *not* to hear the case, but the AP took the unusual step of agreeing with the INS on the desirability of a Supreme Court decision. "The validity of the entire structure of news-collecting, distributing and marketing under modern conditions depends upon it," the AP's lawyers explained. "Nothing but a decision of this Court can assure this great service a sound and indisputable foundation and forestall a great quantity of costly and harassing litigation all over the country."[30] This claim was something of an exaggeration—the Associated Press had been operating profitably for decades without a clearly delineated property right in news—but the fact that the AP would run the risk of reversal in order to get a quick Supreme Court decision suggests how important the issue had become to the AP's managers.

The Supreme Court argument took place in May 1918, while the war in Europe was still ongoing. It matched two of the most prominent lawyers of the era. The INS was represented by Samuel Untermyer, who had recently achieved national renown as counsel to the Pujo investigation, the House of Representatives' inquiry into the existence of a Wall Street "money trust" with undue power over the economy. Speaking for the Associated Press was the St. Louis lawyer Frederick Lehmann, solicitor general in the Taft administration and a former president of the American Bar Association. As is often true, by the time the case reached the Supreme Court there was little new to be said on either side. Untermyer reminded the Court that there could be no copyright in news, and that noncopyrighted material, once published, entered the public domain and became free for all to copy. The AP, he added, was guilty of the very same practices it accused the INS of committing, so if one was at fault, so was the other. And if the AP could hoard its news, Untermyer concluded, it would become an intolerable monopoly, one with the ability to control the flow of information about important public events. Lehmann responded with the already-standard arguments on the other side. The Court had already held that news (at least about prices) was a form of property, regardless of whether it was copyrightable. That property right would be worthless if it evaporated the instant it was first published, because the pennies that could be earned from the sale of a single copy of a newspaper would never justify the expense of gathering and transmitting the news. Without the guarantee of a period of time with the sole right to the news, therefore, no one would invest the money in newsgathering in the first place.

The arguments weren't new, but the audience was. Only eight of the nine justices participated in the case. John Clarke, the newest member of the Court, was a former newspaperman (he was a part owner of the *Youngstown Vindicator*), and he recused himself, apparently for that reason. The remaining justices divided five to three in favor of the Associated Press. Mahlon Pitney's majority opinion relied heavily on the ticker cases and on the AP's assertion that news could not be gathered without some protection from copiers. "The cost of the service would be prohibitive if the reward were to be so limited," Pitney reasoned. "No single newspaper, no small group of newspapers, could sustain the expenditure. Indeed, it is one of the most obvious results of defendant's theory that, by permitting indiscriminate publication by anybody and everybody for purposes of profit in competition with the news-gatherer, it would render publication profitless, or so little profitable as in effect to cut off the service by rendering the cost prohibitive in comparison with the return." The International News Service was "endeavoring to reap where it has not sown," a practice that threatened the very existence of the enterprise.

Pitney was careful not to say that news was property in an absolute sense. He made clear that neither the AP nor the INS had any right to prevent members from the public from copying the news. Once uncopyrighted matter was published in a newspaper, readers were free to spread

that information to others. "The news of current events may be regarded as common property," Pitney explained. "The question here," he
continued, "is not so much the rights of either party as against the public
but their rights as between themselves." In Pitney's view, news "must be
regarded as quasi property," that is, a kind of property right enforceable
only against competitors and not against the world at large. "The right of
the purchaser of a single newspaper to spread knowledge of its contents
gratuitously, for any legitimate purpose not unreasonably interfering
with complainant's right to make merchandise of it, may be admitted,"
he concluded; "but to transmit that news for commercial use, in competition with complainant—which is what defendant has done and seeks
to justify—is a very different matter." The Associated Press had won.[31]

What exactly had it won? Pitney had called the news "quasi property" rather than property. He had taken pains to emphasize that the AP
could only prevent competitors, not newspaper readers, from copying
the news. In practice, however, property and quasi property were
equally valuable to the wire services. The Associated Press did not care
whether its ultimate customers, the readers who bought newspapers,
spread its news to others. It lost little or nothing that way. All the AP
wanted was an injunction prohibiting the INS and its other competitors
from copying and selling its news, and that's just what it got. Despite
Justice Pitney's disclaimers, then, news *was* property for all practical
purposes. From the AP's perspective, crowed Melville Stone, its long-
serving general manager, *International News Service v. Associated Press* "was
a most decisive victory." There was one "chief asset around which is
built the value and permanence of membership in the Associated Press,"
the newspaper publisher Frank Gannett explained a few years after the
case was decided. "This asset is *property in news.*" Even Moses Koenigsberg, the general manager of the INS, had to concede that the case was
the culmination of Stone's "quarter-of-a-century campaign to establish
the claim that news might be held as private property." Koenigsberg had
little patience for Stone's "sanctimonious passion" in "this so-called crusade," which he viewed as a "movement to create the basis for a news
monopoly," but he acknowledged Stone had prevailed.[32]

Two of the three justices in the minority wrote dissenting opinions,
and the way the case has been viewed by later generations has been
heavily influenced by the fact that those two justices were the members
of the 1918 Court who would enjoy the greatest posthumous reputations,

Oliver Wendell Holmes and Louis Brandeis. Holmes disagreed with the majority's implicit Lockean premise, that there was something inherently wrong with reaping where another had sown. "Property, a creation of law, does not arise from value," Holmes argued. "Many exchangeable values may be destroyed intentionally without compensation," as when one business reduced the value of another by competing successfully. "Property depends upon exclusion by law from interference, and a person is not excluded from using any combination of words merely because some one has used it before, even if it took labor and genius to make it." The investment of work or money was not enough to create property; only *law* could create property, and if there was no law protecting the sower, there was nothing wrong with reaping where another had sown. In Holmes's view (and that of Joseph McKenna, who joined his opinion), the only wrong committed by the International News Service was in misrepresenting the source of its news. If the INS had given proper credit to the Associated Press, the AP would have received all it was entitled to.

Brandeis dissented in a characteristically long and fact-laden opinion. While the ticker cases had loosely referred to news as property, he acknowledged, the true ground of those decisions had actually been narrower, because the ticker cases had each involved breaches of a contract to keep the news confidential. The International News Service, by contrast, had no such contract with the Associated Press. Like any other reader of a newspaper, the INS had every right to do what it liked with the AP's news once that news had been published. There was no existing law barring the free use of published news, and Brandeis worried about the consequences of inventing new law that did so. Allowing the AP to monopolize the news, he feared, "would effect an important extension of property rights and a corresponding curtailment of the free use of knowledge and of ideas." A legislature, he pointed out, would have the ability to balance a property right in news with some corresponding obligation on the part of the AP, such as a requirement that the AP sell its news on equal terms to all who wished to buy it. Courts lacked the power to create these sorts of compromises. "Considerations such as these," Brandeis concluded, "should lead us to decline to establish a new rule of law in the effort to redress a newly disclosed wrong."

But Holmes and Brandeis were on the losing side. The Associated Press had tried for decades to secure a property right in news, and in 1918 it finally succeeded.

Another Celerity to News Circulation

Most contemporary legal commentators found Pitney's majority opinion a model of progressive thought. "This case shows the adaptability of the courts to meet new conditions," one writer explained. Another agreed that the Court was "keeping pace with the ever increasing public demand for higher business ethics." The law professor Walter Wheeler Cook happily predicted that "the decision will in the long run have the effect of stimulating the gathering and publication of news." Another lawyer praised the Court for having "gone a long way toward establishing as law the principle that no one shall be permitted to appropriate to himself the fruits of another's labor."[33]

With time, however, the prevailing professional view of *International News Service* turned considerably darker. If the Court meant to declare a broad right to reap the fruits of one's labor, lawyers wondered, how could that right be reconciled with the elaborate statutes governing patents and copyrights, statutes that protected the fruits of one's labor only under certain specific conditions? Clearly the case could not stand for a general right to reap where one had sown. But then how was it possible to distinguish the situations in which one had such a right from the situations in which one did not? Pitney's majority opinion began to seem less like a progressive adjustment of the law to the times, and more like the arrogation of judicial power to create amorphous, indeterminate property rights that rested on nothing but the policy preferences of judges. Seen this way, in an era when judges tended to be more conservative than legislatures, it was Brandeis's deference to legislatures that began to look like the progressive point of view. By 1929 Learned Hand could confidently deny that Pitney "meant to lay down a general rule that a man is entitled to 'property' in the form of whatever he makes with his labor and money." Hand's colleague Thomas Swan agreed that "Brandeis's dissent seems to me a much stronger position than the majority," because "I don't see what bounds we could put on the doctrine if we extend it" beyond the specific facts presented by *International News Service*.[34] Critics like Hand and Swan had no objection as a policy matter to the creation of a property right in news. Their concern was about the lack of any principled way of deciding what other kinds of intangible assets did or did not deserve similar protection, and thus about the lack of judicial authority to create new property rights in the first place. *International News Service* came to be understood as a case about newspapers and nothing else.

And then the tide of professional opinion turned yet again. Technological changes in the twentieth century produced new ways of gathering and transmitting information. Just as the telegraph and the stock ticker had transformed the news business in the nineteenth century, the radio and the computer transformed it in the twentieth. Once again there were new ways of copying information that had been gathered by others. Property in news made a comeback.[35]

In the early 1930s, for example, a radio station in Bellingham, Washington, began producing a program it called the "Newspaper of the Air," in which announcers would read the news from the day's papers. Some of those papers were members of the Associated Press, which promptly sued the station to force it to stop. "Radio has added another celerity to news circulation," the court recognized. If listeners could get their news for free from the radio, they would have no need to buy the newspaper, and the AP would be unable to recoup its investment in gathering and transmitting the news. There was no difference, the court concluded, between pirating news by radio and pirating news by a competing newspaper. In either case, the copier was infringing a property right in news. A few years later a radio station in Pittsburgh began broadcasting unauthorized play-by-play accounts of Pirates baseball games, based on reports of observers peering over the fence from buildings near Forbes Field. A court ordered the station to stop, on the ground that the Pirates had "a property right in such news." Similar midcentury cases came out the same way.[36]

Toward the end of the century, the invention of the pager and then the mobile phone gave rise to a new business: the transmission, almost in real time, of information about games in progress. In 1996 Motorola began selling pagers that could display the scores of professional basketball games, along with other data about the games, with a lag of only two or three minutes between the game itself and transmission of the information. A district judge granted the National Basketball Association's request to shut down Motorola's service. The Court of Appeals reversed, on the ground that Motorola was not copying news gathered by the NBA but was rather investing its own resources to gather the news, much as if the International News Service had been sending its own reporters to Europe to cover the war. The court nevertheless cautioned that when the NBA launched its own pager service, if Motorola began collecting scores from the NBA pagers rather than from its own efforts, Motorola *would* be infringing the NBA's property rights in news about games.[37] The technology was different, but the principle of *International News Service* was still alive.

The first kind of news to be protected as property, back in the late nineteenth century, had been stock and commodity prices. In the late twentieth, the debate was over a more complex kind of financial news. The Standard and Poor's Corporation had long compiled a well-known index of the prices of 500 stocks, to create a single number representative of the overall performance of the stock market. In 1979 Standard and Poor's licensed the Chicago Mercantile Exchange to offer trading in a futures contract based on the S&P index. A year later, a competing exchange called Comex began to offer trading in something it called the Comex 500 Index, which used the same 500 stocks and the same method of calculation as the S&P Index. In S&P's suit against Comex, it argued that "Comex's proposed use is no different than INS' condemned conduct in *International News Service:* Comex is taking S&P's Index, on which S&P expends substantial money, labor and expertise." Meanwhile a very similar lawsuit was taking place over the stock indexes compiled by Dow Jones & Company, another venerable provider of financial information. Without the consent of Dow Jones, the Chicago Board of Trade began offering trading in futures contracts pegged to the Dow Jones Industrial Average and two other Dow Jones indexes. The compilers of the original indexes, S&P and Dow Jones, won both cases. Dow Jones "has a proprietary interest in its indexes and averages," the Illinois Supreme Court held, in an opinion that rested heavily on *International News Service.* As in the ticker cases from a century before, news about prices was a form of property.[38]

In each of these episodes, from the bucket shops of the 1870s through the wire service battles of the turn of the century to the pagers and stock indexes of our own era, property has been an instrumental value, not an end in itself. People have argued that news should or should not be classified as property in order to advance some other goal—in this case, the goal of making money. Judges and legislatures reached decisions, not by inquiring into the true nature of property, but by considering the practical consequences that would flow from a decision one way or the other. Throughout these debates, property proved to be a concept flexible enough to allow for a wide range of argument. It was not *completely* flexible—conventional notions of property did place substantial constraints on the sorts of assertions that would have been deemed reasonable. For example, opponents of a property right in news did not argue that only tangible things could qualify as property, or that property necessarily implied infinite duration, or that the only things classifiable as property were those that had been considered property at some point in the past. Such claims would have been outside the bounds of professionally respectable argument. Property was an instrumental value, but it was not so malleable that it could be put to any old use. The same would be true in later years as well, when further technological change would prompt debates over whether other kinds of assets should be recognized as property.

5

People, Not Things

As THE modern regulatory state gradually formed between roughly 1870 and 1940, contemporaries detected a change in the relationship between government power and private property rights. "With moral progress," one proponent of regulation declared in 1901, "men learn to place the public welfare before the individual interest." When property rights conflicted with human needs, explained Theodore Roosevelt shortly after his presidency ended, "human rights must have the upper hand, for property belongs to man and not man to property." Throughout the period, the federal and state governments created new institutions like regulatory agencies and enacted new laws governing matters like wages, prices, working conditions, building sizes, and the like. These innovations were not entirely unprecedented, but many of them limited the rights of property owners in new ways. "The right of property," one lawyer remarked, seemed to "lose a trifle of its sacredness" and to be "relegated to a lower pedestal."[1]

As with any major historical shift, one can find many reasons for this one, including technological change, growing inequality and class conflict, and changing ideas about the proper role of government.[2] Here the focus will be on a causal factor that has not received as much attention—changes in the way Americans thought about property.

The Law of Nature

Early Americans often described property as a natural right.[3] "We do not derive our property from the State, or from the laws," one resident of Massachusetts insisted in the 1780s; "property is our natural right, and government is intended to support and protect us in the use and enjoyment of it. The dollar I earn is mine, independent of the power of the State, and they can have no right to take it away from me." On this view, property preexisted, in both a logical and a historical sense, the formation of government and the creation of law. Property flowed not from law but from human nature. "The Creator designed that man, as an intelligent moral being, should enjoy not only so much property as will satisfy his mere animal wants," reasoned the New York lawyer E. P. Hurlbut, "but that he should strive for and attain something of wealth also, to minister to the high demands of his moral sentiments." The best evidence of property's naturalness was its ubiquity. It could hardly be a coincidence, the Virginia law professor Henry St. George Tucker explained, that one could find property in nearly every society in the world. Laws protecting property enjoyed "so general a consent of the human race, that there can be but little reason to doubt, that the principles upon which they are founded are planted in the heart, and the laws themselves obligatory upon the conscience."[4] Theorists differed over the details—some located the origin of property in labor, others in the occupancy of previously unoccupied land, still others in a hypothesized social compact—but they agreed on the basic point that property was a natural right.

This way of thinking about property never disappeared, but it grew weaker over the course of the nineteenth and early twentieth centuries. Property gradually came to seem less like a natural right preexisting the law and more like a right *created by* the law.

The earliest American skeptics of property's naturalness pointed out that whether or not property was a natural right in the abstract, the specific kind of property that might exist in a state of nature looked very different from the property enjoyed in a society like that of the United States. Under natural law, Thomas Jefferson argued, land "is the property for the moment of him who occupies it, but when he relinquishes the occupation, the property goes with it." Permanent rights require organization, so "stable ownership is the gift of social law, and is given late in the progress of society." As another lawyer put it, a bit more pithily, in the 1830s, property, "as it respects the *temporary use* of the soil, is the *law of nature;* and, as it respects the right to permanent exclusive property in the substance of the soil, is *the law of the land.*" Joseph Story noted that even if property originated in occupation and use, that principle served to explain very little about the legal systems of countries like the United States, which protected property rights even in assets the owner was not currently occupying or using. "The truth is (though it is a truth rarely brought into discussion among civilized nations), that exclusive sovereignty and ownership of the soil, is a derivative right, resting upon municipal regulations," Story concluded. "If general consent should abolish it tomorrow, it would be difficult to say, that a return to the patriarchal or pastoral state of nations, and the community of property, would be any departure from natural right."[5]

A second wave of skepticism reached American shores around the middle of the nineteenth century, amid a growing concern about the inequality with which property was distributed. "Why these savage hovels by the side of these vast and gorgeous palaces?" an anonymous author in the *United States Magazine* asked in 1845. "Why this squalid, ragged vagrant wandering, homeless and famishing, among these abodes of luxurious opulence?" The author had no doubt that property was a natural right. "A more false and pernicious moral and political heresy was never broached," he declared, "than that which founds the right of property on convention" rather than natural law. But he had in mind a natural law in which "every man must have a right to an equal portion of the earth, or an equivalent, for his subsistence and use." The unequal distribution of wealth in the nineteenth-century United States, on this view, was *contrary* to the natural right of property, which justified a radical reorganization of economic life.[6]

The idea that natural law required some measure of redistribution quickly became a common theme on the American left. The argument was often voiced in religious terms. "No individual man has a right from nature to determine his own share of property independently of equal rights in other men," urged the *Catholic World*. "For nature gives the goods of this earth to all in common." The Presbyterian reformer Charles Henry Parkhurst contended that "the Christian conception of property" was one in which "the proprietary rights of the individual are to be arbitrated from the stand-point of the State, and not the rights of the State from the stand-point of the individual." But there was nothing inherently religious about an egalitarian or communal understanding of the law of nature, which just as often lay beneath secular calls for greater governmental limits on the power of the propertied. "Of the wealth that resides in land the State is certainly the creator and the original and lawful owner," reasoned the economist John Bates Clark. The state thus had the right to apportion that value as it saw fit. "If any theory depreciates . . . the State's reserved right over all wealth," Clark concluded, referring to the older view that natural law limited state power over private property, "so much the worse for that theory."[7]

This egalitarian conception of natural law received a boost from some of the early anthropologists of law, who found that property originated in communities rather than individuals. The most well known in North America was the English lawyer Henry Sumner Maine, whose *Ancient Law* was published in several editions in Britain and the United States. Maine mocked theorists who imagined primitive humans claiming individual property rights in land by virtue of occupancy. "These sketches of the plight of human beings in the first ages of the world are effected by first supposing mankind to be divested of a great part of the circumstances by which they are now surrounded," he scoffed, "and by then assuming that, in the condition thus imagined, they would preserve the same sentiments and prejudices by which they are now actuated,—although, in fact, these sentiments may have been created and engendered by those very circumstances of which, by the hypothesis, they are to be stripped." The anthropologists' strategy was instead to observe actual practices among societies then commonly viewed as primitive, and to assume that those practices offered a window onto the distant past of their own society. Maine focused on India, where he determined that property was held not by individuals but by village communities, who were "an assemblage of joint proprietors, a body of kindred holding a domain in common." The French anthropologist Charles Letourneau studied property arrangements in Indonesia and arrived at the same conclusion. "The genesis of the right of private property in land has been much the same in all parts of the world," Letourneau affirmed. "If it be not a natural law, it is at all events a very general fact, that the soil has at first been everywhere in common, in joint ownership, and that private appropriation has largely arisen out of the progress of agriculture."[8] Among many of those who believed themselves adherents of a newly scientific view of human origins, the existing distribution of property was not a result of natural law but rather a departure from it.

By the late nineteenth century, the law of nature was frequently invoked to support both strong rights of private property and sharp limits on those rights. To skeptics, its indeterminacy as applied to property provided a good reason for doubting its value as an analytical tool. "We can just as well use this argument of natural rights to attack the institution as to uphold it," the economist Richard Ely sneered; "this is because it is dogmatism in any case." If it was a simple game to choose a version of natural law that matched one's preexisting view of property, why should anyone be persuaded by one version or another? "Has every human being, as against others, a natural right to land? and if so, is there any limit to such right?" wondered the New York lawyer Samuel Clarke. But he had no answers for his own questions. "Pretty much all that one man can do for another towards solving them is to present them clearly and ask, 'What do you think?' "[9]

One way out of this thicket was to deny that property had any connection with the law of nature, and to believe instead that property was a human creation. There was already considerable disagreement about the very existence of natural law. American intellectuals were familiar with the English positivists, especially Jeremy Bentham and John Austin, some of whose work was published in the United States. Bentham famously had little patience for any sort of claim based on natural law. "We cannot reason with fanatics armed with *natural right,* which every one understands just as he likes," Bentham complained. Natural law and natural right were just "two sorts of fiction or metaphor" that allowed disputants to "substitute for the reasoning of experience, the chimeras of their imagination." Austin's view was similar: "To say that a human law which conflicts with the law of God, is therefore not *binding,* or not *valid,* is to talk stark nonsense." By the late nineteenth and early twentieth centuries, many American lawyers were saying much the same thing. "The jurists who believe in natural law," Oliver Wendell Holmes diagnosed, "seem to me to be in that naive state of mind that accepts what has been familiar and accepted by them and their neighbors as something that must be accepted by all men everywhere."[10] The concept of natural law was losing some of its hold.

So was its association with property. The view that property was not attributable to nature was again most famously associated with Bentham. "There is no natural property," he insisted. "Property is entirely the creature of law." Simply possessing or even consuming an object did not amount to property. "A piece of cloth which is actually in the Indies may belong to me, whilst the dress which I have on may not be mine," Bentham noted. "The food which is incorporated with my own substance may belong to another, to whom I must account for its use." Property was something more, "an established expectation . . . in the persuasion of power to derive certain advantages from the object." And that expectation, Bentham concluded, "can only be the work of the law. I can reckon upon the enjoyment of that which I regard as my own, only according to the promise of the law, which guarantees it to me." Without law, there could be no property. This view too acquired American adherents by the turn of the twentieth century. The view that property was a natural right, observed the law professor Orrin Mc-Murray, was "a theory so out of keeping with modern conceptions of the relation of the community to the individual" that it "must seriously confuse legal thinking."[11]

Property had firmly been considered a natural right in the late eighteenth century, but by the late nineteenth century that proposition was a matter for debate. Strictly as a logical matter, the weakening naturalness of property need not have implied any particular attitude toward regulation. One who rejected the notion that property was founded in natural law might nevertheless have consequentialist reasons for favoring strong property rights, while a belief in natural rights of property was, as we have seen, not necessarily incompatible with a preference for regulation and even redistribution. Nevertheless, contemporaries recognized that as a practical matter the two issues were linked. Those who believed property to be a natural right tended to disfavor legal incursions on that right, while proponents of regulation tended to minimize or dismiss the naturalness of property.

Sometimes the supporters of regulation made the link explicit. "At every step the right of property is a creation by the social body," one reasoned. "What it gave, it can take away." But the connection was probably drawn more often by the defenders of property rights, who worried that the decline of natural law was hastening the decline of property. "To deny the natural right of property is to throw down the defences against the most odious communism," fretted one correspondent to the *New York Times.* Another observed that opponents of socialism should avoid contending that the right of property "depends upon man-made law, otherwise the Socialist or any other party placed in power might legitimately change the law and abrogate the so-called right." Property felt under attack, and many prominent judges and lawyers felt obliged to defend it.[12] Natural law was one of their weapons.

Christopher Tiedeman, for example, was a conservative law professor best known for his 1886 *Treatise on the Limitations of the Police Power in the United States,* a catalog of tools judges could use to find regulation unconstitutional. Like much legal writing of the era, Tiedeman's books tended to be compilations of court opinions intended for practicing lawyers; he also produced treatises on the law of property, sales, and commercial paper, among other subjects. But Tiedeman occasionally turned to more explicitly theoretical work. In his 1890 book *The Unwritten Constitution of the United States,* he elaborated an argument that foreshadowed some of the constitutional debates of the twentieth century. In assessing the constitutionality of legislation, Tiedeman contended, courts were not limited to the written provisions of constitutions. They were also obliged to consider the "unwritten constitution," that is, "the fundamental principles" that are "found imbedded in the national character and are developed in accordance with the national growth." One such principle, he asserted, was "the so-called *laissez-faire* philosophy," based on "the prevalent doctrine of natural rights," which in his view had until recently so dominated everyday conceptions of legislative power that it was scarcely called into question. "But a change has since then come over the political thought of the country," Tiedeman maintained. "Under the stress of economical relations, the clashing of private interests, the conflicts of labor and capital," natural rights of property "are in imminent danger of serious infringement. The State is called upon to protect the weak against the shrewdness of the stronger, to determine what wages a workman shall receive for his labor, and how many hours he shall labor." As a result, he explained, "the conservative classes stand in constant fear of an absolutism more tyrannical and more unreasoning than any before experienced by man,—the absolutism of a democratic majority." The only security for the natural right of property lay in the unwritten constitution. "In these days of great social unrest," Tiedeman concluded, "we applaud the disposition of the courts to seize hold of these general declarations of rights as an authority for them to lay their interdict upon all legislative acts which interfere with the individual's natural rights, even though these acts do not violate any specific or special provision of the

Constitution."[13] In this battle, natural law was one of property's strongest fortifications.

The conception of property as a natural right thus persisted in part due to its perceived usefulness in fending off regulation. "Though disclaimed by almost all our more careful writers on politics and ethics," observed the philosopher David Ritchie, "it yet remains a commonplace of the newspaper and the platform," particularly in the United States, "where the theory may be said to form part of the national creed." It also remained common in learned journals, where lawyers and others continued to claim that property was founded in nature—if anything, more frequently than ever, now that property's naturalness was thought to have important practical consequences. This persistence was regarded with some amusement by those who considered natural law akin to superstition. "It will probably always continue to be defended," one critic joked, "in company with perpetual motion, circle squaring and the Baconian authorship of Shakespeare."[14] But although it was still alive, the idea that property was a natural right grew weaker in the late nineteenth and early twentieth centuries. Contemporaries believed that this weakening contributed something to a growing acceptance of regulation affecting property rights, and it is hard to say they were wrong.

Power Over People

Meanwhile a second change was just getting under way. For a long time, lawyers had thought of property as a relation between people and the things they owned. The classic definition came from Blackstone, who described property as "that sole and exclusive dominion which one man claims and exercises over the external things of the world." In the early twentieth century, however, among the academic lawyers who thought most about property, this conception was replaced by one in which property was understood, not as a relation between people and things, but simply as a relation between people. Property on this view was not about the powers that people could exercise over objects. It was about the powers they could exercise over other people.[15]

This is an idea of property that is today most associated with the law professor Wesley Hohfeld, but while Hohfeld certainly provided the most detailed account of it, the notion that property is a relation between people has roots extending back to the nineteenth century. The

Vermont judge Nathaniel Chipman observed as early as 1833 that an isolated person surrounded by things could have no sense of property, "for it is essential to any conception of this right, that the subject belongs to one in exclusion of all others." It was the ability to exclude other people from using a thing, not the ability to use the thing itself, that constituted property. Hohfeld's more immediate and likely more causal precursors wrote in the 1880s. One was Oliver Wendell Holmes, who included a discussion of property in the series of Boston lectures he published as *The Common Law*. It was not the law of property that enabled him to use particular objects, Holmes explained. "That is a physical power which I have without the aid of the law. What the law does is simply to prevent other men to a greater or lesser extent from interfering with my use or abuse." The philosopher Thomas Davidson made a similar point a few years later, using language Hohfeld would later take up. An isolated individual might *possess* a thing, he noted, but "possession becomes property solely by being recognized as such by a community. By such recognition the community does two things: (1) It grants a privilege; (2) It undertakes to protect the recipient of that privilege in the exclusive use thereof." Property, on this account, was in the relation between the individual and the community. A Harvard law student named Everett Abbot won a school prize in 1889 for an essay in which he found this conception more accurate than the conventional one. "The error of the ordinary definition of property," Abbot reasoned, "lies in the fact that that phrase declares that the relation between the owner and the thing is legal. It cannot be insisted too strongly that the relation is purely physical." The *legal* relation constituting property, by contrast, "exists, not between a person and a thing, but between persons only, between the owner and the rest of human society."[16] Few ideas, if any, are entirely new, so it is hardly surprising that the conception of property as a relation between people was in the air well before Hohfeld spelled it out in detail.

Hohfeld's well-known discussion of property was first published in two articles in the *Yale Law Journal* in 1913 and 1917.[17] Hohfeld was a law professor in his thirties; a native Californian, he began his teaching career at Stanford and moved to Yale in 1914. He would die of heart failure at the age of thirty-nine a year after publishing the second of the two articles. His main contribution to legal theory was to identify and name eight building blocks—he called them a right, a duty, a privilege, a no-right, a power, a liability, an immunity, and a disability—from which all legal relationships could be built. The building blocks came in pairs, in two distinct ways. First, each was the opposite of one of the others. Rights, for example, were the opposite of privileges, and powers were the opposite of immunities. As Hohfeld explained, "a right is one's affirmative claim against another, and a privilege is one's freedom from the right or claim of another. Similarly, a power is one's affirmative 'control' over a given legal relation as against another; whereas an immunity is one's freedom from the legal power or 'control' of another." Second, each building block was the correlative of one of the others, in the sense that the existence of one in person A implied the existence of another in person B. If A had a right, such as to keep B off A's land, B had a corresponding duty to stay off the land. If A had a privilege, for example to enter the land, B had a corresponding "no-right" (a term of Hohfeld's invention) to prevent A from entering. If A had a power, for instance to transfer his interest in the land to someone else, every other person had the liability to receive the land. (Unlike the ordinary definition of the word, a Hohfeldian liability was not necessarily a bad thing.) Finally, if A had an immunity, say from being taxed, every other person was under the disability of not being able to collect taxes from A. By combining these building blocks in different ways, one could describe a wide variety of legal relationships more clearly than had previously been possible, and one could avoid the terminological and conceptual confusion that Hohfeld found prevalent in court opinions.

By stripping away the conventional thing-centered vocabulary of property, Hohfeld's scheme emphasized the nature of property as relations between people rather than between people and things. To use his own extended example, suppose A owns a parcel of land. "His 'legal interest' or 'property' relating to the tangible object that we call *land*," Hohfeld explained, "consists of a complex aggregate of rights (or claims), privileges, powers, and immunities." One is the "right" to prevent others from entering the land or harming it, a right that imposes a correlative "duty" upon others not to enter or harm the land. A also has "an indefinite number of legal privileges of entering on the land, using the land, harming the land, etc." Because of these "privileges," other people have corresponding "no-rights," because they are not allowed to prevent A from doing any of these things. A also has a variety of "powers," including the power to sell the land, to allow others to use the land, and so on, powers that imply correlative "liabilities" in others. And finally, "A has an indefinite number of legal immunities, using the term immunity in the very specific sense of non-liability or non-subjection to a power on the part of another person. Thus he has the immunity that no ordinary person can alienate A's legal interest or aggregate of jural relations to another person; the immunity that no ordinary person can extinguish A's own privileges of using the land; the immunity that no ordinary person can extinguish A's right that another person X shall not enter on the land or, in other words, create in X a privilege of entering on the land." Because of all these immunities, other people have corresponding "disabilities." Here was the entire bundle of rights constituting A's property expressed in terms of the relations between A and other people.[18]

Hohfeld's idiosyncratic terminology never really caught on. "I don't doubt that his work makes for the side of accurate thinking," Oliver Wendell Holmes confided to Felix Frankfurter, "but the idea of bothering oneself with all that hocus-pocus for daily purpose seems to me superfluous." The sentiment was likely shared by many. Hohfeld's greatest influence was not in the details but rather in how his scheme emphasized the nature of property as relations between people. Within a few years of his death, that understanding of property was already well on its way to becoming standard. "Our concept of property has shifted," the Yale professor Arthur Corbin declared in 1922. " 'Property' has ceased to describe any *res*, or object of sense, at all, and has become merely a bundle of legal relations." Leon Green, the dean of Northwestern's law school, likewise described property as "truly a relational interest, for it is the owner's claim as against other persons."[19] Property was about people, not things.

As with the decline of natural law, the spread of this new conception of property was not linked, as a logical necessity, with any particular view as to the appropriateness of regulation. One could think of property as relations between people and, in principle, either favor or disfavor government intervention in the economy. Nevertheless, as with the decline of natural law, the two issues were often linked in practice. The more one thought about property as relations between people, the less likely one was to oppose regulation that adjusted those relations.

The Columbia law professor Robert Hale, for example, was a sharp critic of the Supreme Court's constitutional decisions protecting businesses against regulation limiting the prices they could charge. The owner of a factory, Hale pointed out, had more at his command than just inanimate machines. "The law has delegated to him a discretionary power over the rights and duties of others," Hale noted. "Ownership is an indirect method whereby the government coerces some to yield an income to the owners." The power wielded over other people by a property owner was no different in this respect from the power exercised by a government official; in both cases, the law authorized one person to coerce other people into performing or not performing particular actions. The income earned by a property owner was thus no more sacrosanct than the salary of a government official. Neither had any natural value deserving constitutional protection. Focusing his attention on public utility companies, the subjects of some then-recent Supreme Court cases strongly protective of property rights, Hale concluded that "it would be as absurd to justify any particular utility values on the ground that their legitimacy is generally recognized in other fields, as it would be for a municipal administration to justify a salary of a sinecure on the ground that some other administration of some other city still pays that sort of salary." By thinking of property as relations between people rather than between people and things (especially their money), Hale was able to depict price regulation as part of the ordinary work of government rather than an abridgment of a constitutional right.[20]

The point that property is a form of delegated governmental power was made even more strongly by the legal philosopher Morris Cohen. If "somebody else wants to use the food, the house, the land or the plow which the law calls mine, he has to get my consent," Cohen observed. "To the extent that these things are necessary to the life of my neighbor, the law thus confers on me a power, limited but real, to make him do what I want." This equation of property and power over others had once been easy to see, in the era when most people had to earn their living from the land, and the practice was that "he who has the legal right over the land receives homage and service from those who wish to live on it." In the modern era, "the character of property as sovereign power compelling service and obedience may be obscured for us in a commercial economy by the fiction of the so-called labor contract as a free bargain and by the frequency with which service is rendered indirectly through a money payment." But while it was harder to see, it was no less real.

"Today I do not directly serve my landlord if I wish to live in the city with a roof over my head," Cohen explained, "but I must work for others to pay him rent with which he obtains the personal services of others," and that work was in turn performed by serving "those to whom the law has accorded dominion over the things necessary for subsistence." In short, "dominion over things is also *imperium* over our fellow human beings." This conclusion, in turn, had implications for how one thought about the permissibility of regulating property. "If the large property owner is viewed, as he ought to be, as a wielder of power over the lives of his fellow citizens, the law should not hesitate to develop a doctrine as to his positive duties in the public interest. The owner of a tenement house in a modern city is in fact a public official and has all sorts of positive duties" such as providing adequate lighting and fire escapes. The same was true of a factory owner, who, as a public official, could be required to provide safe and hygienic working conditions.[21] Again, the more one understood property as power relations among people, the more regulation one was willing to support.

Whether property was best characterized this way was never as widely debated a question as whether property was founded in natural law. There were no newspaper editorials or popular magazine articles insisting that property was or was not a relationship between people. Only lawyers thought about the issue, and even then probably only a very small fraction of the most philosophically inclined. At least within law schools, though, this reconception of property smoothed the way for an acceptance of greater regulatory limits on the use and the value of property. And of course the law schools were the entry point for an increasingly large percentage of the broad policymaking community. All law students took a course in Property, and more and more of them would learn that property was not about things; it was about power over people.

The Disappearing Right

By the early twentieth century, property seemed to be growing weaker every year. In the widely read *North American Review* Daniel Kellogg lamented "the disappearing right of private property." David Kinley, president of the American Economic Association, declared in his annual address for 1914 that "for some twenty-five years" Americans had been moving "from the strong individualism of the early 19th century towards a gradual extension of government authority in economic matters." The economist Ezra Bowen agreed that "the concept of private property has shrunk." New forms of regulation "are sledges that have struck away whole slabs of the gibraltar of private property, making incessant and increasing inroads."[22]

Bowen provided some colorful examples. "A farm, let us say, has been in your family for many generations. Over the week-end, you may have your friends for a clay-pigeon shoot, but not a live-bird shoot, though your father might. Suppose you have a race-course on the place; you may not set up betting booths, though your grand-father had that right. If a member of your family dies, you may not bury him on the place, but your great-grand-father might. If you raise rye, you may not build a still to make your rye into whisky, though your great-great-grand-father might." And that was just rural property; the law had changed even faster in the city. "You own a city lot and you decide to put up a frame building on it. No, you may not; the law forbids because it would increase the fire hazard of your neighbors. Well then, it will be of brick, a loft building. No; loft buildings are not permitted in that section of the city. Then you will build an apartment house, eighteen stories high. No; buildings of more than six stories are forbidden in that zone!" An owner of property was hedged about with law in every direction. "The scope and fullness of the right itself," Bowen concluded, "has been everywhere curtailed."

But Bowen was no critic of these developments. Property was not an immutable fact of nature, he explained; "as old as life, it is however wholly conventional—an artifice, an arrangement." Property had no foundation in natural law. It was merely a human creation, a means to the end of stimulating economic activity. If other ends had come to be seen as more important, "private property has been and will be further modified." The law of property, in any event, was nothing more than a way of adjusting power relationships between people. "Right is correlative to duty," Bowen reasoned, using Hohfeld's vocabulary (although quoting John Chipman Gray). "Everywhere, by judicial decision and by statute, lines are being drawn that give to the features of private property, the aspect of trusteeship." Property owners were being forced to use their property in ways that limited the harm they inflicted on others. "The almost majestic irresponsibility of the ancient right of property is fast waning," Bowen concluded. "Private property, the oldest and, at first, the most uncompromising of social institutions, tends to diminish in force and scope with the growth of civilization."[23]

For a time the Supreme Court was the final wall of defense against the most far-reaching of these changes, but even that wall fell in the 1930s, when a new generation of justices replaced the old. "Regulatory legislation affecting ordinary commercial transactions is not to be pronounced unconstitutional," Justice Harlan Fiske Stone declared, unless "it is of such a character as to preclude the assumption that it rests upon some rational basis," a requirement that would be satisfied only in the rarest of circumstances. The Court would soon turn its attention instead to what Stone called "prejudice against discrete and insular minorities."[24] The regulatory state was here to stay, and with it a distinctly twentieth-century conception of the scope of property rights.

6

Owning Sound

FOR MOST of human history, sound was ephemeral. Once produced it could not be stored or reproduced; it was gone forever. The only way to sell it was as live performance, and that was a task easily handled by existing property law, because rights to hear sound could be sold in the form of tickets to enter concert halls. That changed with the invention of sound recording in the late nineteenth century. When sound could be stored it could be sold in new ways. Now there were gains to be had from establishing a system of property rights in it. But whose rights would they be? And where would their boundaries be located? The answers to these questions would determine how the gains from technological change would be divided.

Music in Solidified Form

Nineteenth-century songwriters made their money from royalties on sheet music sales. Stephen Foster sold more than 130,000 copies of "Old Folks at Home" in the early 1850s. "On the Banks of the Wabash," a hit in the 1890s for the composer Paul Dresser (with lyrics by his younger brother, the novelist Theodore Dreiser), sold more than half a million copies. Of course, few songs were as popular, but to the extent there was any income in composing, it came from publishing sheet music.[1]

The legal foundation for the business of music publishing was the copyright law, which prohibited the copying of musical compositions. In its earliest versions, American copyright law did not explicitly protect music, so pieces of music were often copyrighted as books, charts, or engravings, which did receive protection. In 1831 the law was tidied up to include musical compositions as a separate category of copyrightable works.[2] Even then, however, the composer could prevent only the duplication of the sheet music, not the performance of the composition itself. Having bought the printed notes, a musician was free to play the music in concert without the composer's permission and without sharing any of the revenue with the composer.

For the rest of the century there would be sporadic debate over whether the copyright law should be amended to give composers the right of public performance. Playwrights got such a right in 1856. Before that, playwrights were in the same position as composers: they could prevent the copying of a script, but once the script had been purchased, it was the theater manager and the actors who captured all the income from ticket sales. "If Shakespeare had been an American," one editorialist lamented shortly before the law changed, "it would have been much more profitable for him to have made buttons than plays; unless, indeed, he turned manager, and sparing his own brains, lived on those of other men." But the 1856 amendment to the copyright law did not provide a similar right to composers, most likely because of the differing economics of the theater and music businesses. A playwright could never hope to sell hundreds of thousands of copies of a script. If there was ever to be any money in the theater, it would have to come from performances. Playwrights and their publishers had every reason to push for a change in the law. In nineteenth-century music, by contrast, the money was in sheet music, and there was no better way to promote sheet music sales than by having a composition performed before a large audience. "Composers and publishers generally like to have their music played," one observer pointed out, "in order that a demand may thus be created and more copies of their music sold." Music publishers also worried that customers would be deterred from buying sheet music if the purchase did not include the right of performance. "A piece for which a person has to pay two charges, one for the printed copy, and one for the permission to sing it, does not stand the same chance of popularity and large sales with one which is free to all to sing," reasoned the editor of a Cincinnati music magazine. Because of such concerns, Congress did not extend the right of public performance to musical compositions until 1897, as an afterthought in a bill primarily intended to protect composers of opera and musical theater.[3]

By then the music business was on the cusp of radical change. Thomas Edison had built the first phonograph in 1877. By the 1890s there were already competing phonograph companies and firms selling cylinders and disks containing recorded music. Record sales skyrocketed, from about 500,000 records in 1897 to 2.8 million only two years later. Meanwhile inventors were experimenting with methods of embodying keyboard music in perforated paper, an effort that culminated in the player piano, which came on the market in the first decade of the twentieth century. Consumers no longer had to play the instrument themselves to enjoy piano music; they could simply buy piano rolls and insert them in the piano. Millions of player pianos were sold between 1900 and 1930. They grew so popular, some feared, that "within a few years piano-playing in the home, as we know it to-day, will be a lost art." Sound had once been fleeting, but now it became a commodity capable of being sold.[4]

Sound could thus become property, but whose was it? The music publishers, and the composers they represented, believed it was theirs. "If a man engraves my music and sells it by the sheet, he is a counterfeiter, and I can get money from him and punish him," reasoned the New York lawyer Paul Fuller, who counted the Music Publishers' Association among his clients. "If he does more than that—if he completes that counterfeit to the extent of the reproduction of the actual sound that the composer had in his brain," his sale of the recording was "the ultimate form of piracy." But not everyone agreed. Music boxes had existed since the late eighteenth century. Some played popular songs, but no one thought they infringed the composer's copyright. If the player piano and the phonograph were just more complicated versions of music boxes, some pointed out, it was hard to see why the copyright law should treat them differently. Others noted that the copyright statute only prohibited making copies. A wax cylinder or a roll of perforated paper was not a "copy" of sheet music in the ordinary sense of the word, so if one interpreted the text of the copyright statute strictly, there was nothing illegal about recording a composition the sheet music of which had been copyrighted by someone else.[5] The producers of records and piano rolls unsurprisingly inclined to the latter view. They did not seek the consent of composers before recording their songs, and they did not share their profits afterward.

The issue came before American courts three times around the turn of the century. The composers lost each time. The first was a suit against the inventor John McTammany, who in 1881 patented a precursor to the player piano. McTammany devised a way to produce music by running rolls of perforated paper over an instrument called an organette, a small hand-cranked keyboardless organ that pumped air through reeds. One of McTammany's rolls played "Cradle's Empty, Baby's Gone," a popular song of the 1880s. Harry Kennedy, the song's composer, filed suit in Boston in 1887, but the judge had little trouble dismissing the case. "I cannot convince myself that these perforated strips of paper are copies of sheet music within the meaning of the copyright law," the judge explained. "They are not made to be addressed to the eye as sheet music, but they form part of a machine. . . . Their use resembles more nearly the barrel of a hand organ or music box." A court in Washington, D.C., reached the same result a few years later. The plaintiff was Joseph Stern, who owned the copyrights to "Take Back Your Gold" and "Whisper Your Mother's Name," two songs of the 1890s. The defendant was George Rosey, who made wax cylinders for phonographs. The court again framed the issue as whether the cylinders were copies of the sheet music and again decided they were not. "These prepared wax cylinders can neither substitute [for] the copyrighted sheets of music nor serve any purpose that is within their scope," the court held. "In these respects there would seem to be no substantial difference between them and the metal cylinder of the old and familiar music box."[6]

The third case got the most attention because it reached the Supreme Court. In *White-Smith Music Publishing Company v. Apollo Company*, the Court unanimously held that piano rolls were not copies of sheet music, and thus that Apollo, a manufacturer of player pianos and piano rolls, had not infringed the copyrights owned by White-Smith. "It may be true that in a broad sense a mechanical instrument which reproduces a tune copies it; but this is a strained and artificial meaning," declared Justice William Day. "In no sense can musical sounds which reach us through the sense of hearing be said to be copies, as that term is generally understood." The copyright law simply did not prohibit the creation of piano rolls or sound recordings of other people's songs. In a concurring opinion, Oliver Wendell Holmes urged Congress to change the law. "A musical composition is a rational collocation of sounds," he reasoned. "On principle anything that mechanically reproduces that collocation ought to be held a copy."[7] But it had not been so held yet.

These decisions were widely perceived as unfair to composers. "It is obvious," editorialized the *New York Times*, that "a composer of music can be and is robbed of a property right at least as valid as any other, and is deprived of what ought to be his very best market." The decisions produced several calls to change the law. "If it is true that the copyright act does not furnish protection in cases like the present where there is manifestly a literary piracy," the *American Lawyer* magazine declared, "then the sooner that it is amended the better."[8] The issue, economically insignificant in the 1880s, was of major importance to the music industry by the first decade of the twentieth century, as the markets for piano rolls and sound recordings continued to grow. The question accordingly came before Congress repeatedly between 1906 and 1909: Who should own sound?

The star witnesses on one side were the leading composers of the era. John Philip Sousa had long been a proponent of extending copyright law to prohibit others from recording his compositions. "I myself and every other popular composer are victims of a serious infringement on our clear moral rights," he insisted in 1906. "The composer of the most popular waltz or march of the year must see it seized, reproduced at will on wax cylinder, brass disk, or strip of perforated paper, multiplied indefinitely, and sold at a large profit all over the country, without a penny of remuneration to himself for the use of this original product of his brain." Sousa spent hours entertaining a congressional committee with accounts of how much he was losing by not getting paid for his work. "Last summer and the summer before I was in one of the biggest yacht harbors of the world," he recalled. "Every yacht had a gramophone, a phonograph, an aeolian [a brand of player piano], or something of the kind. They were playing Sousa marches, and that was all right, as to the artistic side of it [here the committee broke into laughter], but they were not paying for them." His songs belonged to him, Sousa insisted, "and I want to be paid for the use they make of my property."[9]

Sousa was joined in Washington by Victor Herbert, who was then at the peak of his popularity as a composer in a wide range of genres. "They are reproducing a part of our brain, of our genius," Herbert testified. "They pay Mr. Caruso $3,000 for each song—for each record. He might be singing Mr. Sousa's song, or my song, and the composer would not receive a cent. I say that that can not be just." Reginald de Koven, who had written several successful comic operas in the previous two decades, reported hearing from an employee of the Aeolian player piano company that in one year alone Aeolian had sold $125,000 of piano rolls embodying his compositions. If he had been entitled to royalties, de Koven estimated, he would have earned around $20,000. Did people buy piano rolls "for the purpose of admiring the roll as a work of art or framing it to hang on a wall?" he asked. "No, gentlemen, it is to hear the music—mark the word, to hear it—and the music is heard, that music which is the property of the composer."[10] The most commercially successful composers and their publishers were the people with the most to gain from a change in the copyright law.

They also feared they had the most to lose from *not* changing the law. If customers bought records and piano rolls instead of sheet music, the composers' primary source of income would dry up. Records "serve the same purpose as sheet music," Victor Herbert argued. "And of necessity with the corresponding increases in the sale of these devices the sale of sheet music decreases." The composer Arthur Penn worried that "people buy records and disks and rolls to-day instead of sheet music. Consequently I lose." The composers' and publishers' worst fears were confirmed by one happy music lover, who told the *New York Times* how much he enjoyed the new possibilities offered by the phonograph and the player piano. "Prior to the advent of either I was what might be termed a constant purchaser of sheet music—in fact a sheet music crank," he confessed. But "since the improvements in the roll and sound reproducing records, if I want a new musical composition I either purchase a roll containing it . . . or more frequently I get it in the form of a disk record." He knew of many others just like him, "people who likewise get their music in this solidified form who used to get it in the form of sheet music."[11] If the new technologies were cutting into sheet music sales, the composers and music publishers pleaded, that was all the more reason to grant them the right to profit from recorded sound.

The composers and music publishers had a powerful ally in the American Copyright League, an organization of book and magazine publishers. The Copyright League's main interest was in strengthening copyright protection for authors (which would increase the publishers' revenue as well), but the League had an eye on a source of income that was barely on the horizon. If composers were denied the right to control sound recording, book authors might be too, and while that was no loss to authors at the time, no one knew what the future would bring. "Phonographic reproductions of their works," explained Richard Rogers Bowker, the editor and publisher of *Publishers Weekly,* "may one of these days become as important an industry as the manufacture of musical records and interfere with printed book production as those are interfering with the production of sheet music." "Canned music" was already a big industry, Bowker noted, and "canned lectures and readings from canned books may come." The Copyright League accordingly lobbied for the recognition of the rights of composers. "After photographs were invented, Congress promptly legislated to include photographic copies as subjects of copyright," the League pointed out in a letter to members of Congress. "It seems right that the Congress should, as in the case of photographs, specifically include under copyright protection mechanical copies of musical works."[12]

On the other side of the debate were the rapidly growing manufacturers of player pianos, piano rolls, phonographs, and phonograph records—"the mechanical music pirates," as critics called them. A change in the copyright law, they argued, would destroy this new industry just as it was getting off the ground. The Victor Talking Machine Company, its lawyer testified, had invested millions of dollars in its plant and its patents, after carefully determining that the sale of records playable on its machines would not infringe any copyrights. It would hardly be fair, he argued, to change the rules of the game after the company had made these irreversible investments. Who would continue to make player pianos, wondered the president of the Automatic Grand Piano Company, if the supply of music rolls was in danger?[13]

These opponents of giving composers the ownership of sound were motivated by self-interest, just like the composers and the music publishers, but like the composers and music publishers they were sophisticated enough to frame their arguments to appeal to the public's sense of fair play. Records and piano rolls would not cut into sheet music sales, they predicted. Instead recordings would *promote* sheet music sales, by serving as a form of free advertising. In fact, the record producers pointed out, the sheet music business had never been better. Sales of sheet music had nearly tripled between 1890 and 1905, just the period when sales should have plummeted if the dire expectations of the composers had any foundation. Some feared the public would abandon their instruments for recorded sound, explained one critic, but "it seems to me that the contrary would be the result." The ability to hear exemplary performances might instead spur amateur musicians to practice all the more. "To the person of real musical instinct and capacity," the critic expected, "the wealth of good music would certainly prove an incentive." Indeed, the new recording companies noted that they were inundated with sheet music from composers and music publishers who begged to have records made of their compositions, without compensation, in the hope that listeners would then go out and buy the sheet music. John Philip Sousa and Victor Herbert might not need the advertising, representatives of the recording companies told Congress, but the vast majority of American composers and publishers were "glad to get the advertisement following from the mechanical reproduction of their music. It is regarded in the trade as the best assistant to the sales of their music of any form of advertising."[14] The music business was in flux. It was not yet clear whether, in the long run, recorded sound would promote or substitute for the sale of sheet music. The most successful composers had economic interests different from those of their less famous colleagues.

Allowing composers and music publishers to exact a toll was likely to make records and piano rolls more expensive, and this provided another argument against changing the law. "It will not be a modern step to place a tax upon the pleasures of the people," suggested the *Musical Age*, a New York trade journal for piano dealers. "This royalty will come from the people and will go into the hands of the few." Music was educational. It refined popular sensibilities. "To restrict the production of cheap music would retard the work; it would be a step backwards." In the view of the New York music publisher Edward Schuberth, this was the anticopyright argument with the biggest effect on members of Congress, who lived "in constant fear that they would be reproached by their constituents" for driving up the cost of entertainment.[15] One did not need to go so far as the editor of the *Musical Age*, who believed that "music everywhere should be as free as the songs of the birds and the whispering of the breezes in the trees," to accept that copyright protection could not be expanded without cost. Recorded sound might become more expensive. Less of it might be produced. If the very purpose of copyright law was to encourage the production of creative work, critics charged, the composers were asking for a counterproductive reform, one that would benefit themselves at the expense of their listeners.

And why should the law be especially solicitous of composers? They were not the only creators of recorded music, the recording industry hastened to point out. There were several steps between printed notes and a record, each of which required just as much talent and hard work, and each of which was just as essential to the finished product. "I can take Mr. Sousa's score," argued the American Graphophone Company's lawyer, "and I can select some person, some alleged musician in this audience, and I can hand him a graphophone and tell him to make that record, and it would not be worth one cent upon the market. It takes the genius of a Sousa to play into the horn. It takes the voice of the magnificent singer to sing into the horn; and it takes the skill of the mechanician who is operating the graphophone to make a fine record that has a marketable value." The composer was just one out of many. And why stop there? Why not include the inventor of the graphophone? And the manufacturer? And the skilled technician who perforates the piano rolls?[16] If being indispensable was enough to own sound, there were many claimants who seemed just as entitled.

As a last resort, the recording industry turned to the Constitution, which authorizes Congress to enact copyright laws granting "authors" the exclusive rights to their "writings." Piano rolls and records were simply not *writings,* industry representatives argued, so Congress had no power to create property rights in them. "A phonograph record is not a writing," declared Frank Dyer of the Edison Phonograph Works, "because it can not be read, not only because of its minuteness and its enormous complexity," but also because of its variability. "That is to say, a phonograph record of a particular piece may be played one day, and the next day the same piece may be played on the phonograph, and the two records will be absolutely dissimilar." Writing, Dyer insisted, implied visibility and consistency. As no one could look at a phonograph record and deduce the sounds it would make when placed on a phonograph, the record must not be a writing. If visibility was not a prerequisite, Dyer asked, then where would the power of Congress stop? Could a pleasing smell be copyrighted? Or an idea that was never written down? There had to be some limit to the definition of a writing, or else anything would be fair game for the copyright law.[17]

But this was not the strongest argument, as even its proponents must have known, because it was at odds with a century of practice. Charts and maps were not literally writings either, but they had been granted copyright protection by the first Congress in 1790. Copyright had later been extended to prints and engravings, and then photographs, which were even more obviously not writings. After Congress expanded copyright to include the right of public performance, first for plays in 1856 and then for music in 1897, without any opposition on constitutional grounds, one could hardly argue that *writing* literally meant writing. "There is nothing in the law or in the constitution that requires a thing to be read to be entitled to copyright protection," concluded the New York lawyer Nathan Burkan, who represented John Philip Sousa and Victor Herbert. "The only test is, Does it embody an intellectual production?" On that definition, the Constitution allowed copyright protection for sound.[18]

Nearly all the phonograph and player piano companies opposed changing the law to benefit composers, but one firm was conspicuously silent. The Aeolian Company of New York was the biggest and most successful producer of player pianos. At its peak Aeolian and its subsidiaries employed five thousand people at piano factories in the United States, England, and Germany.[19] If there was one company that might have been expected to lead the charge against a bill that would raise the price of piano rolls, it was Aeolian. Yet throughout three years of intermittent congressional hearings, not a peep was heard.

It turned out that Aeolian had quietly been preparing to drive its competitors out of business. The firm had entered into contracts with most of the leading music publishers for exclusive rights to produce piano rolls in exchange for royalties on piano roll sales. The contracts would take effect only when the copyright in musical compositions was extended to cover piano rolls; if that ever happened, Aeolian would become something close to a monopolist. The company's incentives were thus aligned with the music publishers rather than the recording industry. Indeed, it came out at the hearings that Aeolian had bankrolled the *White-Smith* case that reached the Supreme Court in 1908, in an effort to have a court declare that piano rolls infringed the copyright in musical compositions. It had been Aeolian, not the White-Smith Music Publishing Company, who had retained Charles Evans Hughes, one of the leading lawyers of the era, to represent White-Smith. (Hughes would go on to become governor of New York, secretary of state, and chief justice of the U.S. Supreme Court.) The prospect of an Aeolian monopoly became yet another argument against changing the law. "You are fostering too great a centralization of power," warned John O'Connell on behalf of the National Piano Manufacturers' Association of America, whose 150 members feared bankruptcy if Aeolian controlled most copyrighted music. "The Aeolian Company and the concerns affiliated with it will have millions of dollars turned into their coffers. And the net result is that the public will pay."[20]

Of all the reasons not to change the law, this was the only one with widespread appeal. That composers should profit from recordings of their compositions seemed intuitively fair to so many people that the phonograph and player piano companies had little chance of continuing to use those compositions for free. That smacked too much of piracy to last for long. But to allow one firm to monopolize the expanding market for piano rolls seemed just as bad. Caught between two unattractive outcomes, Congress did nothing (except to hold more hearings) for years.

The impasse was eventually broken by a compromise brokered by the Massachusetts congressman Charles Washburn.[21] In the Copyright Act of 1909, the holder of a copyright in a musical composition was granted the right to forbid sound recordings, but once he permitted one recording to be made, anyone else was allowed to make a recording as well, upon payment to the copyright holder of a royalty set at two cents per copy. Composers and music publishers thus received a share of the revenues from phonograph records and piano rolls, but not as much as they (or at least the most famous composers) would have received had they been able to negotiate a price. The Aeolian Company was denied the monopoly it had been working so long to arrange. The recording industry continued to grow. Composers owned the right to produce sound, but they could sell it only at a price set by statute, a price that would look lower and lower over time.

Not everyone thought this compulsory license was a good idea. "This is as though copyright should be denied to Mr. Clemens unless he should agree to sell to every other publisher the rights which he has disposed of to Messrs. Harper & Bros.," declared an editorial in the *Century* magazine. "This would be the principle of government paternalism reduced to an absurdity." Indeed, had Congress tried to set prices by statute in most other businesses, there would have been a howl of protest. "Does any farmer want the law to fix the price that he shall receive for a bushel of wheat?" asked Representative Henry Cooper of Wisconsin, while explaining his opposition to the bill. "Does the man who invents a sewing machine want the law to declare the price at which he shall dispose of it?"[22] But the general feeling was that a compulsory license was the only feasible alternative to piracy on one side and monopoly on the other.

This compulsory license is still a part of American copyright law a century later, but it likely would never have been enacted in the first place had the Aeolian Company not attempted to monopolize the sale of piano rolls. Royalty rates would have been a matter for negotiation between composers (represented by music publishers) and recording companies. The most successful composers would have earned more than the statutory rate, and perhaps the less successful would have continued badgering the recording companies to record their compositions for free. The larger story here is the role of contingency in distributing the gains from technological change. Whether composers as a class would benefit from the invention of sound recording was a contested question in the early years, but even when it became clear that they would, there were still open issues of how much they would gain, and how that gain would be allocated across a spectrum of recipients that ranged from Sousa and Herbert on one end to countless unknowns on the other. For these questions, small decisions had big consequences.

Property in Performance

The Copyright Act of 1909 protected composers from the unauthorized recording of their compositions, but did it protect anyone, whether composers, performers, or recording companies, from the unauthorized duplication of a recording? That is, did anyone own sound once it had been recorded? Or was recorded sound in the public domain, free for all to copy?

The question arose immediately, because by 1909 there was already a shadowy industry producing bootleg recordings. In New York, for example, the Continental Record Company would purchase commercially successful records and make duplicates, by using the purchased disk to reverse-engineer a metal matrix, from which it could press multiple copies. The Royal Music Roll Company, among others, found a way to duplicate successful piano rolls. Without the burden of paying musicians, copiers like these could sell their products at a lower cost than the originals. The dust had not yet settled from the debates that led up to the Copyright Act of 1909, but the recording business already faced a new problem.

In the earliest cases to address the issue, courts assumed, without much thought, that copying a sound recording would violate the new copyright law. Henceforth, one judge declared in 1909, record companies would have to be careful to file for a copyright, not just in the printed composition, but also in "the original rendition of the song," by copyrighting "the disc record by which the rendition is preserved." Another judge agreed a few years later that the new copyright law protected a manufacturer of piano rolls as surely as a composer. With time, however, lawyers began to find this position, as one law professor delicately put it, "a little difficult to understand." The Copyright Act of 1909 had said nothing about the copyrightability of sound recordings. Indeed, Congress had rejected various proposals that would have specifically provided for copyright in sound recordings, and the final committee report on the bill that became the Copyright Act disclaimed any such intention to extend copyright to recordings. The Copyright Office accordingly refused to accept sound recordings for copyright registration. Within a few years, courts stopped saying that bootleg recordings violated the copyright law. From the 1920s on, the consensus within the legal profession was that sound recordings could not be copyrighted.[23]

Left without copyright protection for recordings, the recording industry turned to a different strategy. In a case decided a few years before the new copyright law was enacted, a court had found a disk copier liable for the common law wrong of unfair competition. The copier had not merely made copies of the disks produced by the Victor Talking Machine Company (including recordings by Enrico Caruso, the most popular singer of the era). The copier had also tried to pass its disks off as Victor disks, by giving them the same color labels and even including Victor catalog numbers on the labels. Regardless of whether copying disks was illegal, the court concluded, it was clearly illegal to palm one's products off on the public by falsely representing them as having been made by someone else. In subsequent cases, courts began to find unfair competition even without the element of passing off. The Continental

Record Company also copied Victor disks, but Continental did not try to fool the public into thinking Continental disks were made by Victor. Continental gave its disks a different label and made clear in its advertising that it was selling duplicates of Victor disks, not originals. Continental was nevertheless engaging in unfair competition, a court held in 1909. It was taking advantage of Victor's expenditures in recording, just as the bucket shops were taking advantage of the ticker services maintained by the stock exchanges. No one would pay to record Caruso if competitors could simply copy the records and sell the copies. "The education of the public by the dissemination of good music is an object worthy of protection," the court concluded, "and it is apparent that such results could not be attained if the production of the original record was stopped by the wrongful taking of both product and profit by any one who could produce sound discs free from the expense of obtaining the original record."[24] Copying a sound recording, even without any effort to deceive the public, was a form of unfair competition.

When the Federal Trade Commission opened its doors in 1915, one of its responsibilities was to prevent unfair competition. The FTC quickly decided that bootleg recordings fell within its jurisdiction. "A particularly subtle form of competition is the appropriation of the value created by a competitor's expenditures," the agency announced in a memorandum published in 1916. One example was "the making of phonograph records from the commercial records of another company." The FTC accordingly ordered the Orient Music Roll Company to desist from copying the piano rolls produced by its competitors. The copying of sound recordings, although not a violation of the copyright law, was nevertheless coming to be viewed as illegal under the doctrine of unfair competition, as judges and FTC officials filled the gap in the Copyright Act with their own sense of justice.[25]

The recording industry tried repeatedly in the 1920s and 1930s to persuade Congress to amend the Copyright Act to include sound recordings, but these efforts never got far. In the 1920s the industry apparently did not push the issue very hard, because with protection against copying already available under the doctrine of unfair competition there was little to gain from copyright. The recording companies intensified their efforts to obtain copyright in sound recordings in the 1930s, when the possibility of substantial revenue from licensing radio broadcasts came into view. By then, however, they faced a powerful and determined opponent—the radio industry—which managed to prevent any expansion of the copyright law.[26]

The issue of property in sound was transformed by another technological change when radio stations began broadcasting in the 1920s. Much of what they broadcast was recorded music, but at the start they did not pay the owners of copyrights in the underlying compositions. The copyright holders had recently organized as ASCAP, the American Society of Composers, Authors, and Publishers. ASCAP fought back with all it had. Just as composers and publishers had once feared that phonographs and piano rolls would destroy the sheet music business, now they worried that the radio would destroy the phonograph and piano roll business. Why would customers buy disks if they could listen to the same songs on the radio for free? "The situation is serious," ASCAP's general manager complained in 1923. "The radio sets are placed on top of the phonographs, which are never even opened any more." ASCAP's solution was to urge Congress to pass a bill charging listeners an annual tax of five dollars per radio, to compensate composers and publishers for the use of their work.[27]

That idea went nowhere. Instead, the 1920s saw a series of lawsuits filed against radio stations by composers and music publishers. The Copyright Act gave the copyright holder the exclusive right to perform a musical composition for profit. When a record was played on the radio, was that a "performance"? Some courts said it was, but others said it was not, on the theory that "performance" meant only a performance before an audience that was physically present, not an audience of radio listeners. And if it was a performance, was it "for profit" if listeners could tune in for free? By the end of the decade, these uncertainties had been ironed out, in favor of the composers and music publishers. Radio broadcast was a public performance for profit, so stations could not play recorded music without the permission of the copyright holder.[28]

Broadcasters thus had to pay music publishers for their songs. The Copyright Act had specified the royalty rate payable by the recording industry, but there had been no radio in 1909, so there was no comparable statutory rate for radio broadcast. The National Association of Broadcasters lobbied Congress for years to set a broadcast royalty by statute, but Congress never did, largely because of opposition from ASCAP. Broadcast fees were accordingly set in recurring and increasingly acrimonious negotiations between ASCAP and the NAB, two near monopolies locked into a relationship neither could avoid. The cost of recorded music, meanwhile, gave stations an incentive to shift broadcast time to other kinds of programming, like news, sporting events, and dramas.[29]

Composers would profit when recordings of their songs were played on the radio, but what about performers? Did musicians have any property rights in sound? The question was raised in a group of cases filed against radio stations in the late 1930s by two of the most well-known bandleaders of the era, Fred Waring and Paul Whiteman. Waring and Whiteman were both apprehensive about the effects that repeated radio play would have on their record sales. Both also played live on regular radio programs, so they had reason to worry that their radio audiences would be smaller if competing stations could play their records. In the mid-1930s, when Waring was being paid $13,500 per program (more than $200,000 in today's money), disc jockeys on other stations made a point of airing his records at exactly the same time. "I felt it was unfair for them to have our records playing in competition to us," Waring later recalled. "It was a growing menace to all performers."[30] Under Waring's and Whiteman's recording contracts, therefore, their records bore the legend "Not Licensed for Radio Broadcast." Both filed suit when radio stations played the records.

In Waring's cases, courts in Pennsylvania and North Carolina barred the radio stations from playing the records. A performer of recorded music "has undoubtedly participated in the creation of a product in which he is entitled to a right of property," the Pennsylvania Supreme Court reasoned, a right "which in no way overlaps or duplicates that of the author in the musical composition." This property right had to be protected in some way, the court explained, or else "it will be impossible for distinguished musicians to commit their renditions to phonograph records—except possibly for a prohibitive financial compensation—without subjecting themselves to the disadvantages and losses which they would inevitably suffer from the use of the records for broadcasting." Waring thus had the right to decide the uses to which his performance was put. In the North Carolina case, a judge agreed that Waring "has a property right in his performance."[31]

In Whiteman's case, however, a more influential judge on a more prestigious court decided the opposite. Learned Hand, writing for the U.S. Court of Appeals for the Second Circuit in New York, held that whatever property right a musician might have in a recorded performance ended when the record was sold. "It is absurd to say a man has 'property' in all the product of his brains," Hand noted in a memorandum to his colleagues. "The law has never said that or anything like it." And if Whiteman could have a property right in a recorded performance, why not RCA, his record company, "whose skill and experience is equally necessary to the performance as Whiteman's?" How was a court supposed to value their respective contributions? "It seems to me the biggest baloney yet," Hand concluded; "I think they are a bunch of hogs, if you know what I mean." His fellow judges knew exactly what he meant. "I do not question the genius of a Toscanini or even a Whiteman," explained Charles Clark, "but the world has amply repaid such personalities for the beauty they have created." Now Whiteman was at the trough for more. "It is one thing to assure an artist the comforts of life," Clark reasoned; "it is another to make plutocrats out of him and his exploiters. . . . There is no reason for a court to invent a new property right." Robert Patterson, the third judge on the panel, was even more emphatic. "I think that these claims . . . by the orchestra leader are nothing but nonsense," he declared. "It might as well be argued that no one but Al Smith has the right to wear a brown derby, on the ground that the wearing of a brown derby has become a property right belonging to him."[32]

Within a few years little trace remained of Fred Waring's victories. In the early 1940s the recording industry persuaded the legislatures of North Carolina, South Carolina, and Florida to enact statutes explicitly stating that all property rights in a recording passed to the purchaser when a record was sold. That left Pennsylvania as the only state with a rule limiting the radio play of recorded music, but even in Pennsylvania no one ever tried to set up a licensing system to collect royalties for radio play. Radio stations throughout the country played records without paying royalties to anyone except ASCAP, who represented only the composers, not the musicians.[33]

The failure of the bandleaders' suits against the broadcasters prompted many calls for a copyright in sound recordings and caused performers and the recording industry to redouble their lobbying efforts to that end. "Disc making was once a good business," one lawyer recalled, but "this prosperity ended when radio came into the foreground." Proponents of a copyright in sound emphasized the unfairness of allowing radio stations to let the public hear records for free, thus wearing out a song's novelty before the manufacturer of the record had a chance to make sales. They pointed out that the law of many other countries, including Great Britain and Canada, already granted copyright in sound recordings. The issue was before Congress repeatedly through the 1940s and 1950s, but the radio broadcasters were able to beat back all efforts at reform.[34]

Those who stood to gain from a copyright in sound, performers and record manufacturers, were hampered in their lobbying efforts by their inability to agree on whether the copyright should belong to the performers or to the record company. Musicians (often represented before Congress by the American Federation of Musicians) argued that the copyright should belong to them. They were the creators of the music, after all; if the purpose of copyright was to reward artistic creation, the copyright in a recording should belong to the performers. But the idea raised some obvious administrative difficulties. If an orchestra recorded a song, would every member of the orchestra have a share of the copyright? Would the members have to give unanimous consent before the record could be copied or played on the radio? If the copyright were granted to the conductor rather than the entire orchestra, was there any principle by which copyrights could be allocated within smaller and less hierarchical ensembles? Granting the copyright in a recording to the musicians threatened the industry with a host of difficult legal problems.

Granting the copyright to the company that manufactured the record was less intuitively appealing. The technical process of recording involved some artistry, but not as much, most seem to have believed, as that involved in singing or playing an instrument. But centralizing the ownership of sound in a single entity would solve all the administrative problems that would have flowed from trying to divide ownership among the musicians. Granting the copyright to the record company had been the solution adopted by Britain, Canada, and all the other countries that had taken this step. It was the solution the United States itself had adopted in granting copyright in movies—the copyright belonged to the company that produced the movie rather than being divided among all the actors and other creative people who participated in it. Even if musicians did not own the copyright themselves, they could negotiate in advance for royalties from the record company.[35] The performers eventually conceded this issue, but for many years it prevented them from presenting a united front with the record companies in their recurring battles in Congress against the radio broadcasters.

The gains to be had from a copyright in sound recordings were soon magnified, in any event, by further technological change. For many years the recording industry's main opponent had been radio. The old problem of bootleg recordings had been more or less driven into economic insignificance by the law of unfair competition. But the introduction of the long-playing record in 1948 made bootlegging much more profitable. Records had once fit only three to five minutes per side; now the two sides together could play as much as forty-five minutes of music. Customers paid more for the new "LPs," but the records did not cost proportionally more to copy. The major record companies accordingly experienced an epidemic of bootlegging in the late 1940s and early 1950s. They fought back with every weapon they had. They formed a trade association, the Recording Industry Association of America, and lobbied for legislation explicitly prohibiting record piracy. This effort succeeded only in Los Angeles, which enacted an ordinance making it unlawful to reproduce phonograph records without the written consent of the owner of the reproduction rights. The New York legislature twice approved a bill to similar effect, but both times the bill was vetoed by Governor Thomas Dewey, on the ground that the topic was more suitable for federal legislation. Unsuccessful in the legislatures, the record companies filed a barrage of unfair competition suits against the pirates. The suits were mostly successful, but for the recording industry it was not a satisfying resolution of the problem. More bootleggers were certain to arise in the future, and the law of unfair competition was a matter of state common law that might vary from state to state and indeed from judge to judge. The only real solution lay in extending the federal copyright law to sound recordings.[36]

The problem of record piracy got even worse in the mid-1960s, when cassette tapes reached the U.S. market. Copying records became easier and cheaper, because copiers no longer needed equipment for pressing records; a simple tape recorder would do. "The unauthorized duplicator has . . . not been slow to move into the business of manufacturing tapes for automobile and home use," one lawyer remarked in 1966. "A duplicator may even offer an extensive record library for taping purposes, advertising that he has all the latest hits available."[37] Once again, the record companies fought back, but this time with more success. They filed another wave of lawsuits. They persuaded the legislatures of ten states to enact statutes prohibiting record piracy, including the four most populous states—California, New York, Pennsylvania, and Texas.[38] Finally, after decades of trying, they convinced Congress to extend copyright to sound recordings, in a statute that took effect in 1972. Copying sound was at last a violation of copyright law.[39]

The producers of records owned sound—or did they? They had won the ability to sue bootleggers for copyright infringement. But the radio broadcasters were still a powerful opponent. The broadcasters had no reason to support bootlegging, but they had a strong interest in avoiding having to pay copyright holders when they played songs on the radio. As a result, the recording industry won its copyright, but the copyright law explicitly provided that the copyright in sound recordings did not include the right of public performance.[40] Radio stations could continue to play songs for free. They still had to compensate the composer for the copyright in the underlying composition, but performers and record companies earned nothing from radio play. And because "public performance" included the playing of songs on records and in concert as well as on the radio, performers and record companies earned nothing when their songs were recorded or played before audiences by others. But composers and music publishers did.

It is not surprising that musicians have responded to this set of incentives. Composers and performers were once different sets of people, by and large. As late as 1950 only 7 percent of the most popular songs were written by their performers. Over time, however, as the revenue from record sales became an increasingly large fraction of a musician's income, the percentage of performers who wrote their own material grew consistently, as musicians realized they could earn more royalties from writing songs than from merely singing them. Singer-songwriters accounted for 22 percent of the top songs in 1960, 50 percent in 1970, 60 percent in 1980, 64 percent in 1990, 68 percent in 2000, and 88 percent in 2004. The nature of popular music changed as a result. When most musicians performed their own compositions, popular songs were more likely to be understood as vehicles of personal expression rather than (or perhaps as well as) mere commercial products.[41]

By the late twentieth century, property rights in sound were divided in a complex way among a host of players—composers, music publishers, performers, record companies, and broadcasters. This division of ownership was not the result of any rational plan. It was the product of a century of power struggles, in legislatures and in courts, over who would capture the gains from technological change.

7

Owning Fame

THE BLOCKBUSTER performer of the mid-nineteenth century was the Swedish soprano Jenny Lind, whose 1850–1852 tour of the United States packed concert halls from New York to New Orleans and back again. Lind's promoter was P. T. Barnum, no stranger to innovative ways of making money. Everywhere the tour went, shopkeepers were selling Jenny Lind merchandise. "We had Jenny Lind gloves," Barnum later recalled, "Jenny Lind bonnets, Jenny Lind riding hats, Jenny Lind shawls, mantillas, robes, chairs, sofas, pianos—in fact every thing was Jenny Lind." There were Jenny Lind stoves and even Jenny Lind chewing tobacco and cigars, despite Lind's aversion to cigars.[1] Yet none of these products earned Lind or Barnum a cent. Lind's celebrity was obviously a valuable asset, but neither Lind nor Barnum conceived that Lind had any right to prevent others from commercially exploiting her name or image. None of the manufacturers or sellers of Jenny Lind merchandise thought he needed Lind's permission. Indeed, Barnum was *happy* so many people were slapping Lind's name on their products, because it was proof of her popularity, which promised that the concerts would sell out. It apparently never occurred to him that they were taking money out of Lind's pocket.

Before the twentieth century, fame was not something that could be owned. The Austrian ballerina Fanny Elssler performed in New York about a decade before Lind, and she too encountered shops full of merchandise with her name on it—Fanny Elssler boots, Fanny Elssler stockings, Fanny Elssler garters, corsets, shawls, parasols, fans, cigars, boot polish, shaving soap, and even champagne. No one—neither Elssler nor those exploiting her fame—believed her name was a kind of property, much less that it belonged to Elssler. A few decades before that, Benjamin Franklin arrived in France to discover that his portrait was for sale everywhere, as prints, as busts, as clay medallions, and as small pictures on rings and on the lids of snuffboxes. His only reaction was amusement. His face, he told his daughter, was "as well known as that of the moon."[2]

Today, of course, celebrities are not amused to learn that others are selling their names or pictures. Merchandising and endorsements are big businesses, often yielding much more income than whatever it was that made a person famous in the first place. The golfer Tiger Woods, for example, won $6.4 million in golf tournaments in 2004 but earned another $83 million that year in endorsements. In fact, one doesn't need to be working, or living, at all. Each year *Forbes* magazine publishes a list of the top-earning dead celebrities. Some, like 2006 leader Kurt Cobain, still make most of their income from sales of their copyrighted work, but others, like Elvis Presley, who took second place that year, have an income stream from the licensing of their names and images that likely exceeds their revenue from any other source. Perhaps the most surprising person on the list is Albert Einstein, who, entirely from the sale of his name and picture, earns far more, fifty years after his death, than he ever did while he was alive. In 2006, Einstein made approximately $20 million from products like the Baby Einstein line of CDs and DVDs.[3]

Between Jenny Lind and Tiger Woods, between Benjamin Franklin and Albert Einstein, celebrity became a kind of property. Americans began to believe that individuals should control the uses to which their names and pictures were put—that they had the right to stop others from using their names and pictures without their permission, and that they could sell that control to others. Being famous once meant that your name and image belonged to the public in the most literal sense, but now they belong to you, and indeed they may be the most valuable things you own.

The Sacred Right of Privacy

Nineteenth-century Americans often bought pictures of well-known people. Presidents were frequent subjects: one could buy inexpensive images of them as lithographs, on medals, on dishes and cups, on snuff-boxes and whiskey flasks. War heroes, popular entertainers, eminent ministers—all were available for purchase. The subjects of the pictures earned nothing from the sales. They had to consent to sit for an initial portrait, but they do not seem to have tried to prevent others from making copies of the portrait and selling the copies. Nor did they try to claim any right to a share of the proceeds. As Jenny Lind or Benjamin Franklin would have acknowledged, having one's name and image hawked for sale was one of the prices of fame.[1]

The invention of photography in the mid-nineteenth century promised to make the reproduction of images easier and potentially more lucrative, but until the 1880s photography was cumbersome, expensive, and technically complex. Only specialists possessed the necessary equipment and knowledge. In the 1880s, however, George Eastman began selling inexpensive cameras and film that ordinary people could use. Photography changed from an esoteric specialty to a common hobby. "Twelve years ago photography was only practised by a chosen few," one enthusiast remembered in 1892, but with the new equipment photography was an art that "any man of average intelligence can learn from five minutes explanation." Photographs became regular accompaniments to stories in newspapers and magazines. Advertisers had long used drawings, but the near-simultaneous development of new printing methods allowed magazines to fill their pages inexpensively with advertisements incorporating photographs. Advertising cards, posters, catalogs—all placed photographs within sight.[5] Within the space of a few years, the photograph became a ubiquitous part of everyday life.

The photograph created a much larger potential market for the pictures of famous people than had ever been possible before, and that changed the incentives on both sides of the camera. Entrepreneurs had more reason to be aggressive in taking and selling pictures: a snapshot was quick and cheap, and multiple images could be produced from a single negative. The subjects of those pictures—provided they were willing to have their photographs seen by others—likewise had more to gain than ever before. Popular actresses began signing exclusive contracts with photographers, allowing their pictures to be taken in exchange for a royalty upon the sale of each copy. According to the New York theatrical producer Daniel Frohman, this practice did not last long, as actors and actresses eventually figured out that the advertising value of allowing the unrestricted sale of their photographs exceeded whatever could be earned in royalties.[6] But widespread photography had begun to undermine the long-standing assumption that fame implied the public ownership of one's image. As that image was more easily reproduced it became more valuable, and the cost of letting others have it for free correspondingly rose.

To those who did not wish their pictures to appear in the newspaper, photography was less a new opportunity than a new menace. "The illustrated journalism now prevalent finds its finest achievements," scoffed the journalist John Gilmer Speed, "in the publication of photographs surreptitiously taken." At least one New York newspaper, he reported, "keeps a photographer busy in the streets of the metropolis taking 'snap shots' at every person who appears to be of consequence," pictures the paper kept on file to use when a story warranted. If such practices were not stopped, Speed despaired, "vulgarity will envelop the nation." "Something ought to be done about the snapshot artists whose business it is to gather the pictures that embellish our pictorial journals," *Life* magazine agreed. "They are a comparatively new pest." To find one's picture in the press was a shock, an invasion of one's sensibilities, to a degree almost unimaginable today. "The instantaneous photograph," explained one lawyer, had "made it infinitely easier to destroy the privacy of individuals, and to expose the victims of morbid curiosity to a degree of inconvenience and pain that was not dreamed of a few years ago."[7]

Whether one welcomed or deplored the new role of photography, one had a newly powerful reason to exert control over it—either to profit from or to prevent the display of one's picture. In the late nineteenth century, people depicted in photographs accordingly began to argue that they had a right to prevent the unauthorized reproduction of their images. The claim raised "an interesting, and, we believe, a somewhat novel question," one lawyers' magazine noted in 1884. Who owned the right to reproduce a photographic portrait: the photographer or the subject? A photographer might claim a copyright in an ordinary picture, another legal journal observed, but if that picture was a portrait, would its reproduction be "a violation of a sort of natural copyright, possessed by every person of his or her own features"?[8] The answer was not at all clear.

The early cases came out both ways. Sometimes the subject won, on the theory that contracts between sitters and photographers included an implied term prohibiting the photographer from supplying copies to anyone other than the sitter. In an English case from 1888, Alice Pollard discovered her picture on a Christmas card for sale in a local shop window. She had sat for a portrait a few months earlier, and, without her knowledge, the photographer had kept the negative and used it to print Christmas cards. The photographer had done nothing wrong, his lawyer argued. He had been hired to supply prints to Mrs. Pollard and he did just that. Their agreement had said nothing one way or the other about whether he could provide prints to anyone else. "A person has no property in his own features," the lawyer asserted; "short of doing what is libellous or otherwise illegal there is no restriction on the photographer using his negative." But the court disagreed. "The bargain between the customer and the photographer includes, by implication, an agreement that the prints taken from the negative are to be appropriated to the use of the customer only," the judge concluded. In another case two years later the Minnesota Supreme Court reached the same result for the same reason.[9]

This theory of an implied contractual term could not work where the photograph itself was unauthorized, because in such circumstances there was never any contract in the first place. The popular opera singer Marion Manola nevertheless won her 1890 case in New York, after the manager of her opera company hired a photographer to take pictures of her, to Manola's surprise, during a performance. The manager hoped to use the photographs in advertisements, but Manola, who was performing in tights, was unwilling to be seen outside the theater in such a revealing costume. A trial judge in New York enjoined the manager from displaying the pictures. The judge did not write an opinion explaining why, and indeed the manager never even showed up in court to oppose Manola's request for an injunction, but Manola's celebrity was enough for the case to be reported in the newspaper. The following year, when the lawyer Samuel Wandell published his treatise on *The Law of the Theatre*, he cited Manola's case for the proposition that "actors and actresses may control the public exhibition, use or sale of their own photographs."[10]

But not everyone agreed. "No one has a copyright in the picture of himself," insisted the English lawyer Watkin Williams. "The issue in each case," he reasoned, is "whether, when the original photograph was ordered and agreed upon, the bargain really extended to and included the negative of the photograph or merely the photograph itself." In most cases, Williams concluded, "it may be safely said that the customer orders the photographs only," and that the negative was accordingly owned by the photographer, who could do with it what he wished. If people wanted to control their own images, they needed only to bargain with the photographer for the sale of the negative as well. As for the injury that might be suffered from the unauthorized reproduction of one's image, added a New York judge in a case decided shortly after Marion Manola's, it was nothing more than an affront to one's sensibilities, and "the law does not take cognizance of and will not afford compensation for sentimental injury" alone. A father thus had no right to prevent the publication of his daughter's portrait, because he had suffered no loss of money or reputation. E. L. Godkin, editor of the *Nation*, agreed that while unauthorized photography was distasteful, that was not enough to support a lawsuit against the photographer. "Juries," he explained, "are apt to be made up of men who, though they will punish actual damage to a man's reputation, are not disposed to make much account of mere wounds to his feelings or his taste." Some kinds of injuries were simply too insubstantial to be redressed by the legal system.[11]

There was similar uncertainty as to whether people had a right to control the use of their names. Celebrity endorsements were a regular feature of advertising as early as the middle of the nineteenth century. The early endorsements were often in the form of ostensibly unsolicited letters from famous people. The maker of Whitcomb's Asthma Remedy, for example, claimed in an 1866 advertisement to have a letter from Martin Van Buren, written shortly before his death four years before, in which the ex-president expressed his satisfaction with the product. Harriet Beecher Stowe wrote to commend the chocolate manufactured by Walter Baker & Co. Sarah Bernhardt congratulated the firm responsible for American Face Powder ("It is so delicate and pure, and makes the skin to look so beautiful"). James Husted, the former Speaker of the New York State Assembly, reported that after he was thrown from a carriage all his pain had been alleviated by Allcock's Porous Plasters. "There is no humbug about them," Husted declared. "They perform all they promise."[12]

    From the advertisements themselves, there is of course no way to
know whether famous people like these actually wrote the words attributed to them, or, if they did, whether they consented to have their
words used in an advertisement. There are no reported cases involving
complaints of bogus endorsements before the 1890s, and even then the
cases are few and far between. But it is certainly possible that the celebrities involved simply did not sue, or that if there was any litigation it
did not produce a reported opinion. Perhaps the best we can say is that
endorsements were so common that at least *some* of them must have
been printed with the permission of the endorser, no doubt often paid
for by the advertiser. It would have been foolish for advertisers to put
words in the mouths of people so well known in circumstances where
one could be so easily exposed as a fraud.

    By the turn of the century, endorsements often dispensed with the
format of the unsolicited letter, but they still often included direct quotations from the endorser. When Rudyard Kipling praised the Kodak
camera, or when the popular actress Constance Collier told readers
how much she liked Pond's Vanishing Cream, it is possible that Kodak
or Pond's was using their names without their permission, but it would
have been very easy for Kipling or Collier to tell the world that the advertisement was a fake. It would have been just as easy for Emile Zola
to disclaim any endorsement of Vin Mariani, "the famous French tonic
for body, nerves and brain," or for the explorer Henry Stanley to reveal
that in fact he did not enjoy the Liebig Company's extract of beef or the
Williams' Shaving Stick.[13]

    On the other hand, one can find advertisements from the period
that use the names and pictures of famous people in ways that strongly
suggest their permission had not been obtained. An 1889 advertisement for stomach pills, for instance, included a large drawing of President Benjamin Harrison. In the fine print, readers learned that every
order would include a free photograph of the president. Even more suspicious is an advertisement for corset clasps that included drawings and
supposed testimonials, in the form of rhymed poetry, from Queen Victoria and Caroline Harrison, the president's wife. One lawyer lamented
the existence of products like Herbert Spencer cigars and Garfield tea,
because Spencer, who was thousands of miles away in England, most
likely had no idea his name was being used in the United States, and

President Garfield had been assassinated a decade before.[14] If there was a norm requiring a celebrity's consent before using a name or claiming an endorsement, it was not universally followed, particularly where the person involved was unable to complain.

Was it illegal to use the name of a prominent person in an advertisement without his permission? Some believed it was. In 1891, the manufacturer of Soden Mineral Pastilles (a kind of throat lozenges) placed advertisements throughout the United States claiming the endorsement of Sir Morell Mackenzie, the famous English laryngologist. Mackenzie had never actually endorsed the product. A New York judge prohibited the manufacturer of the pastilles from using Mackenzie's name, on the ground that the advertisements were "an infringement of his right to the sole use of his own name." In 1898, when the naval officer George Dewey became a war hero by leading the attack that won the Philippines from Spain, the Patent Office refused to allow a candy company to register "Dewey's Chewies" as a trademark. In the Patent Office, which ruled over trademarks, Dewey's name belonged to Dewey. "No one has the right without the consent of Dewey to appropriate it as a trademark," the Commissioner of Patents insisted. "A living celebrity is entitled to protection from the ordinary trader."[15]

In other cases, however, courts allowed advertisers to continue using the names of people who had never given their consent. The manufacturers of a patent medicine called Sallyco, supposedly a cure for gout, placed advertisements that included the ostensible endorsement of the English physician Morgan Dockrell. Dockrell sued but lost. The advertisements were no doubt fraudulent, the court acknowledged, but Dockrell had not suffered any damage from them. His reputation had not been diminished, nor had he lost any money. So long as no libel was being committed, a person had no right to prevent others from exploiting his name simply because he found it distasteful. "Roger Williams" was a fine brand name for cloth, the Rhode Island Supreme Court observed, "as would be so applied, the names of Washington, Greene, Perry, or, of any other heroes, living or dead."[16]

It was this legal uncertainty about the use of images and names, combined with the unease created by the newly ubiquitous camera and a newly aggressive press, that accounts for the unusual degree of attention paid to an article that appeared in the *Harvard Law Review* in

1890. "The Right to Privacy" was written by Samuel Warren and Louis Brandeis, two young Boston law partners.[17] Warren would leave the law a few years later for a career in Maine as a paper mill magnate, while Brandeis would go on to become a prominent lawyer and a justice of the Supreme Court. The article would become the most well-known piece of legal scholarship in American history. "Instantaneous photographs and newspaper enterprise have invaded the sacred precincts of private and domestic life," they declared. "For years there has been a feeling that the law must afford some remedy for the unauthorized circulation of portraits of private persons." The point of their article was to persuade the legal community that precedent already existed for such a remedy. They did so by collecting cases addressing a variety of analogous questions and then arguing that taken together these cases amounted to judicial recognition of a right of privacy. Courts had long held, for example, that authors and artists had a right to prevent the publication of their unpublished work, that speakers could prevent the unauthorized printing of their oral remarks, and that firms could prevent the disclosure of trade secrets. Such cases, Warren and Brandeis contended, were merely instances "of the more general right of the individual to be let alone." This right to privacy, they concluded, was broad enough to encompass the right not to have one's picture, or even a discussion of one's private affairs, published in the press.

The traditional explanation of the origin of "The Right to Privacy" emphasizes Warren's irritation with sensationalist press coverage of his daughter's wedding. This story apparently originated in Alpheus Mason's 1946 biography of Brandeis. It gained circulation when it was repeated in a widely read law review article by William Prosser, the influential dean of Berkeley's law school. The story turns out not to be true: Warren's oldest daughter was only six years old when "The Right to Privacy" was published. The Warrens and their extended family did appear regularly through the 1880s in gossip columns in the New York and Washington papers, because Warren's wife was the daughter of Thomas Bayard, the senator and secretary of state. Warren may well have been annoyed.[18]

But no personal motive is necessary to explain "The Right to Privacy." In the social circles in which Warren and Brandeis moved, few would have disagreed that the press was becoming too aggressive in invading personal privacy. Their legal argument was new, but in criticizing the press they were merely voicing conventional opinion. The year before Warren and Brandeis wrote, the *New York Times* published an editorial—also called "The Right to Privacy"—complaining about the same menace. In the press "there appear descriptions of the personal appearances, the families, the clothes, and the furniture" of successful people, the *Times* lamented, descriptions "which no doubt sometimes fill the victims with shame and disgust." The paper had no doubt that this was wrong. "The right of privacy with respect to what are properly private affairs is a real right," the *Times* declared, "while curiosity about other people's ways of living is an emotion of which well-bred people are rather ashamed, and which they try to suppress." And this was just one of many similar editorials published at the time. "It is no secret that a good many people think that the newspapers in this blessed land of freedom have too much to say about private people and their private affairs," *Life* magazine observed. "They do not even like to have their likenesses published, nor members of their families." Another magazine despaired that "it is scarcely possible to take up a newspaper without finding in it invasions of the sacred right of privacy."[19] When Warren and Brandeis wrote "The Right to Privacy" there were many readers eager for a legal argument that would confirm what their intuitions already told them.

Warren and Brandeis thus found their arguments praised and repeated by other legal commentators. One New York judge cited the article in holding that a newspaper could not print the name or picture of an actor, for readers to vote on his popularity, without the actor's permission. "An individual is entitled to protection in person as well as property," the judge reasoned, following Warren and Brandeis, "and now the right to life has come to mean the privilege to enjoy life without the publicity or annoyance of a lottery contest."[20] Warren and Brandeis had taken the widely shared sense that something had to be done about the press and molded it into a respectable legal argument that courts, rather than legislatures, were the ones that could do it.

Many, however, perceived a tension between the freedom of the press and a right not to have one's name or picture in the papers. "Is there nothing left in the way of liberty?" wondered one editorialist in the *Atlantic Monthly*. "Is nobody to be fair game for the curiosity, interest, and ridicule of the great public?" *Life* magazine pointed out that "very great wealth means great power, and there would seem to be a legitimate public interest in the possessors' great power, whether they are New York aldermen or multi-millionaires." If a newspaper could be sued for publishing a story or a photograph of a person without his consent, would it be possible to report the news at all? Warren and Brandeis had anticipated this objection and had conceded that "the right to privacy does not prohibit any publication of matter which is of public or general interest," such as information about candidates for public office. But who could say which matters were properly of public interest and which were not? The most extended rebuttal to Warren and Brandeis was an article published in 1894 in the *Northwestern Law Review* by Herbert Spencer Hadley, then a young Kansas City lawyer, later to be governor of Missouri and chancellor of Washington University. "The rights of free speech secured to all by our constitutions," Hadley concluded, would prevent courts from recognizing a right to privacy that would have any teeth, because any information subject to the right would be of so little interest to the public that no newspaper would publish it anyway.[21]

The right to privacy, critics charged, was a cure that would be worse than the disease. "Disgust with the sensationalism of the press leads many into thoughtless and hasty assertions in favor of the alleged right to privacy, just as disgust with certain types of agitators leads many to sympathize with actions or proposals violative of freedom of speech," one observer suggested. But curtailing a free press was an overreaction. "The sensationalism of the press is detestable, but it does not follow that its practices can be properly interfered with. From the standpoint of equal freedom, there is no basis whatever for the alleged right to privacy." The lawyers' magazine *Case and Comment* agreed that the "right of people to speak or publish information about each other, so long as the publication is not defamatory, sufficiently shows that a right to complete privacy cannot exist." And if the law could not prohibit a textual depiction of a person, how could it prohibit a photograph? "It is merely incidental and immaterial whether the printed characters used to describe him are the ordinary letters of the alphabet grouped into words, or mere lines and dots grouped into a picture." "The right of privacy," the magazine concluded, "can have no existence consistent with free speech."[22]

Proponents of the right to privacy had a ready rejoinder. The purpose of the freedom of speech, they argued, "was to prevent a political censorship of the press . . . and not to force upon private individuals a distasteful publicity at the hands of gossiping newspapers." In 1897, when a New York legislator introduced a bill to outlaw the publication of portraits without the subject's consent, the bill's proponents insisted it would be possible to distinguish political cartoons, which had a long and honorable history, from the "mortifying snap-shots by newspaper artists" that the bill would prohibit. But the bill failed, in part because of concerns that it would cut too deeply into the traditional ability of the press to criticize government officials.[23] One could not give individuals control of their images and names without taking rights away from the public, and it was hard to predict what the scope of those lost rights would be.

This worry over the tension between the right of privacy and the freedom of speech played a big role in judges' rejection of the right of privacy in the three leading cases of the 1890s. In *Corliss v. Walker,* a federal judge in Massachusetts refused to suppress the publication of an illustrated biography of the inventor George Corliss, on the ground that such a result "would be a remarkable exception to the liberty of the press." So long as a book was not defamatory, "this constitutional privilege implies a right to freely utter and publish whatever the citizen may please," even without the consent of the subject. The biography included a photograph the publisher had obtained from a negative held by the photographer who had taken Corliss's portrait a few years before. A private individual could prevent the publication of a picture obtained in such circumstances, the judge concluded, "but where an individual becomes a public character the case is different. A statesman, author, artist, or inventor, who asks for and desires public recognition, may be said to have surrendered this right to the public." The price of fame was a loss of control over one's image: "such characters may be said, of their own volition, to have dedicated to the public the right of any fair portraiture of themselves."[24]

A year later the New York Court of Appeals refused to bar the display of a statue of the late philanthropist Mary Hamilton Schuyler, over the objection of her surviving relatives that Schuyler was a sensitive and retiring woman who had been averse to publicity all her life. Schuyler's preferences were irrelevant, held Judge Rufus Peckham, who would be appointed to the U.S. Supreme Court a month later. Whether or not the right to display Schuyler's likeness belonged to her during her lifetime, "whatever right of privacy Mrs. Schuyler had died with her." Images of the dead belonged not to their descendants but to the public.[25]

An asserted right to privacy encompassing the control of one's name and image fared no better in *Atkinson v. Doherty.* John Atkinson was a well-known lawyer and politician in Michigan. When he died in 1898, a cigar company brought out a John Atkinson cigar, which it sold with a label bearing Atkinson's name and picture. His widow sued to stop the sales, but the Michigan Supreme Court allowed them to continue. "No reason occurs to us for limiting the right to apply a name, though borne by another person," the court reasoned. People named their children and their animals after other people; why should inanimate objects be any different? "Why not a John Atkinson wagon, as well as a John Atkinson Jones or horse or dog." John Atkinson would have lost nothing, while he was alive, from the existence of cigars named after him; he was not a competitor in the cigar business, and "we feel sure that society would not think the less of Col. John Atkinson if cigars bearing his name were sold in the shops." Because Atkinson would have had no remedy while alive, his widow could have none after his death. The court explicitly rejected the thesis of Warren and Brandeis that one had a right to prevent the reproduction of one's picture. "We learn of places and things from pictures," the court explained. "They impart information to those who cannot or will not read, and many times more rapidly and effectually than written description would do to those who can and will." Limiting the freedom to publish pictures would thus come at a significant cost. Just as one could not prevent others from photographing one's house or garden, one had no right "to restrain the possessor of a camera from taking a snap shot at the passer-by for his own uses. If we admit the impertinence of the act, it must also be admitted that there are many impertinences which are not actionable" in court.[26]

Despite the prominence of Warren and Brandeis's article, then, and despite the alarm caused by the spread of photography, by the turn of the century American law had not recognized a right to prevent others from using one's picture or one's name. The decided cases "practically negative the existence of any right of privacy that the courts will enforce," concluded the San Francisco lawyer James Hopkins in his review of the law of unfair trade. The Yale law professor George Watrous agreed that "there is little hope of its recognition otherwise than by the legislature," and even that he thought unlikely, because "the practical difficulties in defining and according such a right by statute are too great to make relief even in that manner feasible."[27] The law governing the ownership of names and images was not much clearer in 1900 than it had been in 1880, and to the extent one could discern any direction, it was toward the idea that names and images belonged to the public rather than to the individual.

A Demand for Legal Protection

Already bubbling up through the New York courts, however, was a case that would prompt so much outrage that within two decades the ownership of one's own image would be a firmly established feature of American law. Abigail Roberson was a Rochester teenager who had her portrait taken at a local photographic studio. Somehow her picture ended up on 25,000 posters advertising the flour made by Franklin Mills of nearby Lockport. The photographer most likely sold the negative to whoever designed the posters, but however it happened, no one obtained Roberson's consent. The picture showed Roberson's head and shoulders in profile. Above her head the advertisement read "Flour of the Family." Franklin Mills placed the posters in stores, warehouses, and saloons, including some in Rochester, where Roberson's acquaintances could recognize her. The resulting humiliation caused her to suffer a severe nervous shock, which confined her to bed and required treatment by a physician. Her lawsuit sought $15,000 in damages and an order forbidding Franklin Mills from continuing to use her picture in its advertising.

The defendants (Franklin Mills and the Rochester Folding-Box Company, who apparently produced the posters) sought to have the case dismissed, on the ground that they had the right to use Roberson's picture. "The substance of this contention," responded the trial judge, "is that the feelings of the plaintiff may be outraged with impunity by any person," and that was too much for him to bear. "If such were a fact," he declared, "it would certainly be a blot upon our boasted system of jurisprudence that the courts were powerless to prevent the doing of a wrongful act which would wound in the most cruel manner the feelings of a sensitive person." The case would be different, the judge explained, if the defendants had used the picture of someone who was already in the public eye, because such a person could hardly complain about unwanted publicity. But "any modest and refined young woman might naturally be extremely shocked and wounded in seeing a lithographic likeness of herself posted in public places." Such a display violated the very core of "the sacred right of privacy." If Abigail Roberson's image, "owing to its beauty, is of great value as a trade-mark or an advertising medium," he concluded, "it is a property right which belongs to her."[28]

The case attracted an unusual amount of positive attention, even while it was in the trial court. The trial judge's decision "has elicited general approval from the press," remarked one lawyers' journal. The decision would likely be sustained on appeal, "and we certainly think it ought to be," noted another.[29] There was something disturbing about forcing a young woman into the harsh commercial world, something that grated on conventional ideas about the proper role of women and the sanctity of the home. When the decision was affirmed by New York's intermediate appellate court the following year, another round of approving commentary followed.[30] If ever there was a litigant who could attract public sympathy in favor of a right to control the display of one's image, it was Abigail Roberson.

That sympathy reached its peak in 1902, when the New York Court of Appeals, by a 4–3 vote, reversed the decision and held that Roberson had no right to prevent Franklin Mills from using her picture. "The so-called 'right of privacy' has not as yet found an abiding place in our jurisprudence," Chief Judge Alton Parker decided. Like the earlier judges who had rejected the notion, Parker and his colleagues in the majority were worried about the threat to the freedom of expression posed by allowing people to control the use of their images. "If such a principle be incorporated into the body of the law through the instrumentality of a court," Parker feared, "the attempts to logically apply the principle will necessarily result not only in a vast amount of litigation, but in litigation bordering upon the absurd, for the right of privacy, once established as a legal doctrine, cannot be confined to the restraint of a publication of a likeness, but must necessarily embrace as well the publication of a word picture, a comment upon one's looks, conduct, domestic relations or habits." And that was only the start. If there was a right to privacy that applied to printed matter, "it would necessarily be held to include the same things if spoken instead of printed, for one, as well as the other, invades the right to be absolutely let alone." A legislature might make distinctions between pictures and names, or between print and speech, Parker explained, but because a court had to decide cases on general principles, a decision for Abigail Roberson threatened to swallow up public discourse.[31]

Few court decisions have been so unpopular. One lawyers' magazine lamented that "the ordinary citizen, man or woman, has absolutely no redress against the machinations of any advertising agent who, with a sense of delicacy equal to that of an elephant, may choose to utilize the picture of any reputable and retiring member of the community." Another suggested that some cigar maker should use Parker's picture on a line of "Chief Justice" cigars. "New terrors are added to life," fretted the *New York Times*, while one correspondent to the paper was nervous that if "some enterprising and adventurous advertising agent by fraudulent stealth procures a snapshot of my lady at the bath" the photo might appear in advertisements. Some lawyers criticized the Court of Appeals for grossly overestimating the effects of a decision for Roberson on forms of speech other than advertising. Others criticized the court's timidity in failing to make new law to keep up with the times. After a few months of attacks, Denis O'Brien, one of the judges in the majority on the Court of Appeals, took the extraordinary step of defending the decision in an article in the *Columbia Law Review*.[32] The *Roberson* case had transformed the right to privacy from a novel and uncertain legal issue into a popular cause, among lawyers and in the wider world.

Many responded to the Court of Appeals' decision by calling upon the state legislature for a statute that would empower future Abigail Robersons to keep their pictures out of the marketplace. "The hour is ripe for the legislator to step in," intoned *Harper's Weekly*. "If there be, as Judge Parker says there is, no law now to cover these savage and horrible practices," agreed the *New York Times*, "then the decent people will say that it is high time that there were such a law." Even Elbridge Adams, the lawyer for Franklin Mills, acknowledged that "if we may interpret the comments of the newspaper press upon the decision, as faithfully reflecting public opinion, there is a widespread popular desire for relief."[33]

The legislature responded the following spring with a statute that made New York the first state to recognize a right to control the use of one's name and image, at least in certain circumstances. Section 1 of the statute made it a misdemeanor to use, "for advertising purposes, or for the purposes of trade," the name, portrait, or picture of any living person without that person's consent. Section 2 authorized any person whose name or picture had been so used to file a civil suit to prevent further use and to recover damages. Commentators recognized that the statute had been prompted by all the criticism leveled at the *Roberson* case. "There was a natural and widespread feeling that such use of their names and portraits, in the absence of consent, was indefensible in morals, and ought to be prevented by law," a unanimous opinion of the Court of Appeals recalled a few years later. "Hence the enactment of the statute."[34]

Abigail Roberson had the last laugh. In 1904 Alton Parker resigned from the Court of Appeals to run for president as the Democratic candidate. During the campaign he and his family were so besieged by photographers that Parker declared: "I reserve the right to put my hands in my pockets and assume comfortable attitudes without being everlastingly afraid that I shall be snapped by some fellow with a camera." Roberson promptly wrote a letter to Parker—which she released to the press—reminding him "that you have no such right as that which you assert." If Roberson could not object to the use of her picture on flour advertisements, she asked, on what ground could Parker complain about news photographers? "I am forced to the conclusion," she needled, "that this incident well illustrates the truth of the old saying that it makes a lot of difference whose ox is gored." The story was front page news.[35] Parker lost in a landslide to Theodore Roosevelt and never held public office again.

Once the New York statute was in place, other states followed quickly. In 1904 Virginia enacted a similar statute. In 1905 the Georgia Supreme Court ruled in favor of a man whose picture was used without his consent in an advertisement for a life insurance company. "The body of a person cannot be put on exhibition at any time or at any place without his consent," the court insisted. After reviewing the controversy caused by *Roberson*, the Georgia judges had little doubt they were right. "So thoroughly satisfied are we that the law recognizes, within proper limits, as a legal right, the right of privacy," they declared, "we venture to predict that the day will come that the American bar will marvel that a contrary view was ever entertained." In Indiana a trial judge prohibited a newspaper from printing sketches of a criminal defendant without his permission. The Louisiana Supreme Court barred the police from circulating photographs of people who had not been convicted of a crime. In Wisconsin and Kentucky, courts held that negatives and prints of photographic portraits belonged to the sitter, not to the photographer. A right not to have one's picture used in advertising without one's consent was recognized by courts in Pennsylvania, Missouri, and Kansas. By 1909 even the United States Supreme Court agreed that a person could recover damages where an advertiser had used her picture without her consent, at least where the advertisement caused harm to her reputation. (The advertisement was for whiskey, and the plaintiff was a teetotaler.)[36]

This change in the law did not proceed unanimously. A Providence man's picture had been used without his consent in an advertisement for waterproof "auto coats" to be worn by "autoists" exposed to the weather in the latest method of transportation. The Rhode Island Supreme Court nevertheless threw out his suit in 1909, on the ground that there was no such thing as a right to privacy. The Supreme Court of Washington came to the same conclusion a couple of years later.[37]

By the 1910s, however, commentators acknowledged a clear trend toward recognizing a right to control the use of one's name and image. In his 1908 manual on the law of advertising, Clowry Chapman recommended obtaining written releases from models, in case privacy claims should pop up later. The earliest treatise on the law applicable to the motion picture industry, published in 1918, included an entire chapter on the burgeoning law of privacy. The trend would only grow stronger in later years, as the cases piled up. By the 1930s the *Restatement of Torts*, the profession's leading summary of the law, included a section called "Interference with Privacy" that recognized a civil action against "a person who unreasonably and seriously interferes with another's interest in not having his affairs known to others or his likeness exhibited to the public." Thoughtful lawyers, looking back on three decades of legal change, remembered what had set the change in motion. "The portrayal of the personality by a photograph, painting, caricature, or verbal description (likeness) has only become important since the development of the camera and photographic printing," recalled the law professor Leon Green. "It is the capacity to reproduce the personality of another by photography which has created a demand for legal protection."[38]

A Right of Publicity

The purpose of New York's 1903 privacy statute was to prohibit advertisers from thrusting ordinary people like Abigail Roberson into the public arena. It was not intended to help celebrities capitalize on their fame. The words of the statute, however, did not distinguish between the famous and the nonfamous; they applied equally to everyone. It did not take long before well-known people began bringing suit under the statute, seeking not to avoid the spotlight but to get paid for being in it.

In 1910, for example, Charles Eliot, the former president of Harvard University, sued a book publisher who advertised a set of volumes to be called "Dr. Eliot's Five-Foot Shelf." Eliot had no wish to keep his name out of the public eye. He was already being compensated by a different publishing company for lending his name to a different set of volumes that already bore the name "Dr. Eliot's Five-Foot Shelf." Eliot was not seeking privacy in the ordinary sense of the word, but he won his case. The statute simply barred the use of a person's name in an advertisement without his consent, the court explained, regardless of who that person was.[39]

Many similar cases followed. John Philip Sousa sued a cigar company for using his name and picture. Fred Astaire won an injunction barring the use of his photograph in an advertisement for jewelry. Famous actors, singers, dancers, authors, and professional athletes all brought suit in the New York courts under the statute, and all won. As one lawyer explained, "the New York statute does not in terms discriminate between individuals specially in the public eye and private persons."[40] It empowered both sorts of people to control the use of their names and images.

In most other states the right of privacy had been established by court decision rather than by statute, so there was no statutory text to interpret. The courts were free to decide for themselves whether celebrities could invoke the right along with noncelebrities. Some held that they could. Thomas Edison may have been the most famous person in New Jersey in 1907, but a New Jersey court nevertheless enjoined a medicine company from using Edison's picture on its labels. A man's face was his property, the court reasoned, and "its pecuniary value, if it has one," belonged "to its owner, rather than to the person seeking to make unauthorized use of it." As Edison could hardly complain that he was being dragged into the limelight, one commentator explained, and as the court had not found that the medicine caused any damage to Edison's reputation, his victory "must therefore be based on the broad ground of his right to be free from unjustifiable commercial exploitation of his non-corporeal personality." The Kentucky horseman Jack Chinn, who was famous at least in his home state, won a similar case two years later. "One of the accepted and popular methods of advertising in the present day," the North Carolina Supreme Court determined in another case, "is to procure and publish the indorsement of the article being advertised by some well-known person whose name supposedly will lend force to the advertisement. If it be conceded that the name of a person is a valuable asset in connection with an advertising enterprise, then it must likewise be conceded that his face or features are likewise of value. Neither can be used for such a purpose without the consent of the owner." On one view of the issue, as one lawyer concluded, "it would be impossible to draw an abstract definitive line between public and private characters."[41] If it was wrong to use someone's name or picture in an advertisement without his permission, it was just as wrong where the person was a celebrity.

There was something odd, on the other hand, about allowing people whose names and faces were already in the public eye to invoke a right of *privacy*. "The ordinary individual's personal experiences may richly deserve protection from inquisitive busybodies pandering to the public's appetite for gossip," reasoned the federal judge Charles Clark. "A performer, however, is essentially an exhibitionist. He lives by parading his talent before the public eye. Whatever protection his performance deserves should not be grafted on the right of privacy." When the stage actress Maxine Martin sued a Cleveland theater for using her picture to advertise a burlesque show she had nothing to do with, a local judge found her claim too incongruous to accept. "Persons who expose themselves to public view for hire cannot expect to have the same privacy as the meek, plodding stay-at-home citizen," he argued. "An actress of the accomplishments and reputation claimed for this plaintiff is no longer a private individual, but has become a public character and cannot complain that any right of privacy is trespassed upon by the mere unauthorized publication of a photograph." Courts in Oklahoma and California reached similar conclusions. When the Loose-Wiles Biscuit Company began selling Vassar Chocolates, in packages bearing a pennant, a college seal, and a young woman in mortarboard hat, a federal judge in Missouri denied Vassar College's attempt to put a stop to the sales. "It is quite obvious that the complainant could not well invoke the right of privacy, whatever that right may be determined to be," the judge held. How could a famous public institution like Vassar have a claim to privacy?[42]

The most well-known of these cases involved Texas Christian University's star quarterback Davey O'Brien, who won the Heisman Trophy as the nation's best college football player in 1938. Each year Pabst Blue Ribbon Beer published a football calendar, with schedules of the major college and professional games and photographs of the leading players. The calendar for 1939 included a picture of O'Brien, which Pabst obtained from TCU without notifying O'Brien. O'Brien had turned down endorsement offers from other beer companies and was a member of an organization that sought to prevent young people from trying alcohol. The federal court of appeals nevertheless rejected his claim. The right of privacy belonged only to private people, the court held, but O'Brien "is not such a person and the publicity he got was only that which he had been constantly seeking and receiving."[43]

Cases involving celebrities raised a question going to the very purpose of the new right. Was it supposed to protect only privacy? Or was it also intended to protect something nearly the opposite, the commercial exploitation of one's identity? Lawyers had long recognized that the right of privacy was being invoked by two very different categories of people. Some were genuinely interested in privacy, in preventing or redressing a harm to their feelings caused by unwanted publicity. But others were interested in preserving a market for that very same publicity. Both sorts of people claimed a right to control the use of their own pictures and names, a right lawyers had come to call "privacy," but the nature of that right differed according to the uses for which it was sought. For those who wanted to preserve their ability to sell their names and images elsewhere, the right of privacy was a form of property, something they could offer to the highest bidder. For those who wanted to keep their names and images out of commerce altogether, the right of privacy was more of a civil or personal right, like the right to vote or to speak, something that could not be bought or sold. By becoming famous, celebrities may have "waived" the latter kind of right, but not the former.[44]

This division in the case law was not reflected in the advertising industry, where the normal practice by the early part of the century was to obtain a celebrity's consent before using a name or a picture. The baseball legend Ty Cobb recalled being offered $75 in 1908 for the use of his name on Louisville Slugger bats, and by Cobb's own account, other players had already made similar deals. To this day the rarest and most valuable baseball card in the history of the game is the 1909 card of the Pittsburgh shortstop Honus Wagner, which the manufacturer, the American Tobacco Company, pulled from circulation when Wagner objected to the use of his image. Actresses, who were especially in demand as endorsers of cosmetics, exercised close control over when and how their pictures would be displayed.[45] In the Davey O'Brien case, Pabst believed it *had* obtained O'Brien's permission from TCU's publicity department, which, also believing it had O'Brien's approval, had already furnished hundreds of pictures of O'Brien to other publishers. "No one can doubt," concluded the dissenting judge in the case, "that commercial advertisers customarily pay for the right to use the name and likeness of a person who has become famous." He feared that the court's decision was so "contrary to usage and custom among advertisers" that they would begin taking for free what they had long paid for.

Nor was the division in the case law reflected in the published legal commentary of the period, which was virtually unanimous in asserting that the right of privacy should protect the commercial exploitation of one's fame. "Why should a stranger be permitted to appropriate the value which a party has, by his efforts and industry, caused to become attached to his name?" one writer wondered. "The enormous increase in testimonial advertising has demonstrated beyond a doubt that a name or picture capable of use in such a connection is worth money," declared another. "This economic interest must be recognized, either upon the theory that the plaintiff can sell it himself or upon the theory that the defendant, by his use of it, has admitted its value."[46] Despite the decisions of a few courts, there seems to have been little doubt, within either the legal or the advertising profession, that the famous had as much right as the non-famous to control the use of their names and images.

Testimonials were the focus of legal controversy in the late 1920s and the early 1930s, but the dispute was not about the need for permission, which was assumed; rather, it was about whether there was anything unethical or even fraudulent for a celebrity to get paid to advertise a product he did not genuinely use. "Now Gene Tunney uses a certain laxative," the *Nation* noted in 1929. "Where does salesmanship leave off and dishonesty begin? It is pretty hard to tell. It is just possible that Gene Tunney actually uses the laxative in question and, if true, the assertion has some importance for human irrigation. Should there be some kind of public committee to discover whether Gene is masquerading and is actually a secret devotee of something else?" In 1930 the leading sporting goods manufacturers in the United States, convened by the Federal Trade Commission, declared that they would not use prominent athletes in advertisements for their products unless the athletes "sincerely prefer the product." The trade association of motion picture advertisers condemned the use of movie stars to advertise products the stars in fact knew little about. In 1931 the FTC even required testimonial advertisements to disclose that the endorser was being paid, a policy that remained in effect for only a few months before a court determined it lay outside the FTC's jurisdiction.[47]

If the truthfulness of celebrity endorsements was in doubt, however, the fact that celebrities owned their own names and images was not. A major part of the rapidly growing advertising industry had been built on that assumption. So had the early forms of celebrity merchandising, such as the sale of baseball cards and movie memorabilia.[48] The handful of cases holding that people already in the public eye could not invoke a right of privacy had not prevented celebrities from selling their names and pictures to others.

Lingering doubts about whether privacy could be called a "property" right capable of being bought and sold, or whether it was better understood as an inalienable right personal to the holder, had commercial consequences only in a very narrow class of disputes. What if the lawsuit was brought, not by the celebrity whose name or picture had been used without permission, but by the firm that *did* have permission? Could the licensee of a name or image sue to enforce the celebrity's right of privacy, on the theory that the licensee was now the holder of that right? Or was the right of privacy personal, so that only the celebrity herself could bring the suit? This question did not come up very often. Before 1950 there were only two reported court opinions addressing it. The first was a 1915 New York suit by one poster company, which had contracted with several movie actresses for the exclusive right to sell posters bearing their pictures, against another poster company, which was selling posters of the same actresses. The judge refused to allow the suit. New York's statutory right of privacy, he reasoned, was not "designed to protect the rights of private property," but was rather "based upon the regard of the law for the feelings and sentiments of the individual," and those feelings could not be sold to others. If the pirated posters were to be suppressed, the actresses would have to bring the suit themselves.[49] (The actresses had most likely sold rights to use their pictures to the second poster company as well, despite their prior sale of exclusive rights to the first company. They would not have wanted to sue the second company. In principle the first company could have sued the actresses, but they may have preferred to keep on good terms with the actresses, so they could continue to sell posters in the future.)

The second case received more attention. Since the turn of the century, baseball bats had been endorsed by famous baseball players. The leading bat makers paid for the exclusive right to put a particular player's name on a particular style of bat, normally the type of bat the player actually used. Over time, the names of the most well-known players became associated with certain sizes and proportions of bats—there were Babe Ruth bats, Lou Gehrig bats, and so on. In the early 1930s, a newcomer to the bat business began using the names of players to describe the styles of bats it produced, players who had already granted an exclusive license to an established bat manufacturer. The established bat company sued the newcomer but lost, again on the ground that privacy is a personal right that could not be sold to others. "Fame is not merchandise," the court insisted. "It would help neither sportsmanship nor business to uphold the sale of a famous name to the highest bidder as property." The baseball players themselves could sue the upstart bat company for using their names without permission, but they could not sell the right to do so.[50]

This view, as critics pointed out, was hard to square with conventional business practice, in which the commercial value of a name or a picture was considered an assignable form of property like any other.[51] Although these cases rested on a conception of privacy as a personal right to avoid unwanted publicity rather than a commercial right to exploit one's identity, they did not put a dent in the ever-growing market for celebrity endorsements and merchandise; they affected only the narrow question of who could sue for the unauthorized use of a name or picture, not the broader issue of whether celebrities could license their fame in the first place. This view was put to rest, in any event, in the 1953 case of *Haelan Laboratories v. Topps Chewing Gum,* a case that is widely known but widely misunderstood.

Haelan was a case about baseball cards. One chewing gum company, which had contracted for the exclusive right to use players' photographs on the cards it packaged with its gum, sued another chewing gum company, which was using pictures of the same players. The case came before the federal court of appeals in New York, which at the time was the most influential court in the country other than the U.S. Supreme Court. In an opinion by the well-known judge Jerome Frank, the court decided that one company could sue the other. "A man has a right in the publicity value of his photograph," the court held, and that right could be assigned to another. "This right," Frank continued, in the most famous passage from the opinion, "might be called a 'right of publicity.' For it is common knowledge that many prominent persons (especially actors and ball-players), far from having their feelings bruised through public exposure of their likenesses, would feel sorely deprived if they no longer received money from authorizing advertisements." But that income stream would dry up "unless it could be made the subject of an exclusive grant which barred any other advertiser from using their pictures."[52] By allowing the exclusive right to use names and images, including the right to sue competing users, to be assigned to others, Frank was bringing the law into conformity with commercial practice.

Ever since, Frank's opinion in *Haelan* has frequently been understood as the origin of the "right of publicity," the right of a celebrity in his name and picture.[53] This is true only in a semantic sense, in that the term "right of publicity" does seem to have originated with Frank. In a substantive sense, however, celebrities were selling the rights to use their names and pictures, and courts were recognizing their ability to do so, long before *Haelan*. Lawyers had long been suggesting that the right to "privacy" was a misnomer, because it actually encompassed two or more distinct rights, of which privacy, in the sense of the right to be let alone, was only one.[54] The opinion's only substantive innovation was to allow competing licensees to sue one another rather than requiring the suits to be brought by the celebrities themselves.

Between the late nineteenth century and the middle of the twentieth, a new kind of property had come into existence: the right to control the use of one's name and picture. Jenny Lind had toured the country in the 1850s without profiting from the sale of Jenny Lind merchandise, but when Elvis Presley toured the country in the 1950s, he likely earned more from licensing fees than from ticket sales. There were Elvis shoes, Elvis jeans, Elvis record players, Elvis bracelets, Elvis lipstick, Elvis statues in plaster of Paris, and much more. By 1956, still very early in his career, thirty companies had fifty licenses for Elvis products to be sold in the country's leading department stores. Presley's licensing agent was Henry G. Saperstein of Beverly Hills, whose other clients included Lassie and the Lone Ranger. Back in the 1850s P. T. Barnum had been pleased to discover unauthorized Jenny Lind merchandise. In the 1950s Saperstein sometimes discovered unauthorized Elvis gear, and when he did, "we sue like mad," he explained. "We've never lost a case yet. The courts protect you all the way."[55]

Something Very Dangerous

From the beginning, many had worried that the ownership of names and images would be difficult to reconcile with the freedom of expression. That fear never disappeared. There was something close to a consensus about the cases on the extremes: advertisers should have to pay when they used a person's name or picture, but newspapers shouldn't have to pay for reporting the news when that required naming or showing people.[56] Many cases fell between those extremes, however, and they continued to present difficult questions all through the twentieth century.

For example, what exactly was "news"? If a newsreel showed corpulent women exercising in a gymnasium, with amusing voiceover commentary, had the newsreel company appropriated the women's images without their consent? Or were the women participants in a news story of public interest? When *Time* magazine published, in its "Medicine" section, a story about Mrs. Dorothy Barber of Kansas City, who had checked herself into a hospital because of a condition in which she lost weight despite eating constantly, was that medical news? Or had *Time* stolen Barber's name and image? What about publishing the pictures of divorcing parents and children embroiled in contentious custody litigation? A New York judge held that the corpulent women *were* news; the Missouri Supreme Court determined that the Kansas City overeater was *not* news; and a court in Minnesota concluded that the bewildered children *were* news. Decisions like these seemed to rest on uncomfortably subjective assessments of whether this or that topic was newsworthy. Over time, judges' discomfort in making these kinds of decisions led them to the view that information presented as news was news by definition. Thus when Charlie Chaplin sued NBC for broadcasting on the radio a tape of a conversation between Chaplin and his butler, the court had little trouble rejecting Chaplin's argument that the tape was entertainment rather than news. "This seems to be an argument that matters which ought not to be published as news are not news at all," the judge reasoned. Chaplin was a prominent man whose doings were of broad public interest: "beyond that, courts cannot and should not pass judgment on the value of particular news items."[57] In cases like these, the freedom of the press tended to trump the property rights of the people depicted.

But other hard questions remained. What about fictionalized portrayals of real events? In 1909 two steamships collided off the shore of Massachusetts. A wireless telegrapher named John Binns was aboard one of the ships; his emergency message brought another ship to the rescue and saved hundreds of lives. The incident was of considerable public interest, because it was the first time wireless telegraphy had been used this way. Vitagraph, one of the early film companies, promptly made a series of short movies about the event. The movies were shot in a studio using actors, but they used John Binns's name, and a photograph of the real Binns appeared a few times on screen. The New York Court of Appeals tried to draw a sharp line between fact and fiction. A factual account of Binns's heroism, the court held, would have been lawful, but by converting the story to fiction Vitagraph had illegally appropriated Binns's name and picture to make a profit. The boundary between fact and fiction would prove difficult to maintain, however. John Hersey's Pulitzer Prize–winning novel *A Bell for Adano* recounted real events in the life of an army officer named Frank Toscani, who was not happy that Hersey was profiting from his story. Toscani lost, despite the book's status as fiction, only because Hersey had prudently changed his character's name from Toscani to Joppolo. Warren Spahn, the famous Milwaukee Braves pitcher, sued the publisher of a fictionalized biography and won, but the widow of the actor Jack Donahue, who was portrayed by Ray Bolger in the fictionalized film *Look for the Silver*

Lining, sued the filmmakers and lost.[58] Books and films were not easily compartmentalized into fact or fiction. Many had elements of both, and that made it hard to decide how far the ownership of fame should extend.

A similar conundrum was presented by the use of real people as characters in fiction. It would scarcely have been possible to write fiction without giving characters names that might coincide with the names of real people, so it was recognized early on that such people had no property rights in the use of their names. When a man named Wayne Damron sued the novelist Edna Ferber for including a character named Wayne Damron in *Show Boat,* or when a Mr. and Mrs. Rudy Nebb of Georgia sued the Chicago-based creator of a comic strip called *The Nebbs* (which was about a couple named Mr. and Mrs. Rudy Nebb), judges had little trouble dismissing the suits. The difficult cases arose when authors used the names of people they knew. The author James Jones was an army clerk stationed in Hawaii during the period just before Pearl Harbor. One of the soldiers in his company was named Joseph Anthony Maggio. Jones's 1951 novel *From Here to Eternity,* and the 1953 film based on the novel (which won eight Academy Awards, including Best Picture), were about soldiers stationed in Hawaii just before Pearl Harbor, and both depicted a character named Angelo Maggio. Joseph Maggio sued, alleging that Angelo Maggio was really him, but a judge determined that Jones's use of the name "Maggio" was simply a coincidence. Less fortunate was the novelist Marjorie Kinnan Rawlings, who won the Pulitzer Prize in 1939 for her novel *The Yearling.* A few years after *The Yearling,* Rawlings published *Cross Creek,* which drew on Rawlings's own experiences in the rural Florida town of that name. *Cross Creek* included a character named Zelma, whom Rawlings described as "an ageless spinster resembling an angry and efficient canary." Zelma Cason, the real person behind the character, had been close friends with Rawlings, but she was so offended by her depiction that she sued. The result was more than five years of litigation. The case reached the Florida Supreme Court twice; on both occasions, the court decided in Cason's favor.[59]

There would always be a steady stream of cases in which both sides could legitimately claim sympathy, one by invoking the freedom of expression, the other by noting the unhappy results that could flow from allowing others to exploit one's identity. The Detroit Arctic Expedition

of 1926 was largely financed by the Pathé News Service, which in return received the exclusive right to film the expedition. When a second
film company showed up in Alaska and began filming the preparations
for the trip, in the hope of hitting the theaters before the Pathé News
Service, a court had to make a difficult decision. Which would take
precedence, the public interest in seeing the expedition or a private
company's ostensible property right in images of the expedition, without which there might not be any expedition at all? When a Los Angeles woman committed suicide by leaping from the twelfth floor of a
downtown office building, which was more important, the public interest in seeing the woman's picture or her husband's embarrassment?[60]
Cases like these could not be resolved by relying on precedent or the
words of a statute. They inevitably required judgment as to the relative
worth of two competing interests.

The freedom of expression prevailed in both of these cases, and
indeed in most of the close cases before the late twentieth century.
Judges tended to be circumspect about extending the rights of privacy
and publicity in new directions, for fear of limiting the traditional ability of the media to use names and faces in reporting facts. This circum-
spection began to weaken at the end of the century, however. As celebrity merchandising expanded into an enormous business, and as the
rights of privacy and publicity became familiar, unexceptional parts of
the legal landscape, property rights in fame grew ever larger, at the expense of traditional rights to use the names and pictures of others.

Before the 1970s, for example, a person's name and image entered
the public domain when he died. This was due in part to the early understanding of privacy as a personal right rather than a form of property; once a person was dead, he could not suffer from the publication of
his name or picture. Just as important, there was not yet any significant
merchandising of the identities of dead celebrities, so there was not yet
anyone with an interest in persuading legislatures or courts to allow the
right of publicity to be passed on to one's heirs. The dead were fair game.
Colgate used the name and picture of the late Civil War general Ambrose Burnside to advertise shaving cream, over the objection of his
niece, his only surviving relative. Filmmakers were free to tell the life
story of the composer Walter Schumann, despite the suit filed by his
great-grandchildren, and television broadcasters could do the same for
the gangster Al Capone, despite the complaint of his widow and son.[61]

Motion picture studios sometimes paid surviving family members before they made movies about the lives of famous deceased people, but through the 1960s courts consistently affirmed that the studios were not purchasing any right of publicity the family members might have inherited. MGM paid the estate of the lyricist Lorenz Hart before making the 1948 film *Words and Music,* but, a New York judge held, the payment was not for the right to use Hart's name and image but rather for the copyrights in Hart's songs. Damon Runyon's son earned $25,000 from the sale of motion picture rights to Runyon's life story—the film was never made—and then claimed that for tax purposes the fee was not income but revenue from the sale of a capital asset, his father's right of publicity. His claim was rejected on the ground that Runyon's son had no asset to sell, because Runyon's right of publicity had died with him. The lawyers for Glenn Miller's widow made the same argument in trying to get favorable tax treatment for the $400,000 she earned from the 1953 film *The Glenn Miller Story.* Why would a sophisticated corporation like Universal Pictures pay her so much money, they asked, if Universal could tell the bandleader's story for free? The federal judge Irving Kaufman had an answer: "the 'thing' bought, or more appropriately 'bought off,' seems to have been the chance that a new theory of 'property' might be advanced, and that a lawsuit predicated on it might be successful. It was a purchase, so to speak, of freedom from fear. In effect, it was a hedge against the chance that the Miller 'property' *might* exist."[62]

If so, it was a prescient purchase, because the law soon began to change, under the pressure of a growing investment in merchandising the identities of dead celebrities. The actor Bela Lugosi, famous for his portrayal of Count Dracula, died in 1956, but Universal Pictures continued to license Lugosi's picture. In 1972, a California judge held that the right to sell Lugosi's image belonged to Lugosi's heirs. The decision would soon be reversed by a closely divided California Supreme Court, but the dead were rising. Oliver Hardy died in 1957 and Stan Laurel in 1965. While they were alive they licensed their images for toys and games, and when they died their widows did the same. In 1975, after an unauthorized company began using Laurel and Hardy images, a New York judge allowed the widows to sue. If the right of publicity was a kind of property that could be assigned to others while Laurel and Hardy were alive, the judge reasoned, there was no logical reason it could not pass to their widows upon their death. Over the next three decades state after state reached the same conclusion, some by court decision, others by statute. The forces behind these changes were often very clear. In Tennessee, for example, Elvis Presley Enterprises, stung by a flood of unauthorized Elvis memorabilia, lobbied the state legislature for a statute explicitly stating that the right of publicity survives a celebrity's death.[63] A similar California statute was called the Astaire Celebrity Image Protection Act, in recognition of the lobbying efforts of Robyn Astaire, Fred's widow. Fred Astaire died in 1987; ten years later, after Robyn licensed the necessary film clips, Fred could be seen in a television commercial, dancing with vacuum cleaners.

As property in fame lasted longer, it was also growing broader in scope. Names and pictures had been covered by the rights of privacy and publicity as far back as the original 1903 New York statute. But what about the sound of a voice? A television commercial in the early 1960s for the floor cleaner Lestoil featured an animated duck that sounded like the comic actor Bert Lahr. Lahr sued but lost, on the theory that the right of privacy did not encompass sound. The members of The Fifth Dimension, a popular singing group, lost a similar suit for the same reason a few years later, after a commercial for Trans World Airlines used different singers to imitate the sound of their hit "Up, Up and Away." As critics pointed out, however, a voice can be as strong a marker of identity as a name or a face, particularly if it is the distinctive voice of a well-known entertainer. In 1988 that argument finally carried the day, when a court allowed Bette Midler to recover from the makers of a commercial that included one of the songs for which she was famous, performed by a singer instructed to sound just like Midler. "A voice is as distinctive and personal as a face," reasoned Judge John Noonan. "The human voice is one of the most palpable ways identity is manifested." A few years later Tom Waits, a singer with a voice as distinctive as anyone's, won a similar case.[64]

Once the right of publicity was understood as a property right in one's identity as a whole, rather than protection for particular methods of displaying that identity, new kinds of claims were bound to arise. In the early 1990s the game show hostess Vanna White was awarded $400,000 in damages for an advertisement depicting a robot standing next to two large letters. The robot looked nothing like White, but it was intended to remind readers of White, and that, the court held, was enough to infringe's White's property in her identity. George Wendt and John Ratzenberger, actors famous for sitting at a bar in the television program *Cheers,* won a similar case a few years later against a company that placed robots at airport bars modeled on the bar depicted in the program.[65] Names and faces had been propertized in part to protect the commercial exploitation of identity, but once identity itself was propertized, the range of possible lawsuits was limited only by the imaginations of lawyers.

In cases like these, the old tension between property and free expression was increasingly being resolved in property's favor. "Something very dangerous is going on here," warned Judge Alex Kozinski, dissenting in the Vanna White case. "Overprotecting intellectual property is as harmful as underprotecting it. Creativity is impossible without a rich public domain."[66] A century earlier, opponents of the right to privacy had expressed precisely the same concern.

8

From the Tenement to the Condominium

"IN AMERICA there are so to speak no tenant farmers," Alexis de Tocqueville supposedly discovered while touring the United States in the 1830s. "Every man is the owner of the field he cultivates." Yet by the end of the nineteenth century fewer than half of white Americans, and fewer than a quarter of African Americans, owned their own homes. And by the early twenty-first century the nature of home ownership itself was changing, as nearly six million homes, more than 5 percent of the country's housing stock, were either condominiums or cooperatives, forms of ownership that did not exist in Tocqueville's day.[1] The home is the kind of property with the most meaning to the most people, so the emergence of new types of homes, and new ways of owning homes, has been among the most fundamental changes in the nature of property in the United States.

Like Sheep into Pens

Tocqueville was hardly alone in believing that the early United States was a nation of homeowners. "One of the most remarkable circumstances in our colonial history," Supreme Court justice Joseph Story noted, "is the almost total absence of leasehold estates." Crèvecoeur's representative American Farmer gloried in owning his own land. "The instant I enter on my own land, the bright idea of property, of exclusive right, of independence, exalts my mind," he declared. "What should we American farmers be without the distinct possession of the soil?" Everyone could be a homeowner. Land was so plentiful that "there is room for every body in America." Like the American Farmer, many contrasted the abundance of land in the United States with its scarcity in Europe, where comparatively few could afford to own their own homes. "In Europe the lands are either cultivated, or locked up against the cultivator," Thomas Jefferson explained. "But we have an immensity of land courting the industry of the husbandman." Even Tocqueville, who tended to think democracy was more important than economic conditions, had to agree. "What happens in the United States ought to be attributed much less to the institutions of the country than to the country itself," he conceded. "In America land costs little and each man easily becomes a property owner."[2]

But observations like these were almost surely wrong. One study of six Maryland counties in 1783 finds that only around half of the heads of households owned their own land. In southeastern Pennsylvania in the mid-eighteenth century about 30 percent of married taxpayers owned no land. Some were farmers who rented agricultural land from others, and some were craftsmen who rented homes in town. Thousands of tenants rented land on the great manors of New York.[3] The abundance of land kept purchase prices low, but it kept rents low too. Even farmers who could afford to buy land might face a choice between purchasing worse or more remote land on the one hand, and renting better or closer land on the other. Meanwhile, the poorest farmers could not afford to buy any land at all. And we haven't even accounted for all the slaves and indentured servants who worked on land owned by other people. All told, rates of home ownership, although higher than in Europe, were likely much lower than men like Tocqueville or Story believed. They may not have been personally acquainted with many tenants.

As the country gradually urbanized in the nineteenth century, land prices in cities rose faster than wages. More and more city dwellers had to rent rooms in buildings owned by others. Many lived in boardinghouses—in central Boston, nearly 8 percent of the population were boarders in 1860, and 14 percent were boarders by 1900. In New York that figure seemed higher. "Two-thirds of New York board," the columnist Louise Furniss joked, "and three-thirds take boarders!" Whatever the precise number, the boardinghouse (along with its cousin the

lodging house, which provided rooms but not meals) was a major urban institution in nineteenth-century America. Meanwhile many affluent urbanites lived more or less permanently in hotels, often for
convenience rather than out of strict economic necessity.[4]

Working-class families, unable to afford houses of their own,
sometimes rented rooms in shared houses originally built for a single
family. By the middle of the century, it was a common observation that
housing trickled down the social scale over time, as ever-increasing
numbers of tenants occupied structures that had not been designed for
them. "The wealthy merchant builds himself a palace to-day which
will be inhabited by the son of his porter tomorrow; or at best be used
as a boarding-house by the widow of his clerk," one New Yorker remarked in the 1850s. "There are now remaining in New-York but two
of the fine old mansions which were built before the Revolution, and
one of them is occupied as an emigrant boarding-house, and the other
as a restaurant." As a result, another observed, "the majority of New
York households are living like hermit crabs in other creatures' shells."[5]

New York likely had more renters than any city in the country.
Landowners already formed less than half the electorate in 1790, and by
the election of 1807 more than three-quarters of the voters were renters. "The whole community," explained the lawyer John Taylor, "is, in
fact, divided into the two great classes, of landlords and tenants."[6] This
division was never more evident than on May 1, or "Quarter Day," the
customary moving day on which one year's leases ended and the next
year's began. (The name came from England, where rent was traditionally due quarterly.) Quarter Day was chaos, as New Yorkers all tried to
move at once. According to the poet and journalist Samuel Woodworth
it was

> a scene of tumult, noise, and strife,
> With which compared, old Bable's lofty tower
> Was Order's temple and the shrine of peace.

Woodworth, writing in 1812, explained that "rents increase,"

> And half our population, or for that,
> Or business, or for fashion, must remove,
> And with bright May begin another year.
> 'Tis the strange mania that disclaims a cure.

Woodworth was a tenant himself, a young man in his twenties who had recently moved from Baltimore to New York, married, and had his first child. He knew the tension of Quarter Day all too well.

My LANDLORD is the master of my fate;
And who can tell if next meridian sun
Will not behold me dispossess'd of all
The humble stock of worldly wealth I own?
My wife and boy may—that's digression though—
Are there not thousands, too, who feel like me,
And tremble at the near approach of MAY?
Not for *their* sins—but for the *power* of those
Whom wealth and accident have made their lords.[7]

Long before there were any apartment buildings, New York was already a city of tenants.

As the demand for multifamily housing continued to grow, urban landowners began to build structures specifically for the purpose. The earliest, first built in substantial numbers in the 1840s, were intended for working-class families. The word *tenement* was an ancient legal term originally encompassing any sort of real property holding. By the fifteenth century it was already a colloquial expression for a dwelling, and that meaning crossed the Atlantic. For early nineteenth-century Americans, a *tenement house* was simply a place to live, often a small house on the grounds of a larger one. Thus an 1815 advertisement in a Philadelphia newspaper offered a 174-acre dairy farm for sale, a holding that included "a two story brick house" as well as a "tenement house" and a stable.[8] By the 1850s, however, the word was largely reserved for the new multifamily rental housing sprouting up in the working-class neighborhoods of the nation's largest cities, especially New York. More than half a million New Yorkers lived in tenements by 1864.[9]

The tenements were often crowded and unsanitary. A committee of the state legislature inspecting them in 1856 found some with residents packed "like sheep into pens," with as many as ten people sharing a single small room. "Next to Intemperance and Licentiousness," worried the *New York Times*, "the greatest curse to the lowest class of New-York is, *the houses* they dwell in." The problem, as well-intentioned reformers would insist for decades, was not just the material conditions created by high housing prices. There was also something immoral about having to share a home with others. "The truth is, not even a virtuous and industrious family could long preserve its chastity and good character in company with three other virtuous families, in a room 15 feet by 18. Men are not made to live so near to each other," the *Times* lectured. "But where you add to that, the fact that all four families are by organization and inheritance beggars and profligates; that the room is filthy and never aired; that there are not even the proprieties which accompany better means to separate them; and when to this you unite the consideration, that every other room of a large house is equally packed with idle, dirty, profligate human creatures, and that the cellar is a rum-shop, whose keeper is the agent of the landlord, and therefore has a double hold over the pockets of the wretched tenants, one can see that the natural result would surely be, a horrible wickedness—a sort of geometrically progressing and intensifying depravity."[10] As tenements spread throughout cities, the lesson many would draw was that the government should intervene in the housing market, by prescribing minimum standards of quality or by building or subsidizing housing for the poor.

As the urban population density increased, the problem of high housing prices crept up the economic ladder. By the 1860s, a single-family home was out of reach for more than just the poor. "Whole houses are out of the question," one New Yorker complained, for "book-keepers, artists, editors, clerks, lawyers, copyists, mechanics, and members of other professions and trades." Another agreed that "a professional or business man . . . cannot get a comfortable home in a good quarter in New-York" without paying more than he and his family could afford. Some such families lived in boardinghouses, some rented portions of houses, and some moved outside the city where housing was cheaper, but it was becoming nearly impossible to have a home in the city itself. A middle-class family was too poor for a house but not poor enough to accept a tenement, and many were squeamish about sharing living quarters with others in a hotel or a boardinghouse, an arrangement hard to reconcile with crystallizing Victorian norms of family privacy. "People who do not live under their own roof are ignorant of the most beautiful side of life," one journalist insisted, voicing a common concern. "The husband is but half a husband, the wife but half a wife, the child but half a child, when all three reside in some huge caravansera in common with some hundreds of other persons."[11] Where in the city could a respectable family live?

The solution was the apartment house, first built in substantial numbers in New York in the early 1870s. "There are at the present time a number of 'Apartment Houses' being erected in different parts of our city," *Harper's Weekly* reported in 1870. "People of moderate income are weary of paying enormous rents, and welcome the prospect of cheaper and yet comfortable quarters." The apartment house had some obvious antecedents. American travelers had seen them in European cities, and indeed the earliest American apartments were sometimes called "French flats" or "Parisian flats."[12] At home the apartment house could be seen as both an upscale version of the tenement and a less service-oriented version of the hotel.

The new apartment houses were a big success. "Nearly everyone knows now," one magazine reported in 1872, "that living on a flat has become a fashion." Looking back a decade later, one journalist recalled that "it took at first some considerable effort to overcome the prejudice against the apartment system which existed among our wealthy classes, who only too frequently confounded it with the tenement-house system." But that confusion was quickly dispelled. As one New York judge concluded in 1878, in deciding that a promise not to build a "tenement house" would not prevent the promisor from building an "apartment house," the two structures were nothing alike. Relying on Webster's dictionary, the judge determined that a tenement was "an inferior dwelling-house rented to poor persons," but an apartment house was simply a building with multiple homes rented to different people, and "there is nothing permanently offensive about a rented dwelling-house."[13] New York became a city of apartment dwellers, people who rented homes in multifamily buildings owned by others. Eventually, of course, apartments spread throughout the country.

In 1904, looking back on the past thirty years, Charlotte Perkins Gilman saw the shift from houses to apartments in the largest cities as a sign of greater things to come. "The real estate records show an astonishing ratio of change," she marveled—"private houses being no longer built in numbers worth mentioning compared with apartment-houses." Some critics, she acknowledged, lamented the lost "ideal of the home of our grandmothers," self-sufficient and surrounded by open space. Now "we see our homes lifted clean off the ground—yardless, cellarless, stairless," because of elevators, and sometimes "even kitchenless," because some of the more expensive early apartments were marketed to tenants affluent enough to order their meals from a common kitchen below. But Gilman saw the apartment as a marker of progress, "from the weary housewife making soap and candles, carding, spinning, weaving, dyeing, cutting, sewing, cooking, nursing, sweeping, washing and all the rest, to the handsome, healthy, golf-playing woman who does none of these things . . . for all her former trades are done each and all by expert professionals." In moving from houses to apartments, Gilman expected, families would be outsourcing domestic chores to specialists. The change would be "from a self-centered family life, mainly content with its own members and its immediate neighbors, to a family that is by no means content with its own members, that knows not neighbors though they be as near and numerous as the cells of a honeycomb, and that insists on finding its interests and pleasures in the great outside world."[14] A century later, apartments have kitchens, but Gilman's vision of a different kind of domestic life has largely come true for those who can afford it, especially in large urban areas, even for families who still live in houses. Most of the work that once took place inside the home now takes place outside, and people with friends all over the world may not know their own neighbors. The shift from houses to apartments was not the *cause* of this broader change, but rather, as Gilman observed, simply one aspect of it, a physical manifestation of the deepening specialization and interdependence of modern life.

The Advantages of Co-Operation

One disadvantage of living in apartments was that residents, whether rich or poor, were tenants in a building owned by someone else. They were at the mercy of rising rents. There was no guarantee, when a lease expired, that the landlord would be willing to renew it. Apartment dwellers had traded the security of home ownership for less expensive housing. For most of the nineteenth century, there was no method by which they could become the owners of their own apartments.

The era was thick, meanwhile, with cooperative movements of various sorts, from utopian communities with shared housing to more businesslike agricultural cooperatives. In 1880, when the French-born New York architect Philip Hubert built the first cooperative apartment building in the United States, commentators understood him to be following in this tradition. Indeed, Hubert himself was a product of the cooperative movement: his father had been a follower of the French utopian theorist Charles Fourier, and had designed a Fourierist community in France before emigrating to the United States. Hubert was a prolific author and a successful inventor as well as an architect. He spent most of his life in New York before moving to Los Angeles in 1900, where (at least according to his 1911 obituary) he drove the second automobile ever seen in the city.[15] But of all his accomplishments, the one that has lasted the longest is the cooperative.

Hubert's plan was a simple one. A group of people wishing to own apartments would form a corporation in which they would be the sole shareholders, the corporation would construct an apartment building, and the shareholders would lease their apartments from the corporation at a nominal rent. They would share the expenses of maintaining the building by paying annual fees. Hubert most likely got the idea from the Fourierist communities with which he was familiar, which were organized in a similar way. His first cooperative building was the Rembrandt, built in 1880 for a group of eight shareholders called the Hubert Home Club. It was so successful that he built several more in the next two years. "It is quite a new idea," explained one admirer, but "it is certainly practical, safe, and an admirable example of the advantages of co-operation." The members of a Home Club were, in effect, their own landlords, so they kept the portion of rent that would have represented the landlord's profit in an ordinary apartment building. "This must in the nature of things be an immense saving on the rent," another supporter of the plan suggested. "The advantages of this system, in reduction of rents and independence of landlords, are obvious at a glance."[16]

There were, in principle, other ways to organize co-owners of a single building, but none was as practical as the cooperative. The residents might have dispensed with the corporate structure by co-owning the building directly, as *tenants in common*. (Here the word *tenant* means "holder" rather than "renter.") But co-owning the building directly would have been unwieldy, because the owners of every unit would have had to join together in mortgages, conveyances, and other actions. The corporate form allowed these tasks to be performed more efficiently. Another option, in theory, would have been for each unit in the building to be owned outright by its occupants, with the common areas owned collectively. This plan would eventually exist—as the condominium—in the mid-twentieth century, but before then it was generally thought to be impractical, because, among other things, it would have required separate insurance and property taxation for each unit, and neither the insurance industry nor local government was yet equipped for that.[17] Hubert's cooperative plan was the only feasible way to organize a group-owned apartment building.

A wave of copycat buildings followed, all for relatively affluent residents of New York, the upper tier of the city's apartment dwellers. "The success of the 'Hubert Home Club' in this City has given rise to a deep and appreciative interest in this improved method of co-operative living," the *New York Times* explained in late 1881. Near Central Park one developer was constructing eight luxury cooperatives simultaneously. By 1883, "the vogue is in the direction of 'Home Club' buildings," the *Times* reported. "It is claimed by those who are pushing this plan that it is an assured success." But the Home Club craze was beginning to fizzle out by 1884. The developers of some of the early cooperatives had underestimated construction costs, requiring the clubs to borrow more than had been anticipated. By the end of the decade, a general decline in real estate values resulted in many foreclosures on these mortgages. With foreclosure, ownership shifted from the home clubs to the banks, and the stockholders found themselves tenants once again. Interest in Hubert's plan quickly waned. By 1902, one architect observed, experience with the cooperative was so sour that "no coöperative apartments have been built for many years, and no more are likely to be built, at least in New York."[18] The cooperative appeared to have come to an end.

But it would return. There was a flurry of cooperative construction in New York in the decade before World War I. Park Avenue had been transformed into "a co-operative apartment centre," the *Times* reported in 1910; "in the lower part of the Sixties the development is wholly of the apartment house type, and almost without exception the projected buildings are co-operative apartments." When the war ended, the cooperative spread to cities throughout the country. There were approximately one hundred cooperative buildings in Chicago by 1924. The cooperative was so popular in Los Angeles, one developer boasted, "that the co-operative ownership plan will be adopted for practically every new apartment-house in Southern California." By the mid-1920s there were cooperatives in Boston, Philadelphia, Baltimore, Washington, Detroit, St. Louis, Atlanta, and Seattle. The National Association of Real Estate Boards, the professional organization for real estate brokers, had to establish a special section for all its members who were selling units in cooperative buildings. Financial institutions that had previously been skeptical about lending to cooperatives began doing so. "Coöperative apartment building organisations are springing up all over the country," the Chicago broker Albert Swayne noted in 1925. "It is as if the whole country had suddenly realized that the coöperative apartment house offers one solution to the problem of how to build up the percentage of home owners in our large cities."[19]

Most of these buildings were for affluent purchasers, but cooperatives were also being built for residents with modest incomes. Sunnyside Gardens, constructed in the mid-1920s in Long Island City, New York, a short subway ride from Manhattan, included several hundred units affordable by teachers, nurses, and office workers. Many similar projects followed, typically undertaken by labor unions and other nonprofit organizations. The rationale behind these cooperatives was once again to reduce the cost of housing by cutting out the landlord's profit. There had long been two unattractive means of providing homes for the urban working class—privately owned tenements and public housing. The nonprofit cooperative held out the possibility of a third solution, midway between the public and the private.[20]

In the late 1920s the cooperative seemed to be the wave of the future, but the future never quite arrived. The Great Depression put an end to the cooperative boom of the 1920s. "Mortgage foreclosures took their toll of many of the most carefully organized projects of the fashionable type promoted among the more affluent," one Chicago lawyer recalled, "while unemployment, job fluctuations, and consequent shifts of groups of workers led to the collapse of a number of the low-cost developments." There would be another burst of interest in the 1950s. Many high-end cooperative buildings went up in Florida and in southern California. The federal government encouraged the construction of middle-income cooperatives by providing mortgage insurance and technical advice. Outside of New York, however, the cooperative never amounted to a significant component of the housing stock. By 1975, when the federal government took a census of the nation's housing units, fewer than 1 percent were in cooperatives. Approximately a third of the cooperative units were in New York.[21]

Why wasn't the cooperative more successful? It had some undoubted advantages, as its boosters tirelessly emphasized during the boom of the 1920s. If managed well, a cooperative was cheaper than a comparably situated rental apartment, because there was no landlord to skim rent off the top. "Suppose that, instead of growling about the rent, you had joined with other rent payers and become your own landlord," lectured the *Saturday Evening Post*. "That money will buy you an apartment and cut your rent in two if you have the enterprise to do for yourself what you have been demanding from others."[22] The benefit of owning over renting grew even larger with the expansion of the federal income tax, because the implicit rental value of owner-occupied housing was not included in the tax law's definition of income.[23] Owning a cooperative was also cheaper than owning a comparably sized freestanding house, because the residents of a cooperative could share the expenses of heating, landscaping, maintenance, and the like.[24] Simply as a financial proposition, owning a cooperative combined the best parts of renting an apartment and owning a house.

A cooperative could also be attractive, at least to its residents, from a social point of view. The owner of a house had no control over who bought the other houses on his block, and a tenant in an apartment could not prevent obnoxious people from renting the other apartments on his hall. But cooperatives could, and often did, exclude people with whom the existing residents did not want to live. "Very frequently residential neighborhoods deteriorate in value because one or two house owners sell to undesirables and thereby cause a stampede among the others to get out," the Chicago developer Elmer Claar told his real estate students at Northwestern University's School of Commerce. But there was no danger of that happening in a cooperative. "In a co-operative apartment home one cannot sell or rent to an undesirable and thus deteriorate the tenancy of the building, for the leases cannot be assigned without the consent of the executive committee or board of directors."[25] This concern about "undesirables" encompassed a range of actual motives, from neighborliness to snobbery to outright bigotry. But whether good or bad, the ability to choose one's closest neighbors was a feature unique to the cooperative.

The cooperative also had some disadvantages. Residents had to spend some time on matters of governance, but rarely very much, because in practice buildings tended to hire managers to handle the day-to-day chores involved in operating a building. Ultimate responsibility rested with a board of directors, but even that job seems not to have been very difficult. R. K. Packard was a Chicago physician who served on his building's board of directors in the 1920s. "I purchased a cooperative apartment," Packard explained, "because it made me a home owner instead of a roving flat dweller; because I am assured of having good and respectable neighbors; because it is an economic saving; because the firm I dealt with was highly reputable; because other owners were satisfied with the investment; because the location was satisfactory, and will remain so; and because my wife told me to." He became a director, but "it does not take a great deal of time or work."[26]

But cooperatives did have one very serious downside, and that was the financial interdependence of the residents. The building was subject to a single mortgage. When a resident was unable to pay his proportionate share, the cooperative would default on the loan unless the other residents made up the difference. Cooperatives could accordingly be risky investments, because a purchaser was banking not just on his own continued financial health but that of a group of strangers. In the 1930s, when many cooperatives went under, it was often said that "the owner came out best who defaulted first."[27] Even in better times, awareness of these dangers likely deterred many from living in cooperatives.

The cooperative might eventually have grown more popular despite this disadvantage, because home ownership never lost its cultural status or its financial advantages, and freestanding houses remained out of reach for many, especially in urban areas with high land prices. But the cooperative was mostly superseded in the early 1960s, when something better came along.

The Condominium Concept

Etymology was not often featured in the *Lawyers Title News*, but subscribers in the summer of 1961 could read that "a strange, new word has appeared in the vocabulary of the real estate fraternity. Brokers, promoters, lawyers are using it—'condominium.'" The word itself wasn't new; it had long been used to mean joint rule or sovereignty, as in Sudan, which had been governed by an Anglo-Egyptian condominium until attaining independence just a few years before, or in the New Hebrides, which were still under the rule of an Anglo-French condominium. But the *Lawyers Title News* was not discussing international relations. It was acquainting its readers with the latest thing in real estate, a method of dividing apartment buildings into units, each of which was owned outright by its occupants. William Kerr, the author of the article, was no linguist—he was a lawyer in the New York office of the Equitable Life Assurance Society—so he likely had more confidence than actual knowledge when he claimed that the word's "roots go deep through civil and Roman law to ancient times."[28] For a readership of real estate lawyers, however, the word needed explanation, and so did the concept, because the condominium, in the real estate sense, was something new. "You can buy an apartment in a building and own, mortgage or sell it just as though it were a separate house," marveled the *Los Angeles Times*. Unlike in a cooperative, which was owned by a corporation whose shareholders were tenants, "each owner holds individual title to his apartment."[29]

Today, of course, condominiums are everywhere, and the idea of a condominium seems so obvious that it is hard to understand why we didn't have them before the 1960s. It can't be a simple matter of population density or land prices, because urban crowding produced rental apartments in the first half of the nineteenth century and cooperatives in the second half. Why did the condominium have to wait until nearly a century later?

There was nothing in the law of property that blocked the condominium. American law was based on the law of England, and for centuries English law had allowed different people to own different floors of a building. "There are some, though not many, buildings in England which are owned in this fashion," explained the barrister S. M. Tolson, but one of them was one of the Inns of Court, the buildings where barristers traditionally worked and trained, a fact that must have been widely known among English lawyers. Scottish law was the same. According to the law professor John Erskine, writing in the eighteenth century, many houses in Edinburgh were divided into different floors, each with a different owner. The influential French Civil Code, first published in 1804 and then copied throughout continental Europe, included a provision specifically about disputes that might arise "when the different stories of a house belong to different proprietors." Houses divided in this way had been known in France, Germany, and Switzerland for centuries.[30]

The small number of American lawyers who studied the issue before 1960 were aware of these foreign examples, and they unanimously concluded that American law likewise allowed the ownership of a building to be subdivided by floors. Indeed, they knew of some examples right at home. In 1808 the Massachusetts Supreme Court heard a case involving a house owned by two people, a woman who owned the cellar and one room on the ground floor, and a man who owned the rest of the ground floor and the second floor. The man had fixed the roof and was trying to recover damages from the woman, who had refused to contribute to the repairs. "In legal contemplation," the court explained, "each of the parties has a distinct dwelling-house," one of which happened to sit on top of the other. As the roof belonged to the man who owned the second floor, he had simply fixed his own house, and the woman who lived below had no obligation to chip in. Later cases from other states involved buildings divided the same way. In Jacksonville, Illinois, the man who owned the ground floor removed an interior wall; this caused some cracking and sinking on the second floor, which was owned by someone else. Carrie B. Lilly of Trenton, Missouri, owned a two-story building and then sold to the Knights of Pythias the right to build and own a third story above. The Tuscola Opera House owned and occupied the second and third floors of its building in Tuscola, Illinois; the ground floor was owned by the Madison family. "It is not very unusual, certainly, for one person to own the soil and the first floor of a building, and another the second, and perhaps the third floor of the same building," the Iowa Supreme Court remarked in 1857.[31] Just as property could be divided horizontally, by lines drawn in the ground, it could be divided vertically, by lines drawn in the air.

Buildings, in this respect, were just like the earth itself. Americans were accustomed to dividing land vertically, between one person who owned the surface and another who owned the minerals beneath. As buildings grew taller in the 1920s, the owners of short buildings began doing the reverse, selling the "air rights" above their buildings to others.[32] Property law was not hostile to the condominium.

Before the 1960s, developers occasionally built what would later be called condominiums, although such projects were very rare. One was in New York, a twelve-unit building constructed in 1947 in which each apartment was owned separately. Another, with eleven stories and two apartments on each floor, was built in Great Falls, Montana, a few years later. By 1960 there was one in Washington, D.C., and there were two in Stamford, Connecticut.[33] But these buildings did not inspire emulators. The condominium remained virtually nonexistent in the United States.

When a good idea is available but scarcely anyone takes it up, one should look for institutional obstacles to its implementation. In the case of the condominium there were several, all of which were a result of its novelty. Mortgage lenders, whose trade involved lending for buildings, were afraid to make loans that might require them to foreclose on mere units within buildings. After foreclosure they would be left with apartments for which there was not yet an established market. Title insurers were reluctant to insure a form of real estate that had never received any official legal recognition. Property taxes would have to be imposed separately on each unit, but no local government was equipped to do so. Real estate lawyers wondered how to describe condominium units in deeds. Should they be defined as areas of space, bounded in three dimensions? Or as numbered units within a building that might not yet exist? And what would happen to the ownership of a unit if a condominium building burned down? Would the owner be left with the right to possess a cube of empty space high in the air? "Without legislation" to govern the condominium, one lawyer worried, "condominium instruments in some states might run up to 300 pages in length."[34] None of these obstacles was insuperable, but together they formed a substantial wall of inertia. Someone had to do a lot of organizational work before the condominium could be a viable form of ownership on a significant scale.

Before the late 1950s, there was no one in the United States who had the incentive to take on that task. Meanwhile, however, Latin American countries were enacting statutes explicitly authorizing the condominium—Brazil in 1928, Chile in 1937, Uruguay and Argentina in the late 1940s, Cuba in 1952, and Venezuela in 1958. Puerto Rico, an island with a high population density and thus a natural market for high-rise buildings, passed a similar statute in 1951, thus becoming the first jurisdiction in the United States to give the condominium official legal recognition. Some condominiums were built in Puerto Rico in the 1950s, but the absence of federal mortgage insurance meant that financing for individual units was available only with high down payments and at relatively high interest rates, which put the condominium at a disadvantage relative to other ownership structures. The leading Puerto Rican developers, backed by the Development Bank of Puerto

Rico, accordingly went to Congress in the spring of 1960 to request that mortgage insurance be made available for condominiums.[35]

The ensuing congressional hearings were the first occasions for sustained interest in condominiums in the mainland United States. "This is a new concept, as far as I am concerned, but it is very interesting," remarked Representative Hugh Addonizio of New Jersey. "I am just wondering about the maintenance of these buildings. . . . For example, who sweeps the stairway?" William Widnall, also from New Jersey, was impressed by "the love of a home that the native Puerto Rican has. He doesn't want to rent. He wants a home." Widnall concluded that the condominium "can give the ability to lower income groups to obtain such a home, and within an area where it won't be impossible for them to commute to work." Other members of the House Subcommittee on Housing felt the same way. "I think we ought to give the condominium a try," declared Charles Vanik of Ohio. "It deserves a serious bit of consideration, and we certainly ought to use Puerto Rico as a testing area to see how it works out, to see whether or not the idea might be something that we might import here on the mainland." In the Senate, the Puerto Rican witnesses faced skeptical questioning from Senator Prescott Bush of Connecticut, father of the first President Bush and grandfather of the second. "You take individual mortgages on the individual home in the high rise buildings?" Bush asked. "What about the hallways and common-use facilities? . . . Does the mortgage on the home itself carry the whole deal, so to speak? I mean, you do not need any other mortgage on the common-use property?" But Rafael Pico, the president of the Development Bank of Puerto Rico, put Bush's apprehension to rest. The owner of an individual unit also owned a share of the common areas, and both were wrapped up in the owner's mortgage, Pico explained. "It carries those common elements of the building, and they are inseparable."[36]

The product of these hearings was a small section in a very long statute, the Housing Act of 1961. The relevant section empowered the Federal Housing Administration to provide mortgage insurance for condominium units, just like it did for cooperatives and for freestanding houses.[37] The first hurdle had been overcome.

The next hurdle was to persuade state legislatures to enact statutes like the one in Puerto Rico, authorizing condominiums and setting out the basic rules that would govern them. By the end of 1962 only seven states had passed such statutes, but the process accelerated when the

Federal Housing Administration published model legislation. In early 1964 New York became the fortieth state to authorize the condominium.[38] Within a few years the other ten would do the same, most with close copies of the FHA's model statute. The remaining obstacles fell quickly. With federal mortgage insurance, lenders no longer needed to worry about the condominium's novelty. With explicit statutory authorization, title insurers were willing to write policies. Local governments began taxing condominium units individually. The condominium was in business.

The first FHA-insured condominium outside Puerto Rico was a six-story, sixty-unit building near Miami, completed in 1962. Similar buildings began springing up all over the country—in Newport Beach, Malibu, and Burbank, California; in Richmond, Virginia; in Peekskill, New York; in Lakewood, New Jersey—anywhere with land values high enough to justify apartment living. "Property management experts believe the condominium concept will become a big thing hereabouts before long," declared the real estate editor of the *Los Angeles Times*. "The appeal of a deed to your living quarters is as strong to an apartment dweller as to a suburbanite." The *New York Times* agreed that "nothing since the Federal Housing Administration began insuring home loans 30 years ago has aroused more interest among builders and mortgage lenders than the condominium." Condominiums seemed to be going up everywhere. Perhaps the best indication of how quickly the condominium became an established feature of the landscape can be found in an episode of the Donna Reed Show, a popular situation comedy of the era, broadcast in March 1964. The plot involved neighboring families who attempt to economize by sharing a washing machine and a set of golf clubs. The title: *Pandemonium in the Condominium*.[39]

As the condominium marched across the country, skeptics occasionally raised concerns. The New York developer Norman Tishman was hesitant to switch from cooperatives to condominiums, because in his view a default on a mortgage loan would take much longer to resolve with the condominium. In a cooperative, he explained, "if you default, your equity goes back to the corporation and may be assigned to someone else for no more than what you had owed. It should be in use again very soon under such terms. But in a condominium, if you defaulted," Tishman continued, "nobody would have control of the premises you had title to, and it might be empty and become rundown for an indefinite time since nobody else could assume its management without litigation." The United Housing Foundation, the developer of New York's Co-op City, the world's largest cooperative, declared that the condominium "can never be more than a selling gimmick." The law professor John Cribbet pointed out that a condominium required as many mortgages as it had units, while a cooperative needed only a single mortgage for the entire building. He expected the interest rate for a condominium loan to be half a percent higher than for a cooperative loan, to cover the cost of servicing so many small mortgages. (In an assessment published nearly simultaneously, Curtis Berger, another law professor, expected instead that lenders would *prefer* the condominium over the cooperative, because the condominium allowed the lender to spread the risk of default over many small loans rather than concentrating it in a single large one.)[40]

None of these worries slowed the spread of the condominium. Like the cooperative, the condominium brought home ownership within reach of millions of people who could not afford a freestanding house. But unlike the cooperative, the condominium did not require purchasers to take on the risk that someone else in the building might default on a mortgage loan. By 1972, 27 percent of the nation's housing starts were condominiums, from luxury beach-side high-rises in Key Biscayne to middle-class apartment complexes in Detroit. By 2005 there were over five million condominium units in the United States, more than eight times the number of units in cooperatives. Within the previous four years, new condominium construction had outpaced new cooperative construction by nearly forty to one.[41] The reason was not hard to find: if one took two otherwise identical apartments, one in a condominium and one in a cooperative, the one in the condominium was worth, on average, around 9 percent more.[42]

The cooperative never faded away. This was in part because of the cost of converting existing cooperatives to condominiums, but new cooperatives were still being built—nationwide there were 440,000 units in cooperatives in 1975 and more than 600,000 units in 2005. The cooperative retained one advantage: it was easier for existing residents to exclude newcomers they did not wish to live near. At the top end of the market, this exclusivity was apparently worth a lot.[43]

The ever-changing composition of the housing stock of the United States is in part a straightforward economic story. Where rising land prices have put single-family houses out of reach, there was demand for multifamily housing. Houses were unaffordable for the working class before they became unaffordable for the affluent, so we had tenements before apartment houses or cooperatives. Land prices were highest in the big cities, especially New York, so new kinds of multifamily housing tended to start there and spread to less expensive areas.

The relationship between land prices and wages explains a lot, but it does not explain everything, particularly the long delay between the introduction of the apartment house and the cooperative in the late nineteenth century and the beginnings of the condominium nearly a century later. That is a story of institutional detail, in which the costs of legal change blocked the realization of the condominium until there was someone with the incentive to incur those costs. Mortgage lending, title insurance, property taxes, the drafting of conveyancing documents—each was a subculture with its own established practices that had to be rethought before the first condominium unit could be sold.

Slavery was one of many forms of property that ceased to exist in the United States in the seventeenth and eighteenth centuries. This advertisement was published in a South Carolina newspaper in the 1780s.

LC-USZ62–10293, Prints and Photographs Division, Library of Congress.

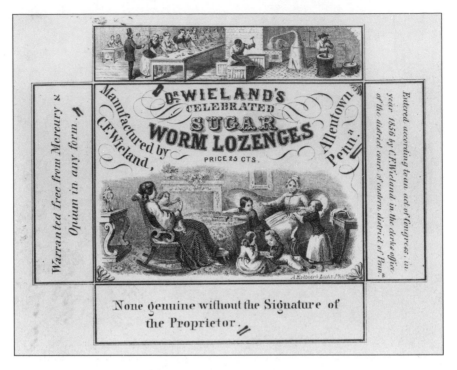

Patent medicines were among the first products to bear trademarks. In the 1850s, when an Allentown doctor marketed these "sugar worm lozenges," trademarks and commercial goodwill were beginning to be recognized as increasingly valuable forms of property.

LC-USZ62–102488, Prints and Photographs Division, Library of Congress.

Had New York constructed its elevated railroads in the first half of the nineteenth century, the owners of adjoining buildings would likely not have been entitled to compensation under the Constitution's takings clause, because no land had been literally taken from them. When the railroads were built in the late nineteenth century, however, property had come to be understood as a bundle of rights, and the takings clause was conventionally interpreted to protect against deprivations of those rights. Adjoining landowners were accordingly entitled to compensation when their buildings were thrown into shadow.

News telegraphers get front-row seats at the 1912 World Series. The Associated Press had recently failed to persuade Congress to create property in news. A few years later it would succeed at the Supreme Court.

LC-B2–2539–14, Prints and Photographs Division, Library of Congress.

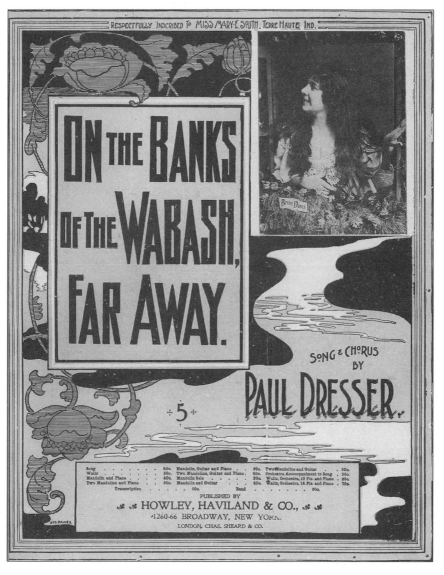

Nineteenth-century composers earned their money from the sale of sheet music. Paul Dresser sold more than half a million copies of "On the Banks of the Wabash," a hit in the 1890s.

Historic American Sheet Music, "On the Banks of the Wabash, Far Away," Music B-945, Duke University Rare Book, Manuscript, and Special Collections Library.

Enrico Caruso listens to himself on the phonograph. Before the Copyright Act of 1909, singers like Caruso were paid to make records but composers were not.

LC-B2–5089–12, Prints and Photographs Division, Library of Congress.

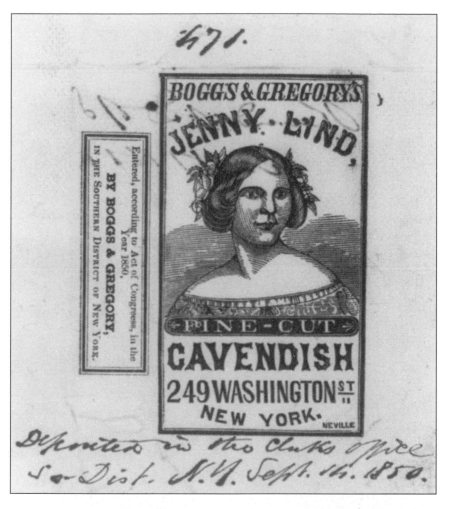

A label for Jenny Lind tobacco, just one of many unauthorized products bearing her name that Lind encountered on her tour of the United States.

Abigail Roberson's picture in an advertisement for Franklin Mills Flour. The Rochester teenager's lawsuit sparked a public debate over whether people should own their names and images.

"The Right of Privacy," Profitable Advertising 12 (1902): 187. Courtesy of the Cincinnati Public Library.

A New York family lives and works in the attic of their crowded tenement, a kind of building first constructed in significant numbers in the 1840s.

LC-USZ62–53130, Prints and Photographs Division, Library of Congress.

The Dakota apartment house in New York, built in the 1880s and shown here in 1903, was one of the early apartment buildings marketed to the affluent. It became a cooperative in the 1960s.

LC-USZ62–101590, Prints and Photographs Division, Library of Congress.

Secretary of Commerce Herbert Hoover listens to the radio. In the 1920s Hoover was the nation's most visible opponent of private property in segments of the electromagnetic spectrum.

LC-USZ62–111716, Prints and Photographs Division, Library of Congress.

9

The Law of the Land

PETER McKone was a house builder in Hartford, Connecticut, in the later part of the nineteenth century. At his place of business on Sheldon Street, near downtown Hartford, he had a few different power saws, two planing machines, a molding machine, and a mortising machine, all powered by an on-site steam engine. Sheldon Street was full of similar enterprises. Right next door was the National Screw Company, which rented parts of its property to the American Paper Barrel Company, the Bailey Letter Press Company, and the Capewell Horse Nail Company, as well as a firm with an exciting if unproven new product, the Mather Electric Light Company. When McKone moved to Sheldon Street in 1884, one reason was doubtless his expectation that the noise and smoke produced by all his machines would be no worse than what the neighborhood already experienced.[1]

George Hurlbut and his family also lived in Hartford, on a residential street called Governor Street. They occupied the first floor of their two-story house and rented the rooms on the second floor to tenants. The problem was that Governor Street and Sheldon Street intersected, and the Hurlbuts were just one lot away from the corner. McKone's building shop fronted on Sheldon, but its lot was at the corner of Sheldon and Governor, which put it next door to the Hurlbuts' house. Once McKone opened his shop, life at the Hurlbuts' was never the same. The shop made so much noise that it was nearly impossible for the Hurlbuts to read or carry on a conversation. McKone's machines vibrated so much that the Hurlbuts' windows rattled and their dishes and glasses shook on their shelves. Smoke and cinders from McKone's steam engine blew through the Hurlbuts' doors and windows and dirtied their floors, carpets, walls, curtains, and sometimes even their food. Mrs. Hurlbut couldn't hang washing on the line without having to wash it all over again. Worst of all, one of the upstairs tenants, a Mrs. White, who was already in a delicate condition, died shortly after McKone moved in next door, and her attendant blamed the noise from McKone's machinery. Mrs. Hurlbut suffered from headaches. The Hurlbuts had great trouble attracting new tenants, and the ones who were willing to stay insisted on paying a reduced rent. McKone's shop was simply incompatible with the Hurlbuts' home. Either McKone would have to build houses elsewhere or the Hurlbuts would have to move.

If this dispute had arisen in the late twentieth century rather than the late nineteenth, it would have raised a few different issues of property law. Did McKone's shop comply with Hartford's zoning laws, or was he running a business in a residential zone? Was McKone's land subject to any restrictive covenants that could be enforced by the Hurlbuts or by a neighborhood association? What obligations did the Hurlbuts owe to their tenants? In the nineteenth century, however, none of these questions would have occurred to the lawyer for either side. They involved forms of regulation that did not yet exist.

On the other hand, the nineteenth-century United States was no Hobbesian free-for-all. Land use *was* regulated, but the most important mode of regulation was judge-created common law, particularly the law of nuisance. A nuisance was simply an unreasonable use of land, considering all the circumstances. As the Connecticut Supreme Court explained in deciding *Hurlbut v. McKone,* "what constitutes a nuisance in one locality may not be in another." A city dweller "must not expect to be surrounded by the stillness which prevails in a rural district. He must necessarily hear some of the noise and occasionally feel slight vibrations produced by the movement and labor of its people and by the hum of its mechanical industries." If living in a city entailed putting up with some annoyances from the neighbors, however, the law certainly did not allow businesses to locate wherever they chose. "Even a cooking stove may be so located and used as to make it a nuisance to the adjacent proprietor," Justice Dwight Loomis reasoned. The reasonableness of a use of land had to be judged on its own facts.

It was *not* reasonable, the court held, for McKone to set up a building shop so close to a residential house. "This surely was no trifling inconvenience which the civilities of a good neighborhood, in a thickly settled and industrious community, required the plaintiff to bear in silence," the court concluded. The noise, vibrations, and smoke emanating from McKone's shop were, "beyond all controversy, a matter of great physical discomfort, powerfully affecting the comfortable enjoyment of the plaintiff's home, and impairing the health of his family and the value of his property." The other businesses on Sheldon Street used loud machines too, but they were much farther from the Hurlbuts' house, so they were no bother. The Hurlbuts won their case. McKone compensated them for their losses, moved his steam engine to the other side of his property, and built a smoke stack that redirected the smoke and cinders away from the Hurlbuts.

This is how disputes about land use were primarily regulated in the nineteenth century, through case by case decisions, by judges, as to whether particular uses of land were reasonable for the location. As cities grew, however, these sorts of controversies multiplied. The law of nuisance had the virtue of simplicity but the fault of being entirely ad hoc and retrospective. From a commercial point of view, it was often difficult to know in advance whether a planned use of land would be found a nuisance. From a residential point of view, there was little one could do to prevent noxious businesses from moving into the neighborhood; one had to let them in and then bring an uncertain lawsuit afterward. The twentieth century would bring new forms of regulation intended to solve these problems.

A Dam to Hold Back the Flood

The first zoning ordinance in the country is conventionally said to be the one enacted by New York City in 1916, but this is true only in a highly qualified sense. Like most legal changes, zoning did not emerge full blown all at once. It crept up gradually, over a very long period.

American governments regulated the use of land from the very beginning, in a piecemeal fashion, to deal with particular problems as they arose. In the colonial period, governments often required owners to improve or use their land, to fence their crops, and to drain wetlands. The colonies placed restrictions on the locations of houses to prevent settlements from growing too dispersed. They limited the height of buildings and the choice of building materials and sometimes even the aesthetic appearance of buildings. State and city governments in the early republic did the same. In Boston, for example, the fronts of new buildings had to form a straight line, while dwelling houses in one Virginia town had to exceed a minimum size.[2]

This tradition of piecemeal local land use regulation continued through the late nineteenth century and into the early twentieth and intensified as cities grew larger and more densely populated. Some of this regulation consisted of ordinances banning noxious activities within the city or restricting them to particular districts. In an effort to combat pollution, for example, Chicago in 1881 prohibited the emission of the worst kinds of smoke from nonresidential chimneys throughout the city. St. Louis banned cow stables; Los Angeles confined gasworks to a designated district; Little Rock outlawed the keeping of horses downtown. Many cities placed limits on the dimensions of buildings, particularly restrictions on height, which had not been necessary before the passenger elevator came into widespread use in the second half of the nineteenth century. Tall buildings did not merely deprive their neighbors of daylight and fresh air; they also posed fire risks, because fire hoses could not reach their top floors. New York accordingly restricted the height of apartment buildings in the 1880s. After 1892 buildings in Boston could be no higher than 125 feet or two and a half times the width of their street, whichever was less. Chicago soon adopted a height ordinance, as did Baltimore, St. Louis, Denver, and Seattle. Some cities, like St. Louis in 1892, designated individual streets as residential only and prohibited businesses from opening there.[3] These ordinances were understood by their backers as resting upon a city's traditional power to proscribe nuisances; the only difference was that now the city was barring them prospectively rather than waiting for them to arise. As the lawyer for St. Louis argued in defending the city's decision to prohibit businesses on a several-block stretch of Washington Boulevard, "a man who builds a livery stable or a rendering establishment, or opens a quarry, or builds a business house on his own land, may benefit himself, but in the doing he may inflict irreparable injury upon his neighbors, and he has no right to do so."

The change that took place in the early twentieth century was not from laissez-faire to regulation, but rather from piecemeal regulation to more comprehensive citywide regulatory schemes, as part of the rise of urban planning more generally. The first was in Los Angeles, which enacted a citywide zoning ordinance in 1908. The ordinance created seven "industrial districts," most along existing railroad lines or the Los Angeles River. Much of the rest of the city was placed within "residence districts," where prohibited activities included "any stone crusher, rolling mill, machine shop, planing mill, carpet beating establishment, public laundry or wash-house, fire works factory, soap factory or any other works or factory where power other than animal power is used." The ordinance was quickly challenged as unconstitutional in several lawsuits, but it was upheld by the California Supreme Court in 1911 and then by the U.S. Supreme Court four years later.[4]

The latter case was brought by J. C. Hadacheck, who had operated a brickyard on his property since 1902, years before the enactment of the ordinance, and indeed well before anyone could have expected such an ordinance to be enacted. The ordinance included no exceptions for land uses that predated its enactment. Hadacheck's land was made of a special kind of clay uniquely suited for brick making. The property was worth $800,000 as a brickyard, he alleged, but no more than $60,000 for any other purpose. He had already made so many excavations that the land was no longer useful for anything else. He had purchased expensive brick-making machinery that had no other use. Hadacheck may have been the one person most severely affected by the city's zoning ordinance. Although the constitutional protections for property rights were at their peak, the Supreme Court unanimously found the ordinance constitutional. Brickyards produced great amounts of smoke and fumes that were bothersome to neighbors. The power to suppress nuisances was "one of the most essential powers of government, one that is the least limitable," the Court concluded. "It may, indeed, seem harsh in its exercise, usually is on some individual, but the imperative necessity for its existence precludes any limitation upon it when not exerted arbitrarily."[5] Zoning had passed its first test.

Once the courts had affirmed the constitutionality of the Los Angeles ordinance, several other California cities adopted similar ordinances of their own. By 1917 there were residential and industrial districts in Redondo Beach, Pasadena, Sacramento, Oakland, San Mateo, Burlingame, Piedmont, and even the small agricultural town of Turlock. Cities in other states did the same, including New Orleans in 1912 and Dallas in 1915.[6] These ordinances prohibited industrial activities within residential zones, but they typically did not prohibit the construction of residences within industrial zones, so while they allowed apartment housing for the poor to be located near industry, they kept industry out of the city's more affluent residential neighborhoods. The rapid spread of zoning suggests that homeowners throughout the nation, at least the ones who would inhabit the new residential zones, agreed on the importance of this goal.

New York's 1916 ordinance was even more comprehensive. It had three use districts, separating residential, commercial, and industrial activities, but it also divided the city into five height districts, each with its own restriction on how tall buildings could be relative to the width of the street, and five area districts, each with its own limits on how much of its lot a building would be allowed to cover. Like residents of other cities, New Yorkers hoped to keep factories and shops away from their homes, but that was not the ordinance's only goal. The height and area districts were intended to protect investors in office buildings, who were threatened by new skyscrapers that blocked light and air, added to street traffic, and competed in the market for rented office space. The several-hundred-page report of the city commission that produced the ordinance was full of photographs showing buildings cast into shadow in the middle of the day and narrow canyonlike streets clogged with automobiles and horse-drawn carriages.[7]

Zoning spread even more quickly after 1916, to cities large and small, in all parts of the country. St. Louis enacted a zoning ordinance in 1918. Omaha got one in 1920. Zoning soon reached Milwaukee, San Francisco, and Montclair, New Jersey; Wichita, Atlanta, and Lowell, Massachusetts; Providence, Portland, and Wilmington, Delaware. "Within the last few years," remarked the Maryland Court of Appeals in 1925, "a veritable flood of so-called 'zoning' legislation has swept over the country." The court was assessing the constitutionality of Baltimore's new ordinance, which had been modeled on New York's. It sorted the city into four use districts (residential, industrial, and two kinds of commercial), five height districts, and six area districts. New York's ordinance served as a template for much of the burst of zoning in the decade following 1916. Even Evanston, Illinois, a quiet town of only 50,000 inhabitants with only one significant employer, Northwestern University, adopted a zoning ordinance in 1921 that included five use districts, three height districts, and three area districts. By 1924, the Commerce Department counted 208 municipalities with zoning ordinances. More than twenty-two million people, or 40 percent of the country's urban population, were living in zoned territory.[8]

These early zoning ordinances were often challenged in the courts by aggrieved property owners, on two grounds. One was that the cities lacked the authority to zone under state law. Some of the early challengers on this basis prevailed, but this lack of authority was easily cured by state legislatures, who simply enacted statutes granting the necessary authority. They were assisted in this effort by the federal government. Herbert Hoover, the secretary of commerce for most of the 1920s, had a personal interest in urban planning. In 1921 he appointed an advisory committee on zoning, consisting of some of the country's leading zoning advocates, including Edward Bassett, counsel to the New York agency responsible for implementing the city's ordinance. The following year the committee published and distributed several thousand copies of a "Zoning Primer" for municipalities to follow and a "Standard State Zoning Enabling Act" for state legislatures to copy. By early 1926, every state but five had passed a zoning enabling act, as had Congress for the District of Columbia.[9] Once zoning had a clear statutory basis, this sort of legal challenge was no longer possible.

The other ground for challenging a zoning ordinance was that it infringed a property owner's constitutional rights. There were many such cases decided by state courts in the early 1920s. In some of them courts found ordinances unconstitutional, particularly where they seemed unreasonably strict. The village of Atherton, California, for example, established a residence district and an "unrestricted district," and limited businesses to the latter, but the unrestricted district contained scarcely more than an acre and was already fully occupied by a restaurant and a gas station. The California Supreme Court, which had already upheld the constitutionality of zoning generally, concluded that Atherton was not really zoning at all, but was rather trying to grant monopolies to two favored property owners. In most of these cases, however, courts sided with the cities. "Zoning statutes are becoming common," the Minnesota Supreme Court recognized in 1925. "A restriction, which years ago would have been intolerable, and would have been thought an unconstitutional restriction of the owner's use of his property, is accepted now without a thought that it invades a private right." The court accordingly overruled its earlier cases and allowed Minneapolis to create a residential district in which apartment buildings were not permitted. "With the crowding of population in the cities," Justice Homer Dibell reasoned, "there is an active insistence upon the establishment of residential districts from which annoying occupations and buildings undesirable to the community are excluded."[10]

Any lingering doubts as to the constitutionality of zoning were removed by the U.S. Supreme Court in 1926, in a case called *Village of Euclid v. Ambler Realty Company*. Euclid was a small suburb adjacent to Cleveland, a village with a population not much over five thousand. Most of Euclid was either farmland or undeveloped land, but enough residents were worried about Cleveland's industrial expansion to prompt Euclid to adopt a New York–style zoning ordinance in 1922, complete with six use districts, three height districts, and four area districts. This was simply prudent planning to some, but not to property owners who hoped to be part of that industrial expansion, including the Ambler Realty Company, which owned sixty-eight acres in a spot its managers thought would be perfect for a factory but which the ordinance placed in a residential zone. "In effect," Ambler charged, Euclid's ordinance "erects a dam to hold back the flood of industrial development and thus to preserve a rural character in portions of the village which, under the operation of natural economic laws, would be devoted most profitably to industrial undertakings."[11] The violation of these natural laws, Ambler alleged, caused the value of its land to decline from $10,000 per acre, its market value as a factory, to a mere $2,500 per acre, its market value for residences.

The case caught Justice George Sutherland in a reflective mood. "Until recent years, urban life was comparatively simple," he recalled in his opinion for a majority of the Court, "but with the great increase and concentration of population, problems have developed, and constantly are developing, which require, and will continue to require, additional restrictions in respect of the use and occupation of private lands." Sutherland was on the Court's conservative wing, and in the most controversial cases he was usually a reliable vote against the constitutionality of legislative intrusions on private property, but progressives and conservatives did not divide cleanly when it came to zoning. Zoning was a form of regulation, but some of its most ardent proponents were conservative too: they were trying to preserve the traditional feel of residential neighborhoods from distasteful aspects of modernity like pollution and crowding. "Regulations, the wisdom, necessity and validity of which, as applied to existing conditions, are so apparent that they are now uniformly sustained, a century ago, or even half a century ago, probably would have been rejected as arbitrary and oppressive," Sutherland concluded. But times had changed. "Such regulations are sustained, under the complex conditions of our day, for reasons analogous to those which justify traffic regulations, which, before the advent of automobiles and rapid transit street railways, would have been condemned as fatally arbitrary and unreasonable." Constitutional principles did not change, Sutherland cautioned, but as conditions changed, so did the way those principles were applied to particular factual situations. "In a changing world," he concluded, "it is impossible that it should be otherwise."[12]

Zoning, Sutherland held, was nothing more than a new means of achieving some traditional ends—preventing nuisances, promoting health, and ensuring safety. An ordinance that prevented an offensive or dangerous factory from opening might also prohibit uses that would not, in themselves, be nuisances, he acknowledged, "but this is no more than what happens in respect of many practice-forbidding laws which this Court has upheld although drawn in general terms so as to include individual cases that may turn out to be innocuous in themselves." The Constitution did not require regulation to be targeted with absolute precision. "The inclusion of a reasonable margin to insure effective enforcement," as in the typical zoning ordinance, "will not put upon a law, otherwise valid, the stamp of invalidity."[13] The last constitutional obstacle to zoning had been removed.

With the blessing of the Supreme Court, zoning continued to spread. By the end of the 1920s nearly eight hundred municipalities had zoning ordinances, laws that governed 60 percent of the nation's urban population. Zoning might still violate the Constitution in individual cases. Only two years after *Euclid*, for example, the Court considered the plight of a landowner in Cambridge, Massachusetts, whose parcel was surrounded by a Ford assembly plant, a soap factory, and railroad tracks. One could hardly imagine a less appealing place to live, but Cambridge placed the parcel in a residential zone, which rendered it nearly worthless. In another opinion by Justice Sutherland, the Court unanimously held that the city had gone too far.[14] But such cases were exceptional. In most of the country, most of the time, zoning became a normal and important function of local government.

From the beginning, zoning was as much about excluding unde-sirable people as about excluding undesirable uses of land. Often the two went hand in hand: tenement buildings, for example, might be objectionable because they brought congestion, but they might also be unwanted because they brought the sort of people who lived in tene-ment buildings. "This invasion of the inferior produces more or less discomfort and disorder, and has a distinct tendency to lower property values," counseled the New York lawyer Frank Williams in his 1922 treatise on the law of zoning. There were early critics of zoning, from the left, on the ground that it benefited the rich at the expense of the poor. "Zoning has been criticised as undemocratic," acknowledged Wil-liam Munro, professor of the new discipline of municipal government at Harvard. "Its critics assert that the policy tends to segregate the well-to-do in one part of the city and the industrial workers in another." Munro himself was a proponent of zoning—he was sure that "people of all classes prefer to live in homogenous neighborhoods"—but this un-ease with the exclusionary side of zoning would be the primary objec-tion to it throughout the century.[15]

Some of the earliest zoning ordinances were intended to enforce racial segregation. In 1910, Baltimore enacted an ordinance establish-ing separate zones for blacks and whites. The idea was quickly copied in other cities, including Atlanta, Louisville, St. Louis, Oklahoma City, and New Orleans. The U.S. Supreme Court declared racial zoning un-constitutional in 1917, not because it denied equal protection of the laws to black residents—that would have been an unsuccessful argument in light of *Plessy v. Ferguson*—but rather because it infringed the property rights of white homeowners who wished to sell to black purchasers. Of course, cities had been segregated long before racial zoning and re-mained so long after. Violence and social sanctions (and in some in-stances restrictive covenants) were strong enough to maintain this system even without formal regulation.[16]

Cities lacked the power to zone by race, but they could, and often did, zone so as to separate the rich and the poor. Occasionally they did so explicitly: Long Branch, New Jersey, for instance, enacted an ordi-nance in the early 1920s requiring all new houses in a certain neigh-borhood to cost at least $15,000. Much more common were provisions requiring minimum lot sizes or minimum floor areas, with the minima set high enough to exclude a significant portion of a city's residents. In one of the zones in Queen Anne's County, Maryland, lots could not be smaller than four acres. More common still were ordinances that restricted certain zones to detached single-family houses, where such houses were out of reach for many. Courts refused to permit minimum-value zoning. They tended to allow minimum lot sizes and floor areas, as in Queen Anne's County, although some of the strictest such requirements were found unconstitutional. Fairfax County, Virginia, for example, was barred from enforcing an ordinance that established a two-acre minimum lot size in the western two-thirds of the county, forcing 90 percent of the county's residents to huddle in the eastern third. "This would serve private rather than public interests," the Virginia Supreme Court held. "Such an intentional and exclusionary purpose would bear no relation to the health, safety, morals, prosperity and general welfare."[17] Single-family housing zones, by contrast, were almost universally allowed and quickly became a ubiquitous feature of zoning ordinances throughout the country.

In the mid-twentieth century, as American judges became more willing to make new law as a remedy for various sorts of inequality, there was a moment when zoning seemed vulnerable on this ground. Mount Laurel, New Jersey, was a partly rural suburb of Philadelphia. Its zoning ordinance, enacted in 1964, established four residential zones, all of which were limited to single-family detached housing, all with minimum lot sizes and floor areas unaffordable to the poor. Mount Laurel was hardly unique. "This pattern of land use regulation has been adopted for the same purpose in developing municipality after developing municipality," the New Jersey Supreme Court lamented. "Almost every one acts solely in its own selfish interest and in effect builds a wall around itself to keep out those people or entities not adding favorably to the tax base." Mount Laurel's ordinance was challenged by a consortium of organizations led by the National Association for the Advancement of Colored People, who argued that it was unconstitutional to exclude the poor in this way. In 1975, near the high-water mark of an era of—depending on one's taste—either judicial creativity or judicial activism, the New Jersey Supreme Court agreed. Every town must "provide, by its land use regulations, the reasonable opportunity for an appropriate variety and choice of housing, including, of course, low and moderate cost housing," the court declared. "It may not adopt regulations or policies which thwart or preclude that opportunity."[18]

Thirty-five years later, litigation spawned by the *Mount Laurel* decision was still ongoing, but low-cost housing was no more plentiful in
New Jersey than elsewhere. Although no other state supreme court followed New Jersey's lead in declaring exclusionary zoning ordinances
unconstitutional, the same concerns led many states to enact legislation facilitating the construction of affordable housing in areas where it
is lacking. There is considerable debate as to whether any of these efforts have succeeded. Zoning remains the primary method by which
homeowners can, in effect, prop up the value of their homes, by making housing scarcer than it would otherwise be, and by excluding unwanted uses and people from their neighborhoods.[19]

Zoning by Private Contract

While municipalities were elaborating systems of public land use regulation, the developers of residential neighborhoods were simultaneously establishing parallel systems of private land use regulation, in the
form of restrictive covenants. These are contractual terms to which
homeowners agree when they purchase property, terms that "run with
the land," as lawyers say, to subsequent owners. By the end of the twentieth century, covenants were at least as important as zoning in restricting land use in much of the country, especially in new residential
neighborhoods.

Like zoning, covenants had very old roots. In the early nineteenth
century there were already fashionable neighborhoods in New York
and Boston where properties were restricted by covenant to residential
use. In 1822, for example, the lots on Hayward Place in Boston were
sold with the provision that "no other building, except one of brick or
stone, of not less than three stories in height, and for a dwelling-house
only" could be built upon them. Forty years later, one of the owners
leased his house to a man who planned to open a restaurant. Neither
the owner nor the would-be restaurateur had been one of the original
purchasers of the land back in 1822, so neither had personally agreed
to the restriction, but the Massachusetts Supreme Court held that they
were nevertheless bound by it, and that it could be enforced by any
neighbor who was also subject to it. "A right or privilege or amenity in
each lot was permanently secured to the owners of all the other lots," the
court explained, a form of security "against annoyances arising from

occupations which would impair the value of the several lots as places of residence."[20] Well before the era of residential zoning, a private alternative was available. The law imposed some requirements—the original parties to the restriction had to intend that it bind subsequent purchasers, for instance, and the subsequent purchasers had to have notice of the restriction when they acquired the land—but these were normally not difficult to satisfy.

Covenants nevertheless remained unusual before the twentieth century, because most neighborhoods were built one house at a time rather than all at once. It was not easy to establish covenants in already-existing neighborhoods. To achieve the benefits of a residence-only restriction, for instance, *all* the neighbors would have had to agree. Even a single holdout would have raised the possibility of an apartment or a factory entering the neighborhood; indeed, were there only a single holdout, such an unwanted use might become more likely, as it would be guaranteed a local monopoly. Covenants were much more feasible where whole neighborhoods were built from scratch. The developer could simply insert the covenants in the deeds to each of the parcels. The initial purchasers of each parcel would still have to agree before buying, but that was an easier obstacle to overcome than securing unanimity in an existing neighborhood.

Covenants became common when residential subdivisions began to be built all at once by real estate developers. The Roland Park subdivision in Baltimore, built in the 1890s, encompassed five hundred acres of houses, all of which were bound by covenants barring businesses of any kind or the construction of more than one house per lot. Roland Park soon became well known as a stable and fashionable place to live. Many high-end subdivisions were built with similar restrictions in the first two decades of the twentieth century, including River Oaks in Houston, Highland Park in Dallas, and the Country Club District in Kansas City. There were single-family covenants in Palos Verdes Estates in Los Angeles and Great Neck Hills on Long Island. "It is the Realtor subdivider who is really planning our cities today, who is the actual city planner in practice," George Ford remarked in 1925.[21] Ford was a city planner, but he recognized that land use was increasingly regulated by covenant rather than law.

Covenants became especially useful after 1917, when the Supreme Court outlawed racial zoning. In Helen Monchow's 1928 study of covenants in eighty-four subdivisions throughout the country, approximately half included racial restrictions, but nearly all the subdivisions built after 1917 did, which suggests that covenants were substituting for zoning. "The device seems to be in rather general use in the vicinity of the larger eastern and northern cities which have experienced a large influx of colored people in recent years," Monchow observed. "But the most pronounced tendency is found on the Pacific Coast where the restriction is directed primarily against the Orientals." This was simply sound public policy, reasoned the lawyer for some Kansas City property owners who were trying to keep their neighborhood white. "Such restrictions," he argued, "tend to promote peace and to prevent violence and bloodshed, and should be encouraged." Racial covenants were the only solution to "the negro problem," agreed Andrew Bruce, a law professor at Northwestern University. "The constant flow of the colored man into the middle and northern states" was producing "not merely a lessening of property values but a constant irritation and ultimate moving out of the original inhabitants who are unwilling to have colored neighbors." Deprived of the ability to zone the newcomers out, Bruce concluded, the best alternative available to cities was what he called "racial zoning by private contract."[22]

Racial restrictions were challenged as unconstitutional, but these challenges failed for decades, because the Constitution only limited the actions of government. When covenants in the District of Columbia barring sale "to any person of the negro race or blood" were brought before the Supreme Court in 1926, the Court determined that the claim was so frivolous that it did not even have jurisdiction to hear the case. "It is obvious," the Court declared, that nothing in the Constitution "prohibited private individuals from entering into contracts respecting the control and disposition of their own property." Of course, even if the Constitution had applied to private contracts, the era was not favorable to claims of discrimination. "As long as the courts recognize the validity of segregation in railway cars and in the public schools," Andrew Bruce remarked, "they can hardly insist upon any inalienable right of a colored person to live in a white neighborhood."[23] If black homeowners had the same right, in principle, to use covenants to keep whites out of black neighborhoods, the doctrine of separate but equal was satisfied.

Racial covenants were also challenged as inconsistent with state property law. There was an old common law doctrine barring unreasonable "restraints on alienation," that is, limits on the ability of a property owner to sell to someone else. In 1919 a California court held that all racial restrictions on sale were void for this reason. The particular covenant at issue, from a Los Angeles subdivision, barred sale to "any person of African, Chinese or Japanese descent." Such a restriction might seem perfectly reasonable, the court explained, but if it were allowed, what would come next? There might be bars on "selling or leasing to persons of Caucasian descent, or to any but albinos from the heart of Africa or blond Eskimos." Where could one draw a line? The only prudent answer was to declare all restrictions unenforceable. This decision might have put an end to racial covenants in California, but a few months later the state Supreme Court effectively overruled it. Restraints on *sale* might be void, the court held, but restraints on *occupancy* were not. Developers had merely to word covenants as restrictions on occupancy rather than sale in order to preserve all-white subdivisions.[24]

Starting in the 1930s, the federal government promoted racial covenants. The Federal Housing Administration, created to insure mortgage loans, recommended racial covenants for the properties it insured, and indeed published a model covenant to that effect for developers to copy. Racial covenants remained very common. In one 1947 study of recently constructed housing in the suburbs of New York, 56 percent of homes were off-limits to African-Americans, and in the larger subdivisions, that figure was 85 percent.[25]

All the while, the National Association for the Advancement of Colored People had been challenging racial covenants as part of its broader legal battle against all kinds of discrimination. Mainstream white attitudes had to change considerably before this effort could pay off, but finally, in 1948, a few years before *Brown v. Board of Education,* the Supreme Court declared racial covenants unconstitutional. *Shelley v. Kraemer* was indistinguishable from any of the earlier cases: it involved a street in St. Louis on which the houses were restricted to members of the "Caucasian race." This time, however, the Court declared that the judicial enforcement of these covenants was enough to constitute state action, and that the Constitution accordingly prohibited courts from enforcing them. The decision scarcely changed the nationwide pattern of residential segregation, which suggests that the racial covenant, like racial zoning before it, was more a symbol of white preferences than a necessary method of putting them into practice. These covenants, now unenforceable, would lurk in property deeds into the twenty-first century, popping up every so often to provoke misunderstanding and embarrassment. Meanwhile the norms of realtors, insurers, lenders, and homeowners themselves were strong enough to ensure that blacks and whites lived by and large separately in much of the nation despite the unenforceability of racial covenants.[26]

Covenants served many purposes other than discrimination, and these purposes expanded over time. Developers realized early on that housing could be made more valuable by attaching not just negative covenants, promises not to use property in a particular way, but also affirmative covenants, obligations to do certain things (typically to pay money) for the benefit of the neighborhood. One of the first such developments was built by the Neponsit Realty Company in the 1910s along Rockaway Beach in New York, a group of upper-class houses with rights to use a private beach. The deed to each house included a covenant requiring the owner to pay an annual fee for maintenance of the beach and the roads. The realty company then set up the Neponsit Property Owners' Association, an organization in which all the homeowners would be members, to own the beach and manage the money collected each year. This kind of arrangement was new enough to raise some difficult questions of property law. Would the annual fee have to be paid by subsequent purchasers of the homes, people who had never themselves promised to pay it? Could it be collected by an organization that did not even exist when the promises were made, one that owned no homes itself? These uncertainties were cleared away by the New York Court of Appeals, which held that homeowners' associations did have the power to collect assessments, and that subsequent purchasers did have to pay.[27]

Given a firm legal basis, the homeowners association became a staple of late twentieth-century American life. Some associations governed neighborhoods made up of single-family houses; many others governed condominium buildings. Before the condominium took root in the early 1960s there were probably fewer than 500 homeowners associations in the country. In 1973 there were approximately 15,000. By 1998, there were more than 200,000 homeowners associations, encompassing more than forty-two million people and nearly 15 percent of the housing in the United States. Most were, in effect, little private governments, regulating matters like the color of paint, the number of occupants, and the design of improvements, normally in more detail than real governments did through zoning ordinances. Some homeowners associations governed developments large enough to resemble private cities, with privately owned streets behind locked gates.[28]

The proliferation of covenants and homeowners associations drew its share of critics, who had no shortage of amusing stories of apparent micromanagement, like the grandmother threatened with a fine for kissing in her own driveway, or the years of litigation over whether a woman in Culver City, California, would be allowed to keep three cats in her condo.[29] But the popularity of these developments reveals how many people are eager to put up with considerable restrictions on their own lives in exchange for enjoying the same restrictions on others. The covenant and the homeowners association, like zoning, are devices for achieving some form of guarantee that one's neighbors will remain as pleasant tomorrow as they are today.

Landlords and Tenants

No part of land law changed faster in the second half of the twentieth century than that governing the relationship between landlords and residential tenants. Perhaps the most important change involved responsibility for maintaining rental housing in a habitable condition. Before 1970, except in a few states, that responsibility was placed squarely on the tenant, who took the premises in whatever condition he found them. "So it has been held," explained Herbert Thorndike Tiffany in his 1912 treatise on landlord-tenant law, "that it is no defense to an action for rent that the premises, though leased for the purpose of pasture, had scattered over them, unknown to the lessor, a poisonous substance which killed the lessee's cattle, that a house leased (unfurnished) was so infested with bugs as to be uninhabitable, that the premises lacked a proper drain, that they were uninhabitable owing to a noxious stench, that the plumbing was defective, or that the building fell owing to the decayed condition of its supports."[30] No matter what the problem was, it was the tenant's problem, not the landlord's. The landlord had no obligations other than to convey to the tenant the possession of a patch of land.

The first influential departure from this rule was in a 1970 case called *Javins v. First National Realty Corporation,* when Judge Skelly Wright declared that the rule could not sensibly be applied to modern urban life. The idea that a lease was nothing more than an interest in land "may have been reasonable in a rural, agrarian society," Wright acknowledged, a society in which access to the land itself was the main purpose of leasing, and in which most tenants were probably more skilled than most landlords at building and fixing houses. "But in the case of the modern apartment dweller, the value of the lease is that it gives him a place to live. The city dweller who seeks to lease an apartment on the third floor of a tenement has little interest in the land 30 to 40 feet below, or even in the bare right to possession within the four walls of his apartment. When American city dwellers, both rich and poor, seek 'shelter' today, they seek a well known package of goods and services—a package which includes not merely walls and ceilings, but also adequate heat, light and ventilation, serviceable plumbing facilities, secure windows and doors, proper sanitation, and proper maintenance."[31] Housing was much more complicated and difficult to maintain than it had once been; most tenants lacked the knowledge to maintain plumbing or electrical systems; and most tenants, in any event, lived in multiunit buildings where they lacked access to those systems. The court accordingly placed the responsibility for maintaining rental housing on the landlord.

This doctrine, soon known as the implied warranty of habitability, spread quickly. At least forty states recognized it by 1983, either by statute or by court decision. The imposition of such obligations on landlords was not entirely new. New York had regulated conditions in tenement housing since 1867, when the state required landlords to provide amenities like fire escapes, working chimneys, and roofs that did not leak. In the early twentieth century a few other states enacted similar laws, and many cities had housing codes establishing minimum standards for tenement housing. But these laws tended to apply only to slum housing in large cities, and they were most likely enforced much less frequently than they could have been.[32] The implied warranty of habitability covered all rental housing, even housing rented by the rich, and it provided tenants with a set of remedies they could implement themselves, like withholding rent or terminating their leases.

Meanwhile, landlords were losing some of *their* remedies. When a tenant did not pay rent, a landlord had traditionally been allowed to enter the apartment and lock the tenant out. He could also seize the tenant's belongings and sell them to make up for the rent he was owed.

By the late 1970s, however, landlords in most states were prohibited from evicting tenants themselves or seizing their property; they had to file lawsuits asking the government to perform those tasks for them. "This growing rule," reflected the Minnesota Supreme Court in 1978, "is founded on the recognition that the potential for violent breach of peace inheres in any situation where a landlord attempts by his own means to remove a tenant."[33] It took time to obtain an order of eviction in court, even under the accelerated procedures available to landlords in most states, so the effect of the change was to give nonpaying tenants extra time before they had to leave.

A far more dramatic change was the Fair Housing Act of 1968, which prohibited discrimination in selling and renting. Landlords had previously been virtually unconstrained in their choice of tenants. Race discrimination in the sale and rental of property had in principle been outlawed by the Civil Rights Act of 1866, but this statute sat dormant on the books for a century, until social conditions caught up. The equal protection clause of the Fourteenth Amendment, ratified in 1868, only prohibited discrimination by the government (except regarding restrictive covenants after *Shelley v. Kraemer*), so it had no application to the vast majority of housing, which was privately owned. The Fair Housing Act prohibited discrimination in privately owned housing on the basis of not just race but also religion and national origin. A 1974 amendment added sex discrimination to the list of prohibited conduct, and in 1988 Congress also prohibited discrimination against the handicapped and families with children. Many states enacted similar statutes, some of which included additional categories of forbidden discrimination, including discrimination on the basis of sexual orientation and discrimination against recipients of public assistance.

Landlords' power to set rent levels was also constrained in many places by the establishment of rent control. Rent control was not completely new: rents were controlled during and shortly after both world wars, as parts of broader systems of emergency price control. The Supreme Court narrowly upheld the constitutionality of rent control in Washington, D.C., just after World War I, by a 5–4 vote. "Have conditions come," wondered the four dissenters, "that socialism, or some form of socialism, is the only permanent corrective?"[34] But these wartime measures were temporary, intended only to prevent profiteering from short-term conditions created by the war. After both wars rent control was

repealed everywhere, with the single exception of New York City, which
retained rent control after World War II. For two decades New York was
the only city in the country with rent control. The federal government
controlled rents for more than a year in the early 1970s as part of President Richard Nixon's wage and price controls, but this was again a temporary program intended to temper inflation.

Rent control—as a permanent measure, not a short-term response
to a crisis—became much more popular in the 1970s. Ordinances establishing rent control were enacted in Los Angeles, Boston, Washington,
and San Francisco, as well as many smaller cities, including Berkeley
and Santa Monica. These ordinances typically allowed landlords to
increase rents by a certain percentage per year, but a rate below the
market rent for uncontrolled apartments. By the mid-1990s somewhere
between 10 and 15 percent of the U.S. rental housing stock was subject
to rent control.[35] Rent control waned a bit in the 1990s and after, as
some jurisdictions (including Massachusetts) abolished it, and others
(including California) softened its impact by allowing landlords to raise
rents to market levels for new tenants.

In these and other more technical respects, the law shifted power
from landlords to tenants, but there is considerable debate over who
gained and who lost from some of the changes, particularly rent control
and the implied warranty of habitability. Certainly many tenants have
benefited from reduced rents and habitable housing. But these are developments that have increased the cost of being a landlord, which
most likely has raised some rents and reduced the supply of rental
housing, which in turn has likely made it more difficult for newer and
poorer tenants to find affordable places to live. The net effect of these
changes, some have argued, has thus been to benefit middle-class tenants, at the expense of landlords and poor tenants alike.[36]

By the end of the twentieth century, landowners had much more
law to reckon with than did landowners from a century before. Zoning
ordinances constrained the dimensions of their houses and the kinds of
activities they could undertake on their land. Restrictive covenants imposed similar prohibitions, often in much finer detail. If they rented to
tenants they bore a variety of new obligations. Of course, all this law
was not imposed on an unwilling population by some distant tyrant. It
was the product of local democracy, of towns and neighborhood associations made up of people voting to accept collective limits on their

actions. On one view, the property rights of homeowners were weakening, because they were barred from doing things they had once been able to do. For every such loss in power, however, homeowners acquired the power to stop their neighbors from doing the same thing. The ubiquity of all this new land use regulation suggests that for most homeowners, most of the time, the trade has been one worth making.

But if regulation helped homeowners by propping up the value of their homes, it harmed those who were not homeowners but wanted to be, by making home ownership less accessible. There would be winners and losers from land use regulation, as from any kind of regulation. Homeowners tend to be more powerful (and in many towns, more numerous) than nonhomeowners, and they have a more palpable stake in raising house prices than nonhomeowners do in lowering them, so it is not surprising that land use regulation has become so pervasive.

10

Owning Wavelengths

By 1910, a mere fourteen years after Guglielmo Marconi secured the first radio patent, the United States Navy counted more than 1,500 transmitting stations throughout the world, including several hundred in the United States or aboard American ships, and the navy was not even including transmitters operated by amateurs. Radio was not yet used for broadcasting. It was a method of point-to-point communication, a substitute for the telegraph that needed no wires and was thus especially useful at sea. The airwaves, however, were already growing congested. Users of the new wireless telegraphy were beginning to interfere with each other's messages when they tried to use the same wavelengths at the same time. Without any law governing the issue, reported the lawyer Edwin Oakes, "it is the man with the more powerful apparatus who gets his message through." But Oakes, like other observers of the growing industry, realized that the problem of interference was only going to get worse as wireless telegraphy became more popular. Some sort of regulation of the airwaves was inevitable.[1]

Congress's first effort to deal with the problem was the Radio Act of 1912, which required operators of radio equipment to obtain a license from the Department of Commerce before transmitting. The license would state the wavelength the station was allowed to use and the hours during which it was allowed to operate. Attorney General George Wickersham promptly advised that the law gave the Commerce Department no authority to *refuse* an application for a license (the department wanted to deny German investors the right to operate a station until American investors were accorded the same right in Germany), but this system of licensing nevertheless worked well enough to permit the emergence of radio broadcasting in the early 1920s.[2] By the middle of the decade, as more and more broadcasters took to the air, it was clear that most people would experience radio passively, as listeners rather than speakers.

The proliferation of radio stations in the early 1920s quickly overwhelmed the licensing scheme established in the Radio Act of 1912. In 1923, the Commerce Department tried to deny a license to the Intercity Radio Company of New York on the ground that all the wavelengths were already taken. The company brought suit, and a federal court held that Attorney General Wickersham had been right: the department had no authority to deny a license to anyone, for any reason, including to prevent interference.[3] The regulatory scheme was beginning to fall apart.

It soon unraveled completely. The Zenith Radio Corporation, one of the early producers of radio equipment, operated a broadcasting station in Chicago called WJAZ. In 1925, when Zenith applied for a broadcasting license, the Commerce Department replied that the only airtime still available anywhere in the spectrum was on a particular wavelength Thursday nights between ten and midnight. The General Electric Company already used the same wavelength for a station in Denver, but not late on Thursday nights. And even that two-hour-per-week license, the Commerce Department cautioned, could be revoked at any time, should General Electric decide to use those hours. After several meetings with Commerce Department staff, Irving Herriott, Zenith's general counsel, threatened to litigate and received a surprising answer. The Coolidge administration's radio lawyer was Stephen Davis, the solicitor of commerce. "Davis informed me," Herriott later recalled, "that the Department of Commerce would welcome such litigation, because, as he stated, it would bring forcibly to the attention of Congress the necessity for adequate radio regulation." Davis asked Herriott to seek a court order requiring the department to issue a license. Back in Chicago, Herriott decided on a different course: he simply advised Zenith to pick a wavelength and begin broadcasting. A month later, the United States attorney in Chicago filed a criminal complaint against Zenith for operating without a license, and Zenith and the government both had the case they wanted. In early 1926 they got the result they wanted too, when the federal court in Chicago dismissed the criminal charge on the ground that the department had no power to punish unauthorized broadcasting.[4]

The *Zenith Radio* decision gave rise to a crisis. "Any station may with impunity operate" at any time and on any wavelength, conceded Acting Attorney General William Donovan. "The present legislation is inadequate to cover the art of broadcasting, which has been almost entirely developed since the passage of the 1912 Act." Without any legal sanctions for interfering with other stations, the only thing restraining established broadcasters from expanding their territories was the knowledge that interference harmed the second user of a frequency as much as the first—that and some stern lecturing from Herbert Hoover, the secretary of commerce. For a short time, that was enough. "Nearly all broadcasters have stuck to their wave lengths," the journalist Silas Bent explained, shortly after *Zenith Radio*. "They realize that to trespass on someone else's front yard would ruin their own programs as well as the other's. A sort of truce thus prevails." Six weeks after *Zenith Radio*, the government's Interdepartmental Radio Advisory Committee had heard of only a single station broadcasting on an unauthorized frequency.[5]

But this informal truce soon broke down. New broadcasters without existing licenses began crowding into frequencies already allocated to others. Existing broadcasters began increasing their power, and thus their geographic range, which brought them into collision with stations in other cities. "There were some stations which deliberately—and I will use a phrase coined by the press—jumped their wavelengths," Irving Herriott remembered. "They were called pirates." Interference became a major source of annoyance. "Sit down before your instrument tonight and tune in a program you want especially to hear," complained an editorial in *The Youth's Companion*, a popular magazine for children.

> You will get it of course, but ten to one it will be spoiled by the whines and whistles that come from the heterodyning of another station operating on an allied wave length, or interrupted by the sound of another program being broadcast from a station of almost exactly similar wave length. The situation is at its worst around Chicago, where there are some thirty stations, all assailing the air at once and getting inextricably in one another's way, every night. If that sort of thing is permitted to continue, no one can be surprised if the disgusted patrons of the radio industry retire their instruments to the attic or to the junk shop.

Everyone agreed that something had to be done. In his annual message to Congress for 1926, even President Coolidge lamented that "many more stations have been operating than can be accommodated within the limited number of wave lengths available," and that radio had "drifted into such chaos as seems likely, if not remedied, to destroy its great value."[6] In late 1926 and early 1927, Congress accordingly turned its attention to the electromagnetic spectrum. How could broadcasters be prevented from interfering with one another?

Property in a Wave-Length

One possibility was to recognize property rights in particular wave-lengths, rights that would allow existing users to stave off trespassers. This was the solution adopted by the Chicago judge Francis Wilson, in a case that arose shortly after the *Zenith Radio* decision. The Chicago station WGN, owned by the *Chicago Tribune* (thus the call letters, which stood for "World's Greatest Newspaper"), had been on the air since 1924. WGN was licensed by the Commerce Department to broadcast at 990 kilocycles. A less popular competitor, the Oak Leaves Broadcasting Station, was licensed to broadcast at 1330 kilocycles. In September 1926, however, after *Zenith Radio* held that the Commerce Department lacked the power to punish unauthorized broadcasters, the Oak Leaves Station switched its frequency to 990 kilocycles and began interfering with WGN's broadcasts. WGN asked for an injunction ordering Oak Leaves to stop.

The case presented "a situation new and novel," Judge Wilson recognized. In the absence of any governing statute, did the common law of Illinois give the first broadcaster at any given frequency the right to suppress the second? Wilson found an answer by examining situations he considered analogous. The first user of a brand name acquired a property right in that name, one that enabled him to stop someone else from using the same name. In some states the first user of running water in a river for mining purposes acquired a right to stop others from taking the same water. The rationale behind such cases, Wilson reasoned, was to protect the investments of the first user. Without a property right, no one would invest in such useful things as brand names or mining, for fear that the value of their investments might be whisked away by a competitor. Wilson concluded that the same logic applied to broadcasting. WGN had invested time and money in building up a radio audience at 990 kilocycles. "Priority in time creates a superiority in right," Wilson held. The first user of a wavelength owned the right to keep using it, a right that authorized a court to enjoin competitors from interfering.[7]

Wilson's *Oak Leaves* decision was, not surprisingly, welcomed by established broadcasters and their listeners. Other stations began to prepare similar lawsuits against interfering competitors. The analogy between the radio spectrum and older forms of property had an intuitive logic that many lawyers found appealing. A would-be broadcaster "is somewhat like the automobile driver wishing to park on a public street, but finding the places already occupied," explained Stephen Davis, the Commerce Department's chief lawyer. "While inherently he has the same privilege as everyone else, he may not remove a car already parked in order to put his in its place. He must travel from block to block until he finds an unoccupied spot." Broadcasters, Davis added, were like holders of general admission tickets in a theater: everyone had an equal right to a given seat, but once a spectator had taken his seat he could not be ousted by another. "So with the individual wishing to engage in radio communication," who had the same obligation to "adjust himself to the existing condition so as not to disturb those whose rights are equal to his and whose status is superior because of priority and possession." The basis of the *Oak Leaves* decision was simply "the familiar doctrine that possession confers a right which is valid as against everyone who cannot show a prior and better right," reasoned Frank Rowley of the University of Cincinnati, one of the first law professors to specialize in the emerging law of radio. "The position that there may be a property in a wave-length is sound." Unless some unforeseen technical advance were to transform the nature of radio, predicted the economist Hiram Jome, the only way to prevent interference would be to allow stations to assert property rights in frequencies.[8]

As Congress considered how to regulate radio, established broadcasters and their lawyers urged the enactment of a statutory scheme that would, in effect, codify and nationalize Judge Wilson's decision, by conferring property rights in existing uses of the electromagnetic spectrum. "It is perfectly fair that those who are in the business first have some rights," declared Paul Klugh, vice president of Zenith Radio's

KJAZ. "Those who come in afterwards certainly cannot have the same rights." Within the government it was recognized as early as 1923 that existing broadcasters "believe their interests would be served better if they were left to acquire by so-called 'squatter rights' as much radio territory of the world as possible." At the National Radio Conference convened by Secretary of Commerce Herbert Hoover, a committee of industry representatives recommended that a station's call letters should be "recognized as representing a property right," and that a license to operate on a given frequency should be presumptively renewable, effectively extending that property right to the continuing use of the frequency itself. Use of the airwaves amounted to "a vested property right in a station," agreed David Podell, speaking on behalf of WMSG, which had been broadcasting from New York's Madison Square Garden since 1924. A committee of the American Bar Association, composed largely of lawyers representing radio interests, cautioned that any legislation would have to allow existing broadcasters to stay on the air. Their clients had a property right in the continued use of their frequencies, the lawyers argued, so any new law that did not acknowledge that right would amount to an unconstitutional taking of property.[9] Radio was not yet lucrative but it promised to be one day. Insiders were well aware that a property right in the use of a wavelength might eventually become the most valuable asset a broadcaster could own.

The industry mounted its most thorough defense of a property regime in a 1926 public statement signed by representatives of the major radio-related trade associations, including the National Association of Broadcasters and the Radio Manufacturers' Association. "It is fair, just and reasonable," the industry argued, that "the right of priority of operation" should govern the allocation of the spectrum. "It would be unfair, in our opinion, to consider a late comer in the business of broadcasting . . . to have equal rights or to be placed upon the same basis as a broadcaster who has served the public well and has a substantial investment." Existing broadcasters "have invested substantial sums of money in broadcasting plant and equipment," they argued, investments that might be rendered worthless if the spectrum were to be allocated from scratch, without any consideration for its existing occupants.[10]

The notion of property in wavelengths, however, was troubling to a wide range of people, for a few different reasons. Many analogized the spectrum to a newly discovered continent and worried about the consequences of letting it slip into private hands. This was a consistent theme in the letters and speeches of Herbert Hoover, who, as secretary of commerce, was the official with the greatest responsibility for governing the airwaves. The spectrum is "a sort of national resource," Hoover argued as early as 1921. He often compared it with older, more tangible forms of public property. It was important to "establish public right over the ether roads," he explained at one 1922 meeting, so that there would be "no national regret that we have parted with a great national asset into uncontrolled hands." Recognizing property in wavelengths, he urged attendees at the 1924 California Radio Exposition, "would be creating a monopoly of a certain road through the ether just as important as if we gave an exclusive right to the navigation of the Sacramento River." Because of his later performance as president, Hoover is sometimes caricatured as a staunch opponent of government involvement in the economy, but as commerce secretary he was the nation's strongest and most visible supporter of public ownership of the airwaves.[11]

Hoover was hardly alone. "The development of these claims of vested rights in radio frequencies," Senator Clarence Dill later recalled, "caused many members of Congress to fear that this one and only remaining public domain in the form of free radio communication might soon be lost unless Congress protected it by legislation." As early as 1924, both houses of Congress considered legislation that would have explicitly declared the airwaves to be owned by the public rather than any individual broadcaster. "The ether and its use within the jurisdiction of the United States may well be considered one of the great and almost untouched natural resources of the Nation," exhorted a report of the Senate Committee on Interstate Commerce. "It would be unthinkable for Congress, through any laches [that is, delay] on its part, to encourage any person or interest to assume the possibility of securing a right to any use of the ether whatever."[12] The broadcasters were not the only ones with their eyes on this prize.

Why were so many worried about property rights in wavelengths? The main concern expressed by lawmakers was the danger that if frequencies could be owned, a few large companies might come to dominate broadcasting. "There are some big interests that hope to claim ultimately a vested right in certain wavelengths," warned Senator Robert Howell of Nebraska. "Not a sufficient time has elapsed to enable them to make the claim now, but if we wait 25 or 50 years we may be confronted with claims of that kind." With such a valuable asset in play, monopoly was worrisome enough in its own right. "The development of radio has opened up a new domain comparable to the discovery of a hitherto unknown continent," one observer cautioned. "Really great stakes are being gambled for. And private interests are trying to obtain control of wave lengths and establish private property claims to them." Members of Congress repeatedly argued that the best way to prevent the monopolization of radio was to declare wavelengths unownable from the start.[13]

But monopoly was especially troubling because of the special nature of broadcasting. Hoover voiced a common intuition when he asserted that "radio communication is not to be considered as merely a business carried on for private gain." Radio was much more than a business. "It is a public concern impressed with the public trust," Hoover continued, "and to be considered primarily from the standpoint of public interest." Radio could be a medium for spreading news, education, and culture to all sorts of people who might not be served otherwise, and these were interests that might be inconsistent with a broadcaster's financial incentives. "It would be most unfortunate for the people of this country, to whom broadcasting has become an important incident of life, if its control should come into the hands of any single corporation, individual, or combination," Hoover declared on another occasion. "It would be in principle the same as though the entire press of the country were so controlled."[14]

Concentrated ownership in the radio industry also raised the specter of censorship, the fear that only certain points of view would be allowed on the air. "Important persons or personages with a message politically acceptable to the companies might well be granted an exclusive right to go on the air, while 'the opposition' could neither share the privilege of existing stations nor erect stations of its own," one journalist worried. "In other words, the owners of stations can do their own censoring in their own way." Charles Caldwell was a lawyer representing the small broadcasters who were trying to elbow aside the established stations and get some spectrum of their own. If big companies were allowed to monopolize the radio, Caldwell told a House committee, "it might well be that some official of the monopoly company, sitting in the quiet of his executive office, surrounded and protected and away from the public, where he can not be seen, will issue the fiat that only one kind of religion shall be talked over the radio; that only one kind of politics shall be talked over the radio; that only one candidate can give messages to the people."[15]

Indeed, others noted, radio was already exhibiting a troubling tendency toward monopoly and censorship. Morris Ernst was a well-known civil rights lawyer who would soon become general counsel to the American Civil Liberties Union. "The Radio Corporation of America has two very good stations in New York City," Ernst pointed out. But "if any organization which is critical of the United States Government wants to get a broadcasting permit, the [Commerce] Department with a great show of reasonableness says, 'Put your name on the list,' and there you will be at the bottom of a list of about 300 applicants." In Chicago, Ernst added, where the *Tribune* was operating two stations, the Commerce Department somehow could not find any wavelengths available for the Chicago Federation of Labor, which wanted a station of its own. A system of property rights in frequencies threatened to make the situation even worse. Edward Nockles, the secretary of the Chicago Federation of Labor, accordingly declared that "organized labor was opposed to property rights on the air." The radio, in Nockles's view, should be developed "for the benefit of all the people and not as a source of profit for corporations."[16]

Meanwhile, government officials in Congress and the executive branch doubtless had motives of their own. A system of property rights in spectrum would have required some initial method of allocating those rights, but once the spectrum had been distributed, wavelengths would have been bought and sold in a market over which government officials could exercise little direct control. In a system without property rights, on the other hand, would-be broadcasters would have to apply for frequencies again and again, and government officials would retain considerable discretionary authority over each allocation. The electromagnetic spectrum thus promised to be a source of political power for the new Federal Radio Commission and the members of Congress who would be overseeing it. Indeed, it did not take long for licensing decisions to become heavily influenced by political factors. As one early study of the commission concluded, "probably no quasi-judicial body was ever subject to so much congressional pressure as the Federal Radio Commission."[17]

Established broadcasters favored property in wavelengths, but they were defeated by a disparate coalition led by the regulators themselves.

The very first sentence of the Radio Act of 1927 accordingly declared that the Act was intended to "provide for the use" of the airwaves "but not the ownership thereof." The Federal Radio Commission was to issue short-term licenses to broadcasters, but "no such license shall be construed to create any right, beyond the terms, conditions, and periods of the license." Before any existing broadcaster could be granted a license, the broadcaster would have to sign "a waiver of any claim to the use of any particular frequency . . . because of the previous use of the same."[18] Similar provisions would be contained in the Communications Act of 1934, which superseded the Radio Act of 1927. Congress was saying, as clearly as it could, that there could be no property in a wavelength.

The Signature of Secretary Hoover

Under the new regulatory scheme, the Radio Commission was supposed to allocate broadcast licenses "as the public convenience, interest, or necessity requires." This was not much of a guide. "If we knew what public convenience, necessity and interest were," admitted H. A. Bellows, one of the first commissioners, "the job of the Commission would be a lot easier than it is." The broadcasters themselves were just as uncertain. Some stations divided their programming into two parts, entertainment and public service, reported Benson Pratt of Chicago's WENR. These stations scheduled lectures and other educational features "so that they may make a record before the Federal Radio Commission and not because they really believe that all of these things are, per se, of real interest or of real value to the listening public." Other stations, Pratt explained, "contend that radio is an entertainment medium only and that if they present only entertainment or other musical features, they will have complied with that portion of the law which refers to public interest, convenience, and necessity."[19] No one could be quite sure.

Without much guidance from the law, the commission tended to give the most powerful stations to the most powerful applicants, companies like General Electric, Westinghouse, and RCA. Many licenses went to the largest urban newspapers. The absence of property rights in spectrum turned out not to make much difference in who was able to broadcast. The Chicago Federation of Labor, for example, one of the most vocal opponents of property rights, applied for a license to broadcast at high power over a long range, day and night, just like the large corporations. It was awarded a weak signal in the daytime only, when its members would be away at work. "Is it in the public interest, necessity and convenience that this marvelous new means of communication should be placed within the control of a few great corporations?" the federation asked in an angry letter to the Senate. "Is it a matter of public necessity that twenty radio stations in one city pound the air with the same jazz tunes? . . . Is it in the public interest, necessity and convenience that all of the 89 channels for radio broadcasting be given to Capital and its friends, and not even one channel to the millions who toil?" The federation had opposed property rights in order to prevent concentration in the radio industry, but concentration was taking place all the same.[20]

As a formal matter, courts and commentators agreed, the Radio Act of 1927 created a system without property rights in wavelengths. In practice, however, things were not so clear. Virtually from the beginning of broadcasting, radio stations had been bought and sold. Before the enactment of the Radio Act, the Commerce Department had not discouraged the transfer of stations and had routinely allowed the purchaser of a station to continue broadcasting. "We take the position," Stephen Davis explained to a Senate committee, "that the license ran to the apparatus; a man can transfer his apparatus, and if there is no good reason to the contrary we will recognize that sale and license the new owner." Some of these sales were for prices far in excess of the value of the station's physical assets, and it was clear to all that the increment represented the expectation of a continuing right to use the airwaves. WEAF in New York, for example, was sold in 1926 for $1 million, only $200,000 of which was for the station itself; the other 80 percent was the value of its license. "I have been offered, in New York City, plants that did not cost over $20,000 for as high as $150,000," Morris Ernst charged, "meaning that the money is for two elements, one the good will established at that station, and the other the signature of Secretary Hoover."[21] If a station could be sold and its broadcasting license would pass with it, broadcasters would enjoy a de facto ability to sell their rights to use particular wavelengths, and the spectrum would in fact be governed by the very sort of property system the Radio Act of 1927 was intended to prohibit.

How to handle the transfer of stations was widely recognized as a looming problem in the debates leading up to the Radio Act. "These franchises are going to become worth not hundreds of thousands of dollars, but a million dollars may be paid for the transfer of a franchise," Robert Howell worried. Some proposed banning the sale of a station during the life of a license, while others suggested scrutinizing sale prices to ensure that they were not any higher than the value of the physical apparatus being sold. In response, broadcasters argued that limiting the sale of stations would only deter investment in radio, by making it impossible for investors to realize any gains. "If a man has spent, say, $100,000 in a station, and perhaps in conducting it another $100,000, and has $200,000 in it on an investment, and he becomes sick or meets with an accident, or he may die, you would not buy that station unless you could operate it," reasoned Norman Baker, the manager of KTNT in Muscatine, Iowa. "Now, we have a 90-day license, and I have used it 30 days. If I die or get sick, there is 2 months left. I believe that I should be authorized to sell that station and transfer the remaining unexpired time of my license over." If the government could revoke or refuse to renew a broadcasting license upon the sale of a station, argued the lawyer for a Cleveland station, "why, you junk their whole million-dollar investment, which I do not think would be proper treatment of an investor. You do not apply the same thing to a railroad or any public utility."[22] Congress had stumbled upon a conundrum. To prevent the emergence of property rights in wavelengths, one had to place strict limits on the sale of radio stations. But the stronger those limits, the fewer radio stations would be established in the first place.

The Radio Act of 1927 did not resolve this problem. Congress simply passed it along to the Radio Commission, by providing that licenses could not be transferred without the consent of the commission. The Communications Act of 1934 gave the same authority, and the same absence of any guidelines for exercising it, to the Radio Commission's replacement, the Federal Communications Commission. The extent to which stations, and thus broadcasting licenses, could be bought and sold would depend on how aggressive these commissions would be in regulating the market.

The Radio Commission began by asserting complete control. The purpose of the Radio Act, declared the commission's general counsel, was to "prevent development of the theory of property rights in the use of a frequency." The commission would accordingly examine all transactions—including sales, leases, and mortgages of radio stations—to ensure that no one concerned was making "any profit based upon the sale of a license." It soon became apparent, however, that actual practice was far more lenient. The Radio Commission, and later the FCC, were faced with repeated applications to approve the sales of stations. The sale price of a station normally far exceeded the appraised value of the physical equipment being sold. John Weare, the treasurer of the Boston Broadcasting Company, operators of WLOE in Boston, was unusually honest in his testimony before the Radio Commission in 1931. The station owned a transmitter with a book value of $28,205, he explained, as well as some office furniture worth around $4,300. The station's license, meanwhile, "should properly be valued at $150,000," or nearly five times the value of the station's physical assets. Most applicants were less candid. They accounted for the disparity between the station's sale price and the value of its physical equipment by emphasizing the intangible values—other than the license—that were being transferred to the buyer. An established station had ongoing contracts for the sale of advertising time. It had an affiliation with a broadcasting network. It had the goodwill of its audience, who had developed the habit of tuning in to particular programs at particular times. All of these assets were clearly worth something, but there was considerable room for creativity in assigning values to them, and applicants were often able to argue that their cumulative value amounted to the full difference between the purchase price and the value of the physical apparatus being conveyed. In some cases the commission refused to accept such valuations, but by the mid-1930s, the commission had approved them in the large majority of cases.[23]

In 1936, for example, the commission approved the sale of KNX, a Los Angeles station, for $1,250,000. The replacement value of the station's entire physical plant was less than $220,000. In explaining its decisions in cases like these, the commission consistently declared that it was ascribing no value to the broadcast license and the associated right to use a particular frequency, but knowledgeable observers were certain that this was not true. "In actual practice," explained the Washington lawyer Harry Warner, "there can be no question but that in negotiations toward the sale or purchase of a radio broadcasting station these are the values which play the greatest part in determining what shall be paid."[24] The commission was unable as a practical matter to second-guess the accounting in all these transactions, but it was also publicly committed to a policy of refusing to recognize the sale of a broadcast license. All it could do was allow disguised sales of licenses while insisting it was not.

By the middle of the century, it was clear that beneath this layer of obfuscation the radio spectrum was governed by a de facto system of property rights. The Federal Communications Commission routinely granted renewals of broadcasting licenses unless the broadcaster had engaged in some form of misconduct. The commission also routinely approved the sale of stations, even where the sale price must have included some increment that represented the value of the license. The law still formally denied the existence of property rights in wavelengths, but broadcasters enjoyed such rights for all practical purposes. A broadcaster might not have had the full bundle of rights associated with other forms of property—he could not lease his license for short periods or let it rest unused, for example—but he had the most important ones. Once a station had a license to use a particular frequency, the station could prevent competitors from using that frequency, and in practice it could convey the frequency to others who would acquire the same right to exclude.[25]

Like Grocery Stores

This mismatch between actual practice and the formal law persisted for a long time—indeed, it still exists today—in part because the worry about allowing property rights in wavelengths that had been so evident in the 1920s never went away. In 1951, as the FCC considered who should get licenses for the new medium of color television, a law student at the University of Chicago named Leo Herzel suggested that the best way would be to put the licenses up for auction. Other scarce goods were allocated by the market rather than the government, Herzel pointed out, because free consumer choice would yield a higher level of total satisfaction. If broadcasters had to bid for color television licenses at recurring intervals, the most popular stations would be able to bid the most. Why not let consumers choose television programs the way they chose other goods? Herzel's proposal drew a sharp rebuke from Dallas Smythe, a professor at the University of Illinois, who voiced the conventional wisdom, in words that echoed those of Herbert Hoover from three decades before. Smythe mocked the notion that one could treat "broadcasting . . . like grocery stores." Herzel's view implied "that the educational and cultural responsibilities of broadcast station operators ought to be no more substantial at the most than those of the operators of the newspapers and magazines," Smythe declared, and that implication was simply wrong. "There is a powerful tradition in the United States that the economic, educational and cultural rights and responsibilities of broadcasting are unique," Smythe concluded. Radio and television were simply too important to be left to the free market. "I for one would take my chances on operating the radio industry like the grocery industry," Herzel replied, "with the hope that those with education and culture in our society will get their hands on a sufficient amount of money to make their needs felt. The existence of certain private universities, colleges, publishing firms and newspapers in this country makes this seem a not too fantastic hope."[26] But the tradition invoked by Smythe, one resting on the fear of a market-imposed uniformity on the airwaves, was still too strong to allow the explicit recognition of property rights in wavelengths.

A similar but much more widely known episode took place a few years later, when the economist Ronald Coase published a proposal much like Herzel's. Radio frequencies were scarce relative to the number of people who wanted to use them, Coase observed, but so were most goods. "Land, labor, and capital are all scarce, but this, of itself, does not call for government regulation," Coase pointed out. "It is true that some mechanism has to be employed to decide who, out of the many claimants, should be allowed to use the scarce resource. But the way this is usually done in the American economic system is to employ the price mechanism." Instead, Coase suggested, the government was granting a valuable resource, the right to broadcast, for free. "Occasionally, when a station is sold, it is possible to glimpse what is involved," he explained. When such sales took place, "there can be little doubt that the purchase price is in fact payment for obtaining the use of the frequency." Why should broadcasters receive a valuable asset for free and then reap the gains from selling it? It would be better, Coase concluded, for the government to do the selling in the first place, by auctioning off the right to broadcast.[27]

Among regulators and academics specializing in broadcasting, Coase's proposal was hardly taken seriously. "Are you spoofing us? Is this all a big joke?" asked Philip Cross, one of the commissioners of the

FCC, when Coase testified at hearings on the future of broadcasting. When Coase, along with two other economists, prepared a draft report for the RAND Corporation favoring property rights in frequencies, the report was viewed so critically within RAND that it was suppressed. "Time has somehow left the authors behind," one critic charged. "I know of no country on the face of the globe—except for a few corrupt Latin American dictatorships—where the 'sale' of the spectrum could even be seriously proposed."[28] Broadcasting was widely understood as an inherently public realm very different from the domains in which property could be bought and sold.

That was the ideological underpinning for the long refusal to recognize property rights in frequencies. Among broadcasters, there was no doubt a much stronger practical reason to prefer the status quo. They were in the habit of receiving an extremely valuable asset for free. Under the proposals of Herzel and Coase, broadcasters would have to start paying for it. Regulators, whether in Congress or the FCC, also had a practical reason to oppose property rights. If licenses were put up for auction, regulators would lose their considerable power to choose who would receive a license. For all these reasons, the legal regime governing broadcasting scarcely changed. Even as new technologies opened up new uses of the electromagnetic spectrum like FM radio and television, the government continued to grant licenses for free and to place formal restrictions, although few practical ones, on their transfer.[29]

Economists, meanwhile, continued to urge reform, but, despite occasional flurries of interest from policymakers, no change would take place for the next few decades. In 1969, for example, the economist Milton Friedman published a short article in *Newsweek* advocating a system of property rights in television broadcast licenses. The article caught the attention of George Schultz, Friedman's former colleague at the University of Chicago, who was then the director of the Office of Management and Budget. Schultz sent it to the White House, where it landed on the desk of John Ehrlichman, President Nixon's chief domestic advisor. Ehrlichman was impressed with "Milton Friedman's suggestion that we change the television and radio licensing system to sell these licenses in fee simple absolute and let the free market take care of the consequences. Has this ever been proposed before?" he asked Peter Flanigan, another of Nixon's domestic policy advisors. "If not, why not?" Flanigan turned the question over to Clay Whitehead, who was in charge of the

Office of Telecommunication Policy. Whitehead had heard this one before. "The idea of a free market in radio and TV licenses was first proposed as early as the 1950s, and has been extensively explored since," he informed Ehrlichman. "There, in fact, already exists a flourishing trade in these licenses," in connection with the sales of radio and television stations, "although exchanges are subject to FCC approval." The new medium of the era was cable television, which relied on wires rather than the electromagnetic spectrum for the transmission of programming, and Whitehead's office was much more interested in formulating policy for cable than in drastically revamping policy for radio and television. "The kind of genuinely free market which Friedman desires can be achieved with cable TV," he explained, "but only if our regulatory approach to cable is quite different from what has evolved for over-the-air broadcasting." Whitehead concluded that "some market-like mechanism is needed throughout" the field of communications, but the more pressing need at the moment was to develop "a realistic cable TV policy which will strongly reinforce the President's theme of diversity and localism."[30] Thus ended the Nixon administration's interest in the issue. From the weary tone of Whitehead's memo, one senses his reluctance even to contemplate the political difficulties of establishing property rights in broadcast frequencies. Theorists like Coase and Friedman might have a good idea in principle, but that was not enough for a busy White House official whose days were already full with more immediate concerns.

Finally, in the 1990s, the government began auctioning nonbroadcast spectrum licenses for technologies like pagers and mobile telephones and allowing some nonbroadcast licensees to sell or lease blocks of the spectrum to others. As far back as 1973, when the regulatory framework for mobile telephony was first being discussed, Clay Whitehead's Office of Telecommunications Policy had seen the possibility for change. The potential for opening up a previously unallocated band of the spectrum "offers an opportunity for experimentation with procedures which would permit market mechanisms to augment the regulatory process," Whitehead reported. "Such methods might include *pro forma* transferability of licenses between mobile users and the adoption of license fee schedules reflecting spectrum value."[31] By the 1990s, policymakers had progressed from license fees to auctions. The first was conducted in 1994: six bidders won ten licenses for wavelengths to be used for paging services, and the government netted $650 million in revenue. There would be approximately seventy-five more auctions through 2008.[32] By 2005, the government had taken in more than $14 billion from completed auctions. The idea of selling property rights in the spectrum had scarcely been taken seriously a half century before, but now, for new technologies, it had become orthodoxy.[33]

The spectrum used for television and radio nevertheless remained governed by the regime established back in 1927. By statute, rights to the airwaves were not a form of property, but they were very much like property in practice. Critics repeatedly pointed out the inefficiencies of a system that resulted in billions of dollars of forgone revenue and large segments of underutilized spectrum.[34] But the combination of material and ideological factors that had created the nominally propertyless system governing the airwaves was simply too strong to dislodge.

11

The New Property

THE MID-TWENTIETH century was an era of profound changes in constitutional interpretation. Some of the major Supreme Court cases of the period are household names, like *Brown v. Board of Education* and *Roe v. Wade*. Others are famous only among lawyers. *Goldberg v. Kelly* is in this second category. In *Goldberg,* decided in 1970, the Court decided that the right to receive government benefits for the poor is a kind of property protected by the Constitution, and thus that officials cannot terminate welfare payments without first holding a hearing to give disappointed claimants a chance to object. *Goldberg* fundamentally changed the way government makes routine decisions. Like many of the big Supreme Court cases of the era, especially the cases expanding the constitutional rights of criminal suspects, *Goldberg* was intended to enhance the power of the weak in their encounters with government bureaucracy.

Goldberg and the cases that followed it were also an important episode in the history of property, because in *Goldberg* the Supreme Court first adopted a view called "the new property," a theory of property rights elaborated a few years earlier by the law professor Charles Reich and much discussed in the legal academic community. That view remains part of our law today, although not to the full extent proposed by Reich and others. The quick rise and partial fall of the new property raise a few questions that can be answered only by placing it in long-run context. What exactly was this new property? How new was it really? Why did it emerge when it did?

The Giant Government Syphon

There could be little doubt, at any time in American history, that a great many forms of property, both old and new, consisted of grants from the government. Ancient intangibles like public office and titles of nobility obviously originated as government grants. So did the forms of commercial property that acquired economic importance in the nineteenth century. Patents, copyrights, and trademarks were government-granted rights of monopoly. Shares in business corporations rested at bottom on corporate charters that were likewise grants from the government of rights to conduct particular kinds of enterprise. By the 1790s, the theorist and politician John Taylor could already distinguish between what he called "natural property," things that exist prior to government and independent of law, and "artificial property," property that exists only because it has been created by the government.[1]

Many of the newer forms of property likewise took the form of government-conferred licenses—to use the airwaves, for instance, or to practice a given profession. Even land, that most physical of assets, was granted by the government: every square inch of the United States had been acquired either directly from the government or at the end of a chain of title that reached back to the government as its first link. Thoroughgoing positivists concluded that *all* property, by its very nature, was a grant from the government, but even the most diehard opponents of this view had to concede that at least *some* kinds of property fit that description.

The government conferred other sorts of benefits too. It paid salaries to its employees. It provided pensions, at first to military veterans and later, with the creation of Social Security, to everyone who had ever been employed. It made regular payments to the poor and the disabled. Everyone agreed that these transfers were a form of property after they occurred—that once the money was in the hands of a government employee or a Social Security recipient, it was that person's property, just like any other money he or she happened to possess. But did he or she have any property rights *before* the transfer, rights in the expectation of continuing to receive payment? If the government were to stop paying an employee's salary or cut off a Social Security recipient's benefits, would the government be depriving that person of property?

Before 1970, the answer was no. In the 1960 case *Flemming v. Nestor,* the Supreme Court decided that Social Security benefits were not a form of property. Ephram Nestor was an immigrant from Bulgaria who had briefly been a member of the Communist Party in the 1930s. He was a sixty-six-year-old retiree when the government deported him in 1956, at the height of the Cold War. His wife Barbara remained in Los Angeles. She continued to receive her monthly Social Security check, but the government stopped her husband's payments, without a hearing, under a recently enacted amendment to the Social Security Act allowing the termination of benefits to recipients deported for "subversive" activities. With the help of two local left-wing lawyers, Barbara Nestor filed suit on Ephram's behalf.[2]

The Nestors won at first. A trial judge determined that Ephram's Social Security benefits were analogous to compensation for services rendered while he was working. "The nature of such benefits make them property rights," he held, "but property cannot be taken from a person without due process of law." The recent amendment to the Social Security Act had deprived Ephram of his benefits after he had already earned them, the judge concluded, and was thus inconsistent with due process.[3]

The Nestors' victory was short-lived, however. The Supreme Court reversed by a 5–4 vote the following year. Social Security benefits were not a form of property, Justice John Harlan explained. "To engraft upon the Social Security system a concept of 'accrued property rights' would deprive it of the flexibility and boldness in adjustment to ever-changing conditions which it demands," he concluded. The government could take benefits away without having to comply with the due process clause. ("People who pay premiums for insurance," Hugo Black remarked in dissent, "usually think they are paying for insurance, not for 'flexibility and boldness.'") William Douglas's notes of the justices' discussion after oral argument suggest that the justices in the majority were worried that if the right to receive benefits was property, Congress would lose the ability to make prospective changes in the program that happened to reduce the future payments to anyone. "Congress could abolish the whole thing," Felix Frankfurter declared to his colleagues, so there could be "no 'vested' interest here."[4]

A year later the Court held that a government job was not a form of property either. Rachel Brawner had been a short-order cook at the

Naval Gun Factory for more than six years until she was fired for being an unspecified security risk. She was never told why she was thought to pose a threat and was never given an opportunity to rebut the charge. Brawner lost too, in another 5–4 decision. "It has become a settled principle," Justice Potter Stewart declared for the majority, "that government employment . . . can be revoked at the will of the appointing officer." Government employees had no property right in continued employment, and thus no right to due process when that employment was taken away.[5]

The legal system, however, was on the cusp of dramatic change. In a wide variety of contexts, Americans were beginning to expect what Lawrence Friedman has called "total justice"—a general right to be treated fairly, especially by the government, and a corresponding right to redress when treated unfairly.[6] Government officials who enjoyed vast realms of unchecked discretion circa 1950—the police, prosecutors, prison guards, hospital workers, teachers, and many others—would be hemmed in with rules by 1980, rules enforceable primarily through litigation. Institutions whose internal workings had once been relatively sheltered from the law were increasingly opened up to legal scrutiny, often in the form of lawsuits. In retrospect, *Flemming v. Nestor* was like a criminal case just before *Gideon* and *Miranda*—the last expression of a view that was about to crumble away.

This change might have swept in government benefits without any consideration of whether they were a kind of property. Despite the text of the due process clause, which literally protects only life, liberty, and property, courts had tended not to inquire very closely into whether any of those three things was present in a given case. In *Flemming v. Nestor*, the Supreme Court disposed of the issue in a single sentence, and only after cautioning that "it is hardly profitable to engage in conceptualizations regarding 'earned rights' and 'gratuities.'" At times the Court showed even less concern about the question. In a 1956 case called *Slochower v. Board of Education*, for example, the Court held that a tenured city college professor could not be summarily fired, without ever pausing to decide whether his job was a form of property.[7] The due process revolution that would take place in the early 1970s could easily have remained within this framework, under the assumption that due process was an obligation that attached to *all* government activity, regardless of whether a claimant had lost any property. But it didn't. Instead, the due process revolution was wrapped up in a debate over the meaning of property.

That was because out of all the many calls for procedural fairness in the 1960s, the most influential bore the title "The New Property." It appeared in the *Yale Law Journal* in 1964, a few years after *Flemming*. The author was Charles Reich, then in his fourth year as a law professor at Yale after a brief career as a lawyer in Washington. Reich was already deeply unhappy with his life. A closeted gay man, he never felt comfortable, either personally or professionally, with the powerful institutions in which he worked. After "The New Property" he would gradually withdraw from Yale. In the late 1960s he began spending much of his time amid the youth culture of the era, both at Yale and in San Francisco during the summers. His 1970 best-seller *The Greening of America* was a critique of the conformity and consumerism of contemporary society and a celebration of what Reich called "Consciousness III," the attitude he ascribed to the youth movement. In the early 1970s he would leave Yale and move to San Francisco, where he would live for the rest of the century and into the next, writing only occasionally.[8]

Reich's interest in the meaning of property was kindled as a law student in the early 1950s, when he edited a classmate's work on the State Department's revocation of passports from those suspected of communism. As he later recalled, it struck him as odd that the government could take something so valuable in an apparently arbitrary manner, without providing any explanation or chance to object. He confronted the issue again as a law clerk to Justice Hugo Black in 1953, when he worked on a case of a physician whose license to practice medicine had been revoked because the physician was found in contempt of the House Committee on Un-American Activities. As a law professor teaching the first-year Property course in the early 1960s, he addressed the perennial question of where property comes from, and realized that passports and licenses (and, he would discover, welfare benefits) were hardly unique in coming from the state. Taking the ascendant positivist view, every kind of property originated in a government grant. "If *all* property comes from the state," Reich wondered, "why should some grants be considered sacred rights, while others, such as welfare, are considered mere privileges?"[9]

Reich began "The New Property" by listing the important ways in which wealth consists of rights and benefits that flow from the government. Many people hold government jobs. Many receive benefits of various kinds, such as Social Security, unemployment compensation, and welfare. Many, from longshoremen to physicians, hold occupational licenses. Many hold franchises, like the right to operate a taxi or to broadcast over a television channel. Many are paid under contracts with the government, and many more receive straight public subsidies, including farmers and shipping lines. Wealth dispensed by the government is an important part of the economy. "Hardly any citizen leads his life," Reich observed, "without at least partial dependence on wealth flowing through the giant government syphon." Some of these forms of government-derived wealth, like franchises and licenses, were recognized by the courts as property, but most, including government benefits, were not. The result, he explained, was the creation of a "new feudalism" in which wealth "is held by its recipients conditionally, subject to confiscation in the interest of the paramount state." Just as "the feudal philosophy of largess and tenure" had given way to a system of property rights, Reich argued, the types of currently important government-created wealth should be classified as property, in order to protect the individual against the government. Government largess might originally have constituted public property, but so once did land, and if land could be redefined as private property so could government benefits. In practice, Reich noted, recognizing benefits as property would require changing how the government doled them out. "The grant, denial, revocation, and administration of all types of government largess should be subject to scrupulous observance of fair procedures," he concluded. "Action should be open to hearing and contest, and based upon a record subject to judicial review. The denial of any form of privilege or benefit on the basis of undisclosed reasons should no longer be tolerated." In a world where government benefits seemed to be replacing other sources of wealth, benefits deserved to be counted as property rights.[10]

This was the "new property," but in what sense was it new? Most of what law professors write consists of exhortations to incremental reform. Academic norms require novelty, but practical legal argument requires precedent, so Reich, like most law professors, had to walk a narrow ledge. If his argument was not innovative enough, it would not impress his academic colleagues, but if it was too innovative, it would be rejected by the lawyers and judges he sought to persuade. Like many law professors, Reich mediated this tension by being old at one level of abstraction and new at another. There was nothing original about classifying the general category of government-derived assets as property; as Reich demonstrated, they had been so classified for some time. It *was* original, on the other hand, to classify the specific subcategory of welfare as property. But not *too* original. Indeed, *Flemming v. Nestor,* the primary case Reich attacked, had been decided by a 5–4 vote. Four of the nine Supreme Court justices, plus the trial judge whose decision the Court reversed, had already adopted Reich's view.

Reich focused on the fact that welfare benefits came from the government, but there was a more intuitive objection to classifying them as the recipients' property that he did not address, which was that they had not yet been paid. Once a payment had been made, the money was clearly the property of the recipient under any definition of the word, and the government could not simply take it away without affording due process. The "new property" was not money already received but rather the expectation of receiving additional payments in the future. All the established forms of government-derived property that Reich cataloged, like licenses and land, had already been granted to their owners. They were like welfare benefits already paid. A closer analogy to the property Reich sought to establish would have been the expectation of receiving land in the future, or the expectation of having a license renewed once it expired. This would not have been an insuperable objection. Reich could have responded with another catalog, this one of all the established forms of property that likewise consisted of expectations. What was a share in a corporation, for example, but the expectation of receiving income in the future? What was the right of publicity but the expectation of exploiting one's fame?

Reich was hardly the first to argue that benefits to the poor should be a matter of right rather than privilege. Nor was he the first to urge greater procedural regularity in the welfare system. His contribution was rather to place both issues within the framework of a broad theory of property, one that suggested parallel reforms in a wide range of fields, such as government employment and government contracting. Among experts on welfare, even those who shared his sympathies for the poor, Reich's views were controversial. The law professor Joel Handler, for example, found that "Reich's strategy is quite clear. What he wants to do, in essence, is elevate the position of the welfare recipient to a position similar to that of a person whose business interests are regulated by government." But Handler thought the strategy doomed to failure, because it ignored the fact that even businesspeople, whose property rights were firmly recognized, were in practice regulated much more by informal and mostly lawless administrative discretion than by formal adjudication. If the law on paper that ostensibly governed knowledgeable and powerful economic actors had little practical effect, Handler asked, why should one expect anything better from welfare?[11]

Despite this skepticism, however, "The New Property" proved extraordinarily influential—by one count, it is the fourth most cited law review article of all time. Part of Reich's influence was no doubt attributable to his timing. The legal culture of the 1960s was unusually receptive to innovative constitutional arguments on behalf of marginalized groups. A new right for the poor proposed twenty years earlier or later would have reached a very different audience. Meanwhile the welfare system was expanding rapidly. Public expenditure on social welfare programs nearly tripled between 1960 and 1970, an increase much faster than that of the population or the GDP. Just as Reich claimed, government benefits really *were* a growing part of the economy, one that was commanding more attention. Questions of how to administer them were more important in the 1960s than they had ever been before.[12]

Much of Reich's influence is also attributable to another contemporary phenomenon, the rise of legal aid for the poor. Fifty years earlier, Reginald Heber Smith had counted only 62 full-time legal aid lawyers in the entire country, but with the arrival of federal funding in the 1960s, there were approximately 400 legal aid lawyers by 1965 and 2,400 by 1968. A theory of property published in an academic law journal would have been of little use to the poor themselves. Few would have read it or possessed the tools to put it to use. The new cohort of lawyers for the poor, on the other hand, *did* read it, and some of them put it to use right away in representing their clients. Changing the law through the courts requires a support structure of lawyers willing and able to litigate a single issue repeatedly. "The New Property" was published just at the moment when, for the first time in American history, there were enough legal aid lawyers to make a difference.[13]

Due Process Run Wild

The lawyers who filed the suit that became *Goldberg v. Kelly* were affiliated with MFY Legal Services in New York. MFY stood for Mobilization for Youth, an organization founded in 1962 to address juvenile delinquency, with funding from the federal government, the City of New York, Columbia University, and the Ford Foundation. Within a few years, MFY's legal unit expanded its field to include poverty generally, and cases involving the denial or termination of welfare benefits formed a major part of its work. In 1967 MFY lawyers began crafting legal arguments to support a requirement of a hearing before benefits could be terminated. Only then did they begin searching for clients.[14]

Poor people with harrowing stories were not hard to find. John Kelly, who would become the lead plaintiff, had become disabled in a car accident in 1966. His only subsistence was a welfare check of $80.05 every two weeks. A city caseworker ordered Kelly to move to a residential hotel, but when Kelly moved out a few days later—the hotel was inhabited by drug addicts and drunkards—the caseworker stopped his checks. Kelly went to visit the caseworker but she refused to see him. The city later claimed that Kelly's case had been closed because he had disappeared. By the time Kelly reached MFY, he was destitute and living on the street. Other clients had similar experiences. Alma Colburn received benefits for herself and her son under the Aid to Families with Dependent Children program, but her benefits were terminated on the grounds that she was living with a man and had a bank account she had failed to report. In fact, she was not living with a man—he had merely driven her to the hospital when she was ill—and she had not reported the bank account because it contained less than five dollars. Juan De Jesus lost his benefits because he ostensibly drank and took drugs, but in fact he did neither. Esther Lett's AFDC benefits were cut off because the city Board of Education erroneously reported that Lett was employed there. When she went to the office where the Board of Education stored its records, to attempt to set the matter straight, she was forced to wait in vain all day. In the afternoon she fainted for lack of food. Stories of bureaucratic mistakes like these were depressingly common, mistakes that could easily lead to homelessness and illness.[15]

The necessary first step of the plaintiffs' legal argument was that the expectation of continuing to receive welfare benefits was a form of property. Had that not been true, the city would have been under no constitutional obligation to provide any sort of process. In perhaps the clearest sign that the new property was not all that new, the city did not even contest this point. The city's lawyers conceded in the trial court that welfare benefits were property and that the due process clause applied; they argued only that the city already *did* provide due process, in the form of hearings after benefits had been terminated. In the Supreme Court the city made the same concession. So did the City of San Francisco in the companion case of *Wheeler v. Montgomery,* argued the same day. So did the federal government, which participated in both cases on the cities' side. As a result, the briefing and oral argument before the Supreme Court scarcely mentioned the new property. The plaintiffs' lawyers in the New York case referred to it only once, in a footnote, while the plaintiffs' lawyers in the San Francisco case did not discuss it at all. The only ones to raise any doubts were the justices themselves. "Suppose a pension has been granted to a recipient, or whatever you call it, and the Congress or the Legislature wants to repeal it," one of the justices asked Peter Sitkin, the lawyer for the San Francisco plaintiffs. "Is it your position that the Constitution forbids it?" Sitkin had to say no.[16] He could not argue that government programs once established could never be changed. But that was a tricky part of the new property: if a pension could not be taken away from one person without first holding a hearing for that person to protest, why could a pension be taken away from thousands of people at once?

When the justices discussed the case after the oral argument, they discovered that no single view of the issue commanded a majority. On one extreme, William Douglas believed that any government gratuity of any kind is a "species of property" that could not be terminated without a hearing. Thurgood Marshall likely felt the same way. On the other extreme was Hugo Black, who felt strongly that welfare benefits are not property at all. The other five justices held a range of positions in the middle. (The Court had only eight members because Harry Blackmun had not yet filled the seat vacated by the resignation of Abe Fortas.) Warren Burger and Potter Stewart were willing to recognize welfare as a form of property, but they viewed the posttermination hearings New York and San Francisco already provided as enough process to satisfy the Constitution. Byron White and John Harlan thought that some kinds of government payments should be terminable without a hearing, but not welfare benefits, because of the harsh consequences to the indigent that could result from a mistaken termination. William Brennan also placed special importance on the fact that welfare recipients were so poor, although he was more certain than White and Harlan that welfare should be classified as property. The result was a 5–3 vote to require some kind of hearing before welfare benefits were terminated, but no rationale that would be completely satisfying to all five justices in the majority.[17]

Justice Brennan's majority opinion thus could not invoke the new property too strongly without losing the votes of White and Harlan. He accordingly trod much more lightly than Charles Reich had a few years earlier. The plaintiffs' constitutional claim "cannot be answered by an argument that public assistance benefits are a 'privilege' and not a 'right,'" Brennan explained. "Relevant constitutional constraints apply." This was a roundabout way of calling welfare property. Brennan used the word *property* only in a footnote, where he observed, in the guise of a tentative suggestion rather than an actual statement of the law, that "it may be realistic today to regard welfare entitlements as more like 'property' than a 'gratuity.' Much of the existing wealth in this country takes the form of rights that do not fall within traditional common-law concepts of property." Brennan followed with a long quotation from Reich, making the same point. Without much fanfare, government benefits had been redefined as a form of property.[18]

Justice Black was very upset. Eighty-three years old, near the end of his thirty-four years on the Court, Black was convinced that the majority was going terribly wrong in following the lead of Reich, his former law clerk. He could not sleep the first two nights after Brennan circulated a draft of his opinion. "He woke up at 3:00 A.M. and got up and talked," his wife recalled. "He said his mind was racing and he was 'writing' an opinion in his mind. . . . Hugo still couldn't sleep at 4:00, and so he got up and took a drink." At the office Black complained to his law clerks that his colleagues "have let their views of due process run wild." Some of that worry made it into his dissenting opinion. "It somewhat strains credulity to say that the government's promise of charity to an individual is property belonging to that individual when the government denies that the individual is honestly entitled to receive such a payment," Black insisted. "Although some recipients might be on the lists for payment wholly because of deliberate fraud on their part, the Court holds that the government is helpless and must continue, until after an evidentiary hearing, to pay money that it does not owe, never has owed, and never could owe. I do not believe there is any provision in our Constitution that should thus paralyze the government's efforts to protect itself against making payments to people who are not entitled to them." Black warned that interpreting the due process clause to require pretermination hearings was only likely to harm the poor, by making the government wary of granting benefits in the first place before making an exhaustive investigation of a claimant's eligibility. "The operation of a welfare state is a new experiment for our Nation," Black concluded. "New experiments in carrying out a welfare program should not be frozen into our constitutional structure."[19]

Goldberg involved a technical legal question, so it did not receive attention in the press proportionate to its importance. The *New York Times,* for example, ran three stories about the Court the day after *Goldberg* was published, but none mentioned *Goldberg*. (The stories were about three new cases the Court agreed to hear, one on whether the Swedish film *I Am Curious (Yellow)* was obscene, one on whether states could constitutionally deny drinks to alcoholics, and one on whether banks could enter the mutual fund business.)[20] The reviews *Goldberg* did receive were sharply divided, unsurprisingly, based on the writer's political inclinations. George W. Beggs of Spokane, Washington, promptly wrote Brennan to express his happiness that there were judges "who are striving to protect and uphold the rights of people who are unfortunate enough to be in the clutches of arbitrary welfare administrators." On the other side, the *New York Daily News* called Brennan's opinion "a masterwork of its type: long on flowery social philosophizing and skimpy on legal precedent." The *Daily News* found in *Goldberg* "further proof, if any were needed, that the high court desperately needs a heavy infusion of strict-constructionist thinking to halt its dangerous practice of making, rather than interpreting, laws." The notion that welfare could be property was "twaddle" and "legalistic nit-picking," snorted the conservative columnist Andrew Tully. "But the times are singular, to put it mildly," Tully observed. "After all, dope addicts are permitted to remain on the relief rolls so they can buy the stuff of their addiction. And this is still a curious, Warren-like Supreme Court, which still seems determined to meddle in

and usurp the functions of the government's other two branches."[21] After more than a decade of rapid constitutional change, the battle lines
were long since drawn.

A Legitimate Claim of Entitlement

One effect of *Goldberg* was to increase the cost of administering welfare
programs. New York City began paying an extra $4 million per month
to recipients the city believed were not eligible for payments but whose
hearings had not yet been held. Requests for hearings were "a new
hustle," complained Jule Sugarman, the city's human resources administrator, an attempt to "virtually smother the system in paperwork."
Then there was the cost of the hearings themselves. Twenty years later,
because of *Goldberg*, the state was holding eight hundred of them every
working day. Maybe this was money that could otherwise have gone
directly to the poor. Then again, maybe it was money well spent: in these
hearings, recipients prevailed 80 percent of the time.[22]

It did not take long for *Goldberg*'s adoption of the "new property" to
prompt lawsuits claiming the status of property for other kinds of
government-derived wealth.[23] Were drivers' licenses a kind of property?
Was government employment property? What about the right to a public
education? Public utility service? A horse-training license? The ability to
file a lawsuit? The new property either promised or threatened, depending on one's political views, to swallow up much of the conduct of government by creating an elaborate body of federal constitutional law
regulating precisely how public benefits could be allocated.

The question of how to define property returned to the Supreme
Court two years after *Goldberg*, in a pair of cases involving state college
professors whose contracts had not been renewed. Robert Sindermann
and David Roth were both political scientists, Sindermann at Odessa Junior College in Texas and Roth at Wisconsin State University–Oshkosh.
Sindermann taught under a series of one-year contracts until 1969,
when the college declined to employ him for another year. Roth had
only a single one-year contract, for the 1968–1969 school year, a contract the university did not renew. Neither Sindermann nor Roth was
given any reasons for not being rehired, and neither was provided a
hearing at which to contest the decision. In both cases there was reason

to suspect retaliation. Both teachers had been outspoken critics of their schools. Sindermann was president of the Texas Junior College Teachers Association, and in that capacity he had publicly criticized the governing board of Odessa Junior College for its decision not to convert the college to a four-year institution. Roth had publicly criticized the administration of his university for suspending ninety-four black students after a protest. The lawsuits filed by Sindermann and Roth both alleged that their teaching jobs were their property, and that by ceasing to employ them without stating reasons or providing a hearing, the states had deprived them of property without due process.[24]

Sindermann's and Roth's cases were just the tip of an iceberg. Reaching the Court at the same time were cases involving more college professors, some high school teachers, a public librarian, and a substitute teacher at a middle school.[25] Many more cases were being litigated in the lower courts, which had reached conflicting outcomes on similar facts. Members of the Supreme Court were acutely aware of what *Goldberg* had unleashed.

Thurgood Marshall thought it a good thing. "In my view, every citizen who applies for a government job is entitled to it," Marshall explained, "unless the government can establish some reason for denying the employment. That is the 'property' right that I believe is protected by the Fourteenth Amendment." His rationale could have been written by Charles Reich. "Employment is one of the greatest, if not the greatest, benefits that governments offer in modern-day life," Marshall reasoned. "When something as valuable as the opportunity to work is at stake, the government may not reward some citizens and not others without demonstrating that its actions are fair and equitable." But most of the justices were nervous about expanding property so far. "To what extent will courts review university determinations?" Byron White asked his colleagues during their discussion of the two cases. He declared that he "would stay out of this as much as possible." Recognizing every government job as the employee's property "would burden the system," Lewis Powell worried, because "it is easy to claim a constitutional right in every case." Warren Burger insisted that "the issue whether teachers—and all other state employees—should have a property interest in re-employment . . . should be determined under state contract law" rather than federal constitutional law.[26] It was clear that a majority of the justices were eager to retreat from some of the implications of the new property.

The Court accordingly discussed property far more carefully than it had two years before in *Goldberg*. "To have a property interest in a benefit," Potter Stewart wrote for the majority in *Roth*, "a person clearly must have more than an abstract need or desire for it. He must have more than a unilateral expectation of it. He must, instead, have a legitimate claim of entitlement to it." The simple fact that a job (or a license, or welfare benefits) might be valuable was not enough to call it property. It would deserve the status of property only if it actually belonged to the person claiming it. And how was a court to know whether it did? "Property interests," Stewart continued, "are created and their dimensions are defined by existing rules or understandings that stem from an independent source such as state law." Property was whatever the law defined as property. On this definition, Roth's job was not property, because he had no legitimate expectation of being rehired for another year. Sindermann's was, but only because his college had an informal practice of conferring permanent tenure on successful teachers, so he *did* have a legitimate expectation of continuing employment.[27]

If the "new property" of *Goldberg* had raised concerns that the term might encompass everything, the newer and more limited property of *Roth* and *Sindermann* raised the opposite concern, that it might encompass nothing at all. Property would not be defined by the conscience of judges; it would be defined instead by "an independent source" such as the law. But the law was the source of procedures as well as substantive benefits. The same law that allowed poor people to receive welfare, for example, also set forth a procedure for evaluating whether claimants were entitled to benefits. The law that established a state college also provided procedures for hiring and firing teachers. Looking to the law for the contours of a property right thus threatened to be a circular enterprise, because a state could always claim that the property right at issue was limited by the procedures it provided for the right's enforcement. We didn't simply promise this person a *job*, the argument would go; we promised him a job with minimal protections against being fired, and that's exactly what he got. If that was to be a winning argument, the due process clause would lack any independent effect. Recipients of government-derived wealth would be entitled only to those procedures the law already provided.

William Rehnquist was one of the two newest members of the Court. He and Lewis Powell had been sworn in only eleven days before *Roth* and *Sindermann* were argued. For the next decade, Rehnquist pressed this argument, that the contours of a property right were defined in part by the procedures the law provided for its enforcement. "Where the grant of a substantive right is inextricably intertwined with the limitations on the procedures which are to be employed in determining that right," he declared in 1974, two years after *Roth* and *Sindermann,* "a litigant . . . must take the bitter with the sweet." Rehnquist was denying a full trial-type hearing to Wayne Kennedy, a federal employee fired under regulations explicitly providing for a more limited kind of hearing in cases like his. But Rehnquist could never persuade a majority of his colleagues to go along with the theory. It would eventually be put to rest in 1985, in a case recognizing as property jobs as a public school security guard and a school bus mechanic. "It is settled that the 'bitter with the sweet' approach misconceives the constitutional guarantee," Justice White wrote for the majority. "The categories of substance and procedure are distinct. Were the rule otherwise, the Clause would be reduced to a mere tautology. 'Property' cannot be defined by the procedures provided for its deprivation any more than can life or liberty."[28] Property under the due process clause would continue to have an independent substantive existence.

The location of its boundaries has remained a matter of controversy right up to the present. The Court has found that drivers' licenses and horse-training licenses are property, that utility service and public education are property, that a job as a probationary police officer is not property, and that the right to file a lawsuit is property but the right to have the police enforce a restraining order is not. None of these decisions has been unanimous. The significance of the property-or-not question has been substantially diminished, in any event, by another line of cases in which the Court has required only minimal procedures for the deprivation of those interests that do amount to property.[29] We have ended up somewhere in the middle, with more procedural requirements than before *Goldberg v. Kelly* but fewer than many people expected in the light of *Goldberg.*

In retrospect, what has been the effect of the "new property"? Some deem it a success: the law professor Owen Fiss, for example, calls *Goldberg* "a tribute to our own little Enlightenment—that extraordinary age of American law when we understood the promise of public reason and boldly acted on that understanding." But others are more critical. Charles Reich lived to be bitterly disappointed with the rightward turn of American political life. "Thirty years later, it is clear that the law has failed to protect the economic citizenship of individuals," he lamented at a symposium marking the anniversary of his article. "The concept of 'new property' for the great mass of working Americans has been rejected." Sylvia Law, who skipped the Woodstock Festival in the summer of 1969 to work on the Supreme Court brief in *Goldberg v. Kelly,* felt the same way. Twenty years after *Goldberg,* she observed, "it is impossible to be sanguine. Poverty may be deeper in the 1990s than ever before in our history. Homelessness, as well as income, divide us. . . . The federal courts, high and low, are as unsympathetic to the claims of the poor as at any time in this century."[30] From the left, the problem with the new property was that it had never been fully implemented.

From the right, the problem was that it had been tried at all. "Use of the courts to expand individual entitlements in this fashion is a prime example of good intentions leading to bad consequences," Francis Fukuyama diagnosed. "Before the application of the 14th Amendment to welfare, social workers had a certain flexibility in distributing benefits: they could demand certain standards of moral behavior from their clients." With the new property, Fukuyama complained, government lost the power to enforce morality among the poor, which he viewed as one of the causes of the "breakdown in American civil society" characterized by "the loosening of moral restraints on sex and drugs."[31]

But the most telling retrospective critiques of the new property were pragmatic rather than ideological. Welfare recipients were poor and poorly educated, and invoking the right to a hearing was difficult and time consuming, so the large majority of recipients never exercised the rights they possessed on paper. The hearings that did take place were conducted by the same overworked welfare departments that made the initial eligibility determinations. In practice, the new property had little effect on the way claimants experienced the welfare system. The system itself became more bureaucratized. The process of applying for benefits became more complex. Social workers exercising professional discretion were largely replaced by clerks applying inflexible rules. Error rates in initial eligibility determinations declined, but administrative expenses increased substantially, which drew resources away from the poor. As one comprehensive review concluded, "it is still the case that the system fails to deliver benefits for a substantial portion of people, including some of the most needy, who meet its substantive standards of need."[32] In the end the new property was simply not as powerful a tool as its proponents hoped or its opponents feared it would be.

—•—

12

Owning Life

SOME of the most difficult property questions of the late twentieth century involved the ownership of living things. Should human body parts be treated as property? Could one own new life-forms, or even portions of the human genome? In one sense these were new questions, thrust into popular consciousness by rapid technological change. In another sense, however, they were not so new. The late twentieth century was not the first time Americans had contemplated the ownership and sale of human bodies and their parts, nor was it the first time they had created new kinds of living organisms. In drawing on more than a century of experience, Americans ended up with some very old answers to some new questions.

Like Fenders in an Auto Junkyard

The first important question concerning property rights in human bodies was about corpses. Whether a human corpse could be property was a question frequently debated in the second half of the nineteenth century. There was a flourishing trade in dead bodies to satisfy the demands of medical schools for cadavers.[1] Corpses were often obtained unlawfully, by digging them up without anyone's consent, but not always; sometimes people sold their own bodies before they died, and over time states increasingly authorized doctors to take the unclaimed bodies of the poor. Was a contract for the sale of a corpse enforceable in court? The question also arose in less dramatic contexts. When a corpse was mishandled in transit, could the next of kin recover for the damage to their property? When family members disagreed about burial arrangements, whose wishes should be respected, and why? By the end of the century, because of recurring cases like these, there was a learned literature on whether dead humans could be owned, and there was nearly a consensus on the answer.

It was a difficult question because instinct and reason pulled in different directions. One the one hand, there was something intuitively unsettling about treating the human body as property. "To make such venerated remains the absolute property of anyone, in the sense of objective appropriation, would be abhorrent to every impulse and feeling of our natures," declared one judge. "Reverence for the dead has become a universal and most sacred sentiment, one which would revolt at the idea of their remains becoming property." This view was so widely shared that virtually all writers concluded that there could be no property in a corpse. A dead body could not be sold like an ordinary commodity, it could not be used as collateral to secure a loan, and it could not be seized to satisfy a debt. "To permit such a contract to be made would be to outrage decency, humanity, and public policy," another judge insisted. The only court in the nation to classify corpses as property was the Indiana Supreme Court. "The bodies of the dead belong to the surviving relations, in the order of inheritance, as property," the court maintained in the course of deciding that an Indianapolis man had the right to bury his deceased son in a cemetery of his choosing. "They have the right to dispose of them as such, within restrictions analogous to those by which the disposition of other property may be regulated."[2] But this statement was roundly criticized, and it was not followed in any other state. In the rest of the country, the dead were not property.

This rule felt right, but it led to some hard questions. What if a body were stolen? It wouldn't be theft, because the supposed thief wouldn't have taken anyone's property. Or what if an undertaker, instead of burying a corpse properly, decided to mutilate it, or to leave it naked out on the highway? He wouldn't be liable for interfering with any property belonging to the next of kin. In one South Carolina case, a man was murdered and his body left on the railroad tracks. Trains ran him over three times before anyone noticed. The administrator of his estate sued the railroad for negligently mutilating the body, but the South Carolina Supreme Court held that no recovery was permissible even if the railroad had run over the body on purpose. "To entitle one to bring action for an injury to any specific object or thing, he must have a property therein," the court reasoned. "If he has no such property, he can have no cause of action, however flagrant or reprehensible the act complained of may be." The administrator was allowed to sue for damage to the deceased's clothing and his watch, which *were* property, but not to the deceased's body.[3]

Calling the body a kind of property seemed to desecrate the notion of being human, but *not* calling it property threatened to remove any legal penalties from the defilement of a corpse. American lawyers resolved this dilemma in two different ways in the late nineteenth century. One technique was simply to assert that whether a corpse was property was irrelevant to deciding concrete cases. "The right to the custody of a thing does not necessarily involve the idea of property in the thing," claimed the New York lawyer John Corwin. The next of kin might have enough *custody* to support a lawsuit for mishandling a dead body, even if they didn't own it. "The question as to whether the remains of the deceased are the subject of property, whichever way it may be answered," Corwin concluded, "need not embarrass or control the decision of any issue as to the right to control the funeral, protect the sacred dust of the dead, or select the place of interment." When Lena Larson's dead husband was dissected without her permission, the Minnesota Supreme Court allowed her suit against the doctor to proceed for this reason. "This whole subject is only obscured and confused by discussing the question whether a corpse is property in the ordinary commercial sense," the court insisted. "In this country it is, so far as we know, universally held that those who are entitled to the possession and custody of it for purposes of a decent burial have certain legal rights to and in it, which the law recognizes and will protect." Whether or not her husband's body was her property, Larson had "a legal right to its possession for the purposes of preservation and burial," and "any interference with that right, by mutilating or otherwise disturbing the body, is an actionable wrong."[4]

The other method of resolving the dilemma was much more common. If a dead person's surviving family members lacked a property right in his body, the Rhode Island Supreme Court held in 1872, they nevertheless had a duty to ensure a proper burial, which implied a corresponding obligation on the part of others to refrain from interfering.

The corpse "may therefore be considered as a sort of *quasi* property," the court concluded, "and it would be discreditable to any system of law not to provide a remedy in such a case." This idea of "quasi property" split the difference between the unacceptable poles of calling the body property and allowing others to defile it. The idea was soon copied by courts in many other states. When Hamp Wilson died in Atlanta, his widow Penina hired the Louisville and Nashville Railroad to transport his body to the town of Warrenton, where it would be buried. The railroad left his coffin out in the rain for several hours en route. By the time it reached Warrenton, Wilson's corpse was in bad condition, and Penina sued the railroad for damages. The human body was not property, the court held, but it was quasi property, and that was enough to allow the suit to proceed. "If this is not true," the court recognized, "for stealing or wrongfully withholding the custody of a dead body there might be . . . no method of recovering or restoring the body to its proper resting place."[5] The concept of quasi property allowed lawsuits to be resolved in ways that were intuitively appealing without having to declare that the human body could be owned.

By 1911, when the Arkansas lawyer W. C. Rodgers summarized the law governing "property rights in human bodies," quasi property was already well established. "The body of a human being after death occupies a somewhat unique position in law," Rodgers explained. "In a sense, it is property, yet in a general sense it is not." Bodies couldn't be bought and sold, but people had a right to direct that their own bodies be donated for scientific research after death. Bodies weren't supposed to have any monetary value, but when a corpse was mutilated the relatives could recover monetary damages for their mental anguish. Bodies couldn't be owned, but a person with rightful custody over a corpse could recover it from someone wrongfully possessing it. In short, "the law recognizes a *quasi* property status of human bodies," a status that mediated between the competing reasons to classify the body as property or as something other than property.[6]

A similar dilemma would recur when technological change permitted living people to sell ever more intimate parts of their bodies to others. There was a very old trade in human hair for wig making, involving professional hair dealers who would travel from town to town offering to pay women for their hair. In one oft-repeated story, Richard Arkwright, the inventor of the spinning frame (an important machine in the early textile industry), got his start as a hair buyer, negotiating with women throughout Lancashire. The New York *Evening Post* reported in the 1870s that hair sold for three dollars per ounce, or twice that for tresses of forty inches or longer. Around the same time a newspaper in Scranton, Pennsylvania, quoted a price of $75 per pound. There was never any call to abolish the hair trade, but it provoked some unease, because selling hair was understood as a last resort of women desperate for money. "There are heart-breaking things we have to do," one dealer admitted. "It is not true, as a rule, that people with money are apt to be in need of hair, and that people without means have abundant crops, but it usually seems so to us." In popular works of fiction like Victor Hugo's *Les Misérables* and Louisa May Alcott's *Little Women*, both first published in the 1860s, and the O. Henry short story "The Gift of the Magi," from 1906, women sell their hair when they have no other way to earn money.[7] The treatment of hair as property could seem unsettling, not because of any higher value placed on hair itself, but because the prospect of selling hair seemed to place pressure on poor women that was not felt by others.

The same was true of human skin. When skin grafting became a common treatment for victims of burns and industrial accidents around the turn of the twentieth century, the demand for skin was satisfied in part by paying donors. "I like the work, if you call it work," one Chicago donor explained in 1910. "Frequently I give up as much as twenty-four inches of skin in one day. Then, of course, I have to rest quietly for a week or two until it grows on again." The surgeons cut the skin in inch-wide strips from his arms and paid three to five dollars per square inch. Skin grew back, like hair, and there was nothing particularly sacred about it, but like hair it was usually sold by those who lacked alternatives, and it was this inequality that drew criticism—probably more in the case of skin because of the pain associated with a procedure in which anesthesia was not always used. The *New York Times* told of "the indigent lady who offered to sell thirty inches of her skin to a hospital for $30," a price the paper thought far too low. "The penury of this woman is pitiable," the story concluded, "and we trust she may find relief."[8]

Breast milk also became a commodity in the early twentieth century. The ancient trade of wet nursing all but disappeared, replaced by the sale of bottled human milk (and later artificial milk). Like wet nurses, the women who supplied milk were often paid for it—in Boston, approximately $4.20 per week for a quart daily, or about half the pay of a live-in wet nurse. Like wet nurses, milk donors were often poor women with few alternatives. The sale of milk thus provoked the same concerns about inequality as the sale of hair and skin, concerns with an even sharper edge because milk suppliers, after earning a living, were sometimes unable to produce enough milk to feed their own infants at home.[9]

When blood transfusion became common after the First World War, the same issue arose. By 1931 the New York City Health Department counted eight thousand people who regularly sold blood to hospitals in the city alone. A few years later the professional blood sellers even unionized, under the umbrella of the American Federation of Labor, in order to bargain for higher prices. "It is the easiest way I know of making $30," remarked Monte Harrington, an undergraduate at the University of California's new southern branch in Los Angeles. "It gives me the feeling that I have not only earned my money, but that I have actually done a good deed." A substantial percentage of the nation's blood donors were compensated in some form well into the second half of the century.[10]

Again, though, many were uncomfortable thinking of blood as an object of commerce. Transfusion was a great advance, one early editorialist reckoned, but "if the selling of one's blood for such a purpose shall ever become a business matter of bargain and sale," he worried, "a new and uncertain factor may enter into the question." Unlike hair or even skin (but like mother's milk), folk tradition suggested that blood bore something of an individual's unique characteristics. Blood felt more like a part of one's body, so selling it seemed uncomfortably close to selling the body itself. "A donor must feel pretty much like a Shylock the first time he sells his blood," one critic charged. "It would be heroic to give it—that would be sacrifice—but selling it—how could that ever be?" Blood could save lives, but was it right to profit from doing so? And many professional blood donors sold blood for want of an alternative, so selling blood once again seemed to impose unfair pressures on the poor. Donors were "unemployed, desperate men forced to sell their blood because it was the only way left to them to earn an honest dollar," one regular donor lamented. "Most of them sold blood for the same reason many women became prostitutes."[11]

Despite this discomfort, blood was unmistakably a kind of property, although judges were at first reluctant to accept the full implications of treating it as such. In the early 1950s, when Gussie Perlmutter sued New York's Beth David Hospital for transfusing tainted blood during an operation, the court conceded that "the property or title to certain items of medical material"—that is, blood—"may be transferred, so to speak, from the hospital to the patient during the course of medical treatment." But the court held that the transaction was not a "sale" of blood, so Perlmutter could not sue under New York's Personal Property Law. Rather, the transfer of blood was incidental to the provision of professional service, a field not covered by the Personal Property Law. The dissenting judge analogized the hospital's provision of blood to a restaurant's provision of food, which *was* recognized as a sale of property. But this sort of squeamishness would soon evaporate. In 1980, the federal Tax Court reviewed the income tax return of Margaret Green, who earned a living from the sale of her blood plasma. This was income from "property held for sale to customers in the ordinary course of business," the court straightforwardly held. "The rarity of petitioner's blood made the processing and packaging of her blood plasma a profitable undertaking, just as it is profitable for other entrepreneurs to purchase hen's eggs, bee's honey, cow's milk, or sheep's wool for processing and distribution. Although we recognize the traditional sanctity of the human body, we can find no reason to legally distinguish the sale of these raw products of nature from the sale of petitioner's blood plasma."[12] Blood, like hair, skin, and milk before it, was property.

One reason was that it was hard to get enough of it without paying donors. It was discomforting to pay for blood, but it was even more discomforting to allow patients to die for want of an adequate supply, so qualms about treating blood as property were a luxury the medical system often could not afford. A second reason was that the recurring concerns about unfair pressures on the poor were not easily translatable into policy. Banning the sale of blood, for example, would hardly have improved the lot of the poor, and indeed it might have made their lives worse, by removing a source of income.

Technological change produced ever more difficult questions. Artificial insemination was first practiced on a significant scale in the 1930s. Almost from the beginning, sperm was purchased from donors and sold to recipients. "Since the human male attains his highest fertility during his twenties," *Time* magazine explained in 1938, a sperm bank's donors were primarily "medical students and interns who are glad to get the $25 fee per insemination." Did that make sperm a kind of property? Within the industry it was treated that way. "We do not own the semen," insisted the director of one sperm bank. "The semen remains the property of the client." In the courts, however, the answer was not so clear. When William Kane committed suicide in 1991, he left behind a partner named Deborah Hecht, two college-age children from a prior marriage, and fifteen vials of frozen sperm in Los Angeles, with directions that the sperm be given to Hecht so that if she wished, the two could have a child. She did want to have a child, but Kane's children sought to have the sperm destroyed. Was the sperm property? If not, the probate court would have lacked any authority to direct its disposition, because the court's jurisdiction extended only to the "property" of a decedent. If it was property, was it subject to the same rules as any other kind of property? The court found a solution midway between property and nonproperty, with reasoning that recalled the "quasi property" courts had devised a century earlier to deal with rights in corpses. Kane "had an interest in his sperm which falls within the broad definition of property," but that did not mean that the law governing other kinds of property would apply. "A man's sperm," the court reasoned, was "not the same as a quarter of land, a cache of cash, or a favorite limousine. Rules appropriate to the disposition of the latter are not necessarily appropriate for the former." Sperm was a unique form of property, governed by its own set of rules. Hecht was entitled to the sperm, the court concluded, but that did not mean she could do with it as she wished. "Even Hecht lacks the legal entitlement to give, sell, or otherwise dispose of decedent's sperm. She and she alone can use it. . . . Thus, in a very real sense, to the extent that sperm is 'property' it is only 'property' for that one person." It was uncomfortable to think of sperm as property but it was impractical not to. Like dead bodies had been, sperm was property for some purposes but not for others.[13]

The 1990s saw the emergence of a similar market in human eggs, which are much more difficult to donate and therefore much more expensive. The same ethical dilemma arose. "If we don't believe in buying and selling babies, then why are we comfortable buying and selling sperm and eggs?" wondered the philosopher Arthur Caplan. The next step in this direction was the ability to store frozen fertilized eggs early in the process of cell division, at a time when they consist of only a few cells, for later transfer to a woman's uterus. Preembryos are not bought and sold, but custody over them has been a disputed issue in some cases, which means the property question has come up yet again. In the first case to raise the issue, the court treated them as property without much discussion, in part because the parties themselves referred to them as their property, and it applied the ordinary rules of property law. A few years later, a different court sharply disagreed. "We conclude that preembryos are not, strictly speaking, either 'persons' or 'property,' but occupy an interim category that entitles them to special respect because of their potential for human life," the court held. In practice, that meant that the court did not apply the ordinary law of property, but rather decided for itself that the interest of one ex-spouse (who wished to have them destroyed) outweighed the interest of the other (who wanted to donate them to a childless couple). The court acknowledged that the case would have been harder if one of the spouses had wished to use them and had no other way of having a child.[14]

From hair to blood to preembryos, medical innovations had allowed for the transfer of parts of the human body from one person to another and had raised increasingly difficult legal questions. Blood had been classified as property, sperm as a sort of quasi property, and preembryos as property in one case and not property in another. There remained one realm of medical practice in which biological material was unambiguously *not* property—organ transplants—but even that decision grew increasingly controversial over time.

Human organ transplants began in the 1950s with kidneys. Successful transplants of other organs followed in the 1960s, including livers, pancreases, and hearts. Organ transplants raised the possibility of all sorts of troubling new transactions, in which the living might sell their kidneys while alive or the use of their other organs upon their death, or the relatives of the recently dead might capitalize on organs no longer in use. Several states moved quickly to ban such transactions. Congress then prohibited the sale of organs as part of the National Organ Transplant Act of 1984. The 1987 revision of the Uniform Anatomical Gift Act, drafted by the National Conference of Commissioners on Uniform State Laws and adopted by most states, made the sale of organs a felony under state law as well. These provisions were uncontroversial. There was scarcely any political support for allowing a market in organs.[15]

Hair, blood, sperm, eggs—these were renewable, but a kidney or a heart was gone forever, and that was enough for most people to draw a line. There were two main reasons for opposing the treatment of transplantable organs as property, both of which were amplified versions of the types of discomfort often felt with selling blood or sperm. The first concern was that there was something immoral about thinking of the human body and its parts as marketable commodities. The body was too sacred to be treated as "ordinary commodity-property like VCR's or designer jeans," maintained one critic. Or as Representative Henry Waxman put it at the hearings on the National Organ Transplant Act, "human organs should not be treated like fenders in an auto junkyard." In popular thought the body, even after death, was still very much the person who inhabited it while alive.[16] Selling organs was too close to selling people.

The second concern with markets in human organs was that they would facilitate the exploitation of the poor, who would face inequitable pressures to sell their own body parts and those of their relatives. "The danger is that poor foreign nationals would be manipulated, no matter how freely they may seem to have consented, into mutilating themselves for the sake of financial gain," testified the bioethicist Warren Reich. "For the profit offered them for sacrificing a kidney (say, $10,000) might be ten to twenty times the per capita income in that country." Meanwhile the prices of organs might make them available only to the affluent, an outcome inconsistent with the often-expressed principle (although one perhaps less often realized in practice) that access to life-saving medical care should not depend on the ability to pay.[17]

This reluctance to treat body parts as property has drawn sharp criticism. The demand for transplantable organs far exceeds the supply, and doubtless the prospect of compensation would persuade more people to be organ donors than are currently willing to volunteer. The prohibition on sales has produced a gruesome black market in cadavers and their components. So far, however, this concern has not prevailed over the apparently widespread revulsion at the thought of markets in body parts.[18]

The question of property in human organs has popped up in a few other contexts, with varying outcomes. In the famous case of *Moore v. University of California,* physicians at the UCLA Medical Center used a leukemia patient's blood samples and excised spleen to produce a cell line that proved to be worth millions of dollars because of its potential for contributing to cancer treatments. John Moore, the patient, found out only after the fact, when his doctors aroused his suspicions by asking him to sign vaguely worded consent forms and insisting that he fly repeatedly from Seattle to Los Angeles for follow-up visits. Moore sued UCLA on several theories, one of which was that by using his cells without his permission, the doctors had taken property from him. A divided California Supreme Court disagreed. "Plaintiff has asked us to recognize and enforce a right to sell one's own body tissue *for profit*," worried Justice Armand Arabian. "He entreats us to regard the human vessel—the single most venerated and protected subject in any civilized society—as equal with the basest commercial commodity. He urges us to commingle the sacred with the profane." The dissenting judges pointed out that declining to classify human cells as property was hardly a way of preventing the emergence of commerce in those cells; it merely shifted the profits from patients to their doctors.[19] For the majority, however, there was something about the human body that rendered such utilitarian calculations distasteful.

Meanwhile there have been several cases in which family members have sued coroners and hospitals for removing corneas from the recently dead for transplant against the wishes of their next of kin. Courts have held that corneas *are* property. "Under traditional common law principles," one court reasoned, "the parents had exclusive and legitimate claims of entitlement to possess, control, dispose and prevent the violation of the corneas and other parts of the bodies of their deceased children. . . . These are all important components of the group of rights by which property is defined."[20] If it was repulsive to contemplate a market in organs, it was even more repulsive to allow them to be snatched away without permission. Whether the human body and its parts were property thus depended heavily on the context. They were property for some purposes but not for others, just as they had always been.

A Better Mouse

There is another way to own life—not the physical body or its parts, but the intellectual property in new kinds of living organisms. In this domain the question of property has been just as controversial, but the law has moved more quickly and more decisively in the direction of recognizing property rights in living things.

The deliberate breeding of new varieties of plants and animals is an ancient practice, but until relatively recently innovators were not awarded exclusive rights in their creations. They could protect their investments with the use of trade names and by keeping their methods secret, but competitors who obtained a new hybrid were free to use it or sell it themselves. In an era when farming was a small-scale local activity, and when farmers obtained their own seeds from the previous year's plants, there were no players who stood to gain much from patents in plants or animals, and there was no organized political force capable of backing an effort to change the law.[21]

Those circumstances changed in the second half of the nineteenth century, as agriculture consolidated, farmers began producing more for the market, and farmers increasingly began to acquire seeds and plants from seed companies rather than generating them on their own. Whether to extend the patent system to new plants became "a prolific source of discussion," as one horticultural magazine put it. By 1881, a special committee of the Missouri Horticultural Society, appointed to report on the question, had to concede that it "has not been able to add anything new to the recent full discussion of the subject" because everything had already been said.[22]

Proponents of patent protection argued that breeders of useful new plants were rarely compensated for all the good they brought into the world. "Very few persons in this country who had originated valuable varieties of fruit had received any direct benefit from it," concluded the American Convention of Nurserymen. Even the Worden grape, "the best black Grape grown in America," had earned Mr. Worden almost nothing. The botanist David Fairchild, who for many years directed the U.S. Agriculture Department's section of foreign seed and plant introduction, lamented that "plant breeders, who are adding countless billions to the wealth of the world," nevertheless received nothing more than "the casual recognition which people generally accord to those who give them something for nothing." It was hardly fair that "inventors have a protected property in their brain-work and skill; authors copyright their books; but originators of new plants and fruits are not encouraged," complained one New York breeder. "And why not?"[23]

The most common argument in favor of property rights in new plants, and the most persuasive, was that plant breeders needed the same encouragement to make investments in useful innovations that the patent law gave to inventors in other fields. The public benefited from more productive strains of wheat, hardier fruit trees, and more beautiful flowers, but such advances were expensive. "If every man who discovered a hardy variety of plant or originated a new kind more valuable than the old, could secure large returns for his work," imagined W. M. Hays, the assistant secretary of agriculture, "we would soon have the needed number doing advanced work." Joseph Rossman, an examiner in the Patent Office, estimated that it "takes from ten to fifteen years to perfect a new plant so that it can be placed on the market. It took [Luther] Burbank 19 years to perfect the amaryllis and over 20 years to give us a new hybrid lily. In developing the white blackberry over 65,000 hybrid bushes were grown and eliminated."[24] But would enough breeders undertake all this painstaking labor without some hope of reward?

Among breeders there was enough opposition to plant patents to delay their enactment for a long time. Part of the opposition stemmed from dissatisfaction with the changing nature of horticulture. With patents, feared one breeder, horticulture would "lose much of its character as a science and art, and lessen its hold upon those who view it not as a commercial speculation but as a source of pure enjoyment and delightful recreation. . . . The mistake" made by advocates of patents "is in admitting that horticulture has no higher aim than dollars and cents." Some opposed patents on the ground that innovation in plant breeding was more a matter of luck than invention. New plants were usually "accidental varieties," insisted one gardener, "that are as much a surprise to the cultivator or producer as to others." Others worried that a system of patents for plants would be impossible to administer, because there would be no way to prove that an ostensibly original flower or fruit was truly new. "Temporary variations occur with all kinds of fruits and plants," charged one critic, "and the greatest horticulturist or botanist that ever lived is very likely to be misled by them, and to pronounce old and familiar plants to be new varieties." How could patent clerks ever do any better?[25] Bills that would have provided patent protection to plant breeders died in Congress repeatedly in the early twentieth century.

Eventually, however, this sort of opposition was overwhelmed by the growth of the firms engaged in providing plants to farmers. Letters poured into Congress from a well-organized coalition of nurseries and trade organizations. Plant patents were "of deep interest to the fruit industry," declared the chairman of the International Apple Shippers Association. Patents would "increase employment on the farm." The result was the Plant Patent Act of 1930, which, for the first time in American history, provided patent protection for new varieties of plants. The statute embodied a compromise: it protected only the right to propagate plants asexually, by cuttings, and not the right to propagate by seeds. It omitted protection for potatoes and Jerusalem artichokes, which were propagated asexually by the same part of the plant that was sold as food, because enforcing the law for these plants would have required making a difficult distinction between sales for planting and sales for eating. These exclusions nevertheless left a wide range of fruits and flowers covered by the Plant Patent Act. Of the first eight plant patents granted in 1931–1932, five were for new kinds of roses, one was for a new carnation, one was for a peach with a ripening period later than other varieties, and one was for a "thornless young dewberry."[26]

The burst of innovation in agriculture in the decades after World War II—the so-called Green Revolution—created incentives for the plant and seed industry to press for the extension of intellectual property rights to plants grown from seeds as well. Once again, the rationale was to encourage the development of new varieties of plants. "The absence of any form of legal protection for the originators of new plants which reproduce sexually has forced many companies to forgo comprehensive research programs," testified Floyd Ingersoll, the president of the American Seed Trade Association. "Experience indicates that when some form of protection is available, research funds are made available by private industry."[27] These lobbying efforts yielded the Plant Variety Protection Act of 1970, which provided patentlike rights to breeders of new seed-grown plants.

Meanwhile a microbiologist named Ananda Chakrabarty, a staff scientist at General Electric in Schenectady, New York, was conducting research that would revolutionize patent law more than biology. Chakrabarty was "tinkering with *Pseudomonas* genes," he later recalled, in an effort to create a bacterium capable of breaking down crude oil into single-cell proteins. The original goal of his research had been to convert oil into food, but the rising cost of oil put an end to that; the goal became instead to invent a bacterium that could clean up oil spills. When Chakrabarty succeeded, GE's patent lawyer, Leo MaLossi, decided to apply for a patent for the new microorganism. This was an unorthodox decision, because the conventional view among patent lawyers was that living things were not patentable. The statute itself did not explicitly exclude living things, but in the political battles over plant patents, everyone on all sides had assumed that new plants were not already eligible for patents. The Patent and Trademark Office upheld this conventional view in 1973, when it rejected MaLossi's patent application on the ground that living organisms were not patentable.[28] But when the Court of Appeals reversed this decision, and held that Chakrabarty's new bacterium *was* patentable, the case arrived at the Supreme Court as the focus of considerable attention.

Diamond v. Chakrabarty (Sidney Diamond was the commissioner of patents and trademarks) raised two difficult questions, one of statutory interpretation and the other of public policy. To be entitled to a patent under the relevant provisions of the statute, an invention had to be a "manufacture" or a "composition of matter" that was "new and useful." There was no additional requirement that an invention be nonliving. If the Court interpreted the words of the statute literally, Chakrabarty would win. There was no dispute that his bacterium was both new and useful, and all agreed that it was not found in nature; rather, Chakrabarty had manufactured it. On the other hand, Congress had enacted the Plant Patent Act of 1930 and the Plant Variety Protection Act of 1970 in the belief that patents could not already be obtained for new kinds of plants. If new and useful plants were already eligible for patents, the two plant acts would have served no purpose. If the Court looked to the intent of Congress rather than the text of the patent law, therefore, Chakrabarty would lose. This was the difficult question of statutory interpretation: when the words of the statute conflicted with Congress's evident understanding of those words, which should prevail?

The policy question, of course, was whether it was wise to grant patents for new forms of life. Strictly speaking, this issue was not before the Supreme Court at all—the Court has authority to interpret the meaning of statutes, not to judge their wisdom—but everyone was aware of its presence, because when the words of the law are ambiguous one cannot help but be guided by a view of which result is more sensible. The federal government, defending the Patent Office's view that living things were not patentable, subtly injected this policy question into its brief wherever it could. The government characterized the question to be decided not as whether a bacterium could receive a patent but much more broadly, as "whether a living organism is patentable," in order to raise the specter of patents on higher forms of invented life. In its brief, the government mentioned the possibility that a ruling in Chakrabarty's favor would lead to the patenting of genetically engineered human life, a prospect sounding dangerously close to slavery. One of the amicus briefs filed on the government's side discussed the dangers of genetic engineering much less subtly. "Genetic engineering will, within the lifetime of many of us, give some individuals or institutions the final and awesome power to irreversibly violate three billion years of evolutionary wisdom through the creation of novel life forms," warned the Peoples Business Commission, an organization formed by Jeremy Rifkin, a prominent critic of science and technology. "Once out of the laboratory, there is no recalling a life form."[29]

These policy concerns were discussed to some degree within the Supreme Court. "There is something a bit unsettling about the reality of the human creation of new living organisms," admitted Bill Murphy, one of Justice Harry Blackmun's law clerks, in a memorandum to Blackmun. He acknowledged that there may be "telling policy arguments which would lead to a conclusion that restrictions or limitations on patent protection are needed in this field." But such arguments, Murphy concluded, "should be addressed to Congress, not this Court." ("Fine memo," Blackmun scrawled at the bottom.)[30] The justices all agreed. They divided five to four, but all nine stuck strictly to the technical question of statutory interpretation.

In an opinion by Chief Justice Warren Burger, the Court decided that living things could be patented. Chakrabarty was not claiming rights in "a hitherto unknown natural phenomenon," Burger declared, but rather "a nonnaturally occurring manufacture," one that was "a product of human ingenuity" just like any invention. Nothing in the patent law excluded living organisms. Its subject matter included "anything under the sun that is made by man." The dissenters, led by William Brennan, responded by emphasizing the incongruity of this view with the existence of the two plant patent acts. And that was all. Writing in a style that to nonlawyers must have seemed curiously narrow and technical given the important question being decided, the Supreme Court opened the door to the patenting of new forms of life.[31]

Chakrabarty was a case about bacteria, but there was no principled ground for distinguishing bacteria from any other form of invented life.

The Patent and Trademark Office soon began granting ordinary patents for new plants, despite the existence of the specialized plant patent statutes. Not long after, the Patent and Trademark Office received a patent application for an oyster developed in a laboratory. This particular oyster was not patentable because the method by which it was created would have been obvious to experts, but the Office was careful to explain, citing *Chakrabarty,* that a more innovative oyster *would* have been patentable. "The Patent and Trademark Office now considers nonnaturally occurring non-human multicellular living organisms, including animals, to be patentable subject matter," it informed the patent bar. The Office warned that it would refuse to consider applications for humans, on the ground that the grant of an "exclusive property right in a human being is prohibited by the Constitution." But all other animals were fair game. In 1988, researchers at Harvard received a patent for a mouse that had been genetically modified to be more susceptible to cancer, and thus more useful in cancer research, than an ordinary mouse.[32]

There was big money in small organisms. One of the amicus briefs in the *Chakrabarty* case, for example, had been filed by a new company called Genentech, which had recently invented microorganisms capable of producing human insulin and human growth hormone, for which they anticipated a large market. Investments in biotechnology companies soared, as genetic engineering became a hot commercial field. The dramatic growth of the biotechnology industry was in part a result of this new form of property, in that patents on living things were the primary assets of these new companies, but before long the industry's growth also became a *cause* of the ongoing recognition of property rights in invented life. The idea that living things could be patented drew its share of critics, who worried about implications like potential patents on bizarre new species like the "humanzee," an imagined cross between a human and a chimpanzee. Congress considered placing limits on the kinds of animals the patent law would cover.[33] But the growing biotechnology firms, who had the most at stake, were becoming powerful enough to beat back all attempts to curtail the property right recognized in *Chakrabarty.*

One could own invented plants and animals. What about genes? The human genome and its components are not patentable in themselves, of course, because they are found in nature. On the other hand, it has long been possible to obtain a patent for a purified or isolated substance if the substance is more useful that way than in its naturally occurring state. One of the earliest such patents, granted in the first decade of the twentieth century, was for purified human adrenaline. As researchers began to isolate segments of the genome, they applied for patents, and the Patent Office began granting them. By 2005, nearly 20 percent of the human genome had been patented. The notion that human genes could be owned as property raised, yet again, all the concerns about desecrating the body and exploiting the weak that had been aroused by earlier episodes of property in parts of the body. In the case of genetic material, these concerns were often presented in a misleading way in the popular press: "Outrageous! They Own Your Body," screamed one representative headline in the *Reader's Digest,* while the science fiction author Michael Crichton warned that "the genes in your body are privately owned." No one owned the genes in anyone else's body; what were owned were genes isolated in a laboratory. A more serious concern raised by gene patents was that they would hinder scientific research, by requiring researchers to obtain the consent of the owners of the various parts of the genome necessary for their research but already patented by others.[34]

As the twenty-first century began, meanwhile, patents for modified versions of living things were attracting increasingly vocal opposition from the societies where those living things originated, societies that typically did not share in the profits. When a company in Texas, for example, received a patent for a form of basmati rice developed from rice that had long been cultivated in India, or when a Colorado company patented a variety of bean originating in Mexico, intense controversies followed. Why, many asked, should the gains from slight variations on well-known plants flow entirely to those who made the last incremental change, when far more effort went into identifying and breeding the organism in the first place? American patent law offered no protection for things that had been known to entire societies for long periods of time. Firms taking advantage of that fact found themselves accused of "biopiracy," the theft of traditional knowledge and practices from less affluent peoples.[35]

So far, however, such concerns have not slowed the use of property as a tool for encouraging the development of new forms of life. Our squeamishness about recognizing property rights in visible parts of the human body has not extended to parts only scientists can see, or to nonhuman forms of life.

In all of these debates, property has, as always, been an instrumental value—a means to an end rather than an end in itself. People have argued passionately on both sides of whether to treat human organs and new forms of life as property because they have had different ends in view. The same had been true a century earlier, when the arguments were about corpses and new breeds of plants. There has always been a widely perceived tension between the sacredness of life and the good reasons for recognizing legal entitlements in living things.

13

Property Resurgent

"You all have come a long way since the old days," Roger Marzulla told the participants at a 2006 symposium held at the Santa Clara University School of Law. Marzulla was a Santa Clara alumnus, he explained, but "we didn't have any get-togethers like this symposium when I was at Santa Clara some thirty-five years ago." The topic of the gathering was the importance of property rights as reflected in recent Supreme Court cases. Similar meetings were taking place across the country, in response to what seemed to be growing support for property in a wide range of contexts, from the birth of an antiregulatory "property rights movement" to the use of property as a tool for protecting the environment. "To put this issue into context," Marzulla reminded his listeners, "it is important to understand that as recently as 20 years ago there was virtually no debate on property rights; it was a musty, back-of-the-library topic fit only for a few professors." Not any more. Marzulla himself had played an important role in making property issues more prominent before Congress and the courts. In the Reagan administration he had been the assistant attorney general in charge of the Justice Department's Environmental Division. "I was sort of known as the property rights guy," Marzulla recalled.[1] After leaving the government he founded a nonprofit organization called Defenders of Property Rights, which participated as an amicus curiae in the Supreme Court's big property cases of the 1990s. By 2006, Marzulla and his colleagues looked back with pride on what they had accomplished. Property rights, felt by many to be weakening for much of the twentieth century, had made something of a comeback by the century's end.

A Market in Pollution Rights

American environmental policy before the twentieth century was primarily intended to promote the exploitation of natural resources rather than their conservation. That began to change in the late nineteenth and early twentieth centuries, first with the establishment of national parks, and then with the enactment of legislation protecting specific resources. By the 1960s and 1970s, amid growing popular interest in preventing air and water pollution and conserving wildlife, environmental protection became a major function of government. Most of this environmental regulation consisted of restrictions on what people could do with their property, such as limits on the amounts of pollutants that could be emitted into the air, or bans on interfering with the natural habitats of endangered species. With this kind of regulation, property rights were antithetical to environmental protection: the stricter the regulation, the more it would have to abridge the rights of property, and the more the legal system was solicitous of property, the less it would help the environment.[2]

Toward the end of the century, however, this opposition started to break down. Property was increasingly understood as a *tool* for protecting the environment. Many began to argue that natural resources were best conserved by *assigning*, rather than restricting, property rights in them, and then letting people buy and sell those rights in a market.[3] Rather than simply banning pollution above a given level, for example, the idea was to allocate property rights in the ability to pollute, and then to allow firms to pollute only to the extent that they had acquired the right to do so, either by receiving pollution credits in the initial allocation or by purchasing such credits from other firms who were not polluting as much as their allocation permitted.

One of the two main intellectual roots of the change was the increasing attention paid at midcentury to the problem of resources owned in common. The tendency of shared resources to be overexploited had of course been known for a very long time. "That which is common to the greatest number has the least care bestowed upon it," Aristotle explained. "Every one thinks chiefly of his own, hardly at all of the common interest." What *was* new, at least among academics and policymakers, was to think of nature as a kind of commons and pollution as a form of overexploitation. "Here it is not a question of taking something out of the commons, but of putting something in," reasoned the biologist Garrett Hardin, in his widely read 1968 article "The Tragedy of the Commons." "The rational man finds that his share of the cost of the wastes he discharges into the commons is less than the cost of purifying his wastes before releasing them. Since this is true for everyone, we are locked into a system of 'fouling our own nest.'"[4]

Once nature was conceptualized as a commons, one obvious solution to the problem of overuse was the allocation of property rights. In the first sustained economic analysis of common property, H. Scott Gordon's 1954 article on fisheries, Gordon had arrived at this conclusion. The "overfishing problem," he realized, was due to the fact that no one owned the fish before they were caught. No fisherman had any incentive to conserve fish, because his competitors would simply take all the fish he did not catch. "The fish in the sea are valueless to the fisherman," Gordon argued, "because there is no assurance that they will be there for him tomorrow if they are left behind today." One way to create value in uncaught fish, or indeed in any common resource, was to "make them private property." If fish could be owned before they were caught, fishing would no longer be a race to deplete the sea. The fisherman's incentive would be to maximize the long-run value of his stock of fish, by leaving some for another day. The problem of overfishing would be solved.[5]

The other important intellectual root of the move toward property rights as a means of protecting the environment was the economic concept of the "externality," first given systematic attention (although not under that name) by the early twentieth-century English economist Arthur Pigou. Many activities incidentally help or harm others, Pigou noticed, in circumstances where it would be impractical to negotiate for payment with all those affected. When a factory was built in a residential neighborhood, for example, the pollution caused harm to the neighbors, and when a property owner planted trees his neighbors received some measure of benefit, but in neither case would it be practical for the neighbors to bargain for the value of what they lost or gained. (It was these incidental gains and losses that would later be called "externalities.") The result, Pigou observed, was a divergence between what was good for the individual and what was good for society as a whole, because in deciding whether to build a factory or to plant trees, the property owner would not be taking into account the effects of his decision on others. The way to remove this divergence, Pigou concluded, was for the government to levy taxes or pay bounties in amounts that would force property owners to bear the true social costs of their decisions.[6]

Pigou's analysis suggested that taxing polluters could be a more efficient way of protecting the environment than prohibiting pollution outright. Over time, this view became conventional among economists. Pigou's treatment of the issue would eventually come in for criticism for ignoring the reciprocal nature of the problem. A factory owner who emitted smoke was harming his neighbors, but the neighbors' desire for clean air was simultaneously harming the factory owner, the economist Ronald Coase pointed out. The question, in Coase's view, was whether the value of clean air exceeded the value of whatever the factory produced by polluting; if it did not, there was no reason to tax the factory.[7] But in a world where clean air and other natural resources were deemed more and more valuable with each passing year, this sort of criticism scarcely slowed the spread of the idea that putting a price on pollution might be the best way of reducing its quantity.

The difficulty with Pigouvian taxes was deciding how large they should be. How was the government to know exactly how much harm a polluter was inflicting on its neighbors, who likely placed different values on the ability to breathe clean air? Economists realized by the 1960s that this obstacle could be surmounted by assigning property rights to clean air or to the ability to pollute and, in effect, letting the parties themselves set the right level of taxation by bargaining. Thomas Crocker was a consultant for the Division of Air Pollution of the United States Public Health Service. Crocker envisioned "a precisely defined system of emission rights which can be purchased and traded by both emitters and receptors." Rather than regulating directly, the government would be creating the very market whose absence gave rise to the externality of pollution in the first place. "Let us try to set up a 'market' in 'pollution rights,'" J. H. Dales proposed in 1968. A government board would begin by "creating a certain number of Pollution Rights, each Right giving whoever buys it the right to discharge one equivalent ton of wastes into natural waters during the current year." These rights would be auctioned to whoever valued them most highly—including polluters of course, but maybe also environmental groups who wanted to prevent them from being used. Pollution rights could be bought and sold among their holders, at whatever prices reflected the value of polluting. There would be difficult questions concerning the details, Dales acknowledged, but in principle, he concluded, "markets *can* be used to implement any anti-pollution policy that you or I can dream up." By the early 1970s, as economists focused their attention on the details, there was a growing theoretical literature on the topic. As economics began to permeate the legal world in the 1960s and 1970s, lawyers paid attention too.[8]

One politically important feature of these proposals was that they were likely to be less expensive for the regulated parties than conventional regulation. A simple ban on pollution above a given level would fall equally on all polluters, but some would be able to comply with the law more cheaply than others. If pollution rights were transferable, the firms able to comply more cheaply could sell their leftover pollution rights to the others, at a price somewhere in the middle, and the total cost of compliance for all firms would be less than under a simple ban. For this reason, the proposals reached a receptive audience in the Nixon administration. The Economic Report of the President for 1971 included a lengthy discussion of the possibility of controlling pollution by setting " 'prices' for the use of the air and water." The report explained that the prices need not be set by the government itself. "Under this system," it explained, "a Government agency would set a specific limit on the total amount of pollutants that could be emitted. It would then issue certificates which would give the holder the right to emit some part of the total amount. Such certificates could be sold by the Government agency at auction and could be resold by owners. The Government auction and private resale market would thus establish a price on use of the environment."[9]

Property-based programs for reducing pollution began to proliferate. In 1974 the Environmental Protection Agency began permitting firms to exceed emissions limits from one source if they made corresponding reductions in pollution from another source. This "netting" policy in effect allowed for the trading of pollution rights within a single firm. The EPA soon expanded the program to allow such trading between firms: a company polluting from one source could purchase emissions credits from another company that had reduced its emissions in the same region. The 1990 amendments to the Clean Air Act established a program for trading permits to emit sulfur dioxide, the pollutant

that causes acid rain. Similar programs were established at the local
and regional levels. Internationally, emissions trading was an important part of the 1997 Kyoto Protocol, which was signed by most nations, although not the United States.[10]

At every step, emissions trading attracted opposition on several
grounds. Many critics found something incongruous in the idea of paying fees to pollute. When the Clean Air Act amendments established
the market in sulfur dioxide emissions, the sociologist Todd Gitlin imagined the sorts of markets that might come next. Would the National
Basketball Association sell fouling rights, and allow teams to trade
them for draft picks? Would states allocate rights to commit crimes like
murder and rape, and permit felons who had not exhausted their quotas to trade them to those who had? The incongruity resulted in part
from the way emissions markets seemed to remove the moral stigma
from pollution. If one viewed pollution as something wrong in itself,
rather than as an inevitable by-product of otherwise useful activities,
there was little distinction between tradeable permits to pollute and
tradeable permits to commit murder. Both were symbolic government
statements endorsing particular activities so long as the requisite fees
were paid. Another source of discomfort with emissions trading was
the way it seemed to equate good and bad intentions. If one were concerned with people's motives as much as their behavior, reducing pollution because of genuine concern for the environment was better than
reducing pollution to save money, and it was wrong for the government
to treat them alike. The environment, meanwhile, was increasingly
valued precisely as a refuge from the marketplace, as a realm with qualities that could not be translated into monetary terms. Buying the right
to despoil the environment, on this view, was like buying babies or
buying love; it was the unwarranted extension of a commodified modernity into one of the few areas still unsullied.[11]

Other critics disagreed not with the implicit philosophy of emissions
trading but with the details of how these programs were implemented.
Pollution credits were often handed out to polluters for free rather than
sold to the highest bidder, a practice hard to defend on theoretical
grounds but often necessary to obtain political support. A market in pollution rights could not work without constant monitoring to make sure
that each polluter was staying within its limits, but accurate monitoring
could be difficult. Within the environmental movement, the use of

market-based programs was thus sometimes viewed as a cover for deregulation.[12]

Emissions trading, finally, threatened to tie the government's hands in the future. A right to pollute that could be bought and sold looked very much like property, and the Constitution forbids the government from confiscating property without paying for it. One can easily imagine a future need to reduce pollution levels. In a world without emissions trading, nothing would prevent the government from regulating more strictly. But once firms hold stocks of emissions credits, would stricter regulation be deemed to infringe their property rights? Government lawyers anticipated this problem and inserted in the legislation establishing the sulfur dioxide emissions market a provision stating that emissions allowances are *not* property rights. Even the EPA, however, admits that "functionally . . . the ownership rights and responsibilities of allowances are similar to property rights."[13] It is not at all clear how this issue would be resolved if it came before a court.

Despite these concerns, property is increasingly being used as a tool for protecting natural resources. There are emissions trading programs for water pollution as well as air pollution. Fisheries are being conserved by the allocation of transferable fishing quotas. Enthusiasts have suggested even more applications of the principle. How about preserving endangered species by assigning property rights in wildlife? Or reducing automobile emissions by privatizing the highways?[14] Such schemes may sound fanciful, but then so did the idea of property in pollution when it was first proposed.

The Liberation of Commerce

Most environmental protection was still accomplished by limiting what people could do with their property, and by the 1980s the accumulation of this sort of regulation gave rise to a self-conscious "property rights movement," a loose collection of activists seeking stronger protections for the expectations of property owners. Ronald Reagan's victory in the 1980 presidential election yielded an administration sympathetic to this view. "When we . . . took office in early 1981," recalled William French Smith, Reagan's first attorney general, "we did so armed with a coherent economic vision," one that included "minimizing the

costs of government intervention in the marketplace." Part of this program involved attempting to dismantle much of the environmental
protection enacted over the previous decades. Such environmental ini-
tiatives were "regulatory monstrosities," argued Secretary of the Interior James Watt, "programs that were costly and without seeming benefit." Watt accordingly proposed opening eighty million acres of virgin
wilderness to drilling and mining.[15]

The other part of the Reagan administration's property agenda was
an effort to reinvigorate property's constitutional protections. "Judicial
deletion of economic rights from the Constitution is a species of activism every bit as deplorable as the unwarranted manufacture of new,
so-called civil rights," declared Edwin Meese, Smith's successor as attorney general. "We must recognize that certain economic rights do exist
and are central to the American constitutional order." The Justice Department accordingly focused its attention on persuading the Supreme
Court to interpret the Fifth Amendment's takings clause as a strong
curb on the government's power to regulate in ways that reduce the
value of property. At times, Meese's lawyers pursued this goal with
enough enthusiasm to alarm even some senior government officials.
Charles Fried, the solicitor general during Reagan's second term, was
no fan of regulation. "Certainly economic liberty, deregulation, and the
fight against unprincipled, ad-hoc, sentimental redistributive adjudication in the federal courts were among the projects that had brought me
to government and the administration in the first place," Fried reflected. "But Attorney General Meese and his young advisers—many
drawn from the ranks of the then fledgling Federalist Societies and often devotees of the extreme libertarian views of Chicago law professor
Richard Epstein—had a specific, aggressive, and, it seemed to me, quite
radical project in mind: to use the Takings Clause of the Fifth Amendment as a severe brake upon federal and state regulation of business
and property." The takings clause requires the government to compensate those whose property is taken for public use. "The grand plan,"
Fried lamented, "was to make government pay compensation as for a
taking of property every time its regulations impinged too severely on
a property right—limiting the possible uses for a parcel of land or restricting or tying up a business in regulatory red tape. If the government labored under so severe an obligation, there would be, to say the
least, much less regulation."[16]

One way to carry out the plan was to file amicus briefs in Supreme Court cases involving the takings clause. In any administration, regardless of party, the Justice Department often files such briefs, because the federal government has an interest in the outcome of all sorts of cases. Normally the federal government's interest is in defending the constitutionality of a statute or some action undertaken by another unit of government. In the takings cases of the 1980s and early 1990s, this ordinary institutional role stood in tension with the antiregulatory views of government lawyers, and ideology won out: the government sided with property owners, against the claims of state governments that their actions did not require compensation under the takings clause. In *Nollan v. California Coastal Commission,* for example, the Justice Department argued that California should have to compensate homeowners denied building permits in a variety of circumstances, while in *Lucas v. South Carolina Coastal Council,* the department supported the claim of a homeowner that he was entitled to compensation when he was not allowed to build. In both cases the federal government's asserted interest was based on the existence of a similar federal program to preserve beaches and other coastal resources, but in both cases the Justice Department took positions that, if accepted by the Supreme Court, would have limited the federal government's ability to do just that.[17]

Another way to beef up the takings clause was to appoint Supreme Court justices who shared an appreciation of the virtues of property rights. Property was crowded out by a host of more salient political issues, especially abortion, whenever a seat opened up on the Supreme Court, so this was a tactic that could not be pursued as earnestly as direct advocacy. Neither the takings clause nor property rights generally were discussed in the confirmation hearings of Sandra Day O'Connor (1981), Antonin Scalia (1986), Anthony Kennedy (1987), or David Souter (1990). Of the four, only Scalia had written anything substantial about property, and even that was ambivalent. On the one hand, just two years before his nomination he had declared that "the free market, which presupposes relatively broad economic freedom, has historically been the cradle of broad political freedom, and in modern times the demise of economic freedom has been the grave of political freedom as well." On the other, he doubted the wisdom of encouraging judges to interpret the Constitution to confer economic rights, for fear that judges empowered to expand rights in one domain would feel more free to expand them in others.[18]

The only Supreme Court nominee of the period with a clear pre-nomination preference for stronger constitutional property rights was Clarence Thomas, who, before his nomination, had given speeches urging the use of natural law as a method of assuring economic liberty. "Natural law when applied to America," he explained, "means not medieval stultification but the liberation of commerce." As he read the Constitution, Thomas argued on another occasion, "economic rights are protected as much as any other rights." Statements like these raised some eyebrows at Thomas's 1991 confirmation hearings, where Senator Joseph Biden repeatedly questioned whether Thomas intended to "strike down laws restricting property rights." Thomas retreated from his earlier views. He claimed to agree with Supreme Court opinions applying a deferential standard to regulations affecting the use of property.[19] In the end, property probably made little difference to Thomas's confirmation, as it was eclipsed by other legal issues, and then all legal issues were eclipsed by the controversy over his relationship with Anita Hill. Nevertheless, the five new justices appointed in the decade between O'Connor and Thomas were all friendlier to the constitutional protection of property rights than any Democratic appointee of the period would have been, and in aggregate they were certainly friendlier than the justices they replaced.

Even with a receptive Supreme Court, there was little that proponents of property rights could do without a supply of cases. In an earlier era, cases would have arisen haphazardly. A case cannot reach the Supreme Court without first being litigated for years at several levels of the court system, which requires so large an expenditure of money and time that only the most committed litigants, or the ones with the most at stake, are willing to persevere. And because the Supreme Court hears only a small fraction of the cases that reach it, normally the ones raising issues as to which lower courts have reached irreconcilable conclusions, the cases the Court chooses to decide typically sit at the tip of an iceberg of similar lawsuits filed all over the country. The cause of constitutional property rights received a crucial boost at just the right time, because the 1980s saw the emergence of the first successful conservative public interest litigating organizations. Just as the "new property" of the 1960s benefited from the new legal services offices of that era, the property rights movement two decades later benefited from new institutions like the Pacific Legal Foundation, which represented the homeowners in *Nollan v. California Coastal Commission*, among other cases, and the Institute for Justice, which likewise represented property owners in many takings cases, the most well known of which would be *Kelo v. City of New London* in 2005. These conservative nonprofits used the same strategy their liberal predecessors had long since perfected. They carefully chose sympathetic clients: not big businesses, but rather middle-class homeowners with whom the public could identify.[20]

All this groundwork paid off in a series of Supreme Court cases finding in the takings clause previously unknown limits on the government's power to regulate without compensating property owners. The Court had not found any regulation to constitute a taking since 1922, when Oliver Wendell Holmes declared that "if regulation goes too far, it will be recognized as a taking." The most well-known recent case, *Penn Central v. New York City* (1978), was not at all promising for property rights advocates. When New York designated Grand Central Terminal as a historic landmark, Penn Central, the terminal's owner, lost the ability to construct an office building in the airspace above, which rendered the property much less valuable than it had been before. The Court nevertheless held that no taking had occurred, in an analysis that strongly suggested that few such claims could ever possibly succeed. Justice Brennan's majority opinion explained that a diminution in the value of property would never, in itself, be enough to establish a taking, no matter how extreme. Nor would the fact that a law imposed burdens on a relatively small number of property owners—in the case of New York's historical landmark program, only a few hundred out of more than a million buildings in the city. The Court's opinion established only the vaguest of guidelines for lower courts to follow in future cases. The only clear implication was that victories for property owners adversely affected by regulation would be very rare indeed.[21]

Rather than trying to overrule *Penn Central* directly, the takings cases of the 1980s and 1990s gradually chipped away at it by carving out categories of cases that would no longer be governed by its lenient standard. The first, decided in 1982, involved a challenge to a New York state law requiring landlords to allow cable television companies to install wiring on the outside of their buildings so that tenants could watch cable TV. Jean Loretto, who owned a five-story brownstone apartment building in Manhattan, brought suit; she argued that the compelled installation of half-inch-thick cable along the roof and in the front of her building was a taking requiring compensation. Loretto conceded that the law had only a very slight effect on the value of her property, and in fact it likely made her building more valuable, because it would be easier to find tenants for apartments with cable television than without. Under *Penn Central*, her claim would have been a clear loser. Yet Loretto won her case. The Court analogized the state law to other, more serious, government-authorized physical invasions of property, like the construction of a dam causing the permanent flooding of land, or the erection of telegraph poles blocking access to a right-of-way, or repeated overflights by very low airplanes. The lesson of these cases, the Court held, was that a law that authorized the permanent physical occupation of property was *always* a taking, regardless of the law's purpose or its negligible economic impact on the owner.[22]

The Court created another new taking rule five years later, in *Nollan v. California Coastal Commission*. The Nollans owned a small, dilapidated beachfront bungalow in Ventura, California. When they applied to the Coastal Commission for a permit to tear down the existing house and replace it with a new three-bedroom home, they were granted permission, but only if they would allow the public to cross their property, to facilitate access to public beaches to the north and south. Under *Penn Central* this condition would not have been deemed a taking. Whatever the Nollans would have lost from allowing beachgoers to walk across their sand was much smaller, no matter how it was measured, than what Penn Central lost from not being able to build above its train station. Again, though, the Court distinguished *Penn Central* and found that the condition was a taking. While the Coastal Commission could have simply denied the Nollans' permit application, Justice Scalia reasoned, a condition imposed on development had to serve the same purpose that an outright ban on building would. Otherwise, he concluded, "the building restriction is not a valid regulation of land use but an out-and-out plan of extortion." Because the only apparent reason to deny the Nollans a building permit was that their proposed house would block the public's view of the ocean, the permit condition—which would have benefited only people who were already at the beach, not those who were looking for it—did not serve the same purpose as a prohibition on building. It was thus a taking, regardless of how large or small its economic impact on the property owner.[23] Local governments had grown accustomed to placing conditions of various kinds on the issuance of building permits. The prospect of having to compensate land-owners would make them think twice.

Nollan was published just two weeks after another takings case in which the Court sided with the property owner, *First English Evangelical Lutheran Church v. Los Angeles.* In *First English* the Court established an-other new principle of constitutional law, that when the government repealed a regulation found by a court to be a taking, the government had to compensate the property owner for losses in the interim. And only three weeks before that, the Court had sided with property own-ers in a third takings case, *Hodel v. Irving.* The timing of the cases was more a coincidence than the product of any plan, but taken together they gave the impression of a Supreme Court eager to expand the con-stitutional rights of property owners. One approving observer was Pres-ident Reagan, who took the opportunity to emphasize the importance of the takings clause in a speech the following month. "There's nothing more encouraging to those who believe in economic freedom than last month's Supreme Court decisions which reaffirm this fundamental guarantee," Reagan declared. "Property rights are central to liberty and should never be trampled upon."[24]

The last of the major cases strengthening the takings clause was *Lucas v. South Carolina Coastal Council,* decided in 1992. David Lucas was another beachfront property owner denied the opportunity to build a house, this time because construction on the beach was contributing to the erosion of the sand. In another opinion by Justice Scalia, the Court held that a regulation denying the owner all economic use of his prop-erty is a per se taking, regardless of the importance of the purpose the regulation serves, unless the government is merely abating a nuisance or enforcing some other already-existing principle of property law. As even this broad-brush summary suggests, the decision left lawyers with several open questions about its scope, but one clear implication was that legislation protecting the environment was likely to require com-pensating property owners unable to build as a result.[25]

From the early 1980s through the early 1990s, the trend in the Supreme Court was unmistakably in the direction of a beefed-up takings clause providing greater protection for property owners against govern-ment regulation. Later cases, however, were disappointing to property rights proponents. Some were victories for regulators; others were wins for property owners, but wins too small or in decisions too fragmented to be of much use. The momentum of the Reagan era had fizzled out. The Supreme Court's retreat was doubtless due at least in part to the 1992 presidential election, which resulted in a Justice Department less hostile to regulation than its predecessors had been. Part of the change may have been caused by the resignation of Byron White in 1993 and his replacement by Ruth Bader Ginsburg, who tended to have less sympathy than White for property owners. Richard Lazarus, who participated in several of these cases as a lawyer on the side of government, places much of the responsibility on Antonin Scalia. Had Scalia been more willing to temper his own strong opinions and build coalitions within the Court, Lazarus argues, he could have done much more to advance his own cause.[26]

The Supreme Court was not the only place where the takings clause could be given more teeth. In his last year in office, Reagan issued Executive Order 12630, titled "Governmental Actions and Interference with Constitutionally Protected Property Rights." The order instructed federal agencies to be "sensitive to" the obligations of the takings clause. Part of that sensitivity simply required complying with the Supreme Court's interpretation of the clause, but the order also imposed a new procedural prerequisite for government action. Whenever an agency contemplated regulating private property, it was now required, in its internal documents and its submissions to the Office of Management and Budget, to identify and assess any possible takings implications.[27] For proponents of property rights this was merely prudent governance. For supporters of stricter environmental regulation, it looked suspiciously like a way to delay new rules by clogging the bureaucracy with extra paperwork.

As the Supreme Court stopped reliably strengthening the takings clause, advocates shifted their attention to state legislatures. Even if restrictions on government power could not be found in the Constitution, state governments remained free to assume those restrictions voluntarily, and in the 1990s many did. By 1997, at least fifteen states had enacted statutes modeled on Executive Order 12630, laws that required state agencies to undertake some form of assessment before regulating property in ways that could plausibly be deemed takings. Many other states went farther, by imposing substantive limits on the extent to which regulation could impose burdens on property owners. Louisiana enacted a law requiring compensation for regulation reducing the value of agricultural land by 20 percent or more, and Mississippi passed a similar law with a threshold of 40 percent. The strictest of these statutes were enacted in Texas, which required compensation for any government action diminishing the value of property by at least 25 percent, and Florida, which mandated compensation whenever regulation "inordinately burdened" the use of property. These statutes went well beyond the Constitution in limiting the scope of government power over property.[28] Similar bills were proposed year after year in the U.S. Congress, but with no success.

By the century's end, property rights clearly received more protection from government regulation than they had a few decades before, but exactly how much more was a matter for debate. A handful of specific government actions limiting the use of property now required compensating its owners, but the vast majority of the regulatory state remained in place, unhindered by the takings clause or any of its statutory supplements. Every day, governments at all levels continued to do all sorts of things that reduced the value of people's property, from enacting zoning ordinances to protecting the environment to choosing the locations of schools or roads, just as they had for a very long time, without any obligation to compensate property owners. In the battle over the takings clause, both sides could claim victory.

The Specter of Condemnation

In the early twenty-first century, controversy over the constitutional protection of property rights shifted from the economic effects of government action to its underlying purposes. The takings clause requires that if private property is to be taken it must be "for public use." Even with compensation, the government cannot take property from one person and give it to another, solely for the second person's private benefit. "Public use" has never been interpreted literally to require that the public be able to *use* the property taken. Governments have routinely condemned land to be used for things like military bases or prisons, places to which the public has no access. Since at least the early twentieth century, the Supreme Court has not interpreted the phrase to require public *ownership* of the property either. During World War I, for example, the federal government requisitioned the electrical power belonging to the International Paper Company, in order to deliver it to other private companies producing things more useful to the war effort. The fact that the power was not ultimately being used by the government itself "did not make the taking any less a taking for public use," Justice Oliver Wendell Holmes reasoned. So long as the International Paper Company was compensated for what it had lost, the government's action satisfied the takings clause.[29]

"Public use" has thus been read to mean something more like "public purpose." Much of the so-called urban renewal of the middle of the twentieth century involved taking land from the owners of substandard housing and giving it to real estate developers who, it was hoped, would put it to more attractive uses. The Supreme Court unanimously held that such transfers amounted to public use. "The public end may be as well or better served through an agency of private enterprise than through a department of government," Justice William Douglas declared. "We cannot say that public ownership is the sole method of promoting the public purposes of community redevelopment projects." The Court likewise unanimously blessed a Hawaii program transferring land from landlords directly to tenants, for the purpose of reducing the concentration of land ownership in the state. "The Court long ago rejected any literal requirement that condemned property be put into use for the general public," Justice Sandra Day O'Connor explained. "Government does not itself have to use property to legitimate the taking; it is only the taking's purpose, and not its mechanics, that must pass scrutiny."[30] Any transfer of property from one private owner to another (assuming the first owner was compensated) could satisfy the takings clause, provided that the purpose of the transfer was to benefit the public rather than merely the second owner.

Of course, what would be of benefit to the public was often in the eye of the beholder. No government program lacks opponents, who often sincerely believe that the program will be of no benefit whatsoever or even detract from the public welfare. Few judges relished the prospect of second-guessing the wisdom of an enormous range of government decisions, and probably fewer still possessed the knowledge even to begin doing so. Courts in the twentieth century thus tended to be exceedingly deferential to legislative findings that particular transfers of property actually were for the public good. "Where the exercise of the eminent domain power is rationally related to a conceivable public purpose, the Court has never held a compensated taking to be proscribed by the Public Use Clause," O'Connor held in the Hawaii case. Courts would not invalidate an asserted public use "unless the use be palpably without reasonable foundation."[31] It was a rare government program that could not satisfy such a lenient standard.

Without much judicial review, the door was open for some episodes of heavy-handed urban planning. Perhaps the most famous was Detroit's destruction of the entire Poletown neighborhood in 1981, and the displacement of thousands of residents, in order to give the land to General Motors, in a desperate and ultimately futile attempt to prevent the city from hemorrhaging jobs. But every part of the country had a comparable story to tell. Los Angeles razed a Mexican-American neighborhood in Chavez Ravine to make room for Dodger Stadium. New York forced the sale of a city block so the New York Times could build a new office building. "The incentives all point in the wrong direction," charged the Institute for Justice in its compilation of hundreds of less well known but similar tales of ordinary homeowners and small businesspeople losing their property to big box retailers and national chains. "Cities love eminent domain because they can offer other people's property in order to lure or reward favored developers. Developers love eminent domain because they don't have to bother with negotiating for property. They can pick anywhere they want, rather than anywhere they can buy."[32]

These might have remained unrelated local grievances but for the work of the Institute for Justice, one of the crop of new conservative public interest organizations. Founded in 1991, the IJ did for public use what the National Association for the Advancement of Colored People had once done for race discrimination, and what the National Rifle Association was simultaneously doing for the right to own guns: it aggregated many small diffuse voices into one sharply focused crusade. The centerpiece of the IJ's campaign to prevent these takings for private development was the case of *Kelo v. City of New London*, decided by the Supreme Court in 2005. Susette Kelo and her fellow plaintiffs lived in modest houses in a waterfront neighborhood of New London, Connecticut. All wished to stay in their homes; one of them, Wilhelmina Dery, was still living in the house in which she had been born, back in 1918. New London was economically stagnant, however, and the city government decided that the best way to attract businesses was to build office space, a hotel, shops, and a marina. To assemble the necessary land, the city had to buy property owned by many people. Some sold voluntarily, but the others, including Kelo, Dery, and the other plaintiffs, refused to move. When the city threatened to acquire their land by eminent domain, they brought suit, alleging that the taking of their property would violate the takings clause because it was for private, not public, use.

Few constitutional lawyers were surprised when they lost. Economic development had been one of the standard public purposes justifying the exercise of eminent domain ever since the days of urban renewal. For decades the Court had refused to scrutinize the claims of local governments that particular development plans would benefit the public or that the acquisition of particular parcels of land was a necessary component of such plans. The majority opinion by Justice John Paul Stevens simply recited the Court's prior decisions on the subject and straightforwardly applied the same rules. To lawyers specializing in the subject, the surprising thing about *Kelo* was not the result but the fact that four Justices dissented. If economic development was a legitimate ground for forcing the sale of property to the government, worried Justice O'Connor, no one's land was safe. "Who among us can say she already makes the most productive or attractive use of her property?" O'Connor wondered. "The specter of condemnation hangs over all property. Nothing is to prevent the State from replacing any Motel 6 with a Ritz-Carlton, any home with a shopping mall, or any farm with a factory." After decades of passivity on this issue, the Supreme Court came very close to placing a significant limit on the power of government with respect to property.[33]

Nearly as surprising was the popular uproar that greeted the decision when it was published in the summer of 2005. Few non-lawyers had paid much attention to the earlier Supreme Court cases on the subject. Few had much sympathy for the slum landlords who lost their land under urban renewal or for the wealthy Hawaiian families who lost theirs when the state transferred it to their tenants. But millions of people could imagine themselves in the position of Susette Kelo or Wilhelmina Dery, middle-class homeowners evicted from their neighborhoods by a coalition of large corporations and powerful politicians. Polls found that 81 percent of Americans disagreed with the decision, and that opposition was nearly equal among Republicans and Democrats. Legislators of both parties rushed to propose bills to counteract *Kelo*. Within a couple of years, all but a few states enacted laws narrowing the circumstances under which the government could take land. Some prohibited takings for the sole purpose of economic development, while others defined "blight" to prevent the taking of property in good condition. Congress considered, but did not pass, a series of bills that would have imposed similar restrictions on the federal government and on federally funded state and local projects. President George W. Bush issued an executive order in 2006 with the same objective. Rarely, if ever, had so much law intended to protect property from government interference been enacted in so short a time. Whether all these new laws would have much practical effect remained an open question. The first systematic study of the post-*Kelo* statutory reforms concluded that most were symbolic at best, and that the ones with real teeth tended to be in the states that did not condemn much property for economic development anyway. For a while people were *talking* about property rights more than they had before, but when the moment had passed it was not clear whether they had done much to make them stronger.[34]

The issue of public use at issue in *Kelo* was, in any event, just a tiny part of the larger question of where to locate the boundary between proper and improper government action with respect to property. As to that broader question, there was little sign of any major change in public opinion or in actual practice. Courts and legislatures had nibbled around the edges, but government after the property rights movement looked a lot like government before. Property remained an important value, but so did sound governance, which sometimes required limiting what some people could do with their property, just as it always had.

14

The End of Property?

"INFORMATION wants to be free," declared the counterculture impresario Stewart Brand in the early years of the personal computer—free in the sense of not costing anything, and free in not being owned.[1] The quotation became something of a motto among Internet-focused intellectuals in the following two decades who shared Brand's sense that the digital revolution would have profound effects on property. "I believe that all generally useful information should be free," agreed Richard Stallman, the computer programmer best known for his view that there should be no property rights in software. "By 'free' I am not referring to price, but rather to the freedom to copy the information." The point was made even more emphatically by John Perry Barlow, the former lyricist for the Grateful Dead. "The future will win; there will be no property in cyberspace," Barlow insisted. "Behold DotCommunism."[2]

Many lawyers made more precise, if equally exuberant, claims. The kind of property that would be most affected by the Internet was copyright, and copyright, they predicted, would have to be drastically overhauled or even abandoned altogether. Copyright was born along with the printing press, recalled Robert Kost, legal advisor to the Congressional Office of Technology Assessment. With the emergence of digital media, Kost explained, "information is reverting to its elemental, nonproperty, form," freed from physical containers like books and "floating in bit streams across national borders." The result, he predicted, would be "the end of copyright." The law professor Raymond Nimmer and the lawyer Patricia Krauthaus agreed that "the advent of high speed, interconnected, large capacity networks capable of moving information around the globe . . . dramatically changes the manner in which information is compiled, transferred, reviewed and used." Because of these changes, they expected, "copyright law will become an anachronism" and "the fundamentals of copyright law will need to be rethought and revised."[3]

Computers allowed information to be copied cheaply and easily, and the Internet allowed it to be sent around the world with the press of a button. Something big was clearly happening. But did information really want to be free? Would there be no property in cyberspace?

The Boundaries of Ownership Are Fraying

For a while it certainly seemed that way, as property came under assault from several directions. In the late 1980s, the advent of inexpensive digital recording popularized a genre of music once familiar only to a tiny group of obscure artists, a style created by *sampling,* or using portions of preexisting recordings in a new one. Some of the most innovative songs of the era were dense collages made up of tiny fragments of earlier works recombined with new material in unexpected ways. A single four-second segment of Public Enemy's "Fight the Power" included at least ten distinct samples. The Beastie Boys fit two hundred samples into the fifteen songs on the CD *Paul's Boutique.* A two-second sample of the drummer Clyde Stubblefield, taken from a 1970 James Brown song, has appeared in nearly two hundred songs. Many of these samples were unrecognizable in their new setting. "We might take a tiny little insignificant sound from a record and then slow it way down and put it deep in the mix with, like, 30 other sounds on top of it," explained Adam Yauch of the Beastie Boys.[4] At the other extreme, some samples were easily recognizable as long sections of instrumental tracks from earlier records.

The underlying recordings being sampled were virtually all under copyright, and some of the owners of those copyrights were not pleased to discover that their work had become the raw material with which others made their fortunes. "I was on a session and the guy pressed one note on the keyboard and it made 'Whooaahh! Good God!' like James Brown," recalled Leo Nocentelli, the guitarist in the influential New Orleans band the Meters. "It blew me away. It was James Brown's voice by the press of a finger and I saw the trouble in that." The Meters would be sampled in several well-known rap songs without receiving any credit or any compensation. "The most you'll get now is, 'I heard your song "Cissy Strut" on an album,' and a pat on the back," Nocentelli lamented. "I don't want just a pat on the back—pat me on the back and stick some dollars in my back pocket." One of the many samples in the Beastie Boys' song "Hold It Now Hit It" consisted of the spoken phrase "Yo Leroy," from a 1977 song by the frequently sampled Jimmy Castor. Castor sued the Beastie Boys in 1987, in what may have been the first sampling-related lawsuit. "I don't deny the creativity of the people putting it together any more than I deny the creativity of the collage artist," explained Castor's lawyer, Bruce Gold. "That doesn't change the question of whether these people have an ownership interest in the underlying works they've used."[5]

Sampling without permission was inconsistent with the formal copyright law, because it infringed the property rights of the owners of the recordings and the musical compositions being sampled, but by the early 1990s sampling was ubiquitous and permission rare. "Probably 99 percent of drum samples out there are not cleared," reported Lawrence Stanley, an attorney who represented hip-hop groups. "Everyone takes beats from other songs, adds things over them, amplifies them, does anything they have to do to make their own track."[6] Actual practice in the music industry was increasingly diverging from the law on paper, because the law had been written at a time when sampling on a large scale was impossible. From one perspective, sampling was opening the gates to an exciting new form of artistic endeavor, one with possibilities that could not have been imagined only a few years before. From another point of view, it was permitting such massive amounts of theft that the very idea of intellectual property was being eroded. What did it mean to own the rights to a song if others could make money by copying and selling parts of it?

Meanwhile, some of the most well-known intellectual enterprises of the 1980s and 1990s were not owned by anyone at all. The first of consequence was the GNU/Linux operating system, begun by Richard Stallman in 1984, and soon the product of thousands of volunteers scattered all over the world who had written or modified portions of it, including the Finnish programmer Linus Torvalds, whose name was attached to it after his work in the early 1990s. Fifteen years later, Linux was a serious competitor with Microsoft's proprietary Windows operating system. Wikipedia, the online encyclopedia founded in 2001, was organized on the same principle of worldwide collaborative volunteer authorship. By 2009, it included more than fourteen million articles in more than 260 languages, written and edited by an enormous number of volunteers. No one made a cent, but a sample of Wikipedia's science articles turned out to be only slightly less accurate than those published in the *Encyclopedia Britannica*.[7] There were many other projects organized along the same lines, including Project Gutenberg, a collective effort to publish electronic versions of books in the public domain, and SETI@ home, a collaboration of millions of home computer users that analyzed radio telescope signals to search for extraterrestrial life.

These enterprises all owed their success to the Internet, which permitted large numbers of small contributors to pool their efforts toward a common goal. Thoughtful observers suggested that this sort of "peer production," as Yochai Benkler put it, might be the wave of the future. "What we are seeing now," Benkler noted, "is the emergence of more effective collective action practices that are decentralized but do not rely on either the price system or a managerial structure for coordination." The Internet promised a third way to get things done, in which information was produced not because it could be sold in the market, and not because someone higher up in a chain of authority ordered its production, but rather as a result of the uncoordinated choices of the producers themselves. Property would have a greatly diminished role in a world characterized by this form of organization.[8]

Perhaps the most conspicuous attack on property rights was Napster, the music file-sharing service released in the summer of 1999 by Shawn Fanning, an undergraduate at Northeastern University. By allowing users to copy the music files on other users' computers, Napster created a mammoth worldwide shared music collection. Within a year and a half there were tens of millions of Napster users all over the world. Colleges found their networks overloaded with the flow of music files. The recording industry worried about a future in which it could no longer sell a product that was so easily obtained for free.

The large majority of the music shared on Napster was under copyright, which meant that most Napster users were breaking the law when they used the site to copy music. Public opinion, however, was at considerable variance with copyright law. In one poll, 58 percent of Americans believed that online music sharing was always or sometimes acceptable;

among young adults, the heaviest users of Napster, the figure was 69 percent.[9] Most users thought they were doing nothing wrong. They knew full well, moreover, that the chances of being sued by the owner of a copyrighted song were infinitesimal. The biggest losers from Napster were the recording companies and publishing houses that held copyrights in the most popular songs. They could not sue tens of millions of copyright infringers. Recorded sound had once threatened the doom of the sheet music business, radio had once threatened to kill the record business, and now file sharing threatened the end of the entire music industry, as copyright—the foundation of the industry's revenue—looked to be on its deathbed.

Yet another challenge came in 2004, when Google announced its plan to scan the contents of several of the biggest academic libraries. The company intended to make available online those titles not under copyright, and to allow searches in, and the display of small portions of text from, books still under copyright. By 2009 the company had scanned more than ten million books. Reactions among authors and publishers varied. Some welcomed the project as an opportunity to sell more books. But many objected, on the ground that this massive project of copying amounted to the greatest copyright infringement ever attempted. Google was of course not scanning all these books as a public service. The company expected to sell advertising on the web pages where the search results appeared. Such profiting from the copying of books, the opponents of the project argued, was a right that belonged to the copyright holders, not Google. Google planned to omit books when copyright holders objected, but opponents insisted that the copyright law placed the burden of obtaining consent on Google, rather than foisting the burden of objecting on authors and publishers. Google quickly found itself the defendant in two copyright infringement suits, one filed by the Authors' Guild and the other by a group of major publishers. The prospect of a universal online library was so appealing to so many people, however, and the outcome of the lawsuits so uncertain, that there was no way to predict what the publishing business would look like in the future. Once again, the Internet seemed to be eroding the importance of intellectual property.

Property was under assault in the digital age, and there was no shortage of explanations as to why. One possibility was that property was a concept best suited to physical entities, while the emerging networked world was made up of nonphysical information. Property is "based on matter," John Perry Barlow proclaimed in his "Declaration of the Independence of Cyberspace." Property had no application in cyberspace, because "there is no matter here." "Intellectual property law cannot be patched, retrofitted, or expanded to contain digitized expression," he concluded. "We will need to develop an entirely new set of methods as befits this entirely new set of circumstances." As value became an attribute of ideas rather than things, agreed the political scientist Debora Halbert, "the fragments of the old and tattered intellectual property system can be discarded and replaced with something more appropriate for the information age." In Halbert's view, "intellectual property law is about protecting property and this function of the law would no longer be needed."[10]

Another theory was that property rights required stable objects of ownership and thus could not accommodate the fluidity of information in electronic form. "Nothing is fixed to anything else," noted Ethan Katsh, one of the earliest experts on the legal implications of the Internet. "Words and images can be moved and edited, lifted off the screen, and put back down." Even the traditional categories of expression had lost their meaning. "Since digital information is fungible and a press of a key can turn text into sound or sound into image, can any traditional frame of reference be valid?" Katsh asked. "What if, although it may be difficult to imagine, there are no longer works with fixed boundaries?" With information constantly in flux, was there any "thing" capable of being owned? "In this shifting view of information, the boundaries of ownership are fraying," Katsh concluded. "It is, therefore, not owning or possessing the information that is valuable but opportunities presented to use and exploit the information that electronic logic encourages." The political scientist Ithiel de Sola Pool made the same point as early as 1983, when personal computers were still new and the Internet was unknown outside a small circle. In a world where texts were constantly being copied and modified, de Sola Pool predicted, "established notions about copyright become obsolete, rooted as they are in the technology of print," where texts were fixed entities. "Electronic publishing is analogous not so much to the print shop of the eighteenth century as to word-of-mouth communication, to which copyright was never applied."[11]

Others focused on the ease of copying in a virtual world, which they expected would make traditional notions of property unworkable.

"The copyright system grew up with printing," Richard Stallman observed, a technology most readers could not use themselves. "Digital
technology is more flexible than the printing press: when information
has digital form, you can easily copy it to share with others. This very
flexibility makes a bad fit with a system like copyright." Property rights
would grow increasingly irrelevant as they plummeted in value. "The
plain economic fact," reasoned the technology journalist and investor
Esther Dyson, "is that even if you can charge for them, the price of copies will go down overall," because when making and distributing copies
was so cheap, the supply of copies would outstrip the demand, which
was limited by the finite amount of consumers' time. As a result, "businesses who make content will have to figure out ways other than selling copies to make money."[12]

In a world where property was meaningless, why would anything
be produced? Some things, perhaps many, would be produced for reasons other than money. Yochai Benkler expected that "nonmarket, non-
proprietary, motivations and organizational forms should in principle
become even more important to the information production system."
Producers with commercial motives would have to sell ongoing services rather than traditional products. "What becomes valuable is the
relationships—sparked by the copies—that tangle up in the network itself," advised Kevin Kelly, the founding editor of *Wired* magazine. "The
relationships rocket upward in value as the parts increase in number
even slightly." At the height of Napster's popularity, the journalist Robert Wright imagined how this business model might work for musicians.
"A band could give away its songs for free on the Web and still eke out a
living by playing concert halls or even small clubs," Wright remarked.
"But, you ask, what kind of people would then be attracted to careers in
music? People who love to play music, that's who—including no small
number of true artists. In a copyrightless world, the Jimi Hendrixes and
Eric Claptons would still be jamming." The industry already offered one
successful example of this strategy, the Grateful Dead, who allowed fans
to record their concerts for free while making money on the sale of concert tickets. "On balance," Wright concluded, "I'd expect a post-copyright
world to spread fame and money more evenly among musicians—and,
in the process, to correlate these things more closely with merit.
What's not to like?"[13]

In the 1960s computers had been understood as the tools of a centralized military-scientific establishment, but by the 1990s the sociology of computer science had changed completely, and computers were the realm of the heirs to the 1960s counterculture.[14] Discussions about property on the Internet were often imbued with a utopian ethic that celebrated communion and disparaged claims to private property. Some of those who made extravagant predictions of the demise of property may have been conflating their expectations of what *would* happen and their preferences as to what *should* happen. But the view that there would be no property, or at least much less property, in cyberspace was not held only by wild-thinking visionaries. It was shared as well by many sober lawyers and academics, who saw property crumbling all around them and sought explanations in the nature of the newly networked world.

Not everyone, however, was so sure that the Internet meant the end of property. No one could know in advance how best to govern the wide range of circumstances that might arise, pointed out the federal judge Frank Easterbrook. Some kinds of information might be best distributed freely, while others might be best paid for. "If you start from property rights, you can negotiate for free distribution," Easterbrook suggested; "if you start from an absence of property rights, it is very hard to get to the best solution when a charge is optimal." Information on the Internet might be nonphysical and ever changing, the law professor Eugene Volokh recognized, but "there is no reason why the dynamic nature of a work would somehow conflict with any underlying copyright principle. The basic policy of the copyright law—to compensate authors so they have more incentive to create—is as applicable to dynamic works as to static ones." When the Commerce Department convened a Working Group on Intellectual Property Rights to address the question, the group concluded that secure property rights were still essential for the creation of new works. "Existing copyright law needs only the fine tuning that technological advances necessitate," the Commerce Department reported, "in order to maintain the balance of the law in the face of onrushing technology." Property rights were being widely flouted on the Internet, but maybe the solution was to make them even stronger. "The only prognosis that's certainly wrong," snorted the lawyer Peter Huber, "is that all boundary-setting law will somehow disappear, because the Workers of the World have united, or because information wants to be free."[15]

Or maybe property would change in unpredictable ways, becoming a bit stronger here and a bit weaker there. Or maybe technological change, which in the recent past had made copying much easier, would in the near future make *preventing* copying much easier, and thus allow copyright holders to assert the same rights in the virtual world that they were accustomed to asserting in the physical world.[16] Everyone agreed that technological change would have some effect on property, but there was little agreement as to what that effect would be.

Information Also Wants to Be Expensive

The golden age of sampling—or the dark age, depending on one's perspective—ended soon after it began. The first court opinion on the legality of sampling was written in 1991 by Judge Kevin Duffy, a white, fifty-eight-year-old Nixon appointee with no apparent interest in the artistic possibilities of the new technology. The case involved the rapper Biz Markie's song "Alone Again," which incorporated a loop of the easily recognizable piano chords from "Alone Again (Naturally)," by the Irish singer Gilbert O'Sullivan, the best-selling song in the United States for six weeks in 1972. "Thou shalt not steal," Duffy began, and that set the tone for what followed, a thorough rebuke for what the judge called a "callous disregard for the law and for the rights of others." In response to the argument that sampling was a common and accepted practice in the music industry, Duffy expressed only astonishment that "the defendants in this action for copyright infringement would have this court believe that stealing is rampant in the music business and, for that reason, their conduct here should be excused." He concluded that "the mere statement of the argument is its own refutation," and indeed referred the case to the United States Attorney for criminal prosecution.[17] "Alone Again" was pulled from circulation. Biz Markie titled his next album *All Samples Cleared!*

This was just one opinion by one trial judge, but later cases reached similar outcomes. In 2005 a federal court of appeals concluded that *any* unauthorized sampling, no matter how small, was a violation of copyright law. Popular music had already changed. Musicians could no longer incorporate samples from dozens of sources in a single song, because it was impractical and expensive to obtain permission from so many copyright holders. They began instead to use just one source per song. Sampling, at its best, had once been a new collage-like form of music, but it was reduced to the straightforward reproduction of familiar passages from earlier songs.[18] If technology was at war with traditional notions of property, property won the first battle.

More reassertions of property followed. Napster had to shut down after it was held liable for copyright infringement. New companies tried a variant of Napster's model: rather than storing copies of music files centrally, services like Kazaa and Grokster kept the files on users' own computers, in the hope that by not engaging in any copying themselves, they might escape liability. In simply producing a tool that *others* could use to make copies, Grokster's lawyers argued, these services were like the manufacturers of videocassette recorders. In 1984, when taping television programs was as new and controversial as file sharing would be twenty years later, the Supreme Court had held that VCR manufacturers could not be held liable for the copyright violations of VCR owners. The Court unanimously rejected the analogy. "One who distributes a device with the object of promoting its use to infringe copyright," Justice David Souter reasoned, "is liable for the resulting acts of infringement by third parties." Grokster and Kazaa shut down too. Smaller file-sharing services continued to proliferate in the shadows. Every so often the recording industry brought suit against an individual user, sometimes with startling results. In 2009, for example, a court ordered a graduate student at Boston University to pay $675,000 to four record companies for illegally downloading songs. But the Napster and Grokster cases blunted much of the economic impact of file sharing. Consumers turned instead to pay sites like Apple's iTunes, where copyrighted material was available for a small fee, with the consent of its owners.[19]

Copyright itself, meanwhile, was growing stronger. Under the Copyright Act of 1976, copyright protection lasted for fifty years after the death of the author. In the case of a corporate author, copyright lasted for seventy-five years from publication. As the twentieth century neared its end, copyrights in works from the early part of the century were soon to expire, including some that still earned significant royalties for their owners, such as the early Disney animated films and the songs of George Gershwin. These copyright holders lobbied for a longer copyright, and the result was the Copyright Term Extension Act of 1998, which added twenty years to the duration of copyrights, including those in works created prior to 1998. "Steamboat Willie," the first Mickey Mouse cartoon with synchronized sound, would have entered the public domain in 2003. With its copyright extended, it remains Disney's property until 2023.

The Copyright Term Extension Act was quickly challenged on constitutional grounds by Eric Eldred, a retired computer programmer in New Hampshire whose hobby was to scan public domain classics and make them available on the Internet. The extension of copyright meant that no works would enter the public domain for the next twenty years. One of the books Eldred wanted to scan was Robert Frost's *New Hampshire*, the copyright to which would have expired in 1998, but for the Copyright Term Extension Act. Eldred was represented by the law professor Lawrence Lessig, an outspoken opponent of the expansion of copyright. Lessig argued that a copyright that lasted seventy years after the author's death was functionally equivalent to one that lasted forever, and was thus inconsistent with the copyright clause of the Constitution, which grants to Congress the power to enact copyright laws "for limited times." He also argued that by extending copyrights for works already in existence, the law was inconsistent with the preamble of the copyright clause, which explains that the purpose of copyright is "to promote the progress of science." A longer term, after all, could hardly encourage the production of works already written before the longer term came into effect. The weakness in the argument was that for two centuries, in prior copyright acts, Congress had done the same thing: it had extended the terms of copyrights for new works and for works already in existence. If constitutional interpretation relied as much on past practice as on the literal meaning of the Constitution's text, Lessig and Eldred faced an insurmountable hurdle. That was enough for the Supreme Court, which rejected Eldred's claim. Copyright had grown longer.[20]

Copyright also grew more powerful. Media companies fought back against the widespread copying of their intellectual property by pressing for harsher punishments for infringers. These efforts bore fruit in the late 1990s. In the No Electronic Theft Act of 1997, Congress expanded criminal penalties for copyright infringement, even for hobbyists like Eric Eldred who had no expectation of making any profit. The Digital

Millennium Copyright Act of 1998 criminalized the creation and dissemination of software intended to circumvent the protections against copying that were increasingly being added to music and video files. In the 1980s copyright had seemed imperiled by technological change, but by the turn of the century copyright was stronger than ever.

A series of court decisions in the first few years of the century reinforced other kinds of property rights in cyberspace. Were unauthorized robotic searches of a website a form of trespass? Yes, said a court in 2000, in response to a suit filed by eBay against one of its early competitors. "If eBay were a brick and mortar auction house with limited seating capacity," the court reasoned, "eBay would appear to be entitled to reserve those seats for potential bidders, [and] to refuse entrance to individuals (or robots) with no intention of bidding." Were unwanted e-mail messages trespassers too? When a disgruntled former Intel employee vented his grievances in six e-mails, each sent to thousands of current employees, Intel sued for trespass. The California Supreme Court, by a 4–3 vote, held that the e-mails were not trespassing, but only because they did not impair the functioning of Intel's computer system. The court made clear that unwanted e-mail *would* be a trespass if it was frequent enough to slow the recipient's computer. Was a domain name a kind of property? Yes, said a federal court of appeals, in a case involving the extremely valuable domain name *sex.com*. "Like a share of corporate stock or a plot of land, a domain name is a well-defined interest," the court held. "Like other forms of property, domain names are valued, bought and sold, often for millions of dollars."[21] Property was just as ubiquitous in cyberspace as in real space.

Even the Google Books project, perhaps the greatest of all the Internet's threats to property rights, took an unexpected turn. In 2008 Google announced that it had reached a settlement with the two groups of plaintiffs that had filed copyright infringement suits three years before. Under the settlement, Google would receive permission to commercially exploit *all* out-of-print books, even those still under copyright. Google would become, in effect, something close to a monopolist for a significant percentage of the books published in the United States. This was a much greater role, and likely a far more lucrative role, than even Google originally envisioned for Google Books. As critics pointed out, it was a very unusual settlement agreement that allowed a defendant to do *more* than it had been doing when it was sued. The agreement drew objections from a wide range of parties. The U.S. Department of Justice complained that the settlement would violate the antitrust laws. The Copyright Office objected that the settlement was inconsistent with copyright law. A group of authors insisted that in reaching a settlement on behalf of all authors, the lead plaintiffs had failed to protect the interests of the class it was purportedly representing. The governments of Germany and France declared that the settlement would harm their own nationals (many of whom held U.S. copyrights) and would breach the United States' obligations under international copyright treaties. Privacy advocates worried about what Google would do with its records of who was reading what. In the fall of 2009 the parties bowed to all this pressure and announced that the deal was off. They began to negotiate a new settlement agreement.[22]

"Information wants to be free," Stewart Brand had famously said, but the rest of his remarks were less well remembered. "Information also wants to be expensive," Brand continued. "It wants to be expensive because it can be immeasurably valuable to the recipient." Information wanted to be free, but it also wanted to be property. "That tension will not go away," Brand predicted. "It leads to endless wrenching debate about price, copyright, 'intellectual property,' and the moral rightness of casual distribution, because each round of new devices makes the tension worse, not better."[23] By making copying so easy, the computer and the Internet had made the enforcement of property rights more difficult, but by opening up new ways of selling intellectual property, they had also boosted the incentives to enforce property rights. The stakes were higher on both sides.

The result was not the end of property, as some had expected. Rather, the scope and the strength of property rights changed here and there, in response to changing conditions. If we place this episode in long-term perspective, the outcome is not very surprising. The Internet was not the first technological change that threatened to upset established notions of property.[24] It will not be the last. Property in the digital age ended up stronger in some ways and weaker in others. DotCommunism never arrived.

Means and Ends

In the end, neither of Stewart Brand's claims was quite right. Information does not want to be free *or* to be expensive, because information does not want anything. *People* want things. The things they want, and the intensity with which they want them, change over time in response to changing material and intellectual circumstances. Those changing desires often cause them to think new thoughts about property. From the abandonment of feudal land tenure in colonial times to the expansion of copyright at the turn of the twenty-first century, our ideas about property have always been in flux.

What will come next? Recent years have seen claims that whiteness (in the racial sense) is a form of property, that indigenous culture is a form of property, that human capital is a form of property, that marital status is a form of property, and that a job is both a form of property and a reason for giving employees a property right in the ongoing operation of a factory. Animals have been classified as property for millennia, but two centuries ago we could have said the same about fellow human beings, and some have recently argued that this way of thinking about animals is a tragic mistake similar to slavery.[25] Some hope for a world in which property is constitutionally protected against virtually any government action reducing its value, some for a world in which property receives scarcely any protection, and some for every point between. A few of these arguments may prevail and most probably will not, but the one thing we can safely predict is that such arguments will continue to push our understanding of property in one direction or another.

Philosophers and law professors sometimes try to discern property's "true" nature, but the stories this book has told suggest that property is not something that *has* a true nature. It is a human institution that exists to serve a broad set of purposes. Those purposes have changed over time, and as they have, so too has the conventional wisdom about what property is "really" like. Is it a thing or a bundle of rights? Is it a relationship between people and things or a relationship between people and other people? Is it something we find in nature or something we create through law? What one thinks property *is* depends on what one wants property to *do*—that is, what goals one is trying to advance by thinking of property in a particular way. For those who wanted to help welfare recipients stand up to government bureaucracies, it was useful to think of welfare benefits as property, so they were well disposed toward an understanding of property that encompasses welfare. Those who were more concerned about the costs of hearings, on the other hand, tended toward a definition of property that excludes welfare. People who wanted celebrities to be able to earn money from endorsing products found it useful to think of fame as property, while those who worried more about an impoverished public domain disagreed. Property is not an end in itself but rather a means to many other ends. Because we have never had unanimity on how to prioritize those other ends, we have never had unanimity on an understanding of property. Our conceptions of property have always been molded to serve our own particular purposes.

Over time, as new coalitions formed around particular goals, they pushed conventional understandings of property in one direction or another. Sometimes these coalitions were explicitly organized for that purpose, like the property rights movement of the late twentieth century. Sometimes they were easily identifiable interest groups, like the newspapers who were members of the Associated Press, which spent years lobbying and litigating to create property in news. Often, however, these coalitions were neither organized nor easily identifiable, but simply patterns of individuals or groups with similar interests that happened to push in the same direction. There was no trade association of celebrities making any concerted effort to establish the right of publicity, for example. Fame became property because all the scattered individuals who could profit from it were able to appeal to the widely shared intuition that they should.

Sometimes these coalitions formed because there was money to be made in redefining property. The more valuable an asset becomes, the more there is to gain in creating and enforcing property rights in that asset. When technological change has increased the value of a resource, property has often followed.[26] Sound was never property until the invention of sound recording; fame was never property until the invention of the camera; the electromagnetic spectrum was never property until the invention of radio. The actors driving these changes have unsurprisingly been the people to whom the gains would flow.

Sometimes, however, these coalitions formed for reasons more ideological than economic. Public office and human labor ceased to be property, but not because they became less valuable. Rather, it became intellectually unpalatable to think of offices and people as something capable of being owned. Welfare benefits may have been growing more valuable when they came to be conceived as property in the 1960s and 1970s, but the main reason for thinking of them as property was a political one, the desire to help the poor stand up to an unfeeling and error-prone bureaucracy. Body parts became much more valuable when they could be transplanted, but so far, at least, attempts to classify them as property have been defeated by noneconomic concerns.

In the course of this push and pull, advocates on all sides have made, and still make, claims about property—about its origins, about its attributes, about its purposes, and about its outer limits. Almost all of our discourse about property has consisted, and still consists, of such claims. The "property" we talk about now, however, is not the same as the property of 1900, which was not the same as the property of 1800, and so on. Our conceptions of property have changed over time, to match the changes in the goals we think are worth pursuing. Those changes have been contested at each step along the way, but the debates have never been about the nature of property in the abstract. Property has always been a means rather than an end.

Abbreviations

HHL Herbert Hoover Presidential Library, West Branch, Iowa

HLS Historical and Special Collections Department, Harvard Law School Library, Cambridge, Mass.

LC Manuscript Division, Library of Congress, Washington, D.C.

NA National Archives, College Park, Md.

NL Newberry Library, Chicago, Ill.

NYPL Manuscripts and Archives Division, New York Public Library, New York, N.Y.

NYSE New York Stock Exchange Archives, New York, N.Y.

Notes

Introduction

1. *Los Angeles Times*, 2 Nov. 1997, 1; *Newman v. Sathyavaglswaran*, 287 F.3d 786 (9th Cir. 2002).

2. Michael F. Brown, *Who Owns Native Culture?* (Cambridge: Harvard University Press, 2003); Kristen A. Carpenter, Sonia K. Katyal, and Angela R. Riley, "In Defense of Property," *Yale Law Journal* 118 (2009): 1024–1125.

3. *Sony Corporation of America v. Universal City Studios*, 464 U.S. 417 (1984); *A&M Records v. Napster*, 239 F.3d 1004 (9th Cir. 2001).

4. William Blackstone, *Commentaries on the Laws of England*, 8th ed. (Oxford: Clarendon Press, 1778), 2:2.

5. Specialists will also recognize that the book mostly stays at the level of practice, below the intellectual debates so well laid out in Gregory S. Alexander, *Commodity & Propriety: Competing Visions of Property in American Legal Thought 1776–1970* (Chicago: University of Chicago Press, 1997).

1. Lost Property

1. "Law of Real Property," *American Jurist* 1 (1829): 98; John Pickering, "A Lecture on the Alleged Uncertainty of the Law," *American Jurist* 12 (1834): 309 (lecture delivered in March 1830).

2. St. George Tucker, ed., *Blackstone's Commentaries* (Philadelphia: William Young Birch and Abraham Small, 1803), 1:x, v.

3. William Blackstone, *Commentaries on the Laws of England*, 8th ed. (Oxford: Clarendon Press, 1778), 2:53; A. W. B. Simpson, *A History of the Land Law*, 2nd ed. (Oxford: Clarendon Press, 1986), 1–24; Jesse Root, *Reports of Cases Adjudged in the Superior Court and Supreme Court of Errors* (Hartford, CT: Hudson and Goodwin, 1798), 1:xxxix; Tucker, ed., *Blackstone's Commentaries*, 3:44; James Kent, *Commentaries on American Law*, 2nd ed. (New York: O. Halsted, 1832), 3:514.

4. Viola Florence Barnes, "Land Tenure in English Colonial Charters of the Seventeenth Century," in *Essays in Colonial History Presented to Charles McLean Andrews by His Students* (New Haven: Yale University Press, 1931), 4–40; Beverley W. Bond, Jr., *The Quit-Rent System in the American Colonies* (New Haven: Yale University Press, 1919); Zephaniah Swift, *A System of the Laws of the State of Connecticut* (Windham, CT: John Byrne, 1795), 1:239; William R. Vance, "The Quest for Tenure in the United States," *Yale Law Journal* 33 (1924): 248–271; Charles W. McCurdy, *The Anti-Rent Era in New York Law and Politics, 1839–1865* (Chapel Hill: University of North Carolina Press, 2001).

5. Swift, *A System of the Laws,* 1:238; James Sullivan, *The History of Land Titles in Massachusetts* (Boston: I. Thomas and E. T. Andrews, 1801), 66; Timothy Walker, *Introduction to American Law* (Philadelphia: P. H. Nicklin and T. Johnson, 1837), 261–262, 258, 262.

6. Walker, *Introduction to American Law,* 264; "Personal Hereditaments," *American Law Magazine* 2 (1843): 68.

7. Samuel G. Drake, *The History and Antiquities of Boston* (Boston: Luther Stevens, 1856), 100; William Smith, *History of New-York* (Albany: Ryer Schermerhorn, 1814), 294; Tucker, ed., *Blackstone's Commentaries,* 3:21n1; Kent, *Commentaries,* 3:402.

8. Tucker, ed., *Blackstone's Commentaries,* 3:24n2; Kent, *Commentaries,* 3:403; *In re Corporation of St. Mary's Church,* 7 Serg. & Rawle 517 (Pa. 1822); Henry St. George Tucker, *Commentaries on the Laws of Virginia* (Winchester, VA: Winchester Virginian, 1831), 1:12.

9. Kent, *Commentaries,* 3:402n; Tucker, ed., *Blackstone's Commentaries,* 3:36n11; *Bank of Toledo v. City of Toledo,* 1 Ohio St. 622, 660 (1853).

10. K. W. Swart, *Sale of Offices in the Seventeenth Century* (Utrecht: HES Publishers, 1980); William Doyle, *Venality: The Sale of Offices in Eighteenth Century France* (Oxford: Clarendon Press, 1996); Blackstone, *Commentaries,* 2:36–37.

11. Harold C. Syrett, ed., *The Papers of Alexander Hamilton* (New York: Columbia University Press, 1961–1987), 25:532–533.

12. *Hoke v. Henderson,* 15 N.C. 1 (1833).

13. *Writings of Levi Woodbury, Ll.D.* (Boston: Little, Brown, 1852), 1:125 (remarks delivered in 1830); Kent, *Commentaries,* 3:454; Francis Hilliard, *An Abridgment of the American Law of Real Property* (Boston: Charles C. Little and James Brown, 1838–1839), 2:114; *In re Brown,* 4 F. Cas. 332 (S.D.N.Y. 1842); *Conner v. New York,* 5 N.Y. 285 (1851); *Knoup v. Piqua Bank,* 1 Ohio St. 603 (1853).

14. Blackstone, *Commentaries,* 2:32–35; J. M. Neeson, *Commoners: Common Right, Enclosure and Social Change in England, 1700–1820* (Cambridge: Cambridge University Press, 1993).

15. Tucker, ed., *Blackstone's Commentaries,* 3:32n; *Trustees of the Western University of Pennsylvania v. Robinson,* 12 Serg. & Rawle 29 (Pa. 1824); *Van Rensselaer v. Radcliff,* 10 Wend. 639 (N.Y. 1833).

16. *Watts v. Coffin,* 11 Johns. 495 (N.Y. Sup. 1814); *Livingston v. Ten Broeck,* 16 Johns. 14 (N.Y. Sup. 1819); *Executors of Livingston v. Livingston,* 4 Johns. Ch. 287 (1820); *Thomas v. Marshfield,* 27 Mass. 364 (1830); Kent, *Commentaries,* 3:405; Shawn Everett Kantor, *Politics and Property Rights: The Closing of the Open Range in the Postbellum South* (Chicago: University of Chicago Press, 1998).

17. Blackstone, *Commentaries,* 1:429; Robert J. Steinfeld, *The Invention of Free Labor: The Employment Relation in English and American Law and Culture, 1350–1870* (Chapel Hill: University of North Carolina Press, 1991).

18. Blackstone, *Commentaries,* 3:143; *Benson v. Remington,* 2 Mass. 113 (1806); *Day v. Everett,* 7 Mass. 145 (1810); *Gale v. Parrot,* 1 N.H. 28 (1817); Tapping Reeve, *The Law of Baron and Femme,* 2d ed. (Burlington, VT: Chauncey Goodrich, 1846), 290–291; Holly Brewer, *By Birth or Consent: Children, Law, and the Anglo-American Revolution in Authority* (Chapel Hill: University of North Carolina Press, 2005), 333; Michael Grossberg, *Governing the Hearth: Law and the Family in Nineteenth-Century America* (Chapel Hill: University of North Carolina Press, 1985), 235; Mary Ann Mason, *From Father's Property to Children's Rights: The History of Child Custody in the United States* (New York: Columbia University Press, 1994), 6–7.

19. David W. Galenson, "The Rise and Fall of Indentured Servitude in the Americas: An Economic Analysis," *Journal of Economic History* 44 (1984): 1–26; David Hoffman, *Legal Outlines* (Baltimore: Edward J. Coale, 1829), 156; Kent, *Commentaries,* 2:205; Edward D. Mansfield, *The Legal Rights, Liabilities and Duties of Women* (Salem, MA: John P. Jewett and Co., 1845), 321–322.

20. E. N. Elliott, *Cotton Is King, and Pro-Slavery Arguments* (Augusta, GA: Pritchard, Abbott and Loomis, 1860), vii; Albert Taylor Bledsoe, *An Essay on Liberty and Slavery* (Philadelphia: J. B. Lippincott and Co., 1856), 89–91; John H. Power, *Review of the Lectures of Wm. A. Smith, D.D., on the Philosophy and Practice of Slavery* (Cincinnati: Swormstedt and Poe, 1859), 61; Walter Johnson, *Soul by Soul: Life Inside the Antebellum Slave Market* (Cambridge: Harvard University Press, 1999).

21. E.g., Morton J. Horwitz, *The Transformation of American Law, 1870–1960: The Crisis of Legal Orthodoxy* (New York: Oxford University Press, 1992), 145–167; Kenneth J. Vandevelde, "The New Property of the Nineteenth Century: The Development of the Modern Conception of Property," *Buffalo Law Review* 29 (1980): 325–367; Thomas C. Grey, "The Disintegration of Property," in J. Roland Pennock and John W. Chapman, eds., *Nomos XXII: Property* (New York: New York University Press, 1980), 69–85.

22. Robert W. Gordon, "Paradoxical Property," in John Brewer and Susan Staves, eds., *Early Modern Conceptions of Property* (London: Routledge, 1995), 95–110; Paul Langford, *Public Life and the Propertied Englishman 1689–1798* (Oxford: Clarendon Press, 1991), 14–70.

23. *Tonson v. Collins,* 96 Eng. Rep. 180, 187 (K.B. 1762).

24. Richard B. Morris, "Primogeniture and Entailed Estates in America," *Columbia Law Review* 27 (1927): 24–51; George L. Haskins, "The Beginnings

of Partible Inheritance in the American Colonies," *Yale Law Journal* 51 (1942): 1280–1315; Lee J. Alston and Morton Owen Schapiro, "Inheritance Laws Across Colonies: Causes and Consequences," *Journal of Economic History* 44 (1984): 277–287; Carole Shammas, "English Inheritance Law and Its Transfer to the Colonies," *American Journal of Legal History* 31 (1987): 145–163.

25. Noah Webster, *Sketches of American Policy* (Hartford, CT: Hudson and Goodwin, 1785), 24; Peres Fobes, *A Sermon, Preached Before His Excellency Samuel Adams, Esq.* (Boston: Young and Minns, 1795), 25; Thomas Paine, *Rights of Man,* 4th ed. (Boston: I. Thomas and E. T. Andrews, 1791), 35; Benjamin Rush, *Medical Inquiries and Observations* (Philadelphia: Prichard and Hall, 1789), 54.

26. Holly Brewer, "Entailing Aristocracy in Colonial Virginia: 'Ancient Feudal Restraints' and Revolutionary Reform," *William and Mary Quarterly* 54 (1997): 307–346; Tucker, ed., *Blackstone's Commentaries,* 3:119n; Stanley N. Katz, "Republicanism and the Law of Inheritance in the American Revolutionary Era," *Michigan Law Review* 76 (1977): 1–29; John F. Hart, "'A Less Proportion of Idle Proprietors': Madison, Property Rights, and the Abolition of Fee Tail," *Washington & Lee Law Review* 58 (2001): 167–194; Thomas Jefferson Randolph, ed., *Memoir, Correspondence, and Miscellanies, from the Papers of Thomas Jefferson* (Charlottesville, VA: F. Carr and Co., 1829), 1:30; Sullivan, *History of Land Titles,* 78; Joel Barlow, *The Political Writings of Joel Barlow* (New York: Mott and Lyon, 1796), 30.

27. Kent, *Commentaries,* 4:19; Swift, *System of the Laws,* 247; Edward D. Mansfield, *American Education, Its Principles and Elements* (New York: A. S. Barnes and Co., 1851), 25n; "The Effect of Commerce in Abolishing Restrictions Upon the Transfer of Property," *Merchants' Magazine and Commercial Review* 22 (1850): 385–388.

28. Francis Hilliard, *The Elements of Law* (Boston: Hilliard, Gray, and Co., 1835), 7.

29. *Caines v. Grant,* 5 Binn. 119 (Pa. 1812); *Sergeant v. Steinberger,* 2 Ohio 305 (1826); Kent, *Commentaries,* 4:361–362; Peter S. du Ponceau, *A Dissertation on the Nature and Extent of the Jurisdiction of the Courts of the United States* (Philadelphia: Abraham Small, 1824), 114–115.

30. Joseph K. Angell, *An Inquiry into the Rule of Law Which Creates a Right to an Incorporeal Hereditament, by an Adverse Enjoyment of Twenty Years* (Boston: Hilliard, Gray, Little and Wilkins, 1827), 103; *McCready v. Thomson,* 23 S.C.L. 131 (1838); *Mahan v. Brown,* 13 Wend. 261 (N.Y. 1835); *Robeson v. Pittenger,* 2 N.J. Eq. 57 (1838).

31. Kent, *Commentaries,* 3:446n; *Parker v. Foote,* 19 Wend. 309 (N.Y. 1838); *Myers v. Gemmel,* 10 Barb. 537 (N.Y. Sup. 1851).

32. *Hoy v. Sterrett,* 2 Watts 327 (Pa. 1834); *Pierre v. Fernald,* 26 Me. 436 (1847); *Cherry v. Stein,* 11 Md. 1 (1858); *Napier v. Bulwinkle,* 39 S.C.L. 311 (1852); *Gerber v. Grabel,* 16 Ill. 217 (1854); *Klein v. Gehrung,* 25 Tex. Supp. 232 (1860);

Emory Washburn, *A Treatise on the American Law of Real Property* (Boston: Little, Brown and Co., 1860–1862), 2:63.

33. Morton J. Horwitz, *The Transformation of American Law, 1780–1860* (Cambridge: Harvard University Press, 1977), 31–62; *Holmes v. Tremper,* 20 Johns. 29 (N.Y. Sup. 1822); *Van Ness v. Pacard,* 27 U.S. 137 (1829).

34. *Jackson v. Brownson,* 7 Johns. 227 (N.Y. Sup. 1810); *Findlay v. Smith,* 20 Va. 134 (1818); Sullivan, *History of Land Titles,* 334–335; *Hastings v. Crunckleton,* 3 Yeates 261 (Pa. 1801); Nathan Dane, *A General Abridgment and Digest of American Law* (Boston: Cummings, Hilliard and Co., 1823–1829), 3:214.

35. Book Review, *American Jurist* 19 (1838): 487.

36. Charles Watts to William Sampson, in William Sampson, *Sampson's Discourse* (Washington, DC: Gales and Seaton, 1826), 90; *Farrar v. Stackpole,* 6 Me. 154 (1829).

37. Tucker, ed., *Blackstone's Commentaries,* 1:x; "Honestus" [Benjamin Austin], *Observations on the Pernicious Practice of the Law* (Boston: Adams and Nourse, 1786), 12.

38. Henry Dwight Sedgwick, Book Review, *North American Review* 19 (1824): 417.

2. The Rise of Intellectual Property

1. "Conclusion of the Account of Dr. Smith's *New and General System of Physic,*" *Monthly Review* 41 (1769): 290.

2. John Clayton, *The Snares of Prosperity* (London: J. Buckland and T. Pitcher, 1789), 32; Constantia [Judith Sargent Murray], *The Gleaner* (Boston: I. Thomas and E. T. Andrews, 1798), 1:69; *Prospectus of Delaplaine's National Panzographia* (Philadelphia: William Brown, 1818), 7; "Literary Societies," *Southern Literary Gazette* 1 (1828): 59; James T. Austin, *An Oration, Delivered on the Fourth of July, 1829* (Boston: John H. Eastburn, 1829), 22.

3. *Annals of Congress* 22 (1811): 648; John W. Francis, *An Inaugural Dissertation on Mercury* (New York: C. S. Van Winkle, 1811), viii.

4. For English examples, see "An Address to the Parliament of Great Britain, on the Claims of Authors to Their Own Copy-Right," *The Pamphleteer* 2 (1813): 176; Richard Ryan, *Dramatic Table Talk* (London: John Knight and Henry Lacey, 1825), 206; Robert Maugham, *A Treatise on the Laws of Literary Property* (London: Longman, Rees, Orme, Brown, and Green, 1828), 189.

5. *Richmond Enquirer,* 6 May 1831, 2; "Rights of Authors," *Southern Literary Messenger* 3 (1837): 37; E. P. Hurlbut, *Essays on Human Rights and Their Political Guarantees* (New York: Greeley and McElrath, 1845), 198; *Davoll v. Brown,* 7 F. Cas. 197 (C.C.D. Mass. 1845); Lysander Spooner, *The Law of Intellectual Property* (Boston: Bela Marsh, 1855). In Europe, versions of the phrase in French, Italian, and Spanish were in wide circulation at approximately the same time. Justin

Hughes, "Notes on the Origin of 'Intellectual Property': Revised Conclusions and New Sources" (July 2009), http://ssrn.com/abstract=1432860.

6. The best discussion of the history of patents and copyrights in England and the early United States is Oren Bracha, *Owning Ideas: A History of Anglo-American Intellectual Property* (S.J.D. dissertation, Harvard Law School, 2005).

7. Thorvald Solberg, ed., *Copyright Enactments of the United States* (Washington, DC: Government Printing Office, 1906), 11–12.

8. U.S. Constitution, article I, section 8; 1 Stat. 124 (1790); 1 Stat. 109 (1790).

9. 1 Stat. 318 (1793); 5 Stat. 117 (1836).

10. George Ticknor Curtis, *A Treatise on the Law of Copyright* (Boston: Charles C. Little and James Brown, 1847), 11; "International Copyright," *Southern Quarterly Review* 4 (1843): 8; *Hovey v. Henry,* 12 F. Cas. 603 (C.C.D. Mass. 1846); *Ex parte Wood,* 22 U.S. 603, 608 (1824).

11. B. Zorina Khan, *The Democratization of Invention: Patents and Copyrights in Economic Development, 1790–1920* (New York: Cambridge University Press, 2005), 35, 62; Edward A. Byrn, "The Progress of Invention During the Past Fifty Years," *Scientific American* 75(4) (1896): 82.

12. *Stowe v. Thomas,* 23 F. Cas. 201 (C.C.E.D. Pa. 1853); Bracha, *Owning Ideas,* 319–373.

13. James J. Barnes, *Authors, Publishers and Politicians: The Quest for an Anglo-American Copyright Agreement, 1815–1854* (Columbus: Ohio State University Press, 1974); Aubert J. Clark, *The Movement for International Copyright in Nineteenth Century America* (Washington, DC: Catholic University of America Press, 1960); "Copyright," *Maine Monthly Magazine* 1 (1837): 364.

14. Frank I. Schechter, *The Historical Foundations of the Law Relating to Trade-Marks* (New York: Columbia University Press, 1925); F. A. Girling, *English Merchants' Marks* (London: Oxford University Press, 1964); Abraham S. Greenberg, "The Ancient Lineage of Trade-Marks," *Journal of the Patent Office Society* 33 (1951): 876–887; Gary Richardson, "Brand Names Before the Industrial Revolution" (2008), http://www.nber.org/papers/w13930.pdf; Benjamin J. Paster, "Trademarks—Their Early History," *Trademark Reporter* 59 (1969): 551–572; Giles Jacob, *A New Law-Dictionary* (London: E. and R. Nutt, 1729), unpaginated (entry for "Mark to Goods").

15. *Boston News-Letter,* 17 Mar. 1711, 2; *American Weekly Mercury* [Philadelphia], 1 Sept. 1737, 4; W. W. Abbot et al., eds., *The Papers of George Washington, Colonial Series* (Charlottesville: University Press of Virginia, 1983–1995), 9:156.

16. *Columbian Centinel* [Philadelphia], 24 Dec. 1791, 157; Julian P. Boyd et al., eds., *The Papers of Thomas Jefferson* (Princeton: Princeton University Press, 1950–), 22:384–385.

17. *Millington v. Fox,* 40 Eng. Rep. 956, 961 (Ch. 1838); "Trade Marks," *American Jurist* 25 (1841): 269–280; Charles Stewart Drewry, *A Treatise on the*

Law and Practice of Injunctions (London: S. Sweet, 1841), 228; *Taylor v. Carpenter*, 23 F. Cas. 742, 744 (C.C.D. Mass. 1844); *Taylor v. Carpenter*, 11 Paige Ch. 292 (N.Y. Ch. 1844).

18. *Albion*, 8 May 1847, 224; *Farmers' Cabinet*, 18 Feb. 1858, 3; Francis Wharton, *A Treatise on Theism* (Philadelphia: J. B. Lippincott and Co., 1859), 51; Mark Twain, *The Innocents Abroad* (Hartford, CT: American Publishing Co., 1869), 238.

19. "Counterfeiting Marks and Names on Merchandise," *Merchants' Magazine and Commercial Review* 14 (1846): 330; "Counterfeit Trade Marks," *Scientific American* 12 (1857): 386; H.R. Rep. No. 527, 36th Cong., 1st Sess. (1860), 1; S. Doc. No. 20, 56th Cong., 2nd Sess. (1900), 59; 16 Stat. 198 (1870); *Trade-Mark Cases*, 100 U.S. 82 (1879); Joseph Story, *Commentaries on Equity Jurisprudence* (Boston: Hilliard, Gray, and Co., 1836), 2:223; *Snowden v. Noah*, Hopk. Ch. 347 (N.Y. Ch. 1825); *Thomson v. Winchester*, 36 Mass. 214 (1837); *Bell v. Locke*, 8 Paige Ch. 75 (N.Y. Ch. 1840); *Coats v. Holbrook, Nelson & Co.*, 2 Sand. Ch. 586 (N.Y. Ch. 1845).

20. Mark P. McKenna, "The Normative Foundations of Trademark Law," *Notre Dame Law Review* 82 (2007): 1839–1916; *Falkinburg v. Lucy*, 35 Cal. 52, 64–65 (1868); *Boardman v. Meriden Britannia Co.*, 35 Conn. 402 (1868).

21. Charles Stewart Drewry, *A Treatise on the Law and Practice of Injunctions* (Philadelphia: John S. Littell, 1842), 159; *Walton v. Crowley*, 29 F. Cas. 138, 141 (C.C.S.D.N.Y. 1856).

22. *Amoskeag Manufacturing Co. v. Spear*, 4 N.Y. Super. 599, 604, 608 (1849); *Clark v. Clark*, 25 Barb. 76 (N.Y. Sup. 1857); *Derringer v. Plate*, 29 Cal. 292, 295 (1865); "Trade Marks," *Scientific American* 16 (1867): 125. See also *Bradley v. Norton*, 33 Conn. 157 (1865); *Curtis v. Bryan*, 36 How. Pr. 33 (N.Y. Com. Pl. 1867); "Trade-marks at Law," *Scientific American* 14 (1859): 316.

23. *Samuel v. Berger*, 13 How. Pr. 342 (N.Y. Sup. 1856); Francis H. Upton, *A Treatise on the Law of Trade Marks* (Albany, NY: Weare C. Little, 1860), 14–15; *Congress and Empire Spring Co. v. High Rock Congress Spring Co.*, 57 Barb. 526 (N.Y. Sup. 1867); *Canal Co. v. Clark*, 80 U.S. 311, 322 (1871).

24. *Stokes v. Landgraff*, 17 Barb. 608 (N.Y. Sup. 1853); *Merrimack Manufacturing Co. v. Garner*, 2 Abb. Pr. 318 (N.Y. Sup. 1855); *Town v. Stetson*, 5 Abb. Pr. 218 (N.Y. Sup. 1868); *Fetridge v. Merchant*, 4 Abb. Pr. 156 (N.Y. Sup. 1857); *Fetridge v. Wells*, 13 How. Pr. 385 (N.Y. Super. 1857); *Caswell v. Davis*, 35 How. Pr. 76 (N.Y. Super. 1867).

25. Nancy F. Koehn, "Henry Heinz and Brand Creation in the Late Nineteenth Century: Making Markets for Processed Food," *Business History Review* 73 (1999): 349–393; Horace Greeley et al., *The Great Industries of the United States* (Hartford, CT: J. B. Burr and Hyde, 1873), 142; Mark Bartholomew, "Advertising and the Transformation of Trademark Law," *New Mexico Law Review* 38 (2008): 1–48.

26. *American Washboard Co. v. Saginaw Manufacturing Co.*, 103 F. 218, 284 (6th Cir. 1900); Milton Handler and Charles Pickett, "Trade-Marks and Trade Names—An Analysis and Synthesis: II," *Columbia Law Review* 30 (1930): 781–782.

27. *McGill v. Gorman*, 1 Ky. Op. 352 (1866); *Hobbs v. Francais*, 19 How. Pr. 567 (N.Y. Super. 1860); *Barrows v. B.B. & R. Knight*, 6 R.I. 434 (1860); *Messerole v. Tynberg*, 36 How. Pr. 14 (N.Y. Super. 1868); *Amoskeag Manufacturing Co. v. Garner*, 55 Barb. 151 (N.Y. App. Div. 1869); William Henry Browne, *A Treatise on the Law of Trade-Marks and Analogous Subjects* (Boston: Little, Brown, and Co., 1873), 44.

28. *Aunt Jemima Mills Co. v. Rigney & Co.*, 247 F. 407, 409 (2nd Cir. 1917); *Vogue Co. v. Thompson-Hudson Co.*, 300 F. 509, 512 (6th Cir. 1924); *Wall v. Rolls-Royce of America, Inc.*, 4 F.2d 333, 334 (3rd Cir. 1925); Frank I. Schechter, "The Rational Basis of Trademark Protection," *Harvard Law Review* 40 (1927): 814, 825, 831.

29. *E.I. du Pont de Nemours Powder Co. v. Masland*, 244 U.S. 100, 102 (1917); Felix S. Cohen, "Transcendental Nonsense and the Functional Approach," *Columbia Law Review* 35 (1935): 814–815.

30. *DHL Corp. v. Commissioner*, T.C. Memo 1998-461; "Best Global Brands," *Business Week*, 18 Sept. 2008; Steve Rivkin and Fraser Sutherland, *The Making of a Name: The Inside Story of the Brands We Buy* (New York: Oxford University Press, 2004), 8.

31. Mark A. Lemley, "The Modern Lanham Act and the Death of Common Sense," *Yale Law Journal* 108 (1999): 1696, 1712.

32. There are many examples in eighteenth-century English cases. Early American examples include William Watson, *A Treatise on the Law of Partnership* (Philadelphia: William P. Farrand and Co., 1807), 266; and "Of the Copy-Right and Good Will of Newspapers," *United States Law Intelligencer & Review* 3 (1831): 443.

33. Joseph Story, *Commentaries on the Law of Partnership* (Boston: Charles C. Little and James Brown, 1841), 139.

34. Ibid., 139–140.

35. *Atkinson v. Ball*, 26 Va. 446 (1827); "Case and Opinion Respecting the 'Good Will' of a Newspaper Establishment," *American Jurist* 16 (1836): 87–92.

36. *Dougherty v. Van Nostrand*, Hoff. Ch. 68 (N.Y. Ch. 1839); *Williams v. Wilson*, 4 Sand. Ch. 379 (N.Y. Ch. 1846).

37. *Dayton v. Wilkes*, 17 How. Pr. 510 (N.Y. Super. 1859); *Musselman and Clarkson's Appeal*, 62 Pa. 81 (1869); *Hines v. Driver*, 72 Ind. 125 (1880); *Maxwell v. Sherman*, 55 So. 520 (Ala. 1911); *Burkhardt v. Burkhardt*, 5 Ohio Dec. Reprint 185 (Ohio Super. 1874); A. S. Biddle, "Good-Will," *American Law Register* 23 (1875): 8.

38. Adelbert Hamilton, "Good-Will," note appended to *Barber v. Connecticut Mutual Life Insurance Co.*, 15 F. 312 (C.C.N.D.N.Y. 1883), at 317; "Good-Will,"

Nebraska Law Journal 1 (1891): 589; "The Nature of Business Goodwill," *Harvard Law Review* 16 (1902): 136; "Good Will—Good Will as Property," *Harvard Law Review* 19 (1906): 538; John E. Hale, "Good Will as Property," *St. Louis Law Review* 10 (1924): 62.

39. *Haugen v. Sundseth,* 118 N.W. 666, 667 (Minn. 1908); "How the Good-Will Is to Be Dealt with in Partnerships," *American Law Register* 18 (1870): 65.

40. *Elliot's Appeal,* 60 Pa. 161 (1869); *Metropolitan National Bank v. St. Louis Dispatch Co.,* 36 F. 722, 724 (C.C.E.D. Mo. 1888); *Hart v. Smith,* 64 N.E. 661 (Ind. 1902). In *Hart,* this conundrum led the Indiana Supreme Court to declare that goodwill is *not* property, in order to exempt it from property taxation.

41. *Adams Express Co. v. Ohio State Auditor,* 165 U.S. 194, 222–223 (1897); *Adams Express Co. v. Ohio State Auditor,* 166 U.S. 185, 218–219, 222 (1897).

42. Story, *Commentaries on Equity Jurisprudence,* 1:290; *Vickery v. Welch,* 36 Mass. 523 (1837); *Jarvis v. Peck,* 10 Paige Ch. 118 (N.Y. Ch. 1843).

43. Willard Phillips, *The Law of Patents for Inventions* (Boston: American Stationers' Co., 1837), 333, 340.

44. *Peabody v. Norfolk,* 98 Mass. 452, 459–460 (1868); *Champlin v. Stoddart,* 30 Hun. 300, 302 (N.Y. App. Div. 1883); *Salomon v. Hertz,* 2 A. 379, 380 (N.J. Ch. 1886); Jairus Ware Perry, *A Treatise on the Law of Trusts and Trustees* (Boston: Little, Brown, and Co., 1872), 38; *Eastman Co. v. Reichenbach,* 20 N.Y.S. 110 (N.Y. Sup. 1892); *Tabor v. Hoffman,* 23 N.E. 12 (N.Y. 1889); *Bristol v. Equitable Life Assurance Society,* 30 N.E. 506 (N.Y. 1892).

45. *Garst v. Scott,* 220 P. 277, 278 (Kan. 1923); Catherine L. Fisk, "Working Knowledge: Trade Secrets, Restrictive Covenants in Employment, and the Rise of Corporate Intellectual Property, 1800–1920," *Hastings Law Journal* 52 (2001): 441–535.

46. *Cincinnati Bell Foundry Co. v. Dodds,* 10 Ohio Dec. Reprint 154 (1887).

47. *Ruckelshaus v. Monsanto,* 467 U.S. 986 (1984).

48. Francis J. Swayze, "The Growing Law," *Yale Law Journal* 25 (1915): 10–11; Kenneth J. Vandevelde, "The New Property of the Nineteenth Century: The Development of the Modern Concept of Property," *Buffalo Law Review* 29 (1980): 325–367; "Exemption from Taxation as Property Under the Fifth and Fourteenth Amendments," *Columbia Law Review* 12 (1912): 725; *Hoover v. McChesney,* 81 F. 472 (C.C.D. Ky. 1897); *Choate v. Trapp,* 224 U.S. 665 (1912).

49. *Plessy v. Ferguson,* 163 U.S. 537, 549 (1896).

3. A Bundle of Rights

1. Jesse Dukeminier et al., *Property,* 6th ed. (New York: Aspen, 2006), 81.

2. E.g., Denise R. Johnson, "Reflections on the Bundle of Rights," *Vermont Law Review* 32 (2007): 250–252; Abraham Bell and Gideon Parchomovsky, "A Theory of Property," *Cornell Law Review* 90 (2005): 544–545; Adam Mossoff,

"What Is Property? Putting the Pieces Back Together," *Arizona Law Review* 45 (2003): 372–373, 395.

3. James Madison, "Property," *National Gazette,* 29 Mar. 1792, 174; *Vanhorne's Lessee v. Dorrance,* 2 U.S. 304 (C.C. Pa. 1795); Jennifer Nedelsky, *Private Property and the Limits of American Constitutionalism: The Madisonian Framework and Its Legacy* (Chicago: University of Chicago Press, 1990), 16–66.

4. William J. Novak, *The People's Welfare: Law and Regulation in Nineteenth-Century America* (Chapel Hill: University of North Carolina Press, 1996); John F. Hart, "Land Use Law in the Early Republic and the Original Meaning of the Takings Clause," *Northwestern University Law Review* 94 (2000): 1099–1156.

5. *Calder v. Bull,* 3 U.S. 386, 388 (1798).

6. William Michael Treanor, "The Original Understanding of the Takings Clause and the Political Process," *Columbia Law Review* 95 (1995): 792–794; *Monongahela Navigation Co. v. Coons,* 6 Watts & Serg. 101 (Pa. 1843).

7. *Davidson v. Boston & Maine Railroad,* 57 Mass. 91, 106 (1849); *Cushman v. Smith,* 34 Me. 247 (1852); "On the Liability of the Grantee of a Franchise to an Action at Law for Consequential Damages, From Its Exercise," *American Law Magazine* 1 (1843): 55; Isaac F. Redfield, *The Law of Railways* (Boston: Little, Brown, and Co., 1867), 294.

8. *Hollister v. Union Co.,* 9 Conn. 436 (1833); *Legal Tender Cases,* 79 U.S. 457, 551 (1870); *Shrunk v. Schuylkill Navigation Co.,* 14 Serg. & Rawle 71 (Pa. 1826); *Radcliffe's Executors v. Brooklyn,* 4 N.Y. 195, 206–207 (1850); *Hatch v. Vermont Central Railroad Co.,* 25 Vt. 49 (1852).

9. *Callender v. Marsh,* 18 Mass. 418, 438 (1823); *In re Opening of Hamilton Avenue,* 14 Barb. 405 (N.Y. Sup. 1852); *McKeen v. Delaware Division Canal Co.,* 49 Pa. 424 (1865).

10. *Paxson v. Sweet,* 13 N.J.L. 196 (1832); *Lansing v. Smith,* 8 Cow. 146 (N.Y. Sup. 1828); *Smith v. Corporation of Washington,* 61 U.S. 135, 148 (1857).

11. *Charles River Bridge v. Warren Bridge,* 36 U.S. 420, 638 (1837) (Story, J., dissenting); James Kent, *Commentaries on American Law,* 6th ed. (New York: William Kent, 1848), 2:340; *O'Connor v. Pittsburgh,* 18 Pa. 187 (1851); "The Right of Eminent Domain," *American Law Register* 5 (1856): 11–12; *Alexander v. City of Milwaukee,* 16 Wis. 247 (1862); Theodore Sedgwick, *A Treatise on the Rules Which Govern the Interpretation and Application of Statutory and Constitutional Law* (New York: John S. Voorhies, 1857), 525.

12. *Gardner v. Village of Newburgh,* 2 Johns. Ch. 162 (1816); *Patterson v. Boston,* 37 Mass. 159 (1838).

13. The judge's opinion is not officially reported but it appears in "Rights of Municipal Corporations," *American Jurist* 2 (1829): 203–214 (quoted language at 212). The decision was reversed in an unreported opinion of the Maryland Court of Appeals and then reached the U.S. Supreme Court as *Barron v. Baltimore,* 32 U.S. 243 (1833), in which the Court held that the takings

clause of the U.S. Constitution limits only the federal government, not the states.

14. *Hooker v. New-Haven and Northampton Co.,* 14 Conn. 146 (1841); *Crawford v. Village of Delaware,* 7 Ohio St. 459, 465 (1857); Theodore Sedgwick, *A Treatise on the Measure of Damages,* 2nd ed. (New York: John S. Voorhies, 1852), 111n*.

15. *Bank of Columbia v. Okely,* 17 U.S. 235, 244 (1819); *Bank of the State v. Cooper,* 10 Tenn. 599 (1831); *Hoke v. Henderson,* 15 N.C. 1 (1833); *Taylor v. Porter & Ford,* 4 Hill. 140 (N.Y. Sup. 1843).

16. James Kent, *Commentaries on American Law* (New York: O. Halsted, 1826–1830), 2:276; *Baker v. City of Boston,* 29 Mass. 184, 198 (1831); *Jordan v. Overseers of Dayton,* 4 Ohio 294, 309 (1831).

17. *Thurlow v. Massachusetts,* 46 U.S. 504, 583 (1847); *Thorpe v. Rutland and Burlington Railroad Co.,* 27 Vt. 140 (1854); *Ohio and Mississippi Railroad Co. v. McClelland,* 25 Ill. 140 (1860); *Mobile v. Yuille,* 3 Ala. 137 (1841).

18. *Stuyvesant v. City of New York,* 7 Cow. 588 (N.Y. Sup. 1827); *Commonwealth v. Alger,* 61 Mass. 53, 84–85 (1851).

19. *Wadleigh v. Gilman,* 12 Me. 403 (1835).

20. John Austin, *Lectures on Jurisprudence,* 3rd ed., ed. Robert Campbell (London: John Murray, 1869), 2:818, 2:836.

21. Robert Green McCloskey, ed., *The Works of James Wilson* (Cambridge: Harvard University Press, 1967), 2:711; *Morrison v. Semple,* 6 Binn. 94 (Pa. 1813); Edward Coke, *The First Part of the Institutes of the Laws of England* (1628; Philadelphia: Johnson and Warner, 1812), 1:1.

22. *Papers Read Before the Juridical Society* (London: V. & R. Stevens & G. S. Norton, 1858–1874), 83; Robert Campbell, *The Law Relating to the Sale of Goods and Commercial Agency* (London: Stevens & Haynes, 1881), 30.

23. E.g., F. W. Maitland, "The Mystery of Seisin," *Law Quarterly Review* 2 (1886): 489; John Herbert Williams and William Morse Crowdy, *Goodeve's Modern Law of Personal Property,* 4th ed. (London: Sweet and Maxwell, 1904), 17; Alfred Nixon and Robert W. Holland, *Commercial Law* (London: Longmans, Green, and Co., 1907), 147.

24. Henry Dunning Macleod, *The Elements of Economics* (London: Longmans, Green, and Co., 1881), 1:141–142.

25. *Cincinnati v. Williams,* 8 Ohio Dec. Reprint 718 (1883); Lewis H. Bisbee and John C. Simonds, *The Board of Trade and the Produce Exchange* (Chicago: Callaghan and Co., 1884), 198–199; John Lewis, *A Treatise on the Law of Eminent Domain in the United States* (Chicago: Callaghan and Co. 1888), 43–44.

26. E.g., Samuel Williston, "History of the Law of Business Corporations Before 1800," *Harvard Law Review* 2 (1888): 151; John R. Commons, *The Distribution of Wealth* (New York: Macmillan and Co., 1893), 92; Robert Ludlow Fowler, *The Real Property Laws of the State of New York* (New York: Baker, Voorhis and Co., 1904), 469.

27. Joseph K. Angell, *A Treatise on the Law of Watercourses,* 5th ed. (Boston: Little, Brown and Co., 1854), 531; Thomas Cooley, *A Treatise on the Constitutional Limitations Which Rest Upon the Legislative Power of the States of the American Union* (Boston: Little, Brown and Co., 1868), 544–545; *Glover v. Powell,* 10 N.J. Eq. 211 (1854); *Evansville and Crawfordsville Railroad Co. v. Dick,* 9 Ind. 433 (1857); *Nevins v. Peoria,* 41 Ill. 502 (1866); *Lee v. Pembroke Iron Co.,* 57 Me. 481 (1867).

28. *Pumpelly v. Green Bay Co.,* 80 U.S. 166, 177–178, 181 (1871).

29. *Eaton v. Boston, Concord, and Montreal Railroad,* 51 N.H. 504 (1872). I have removed internal quotation marks from some of the quotations.

30. John F. Dillon, *The Law of Municipal Corporations,* 2nd ed. (New York: James Cockroft and Co., 1873), 2:900; Theodore Sedgwick, *A Treatise on the Rules Which Govern the Interpretation and Construction of Statutory and Constitutional Law,* 2nd ed. (New York: Baker, Voorhis and Co., 1874), 458; *Grand Rapids Booming Co. v. Jarvis,* 30 Mich. 308 (1874); *Thurston v. St. Joseph,* 51 Mo. 510 (1873); *Kemper v. Louisville,* 77 Ky. 87 (1878); *Weaver v. Mississippi & Rum River Boom Co.,* 28 Minn. 534 (1881); *Foster v. Stafford National Bank,* 57 Vt. 128 (1884); *Conniff v. San Francisco,* 67 Cal. 45 (1885); *Station v. Norfolk & Carolina Railroad Co.,* 111 N.C. 278 (1892).

31. Henry E. Mills, *A Treatise on the Law of Eminent Domain* (St. Louis: F. H. Thomas and Co., 1879), 33; Christopher G. Tiedeman, *A Treatise on the Limitations of Police Power in the United States* (St. Louis: F. H. Thomas Law Book Co., 1886), 397; Charles C. Dickinson, "Leading Limitations Upon the Exercise of the Right of Eminent Domain," *Cornell Law Journal* 1 (1894): 11; Carman F. Randolph, *The Law of Eminent Domain in the United States* (Boston: Little, Brown and Co., 1894), 128–129.

32. *Transportation Co. v. Chicago,* 99 U.S. 635, 642 (1878); *Cumberland v. Willison,* 50 Md. 138 (1878).

33. *Story v. New York Elevated Railroad Co.,* 90 N.Y. 122, 186 (1882) (Earl, J., dissenting); Charles S. Haight and Arthur M. Marsh, *Questions and Answers for Bar-Examination Review* (New York: Baker, Voorhis and Co., 1909), 86; A. Knauth, "Constitutional Protection of Property Rights," *Albany Law Journal* 26 (1882): 328; F. R. T., Book Review, *Harvard Law Review* 14 (1901): 471.

34. "Additional Compensation for Additional Burdens to Owners of Property Abutting on Streets," *Central Law Journal* 19 (1884): 384; *New York Times,* 18 Oct. 1882, 4; David J. Brewer, "Protection to Private Property from Public Attack," *New Englander and Yale Review* 19 (1891): 103.

35. Arthur G. Sedgwick, "Constitutional Protection of Property Rights," *North American Review* 135 (1882): 253–265.

36. Lewis, *A Treatise on the Law of Eminent Domain,* 45–46.

37. Ill. 1870, art. II, sec. 13; W. Va. 1872, art. III, sec. 9; Ark. 1874, art. II, sec. 22; Pa. 1874, art. XVI, sec. 8; Ala. 1875, art. XIII, sec. 7; Mo. 1875, art. II, sec. 21; Neb. 1875, art. I, sec. 21; Colo. 1876, art. II, sec. 15; Tex. 1876, art. I, sec.

17; Ga. 1877, sec. 3; Cal. 1879, art. I, sec. 14; La. 1879, art. 156; Mont. 1889, art. III, sec. 14; N.D. 1889, art. I, sec. 14; S.D. 1889, art. VI, sec. 13; Wyo. 1889, art. I, sec. 33; Miss. 1890, art. 3, sec. 17.

38. R. Mason Lisle, "An Interesting Question in Eminent Domain Under Constitutional Law," *American Law Register* 36 (1888): 1–3; Frank Hagerman, "When Property Is Damaged for Public Use," *American Law Review* 25 (1891): 924–939.

39. *Welch v. Swasey*, 214 U.S. 91 (1909); *Block v. Hirsh*, 256 U.S. 135, 156 (1921).

40. *Pennsylvania Coal Co. v. Mahon*, 260 U.S. 393 (1922).

41. Richard F. Hamm, *Shaping the Eighteenth Amendment: Temperance Reform, Legal Culture, and the Polity, 1880–1920* (Chapel Hill: University of North Carolina Press, 1995), 20; *Wynehamer v. People*, 13 N.Y. 378, 396–397 (1856).

42. *Wynehamer*, 468–469.

43. *People ex rel. Manhattan Savings Institution v. Otis*, 90 N.Y. 48, 51–52 (1882); *In re Jacobs*, 98 N.Y. 98, 105 (1885).

44. *State v. Allmond*, 7 Del. 612 (1856); *State v. Paul*, 5 R.I. 185 (1858).

45. Cooley, *Constitutional Limitations*, 356; *District of Columbia v. Saville*, 8 D.C. 581 (1874); *State v. Goodwill*, 10 S.E. 285 (W.Va. 1889); *State v. Scougal*, 51 N.W. 858 (S.D. 1892); *Ex parte Whitwell*, 32 P. 870 (Cal. 1893); *St. Louis v. Hill*, 22 S.W. 861 (1893); *Ritchie v. People*, 40 N.E. 454 (Ill. 1895).

46. *Goodwill*, 287; *Scougal*, 865; *Hill*, 862.

47. *Davidson v. New Orleans*, 96 U.S. 97, 104 (1877).

48. *Slaughter-House Cases*, 83 U.S. 36, 127 (1872) (Swayne, J., dissenting); *Munn v. Illinois*, 94 U.S. 113, 143 (1876) (Field, J., dissenting).

49. The early economist John Commons explained this transition in similar but not identical terms, as a shift from a conception of property as "use-value" to one of "exchange-value." John R. Commons, *Legal Foundations of Capitalism* (New York: Macmillan, 1924), 11–21.

50. *Chicago, Milwaukee & St. Paul Railway Co. v. Minnesota*, 134 U.S. 418, 458 (1890); *Smyth v. Ames*, 169 U.S. 466 (1898).

51. William H. Taft, "The Right of Private Property," *Michigan Law Journal* 3 (1894): 219.

52. *Rippe v. Becker*, 57 N.W. 331, 336 (Minn. 1894); *Woods's Appeal*, 75 Pa. 59 (1874); *Pollock v. Farmers' Loan & Trust Co.*, 157 U.S. 429, 607 (1895) (Field, J., concurring).

53. Howard Gillman, *The Constitution Besieged: The Rise and Demise of Lochner Era Police Powers Jurisprudence* (Durham, NC: Duke University Press, 1993), 10; James W. Ely, Jr., *The Guardian of Every Other Right: A Constitutional History of Property Rights*, 3rd ed. (New York: Oxford University Press, 2008), 83–105.

54. Morton J. Horwitz, *The Transformation of American Law 1870–1960: The Crisis of Legal Orthodoxy* (New York: Oxford University Press, 1992), 145–151; Kenneth J. Vandevelde, "The New Property of the Nineteenth Century: The

Development of the Modern Concept of Property," *Buffalo Law Review* 29 (1980): 357–359.

55. Thomas C. Grey, "The Disintegration of Property," in J. Roland Pennock and John W. Chapman, eds., *Nomos XXII: Property* (New York: New York University Press, 1980), 81, 85n40; Horwitz, *Transformation*, 151–156.

4. Owning the News

1. Quoted in Jeffrey L. Pasley, *"The Tyranny of Printers": Newspaper Politics in the Early American Republic* (Charlottesville: University Press of Virginia, 2001), 9.

2. Richard R. John, *Spreading the News: The American Postal System from Franklin to Morse* (Cambridge: Harvard University Press, 1995), 31–42; Richard B. Kielbowicz, *News in the Mail: The Press, Post Office, and Public Information, 1700–1860s* (New York: Greenwood Press, 1989); Charles G. Steffen, "Newspapers for Free: The Economies of Newspaper Circulation in the Early Republic," *Journal of the Early Republic* 23 (2003): 409–410.

3. Menahem Blondheim, *News Over the Wires: The Telegraph and the Flow of Public Information in America, 1844–1897* (Cambridge: Harvard University Press, 1994), 11–67.

4. "How We Get Our News," *Harper's New Monthly Magazine* 34 (1867): 513; Melville E. Stone, *Fifty Years a Journalist* (Garden City, NY: Doubleday, Page and Co., 1921), 63–64; Fred Fedler, "Plagiarism Persists in News Despite Changing Attitudes," *Newspaper Research Journal* 27(2) (2006): 24–37.

5. Quoted in Victor Rosewater, *History of Cooperative News-Gathering in the United States* (New York: D. Appleton and Co., 1930), 279.

6. Richard A. Schwarzlose, *The Nation's Newsbrokers* (Evanston, IL: Northwestern University Press, 1989–1990), 2:248.

7. Quoted in Schwarzlose, *Nation's Newsbrokers*, 2:59, 2:150–151.

8. Circular, 1 Nov. 1890, Melville E. Stone Papers, box 8, folder 530, NL; Circular, 3 Sept. 1895, Victor Lawson Papers, box 112, folder 729, NL.

9. *Clayton v. Stone*, 5 F. Cas. 999 (C.C.S.D.N.Y. 1829); James Schouler, *A Treatise on the Law of Personal Property* (Boston: Little, Brown, and Co., 1873), 672.

10. James Appleton Morgan, *The Law of Literature* (New York: James Cockroft and Co., 1875), 2:382; *Harper v. Shoppell*, 26 F. 519 (C.C.S.D.N.Y. 1886); "What Matter Is Entitled to Copyright Protection in the United States Statutes," *Central Law Journal* 56 (1903): 493; *Tribune Co. of Chicago v. Associated Press*, 116 F. 126 (C.C.N.D. Ill. 1900).

11. "Stealing News," *Nation* 38 (1884): 159.

12. *New York Times*, 5 Mar. 1884, 3; 15 Mar. 1884, 4; *Copyright in Congress 1789–1904* (Washington, DC: Government Printing Office, 1905), 226–229; Robert Brauneis, "The Transformation of Originality in the Progressive-Era

Debate over Copyright in News" (2009), http://ssrn.com/abstract=1365366; *New York Times*, 2 Feb. 1884, 4; Joseph Frazier Wall, *Henry Watterson: Reconstructed Rebel* (New York: Oxford University Press, 1956), 181; Henry Watterson, *"Marse Henry": An Autobiography* (New York: George H. Doran Co., 1919), 2:104–105; *New York Times*, 19 Apr. 1884, 1; Oliver Gramling, *AP: The Story of News* (New York: Farrar and Rinehart, 1940), 284.

13. "Current Topics," *Albany Law Journal* 60 (1899): 132; "Copyright in Telegraphic News," *Journal of the Society of Comparative Legislation* 1 (n.s.) (1899): 472; "Legislation of the Empire, 1895," *Journal of the Society of Comparative Legislation* 1 (1896–1897): 98; Lionel Bently, "Copyright and the Victorian Internet: Telegraphic Property Laws in Colonial Australia," *Loyola of Los Angeles Law Review* 38 (2004): 71–176; Acland Giles, "Literary and Artistic Copyright in the Commonwealth," *Commonwealth Law Review* 3 (1906): 153; *New York Times*, 2 July 1898, 2; 11 Aug. 1899, 6; Warwick H. Draper, "Copyright Legislation," *Law Quarterly Review* 17 (1901): 48–49.

14. E. Fulton Brylawski and Abe Goldman, eds., *Legislative History of the 1909 Copyright Act* (South Hackensack, NJ: Fred B. Rothman and Co., 1976), 1:C21–C22; 2:D203; Richard Rogers Bowker, *Copyright: Its History and Its Law* (Boston: Houghton Mifflin Co., 1912), 88–89.

15. *Tribune Co. of Chicago v. Associated Press*, 116 F. 126 (C.C.N.D. Ill. 1900); *New York Times*, 9 Sept. 1909, 1; 10 Sept. 1909, 1, 8; 11 Sept. 1909, 1.

16. Stuart Banner, *Anglo-American Securities Regulation: Cultural and Political Roots, 1690–1860* (Cambridge: Cambridge University Press, 1998), 261–262.

17. David Hochfelder, "'Where the Common People Could Speculate': The Ticker, Bucket Shops, and the Origin of Popular Participation in Financial Markets, 1880–1920," *Journal of American History* 93 (2006): 335–358.

18. Cedric B. Cowing, *Populists, Plungers, and Progressives: A Social History of Stock and Commodity Speculation 1890–1936* (Princeton: Princeton University Press, 1965), 28–30; Ann Fabian, *Card Sharps, Dream Books, & Bucket Shops: Gambling in 19th-Century America* (Ithaca, NY: Cornell University Press, 1990), 188–193.

19. Special Committee on Bucket Shops, "Digest of the Preliminary Work of the Special Committee of June 25, 1913," 7, 12–13, NYSE.

20. Special Committee on Bucket Shops, "Digest," 154, 35.

21. *Kiernan v. Manhattan Quotation Telegraph Co.*, 50 How. Pr. 194 (N.Y. Sup. 1876).

22. Jonathan Ira Levy, "Contemplating Delivery: Futures Trading and the Problem of Commodity Exchange in the United States, 1875–1905," *American Historical Review* 111 (2006): 329–335; *New York & Chicago Grain & Stock Exchange v. Board of Trade*, 19 N.E. 855 (Ill. 1889); *National Telegraph News Co. v. Western Union Telegraph Co.*, 119 F. 294 (7th Cir. 1902).

23. *Board of Trade v. Hadden-Krull Co.*, 109 F. 705 (C.C.E.D. Wis. 1901); *F. W. Dodge v. Construction Information Co.*, 66 N.E. 204 (Mass. 1903).

24. *Chicago Board of Trade v. Christie Grain & Stock Co.,* 198 U.S. 236 (1905); *Hunt v. New York Cotton Exchange,* 205 U.S. 322 (1907).

25. J. Harold Mulherin, Jeffry M. Netter, and James A. Overdahl, "Prices Are Property: The Organization of Financial Exchanges from a Transaction Cost Perspective," *Journal of Law & Economics* 34 (1991): 591–644; Victor Lawson to Albert J. Barr, 2 Nov. 1892, Victor Lawson Papers, box 2, folder 4, p. 287, NL.

26. Schwarzlose, *Nation's Newsbrokers,* 2:233; Gramling, *AP,* 285; Kent Cooper, *Kent Cooper and the Associated Press: An Autobiography* (New York: Random House, 1959), 198; *Law of the Associated Press* (New York: Associated Press, 1917), 2:31–32, 2:107–108.

27. *Law of the Associated Press,* 2:10–15.

28. *Law of the Associated Press,* 2:162–163; *Associated Press v. International News Service,* 240 F. 983 (S.D.N.Y. 1917).

29. *Associated Press v. International News Service,* 245 F. 244 (2nd Cir. 1917).

30. Memorandum of Respondent Regarding Petition for Writ of Certiorari, 2–3, *International News Service v. Associated Press,* 248 U.S. 215 (1918).

31. *International News Service v. Associated Press,* 248 U.S. 215 (1918). For discussions of the case that focus on issues different from those highlighted here, see Douglas G. Baird, "The Story of *INS v. AP:* Property, Natural Monopoly, and the Uneasy Legacy of a Concocted Controversy," in Jane C. Ginsburg and Rochelle Cooper Dreyfus, eds., *Intellectual Property Stories* (New York: Foundation Press, 2006); Richard A. Epstein, "*International News Service v. Associated Press:* Custom and Law as Sources of Property Rights in News," *Virginia Law Review* 78 (1992): 85–128.

32. Stone, *Fifty Years a Journalist,* 361; Frank E. Gannett, "What Is Your Associated Press Membership Worth to You?" (1924), Victor Lawson Papers, box 113, folder 736, NL; Moses Koenigsberg, *King News: An Autobiography* (1941; Freeport, NY: Books for Libraries Press, 1972), 455.

33. Alexander M. Bickel and Benno C. Schmidt, Jr., *The Judiciary and Responsible Government 1910–21* (New York: Macmillan, 1984), 701; Edward S. Rogers, "Unfair Competition," *Michigan Law Review* 17 (1919): 491; Benjamin Pepper, "Unfair Competition: Application to News Service," *Cornell Law Quarterly* 4 (1919): 226; Walter Wheeler Cook, "The Associated Press Case," *Yale Law Journal* 28 (1919): 390; "Property in News," *Harvard Law Review* 32 (1919): 566.

34. W. Edward Sell, "The Doctrine of Misappropriation in Unfair Competition: The *Associated Press* Doctrine After Forty Years," *Vanderbilt Law Review* 11 (1958): 494–496; Learned Hand to Martin Manton and Thomas Swan, 8 Oct. 1929, and Thomas Swan to Learned Hand and Martin Manton, 8 Oct. 1929, *Cheney Bros. v. Doris Silk Corp.,* Learned Hand papers, box 186, folder 17, HLS.

35. Victoria Smith Ekstrand, *News Piracy and the Hot News Doctrine: Origins in Law and Implications for the Digital Age* (New York: LFB Scholarly Publishing, 2005).

36. *Associated Press v. KVOS, Inc.*, 80 F.2d 575 (9th Cir. 1935); *Pittsburgh Athletic Co. v. KQV Broadcasting Co.*, 24 F. Supp. 490 (W.D. Pa. 1938); *Twentieth Century Sporting Club v. Transradio Press Service, Inc.*, 300 N.Y.S. 159 (N.Y. Sup. 1937); *National Exhibition Co. v. Fass*, 143 N.Y.S.2d 767 (N.Y. Sup. 1955).

37. *National Basketball Association v. Motorola, Inc.*, 105 F.3d 841 (2nd Cir. 1997).

38. *Standard & Poor's Corp. v. Commodity Exchange, Inc.*, 683 F.2d 704 (2nd Cir. 1982); *Board of Trade of the City of Chicago v. Dow Jones & Co.*, 456 N.E.2d 84 (Ill. 1983).

5. People, Not Things

1. "Private Property and Public Interest," *Independent* 53 (1901): 573; Theodore Roosevelt, "Duties of the Citizen" (1910), in Maurice Garland Fulton, ed., *Roosevelt's Writings* (New York: Macmillan, 1920), 227; "The Right of Property vs. the Right of Self-Preservation," *American Lawyer* 11 (1903): 2.

2. An enormous amount has been written on this subject, including, for example, Morton Keller, *Regulating a New Economy: Public Policy and Economic Change in America, 1900–1933* (Cambridge: Harvard University Press, 1990).

3. Richard Schlatter, *Private Property: The History of an Idea* (New Brunswick, NJ: Rutgers University Press, 1951), 187–205; for examples, see *The Works of the Honourable James Wilson, L.L.D.* (Philadelphia: Bronson and Chauncey, 1804), 2:467; "Restrictions Upon State Power in Relation to Private Property," *United States Law Intelligencer and Review* 1 (1829): 59.

4. "On Publick and Private Credit," *Worcester Magazine* 3 (1787): 135; James Schouler, "Property and Its Origin," *United States Jurist* 2 (1872): 317; E. P. Hurlbut, *Essays on Human Rights and Their Political Guarantees* (New York: Greeley and McElrath, 1845), 178; Henry St. George Tucker, *A Few Lectures on Natural Law* (Charlottesville, VA: James Alexander, 1844), 12.

5. Albert Ellery Bergh, ed., *The Writings of Thomas Jefferson* (Washington, DC: Thomas Jefferson Memorial Association, 1907), 13:333; Gregory S. Alexander, *Commodity & Propriety: Competing Visions of Property in American Legal Thought 1776–1970* (Chicago: University of Chicago Press, 1997), 26–29; "Origin of Property—Cherokee Titles," *American Jurist* 6 (1831): 282; Joseph Story, *A Discourse Pronounced at the Request of the Essex Historical Society* (Boston: Hilliard, Gray, Little, and Wilkins, 1828), 69–70.

6. "What Is the Reason?" *United States Magazine and Democratic Review* 16 (1845): 17–19.

7. Timothy Walker, *Introduction to American Law* (Philadelphia: P. H. Nicklin and T. Johnson, 1837), 257; "How Exclusive Ownership in Property First Originated: Communism," *American Catholic Quarterly Review* 3 (1878): 13; James A. Cain, "The Origin of Private Property," *Catholic World* 47 (1888): 547; C. H.

Parkhurst, "The Christian Conception of Property," *New Princeton Review* 1 (1886): 37; J. B. Clark, "The Moral Basis of Property in Land," *Journal of Social Science* 27 (1890): 21.

8. Henry Sumner Maine, *Ancient Law* (1861; Boston: Beacon Press, 1963), 246–247, 254; Charles Letourneau, *Property: Its Origin and Development* (New York: Charles Scribner's Sons, 1907), 115.

9. Richard T. Ely, *Property and Contract in Their Relations to the Distribution of Wealth* (New York: Macmillan, 1914), 2:534; Samuel B. Clarke, "Criticisms Upon Henry George, Reviewed from the Stand-point of Justice," *Harvard Law Review* 1 (1888): 271–272.

10. Jeremy Bentham, *Principles of Legislation* (Boston: Wells and Lilly, 1830), 307, 304; John Austin, *The Province of Jurisprudence Determined,* 2nd ed. (London: John Murray, 1861), 234; John W. Burgess, *Political Science and Comparative Constitutional Law* (Boston: Ginn and Co., 1891), 88; T. Dabney Marshall, "What Law Is," *American Law Review* 27 (1893): 544; John Chipman Gray, *The Nature and Sources of the Law* (New York: Columbia University Press, 1909), 213; Oliver Wendell Holmes, "Natural Law," *Harvard Law Review* 32 (1918): 41.

11. *The Works of Jeremy Bentham* (Edinburgh: William Tait, 1843), 1:308; Orrin K. McMurray, "Liberty of Testation and Some Modern Limitations Thereon," in *Celebration Legal Essays* (Chicago: Northwestern University Press, 1919), 539.

12. "Property: Its Origin and Development," *Literary World* 23 (1892): 290; *New York Times,* 17 Aug. 1902, 8; 19 June 1910, 10; Henry B. Brown, "The Distribution of Property," *Annual Report of the American Bar Association* 16 (1893): 213–242; John F. Dillon, "Property—Its Rights and Duties in Our Legal and Social Systems," *American Law Review* 29 (1895): 161–188; Arthur Twining Hadley, "The Constitutional Position of Property in America," *Independent* 64 (1908): 834–838.

13. Christopher G. Tiedeman, *The Unwritten Constitution of the United States* (New York: G. P. Putnam's Sons, 1890), 16, 78–81.

14. David G. Ritchie, *Natural Rights* (New York: Macmillan, 1895), ix; William Tucker, "The Evolution of Property," *Universalist Quarterly and General Review* 22 (1885): 465; George B. Newcomb, "Theories of Property," *Political Science Quarterly* 1 (1886): 19; William E. Simonds, "Natural Right of Property in Intellectual Production," *Yale Law Journal* 1 (1891): 16–17; George H. Smith, "The Unwritten Constitution of the United States," *American Law Review* 27 (1893): 57; John E. Keeler, "Survival of the Theory of Natural Rights in Judicial Decisions," *Yale Law Journal* 5 (1892): 25.

15. William Blackstone, *Commentaries on the Laws of England* (Oxford: Clarendon Press, 1765–1769), 2:2; Alexander, *Commodity & Propriety,* 311–351.

16. Nathaniel Chipman, *Principles of Government* (Burlington, VT: Edward Smith, 1833), 70; Oliver Wendell Holmes, Jr., *The Common Law* (Boston: Little,

Brown and Co., 1881), 220; Thomas Davidson, "Property," *Journal of Social Science* 22 (1887): 107; Everett V. Abbot, "The Police Power and the Right to Compensation," *Harvard Law Review* 3 (1889): 190.

17. Wesley Newcomb Hohfeld, "Some Fundamental Legal Conceptions as Applied in Judicial Reasoning," *Yale Law Journal* 23 (1913): 16–59; Wesley Newcomb Hohfeld, "Fundamental Legal Conceptions as Applied in Judicial Reasoning," *Yale Law Journal* 26 (1917): 710–770.

18. Hohfeld, "Fundamental Legal Conceptions," 746–747.

19. Oliver Wendell Holmes, Jr., to Felix Frankfurter, 20 Feb. 1922, *The Oliver Wendell Holmes, Jr., Papers* (Frederick, MD: University Publications of America, 1985), reel 21, frame 909; Arthur L. Corbin, "Taxation of Seats on the Stock Exchange," *Yale Law Journal* 31 (1922): 429; Leon Green, "Relational Interests," *Illinois Law Review* 30 (1935): 37.

20. Barbara H. Fried, *The Progressive Assault on Laissez Faire: Robert Hale and the First Law and Economics Movement* (Cambridge: Harvard University Press, 1998); Robert L. Hale, "Rate Making and the Revision of the Property Concept," *Columbia Law Review* 11 (1922): 214.

21. Morris R. Cohen, "Property and Sovereignty," *Cornell Law Quarterly* 13 (1927): 12, 26.

22. Daniel F. Kellogg, "The Disappearing Right of Private Property," *North American Review,* Jan. 1914, 55; David Kinley, "The Renewed Extension of Government Control of Economic Life," *American Economic Review: Papers and Proceedings* 4 (1914): 3; Ezra Bowen, "The Concept of Private Property," *Cornell Law Quarterly* 11 (1925): 46.

23. Bowen, "Concept of Private Property," 46–48.

24. Barry Cushman, *Rethinking the New Deal Court: The Structure of a Constitutional Revolution* (New York: Oxford University Press, 1998); *United States v. Carolene Products,* 304 U.S. 144, 152 and n4 (1938).

6. Owning Sound

1. Russell Sanjek, *American Popular Music and Its Business: The First Four Hundred Years* (New York: Oxford University Press, 1988), 2:49, 77; Lisa Gitelman, "Reading Music, Reading Records, Reading Race: Musical Copyright and the U.S. Copyright Act of 1909," *Musical Quarterly* 81 (1997): 273.

2. Sanjek, *American Popular Music,* 2:4; 4 Stat. 436 (1831).

3. Zvi S. Rosen, "The Twilight of the Opera Pirates: A Prehistory of the Exclusive Right of Public Performance for Musical Compositions," *Cardozo Arts & Entertainment Law Journal* 24 (2007): 1157–1218; 11 Stat. 138 (1856); *New York Daily Times,* 24 June 1856, 4; David Suisman, *Selling Sounds: The Commercial Revolution in American Music* (Cambridge: Harvard University Press, 2009), 56–89; "Amendments to the Copyright Law," *Scientific American* 76 (1897): 227;

"The Musical Copyright Act," *Church's Musical Visitor* 11 (1882): 353; 29 Stat. 481 (1897).

4. Walter L. Welch and Leah Brodbeck Stenzel Burt, *From Tinfoil to Stereo: The Acoustic Years of the Recording Industry, 1877–1929* (Gainesville: University Press of Florida, 1994), 28–102; Andre Millard, *America on Record: A History of Recorded Sound* (New York: Cambridge University Press, 1995), 49; Arthur W. J. G. Ord-Hume, *Pianola: The History of the Self-Playing Piano* (London: George Allen and Unwin, 1984), 27–28; Littell McClung, "Player-Pianos for Piano-Players," *Lippincott's Monthly Magazine* 91 (1913): 248; Jonathan Sterne, *The Audible Past: Cultural Origins of Sound Reproduction* (Durham, NC: Duke University Press, 2003).

5. E. Fulton Brylawski and Abe Goldman, eds., *Legislative History of the 1909 Copyright Act* (South Hackensack, NJ: Fred B. Rothman and Co., 1976), H31–32; "Current Topics," *Albany Law Journal* 48 (1893): 442; "Machines and Copyright," *Current Literature* 27 (1900): 97.

6. *Kennedy v. McTammany,* 33 F. 584 (C.C.D. Mass. 1888); *Stern v. Rosey,* 17 App. D.C. 562 (C.A.D.C. 1901).

7. *White-Smith Music Publishing Co. v. Apollo Co.,* 209 U.S. 1 (1908).

8. *New York Times,* 26 Feb. 1908, 6; "Is the Copyright in a Musical Composition Infringed by Its Phonograph?" *American Lawyer,* Apr. 1901, 154.

9. John Philip Sousa, "The Menace of Mechanical Music," *Appleton's Magazine* 8 (1906): 278–284; Brylawski and Goldman, *Legislative History,* H24.

10. Edward N. Waters, *Victor Herbert: A Life in Music* (New York: Macmillan, 1955), 333–344; Brylawski and Goldman, *Legislative History,* H26, J198–199.

11. *New York Times,* 19 Dec. 1907, 8; 16 Dec. 1907, 8; 22 Dec. 1907, 13.

12. Richard Rogers Bowker to Frank D. Currier, 27 Dec. 1907, Richard Rogers Bowker papers, box 80, NYPL; Richard Rogers Bowker to Charles G. Washburn, 12 Dec. 1908, Richard Rogers Bowker papers, box 81, NYPL; Draft of letter from American Copyright League to the 60th Congress, n.d. 1907, Richard Rogers Bowker papers, box 79, NYPL.

13. "The Copyright Question," *Dial* 45 (1908): 444; Brylawski and Goldman, *Legislative History,* K264–265, J335.

14. Brylawski and Goldman, *Legislative History,* K291; Philip G. Hubert, Jr., "What the Phonograph Will Do for Music and Music-Lovers," *Century Illustrated Magazine* 46 (1893): 153; Brylawski and Goldman, *Legislative History,* J310.

15. Brylawski and Goldman, *Legislative History,* J352; Edward Schuberth & Co. to Robert Underwood Johnson, 14 Mar. 1907, Robert Underwood Johnson papers, box 11, NYPL.

16. Brylawski and Goldman, *Legislative History,* H140–141, H186–187, J254.

17. Ibid., J286–288.

18. Ibid., J207.

19. Ord-Hume, *Pianola,* 270.

20. Brylawski and Goldman, *Legislative History,* H167, H115–116.

21. Charles G. Washburn to Richard Rogers Bowker, 13 Apr. 1914, Richard Rogers Bowker papers, box 81, NYPL; N. A. Livingstone to George Haven Putnam, 31 Mar. 1908, George Haven Putnam papers, box 5, NYPL.

22. Brylawski and Goldman, *Legislative History*, K361, M111–112.

23. Arthur W. Weil, *American Copyright Law* (Chicago: Callahan and Co., 1917), 229; *Fonotipia Ltd. v. Bradley*, 171 F. 951, 963 (C.C.E.D.N.Y. 1909); *Aeolian Co. v. Royal Music Roll Co.*, 196 F. 926 (W.D.N.Y. 1912); Richard C. De Wolf, *An Outline of Copyright Law* (Boston: John W. Luce and Co., 1925), 102; Barbara A. Ringer, "The Unauthorized Duplication of Sound Recordings" (1957), published in *Copyright Law Revision* (Washington, DC: Government Printing Office, 1961), 4–5; *Capitol Records, Inc. v. Mercury Records Corp.*, 221 F.2d 657 (2nd Cir. 1955).

24. *Victor Talking Machine Co. v. Armstrong*, 132 F. 711 (C.C.S.D.N.Y. 1904); *Fonotipia*, 171 F. at 963.

25. *Memorandum on Unfair Competition at the Common Law* (Washington, DC: Government Printing Office, 1916), 72; *Federal Trade Commission v. Orient Music Roll Co.*, 2 F.T.C. 176 (1919); *Metropolitan Opera Association v. Wagner-Nichols Recorder Corp.*, 101 N.Y.S.2d 483 (N.Y. Sup. 1950).

26. Ringer, "Unauthorized Duplication," 22–34.

27. W. Jefferson Davis, *Radio Law*, 2nd ed. (Los Angeles: Parker, Stone and Baird Co., 1930), 91; *New York Times*, 22 Mar. 1923, 1; 25 Mar. 1923, E3.

28. *Jerome H. Remick & Co. v. American Automobile Accessories Co.*, 5 F.2d 411 (6th Cir. 1925); Stephen Davis, *The Law of Radio Communication* (New York: McGraw-Hill, 1927), 136–139; "Infringement of Musical Copyright by Radio Broadcasting," *University of Pennsylvania Law Review* 75 (1927): 549; A. L. Ashby, "Legal Aspects of Radio Broadcasting," *Air Law Review* 1 (1930): 342; *Buck v. Jewell-La Salle Realty Co.*, 283 U.S. 191 (1931).

29. John Ryan, *The Production of Culture in the Music Industry: The ASCAP-BMI Controversy* (Lanham, MD: University Press of America, 1985); Michele Hilmes, *Radio Voices: American Broadcasting, 1922–1952* (Minneapolis: University of Minnesota Press, 1997), 72–73, 83.

30. Virginia Waring, *Fred Waring and the Pennsylvanians* (Urbana: University of Illinois Press, 1997), 138.

31. *Waring v. WDAS Broadcasting Station, Inc.*, 194 A. 631, 635, 638 (Pa. 1937); *Waring v. Dunlea*, 26 F. Supp. 338, 340 (E.D.N.C. 1939).

32. *RCA Manufacturing Co. v. Whiteman*, 114 F.2d 86 (2nd Cir. 1940); Learned Hand to Charles Clark and Robert Patterson, 20 June 1940, Charles Clark to Learned Hand and Robert Patterson, 21 June 1940, Robert Patterson to Learned Hand and Charles Clark, 29 June 1940, *RCA Manufacturing Co. v. Whiteman*, Learned Hand papers, box 202, folder 3, HLS.

33. Ringer, "Unauthorized Duplication," 8–9; Sidney A. Diamond, "Copyright Problems of the Phonograph Record Industry," *Vanderbilt Law Review* 15 (1962): 431; William Howland Kenney, *Recorded Music in American*

Life: The Phonograph and Popular Memory, 1890–1945 (New York: Oxford University Press, 1999), 189–190.

34. Nathan Bass, "Interpretative Rights of Performing Artists," *Dickinson Law Review* 42 (1938): 67–68; "Rights of Performers Against Unlicensed Radio Broadcasts," *Yale Law Journal* 49 (1940): 563–568; Rudolf M. Littauer, "The Present Legal Status of Artists, Recorders and Broadcasters in America," *Geistiges Eigentum* 3 (1938): 217; Joseph S. Dubin, "Copyright Aspects of Sound Recordings," *Southern California Law Review* 26 (1953): 141–142; Ringer, "Unauthorized Duplication," 34–37.

35. Milton Diamond and Jerome H. Adler, "Proposed Copyright Revision and Phonograph Records," *Air Law Review* 11 (1940): 51–55.

36. Ringer, "Unauthorized Duplication," 9n84; "Piracy on Records," *Stanford Law Review* 5 (1953): 433–458.

37. Millard, *America on Record,* 316–321; Paul Frederick Helfer, "Copyright Revision and the Unauthorized Duplication of Phonograph Records—A New Statute and the Old Problems: A Job Half Done," *Bulletin of the Copyright Society of the U.S.A.* 14 (1966): 144.

38. These cases and statutes are summarized in the amicus brief filed by the Recording Industry Association of America in *Goldstein v. California,* 412 U.S. 546 (1973), the case in which the Supreme Court upheld the constitutionality of California's antipiracy statute.

39. 85 Stat. 391 (1971).

40. William H. O'Dowd, "The Need for a Public Performance Right in Sound Recordings," *Harvard Journal on Legislation* 31 (1994): 251–254.

41. Shourin Sen, "The Denial of a General Performance Right in Sound Recordings: A Policy that Facilitates Our Democratic Civil Society?" *Harvard Journal of Law & Technology* 21 (2007): 235, 256–262.

7. Owning Fame

1. Phineas T. Barnum, *The Life of P. T. Barnum, Written by Himself* (1855; Urbana: University of Illinois Press, 2000), 309; W. Porter Ware and Thaddeus C. Lockard, Jr., *P. T. Barnum Presents Jenny Lind: The American Tour of the Swedish Nightingale* (Baton Rouge: Louisiana State University Press, 1980), 9, plate between pages 70 and 71.

2. Ivor Guest, *Fanny Elssler* (London: Adam and Charles Black, 1970), 133; Leonard W. Labaree, ed., *The Papers of Benjamin Franklin* (New Haven: Yale University Press, 1959–), 29:613.

3. Ron Sirak, "Golf's First Billion-Dollar Man," *Golf Digest,* Feb. 2006; Lacey Rose, Louis Hau, and Amanda Schupak, "Top-Earning Dead Celebrities," *Forbes,* 24 Oct. 2006.

4. Noble E. Cunningham, Jr., *Popular Images of the Presidency from Washington to Lincoln* (Columbia: University of Missouri Press, 1991), 241–280;

Wendy Wick Reaves and Sally Pierce, "Translations from the Plate: The Marketplace of Public Portraiture," in Grant B. Romer and Brian Wallis, eds., *Young America: The Daguerreotypes of Southworth & Hawes* (Göttingen, Germany: Steidl, 2005), 89–103; Leo Braudy, *The Frenzy of Renown: Fame and Its History* (New York: Oxford University Press, 1986), 453–455.

5. Reese V. Jenkins, "Technology and the Market: George Eastman and the Origins of Mass Amateur Photography," *Technology and Culture* 16 (1975): 1–19; John Carbutt, "Photography and the Manufacturing Arts," *American Architect and Building News* 35 (1892): 152A; Robert Taft, *Photography and the American Scene: A Social History, 1839–1889* (1938; New York: Dover Publications, 1964), 419–450; James D. Norris, *Advertising and the Transformation of American Society, 1865–1920* (New York: Greenwood Press, 1990), 35–36; William Leach, *Land of Desire: Merchants, Power, and the Rise of a New American Culture* (New York: Pantheon, 1993), 44–49.

6. Daniel Frohman, "Actress Aided by Camera," *Cosmopolitan* 22 (1897): 414.

7. John Gilmer Speed, "The Right of Privacy," *North American Review* 163 (1896): 73–74; "A Nuisance," *Life* 47 (1906): 271; "The Right to Privacy," *Harvard Law Review* 7 (1893): 182.

8. Michael Madow, "Private Ownership of Public Image: Popular Culture and Publicity Rights," *California Law Review* 81 (1993): 147–167; "Portrait Right," *Washington Law Reporter* 12 (1884): 353; J. A. J., "The Legal Relations of Photographs," *American Law Register* 17 (1869): 8.

9. *Pollard v. Photographic Co.*, 40 Ch. Div. 345 (1888); *Moore v. Rugg*, 46 N.W. 141 (Minn. 1890).

10. Dorothy Glancy, "Privacy and the Other Miss M," *Northern Illinois Law Review* 10 (1990): 401–440; *New York Times*, 15 June 1890, 2; 18 June 1890, 3; 21 June 1890, 2; Samuel H. Wandell, *The Law of the Theatre* (Albany, NY: James B. Lyon, 1891), 110.

11. Watkin Williams, "The Sale of Photographic Portraits," *Solicitors' Journal*, 1 Nov. 1879, 4–5; *Murray v. Gast Lithographic and Engraving Co.*, 31 Abb. N.C. 266 (N.Y. Sup. 1894); E. L. Godkin, "The Rights of the Citizen," *Scribner's Magazine* 8 (1890): 67; "The Right to Privacy," *Nation* 51 (1890): 496.

12. *Harper's Weekly*, 6 Jan. 1866, 14; 26 May 1877, 414; 18 Dec. 1880, 818; 8 Dec. 1877, 970.

13. *Emergence of Advertising in America: 1850–1920*, http://scriptorium.lib.duke.edu/eaa/index.html, images K0550, P0027; Leonard de Vries and Ilonka van Amstel, *The Wonderful World of American Advertisements 1865–1900* (Chicago: Follett Publishing Company, 1972), 28, 57, 24.

14. Edgar R. Jones, *Those Were the Good Old Days: A Happy Look at American Advertising, 1880–1930* (New York: Simon and Schuster, 1959), 32, 39; "Advertising Brigands," *Case and Comment*, Dec. 1895, 3.

15. *Mackenzie v. Soden Mineral Springs Co.*, 18 N.Y.S. 240 (N.Y. Sup. 1891); *Official Gazette of the United States Patent Office* 85 (1898): 149.

16. *Dockrell v. Dougall,* 78 L.T. Rep. 840 (Q.B. Div. 1898); *Barrows v. B.B. & R. Knight,* 6 R.I. 434 (1860).

17. Samuel D. Warren and Louis D. Brandeis, "The Right to Privacy," *Harvard Law Review* 4 (1890): 193–220.

18. Alpheus Thomas Mason, *Brandeis: A Free Man's Life* (New York: Viking, 1946), 70; William L. Prosser, "Privacy," *California Law Review* 48 (1960): 383; James H. Barron, "Warren and Brandeis, *The Right to Privacy,* 4 Harv. L. Rev. 193 (1980): Demystifying a Landmark Citation," *Suffolk University Law Review* 13 (1979): 875–922; Amy Gadja, "What if Samuel D. Warren Hadn't Married a Senator's Daughter?: Uncovering the Press Coverage that Led to *The Right to Privacy*" (2007), http://papers.ssrn.com/abstract=1026680.

19. Robert E. Mensel, "'Kodakers Lying in Wait': Amateur Photography and the Right of Privacy in New York, 1885–1915," *American Quarterly* 43 (1991): 24–45; *New York Times,* 15 Mar. 1889, 4; "Current Topics," *Open Court* 5 (1891): 223; "Editorial Notes," *Outlook* 49 (1894): 166; "The Right to Privacy," *Congregationalist* 82 (1897): 321; "Highways & Byways," *Chautauquan* 30 (1899): 120; "Newspaper Publicity," *Friends' Intelligencer* 56 (1899): 998; *Life,* 1 Jan. 1891, 4; "The Right to Privacy," *Youth's Companion* 64 (1891): 641.

20. "The Right to Privacy," *Green Bag* 6 (1894): 498–501; Wordsworth Donisthorpe, *Law in a Free State* (London: Macmillan and Co., 1895), 21; Augustus N. Hand, "Schuyler Against Curtis and the Right to Privacy," *American Law Register* 45 (1897): 752; Guy H. Thompson, "The Right of Privacy as Recognized and Protected at Law and in Equity," *Central Law Journal* 47 (1898): 150; *Marks v. Jaffa,* 26 N.Y.S. 908 (N.Y. Super. 1893).

21. "The Right to Be Let Alone," *Atlantic Monthly* 67 (1891): 429; *Life* 18 (1891): 240; Warren and Brandeis, "The Right to Privacy," 214–215; Herbert Spencer Hadley, "The Right to Privacy," *Northwestern Law Review* 3 (1894): 3.

22. "The Right to Privacy," *Liberty* 11 (1896): 2; "The Miscalled Right of Privacy," *Case and Comment* 7 (1900): 39–40; "Rights in a Portrait," *Case and Comment* 9 (1902): 15–16.

23. "Department of Equity," *American Law Register* 43 (1895): 139; "Prevention of the Publication of Portraits of Persons," *Central Law Journal* 44 (1897): 294–295; *New York Times,* 2 Apr. 1897, 6; 21 Jan. 1900, 22.

24. *Corliss v. E. W. Walker Co.,* 57 F. 434 (C.C.D. Mass. 1893); *Corliss v. E. W. Walker Co.,* 64 F. 280 (C.C.D. Mass. 1894).

25. *Schuyler v. Curtis,* 42 N.E. 22 (N.Y. 1895).

26. *Atkinson v. John E. Doherty & Co.,* 80 N.W. 285 (Mich. 1899).

27. James L. Hopkins, *The Law of Unfair Trade* (Chicago: Callaghan and Company, 1900), 165; George D. Watrous, "Torts," in *Two Centuries' Growth of American Law 1701–1901* (New York: Charles Scribner's Sons, 1901), 97–98.

28. *Roberson v. Rochester Folding-Box Co.,* 65 N.Y.S. 1109 (N.Y. Sup. 1900).

29. "A Sensible Decision," *Christian Advocate* 75 (1900): 1281; "Property in a Face," *Youth's Companion* 74 (1900): 434; "Public Characters and the Right of Privacy," *Virginia Law Register* 6 (1900): 495; "Current Topics," *Albany Law Journal* 62 (1900): 83.

30. *Roberson v. Rochester Folding-Box Co.,* 71 N.Y.S. 876 (App. Div. 1901); "Equity—The Right of Privacy," *Columbia Law Review* 1 (1901): 491; "The Right to Privacy," *Harvard Law Review* 15 (1901): 227; "Likenesses—Use for Advertising," *Yale Law Journal* 11 (1901): 60.

31. *Roberson v. Rochester Folding Box Co.,* 64 N.E. 442 (N.Y. 1902).

32. "Right to Privacy," *Harvard Law Review* 16 (1902): 72; "Exit the Right of Privacy," *Law Notes* 6 (1902): 80; "The Right of Privacy," *Outlook* 71 (1902): 716; "The Miscalled Right of Privacy," *American Lawyer* 10 (1902): 293; "Current Topics," *Albany Law Journal* 64 (1902): 226; *New York Times,* 3 July 1902, 8; 13 July 1902, 8; "Injunction—Rights of Privacy," *American Law Register* 50 (1902): 675; "Publication of Photograph as an Advertisement," *Columbia Law Review* 2 (1902): 487; William Seton Gordon, "The Right of Privacy," *Canadian Law Times* 22 (1902): 289; Denis O'Brien, "The Right of Privacy," *Columbia Law Review* 2 (1902): 437.

33. "No Right to 'Privacy'," *Chautauquan* 35 (1902): 541; "The Camera and the Prominent Person," *Current Literature* 34 (1902): 390; *Harper's Weekly* 46 (1902): 984; *New York Times,* 23 Aug. 1902, 8; Elbridge L. Adams, "The Law of Privacy," *North American Review* 175 (1902): 367; see also Elbridge L. Adams, "The Right of Privacy and Its Relation to the Law of Libel," *Journal of Social Science* 41 (1903): 90.

34. N.Y. Laws 1903, c. 132; "Legal Notes," *Scientific American* 88 (1903): 434; "Property Right in One's Name and Picture," *Yale Law Journal* 13 (1903): 46; *Rhodes v. Sperry & Hutchinson Co.,* 85 N.E. 1097 (N.Y. 1908).

35. *New York Times,* 27 July 1904, 1.

36. "Right of Privacy," *Virginia Law Register* 11 (1906): 938; *Pavesich v. New England Life Insurance Co.,* 50 S.E. 68 (Ga. 1905); "The Right to Print Portraits," *American Lawyer* 13 (1905): 126; *Itzkovich v. Whitaker,* 39 So. 499 (La. 1905); *Klug v. Sheriffs,* 109 N.W. 656 (Wis. 1906); *Douglas v. Stokes,* 149 S.W. 849 (Ky. App. 1912); *Von Thodorovich v. Franz Josef Beneficial Association,* 154 F. 911 (C.C.E.D. Pa. 1907); *Munden v. Harris,* 134 S.W. 1076 (Mo. App. 1911); *Kunz v. Allen,* 172 P. 532 (Kans. 1918); *Peck v. Tribune Co.,* 214 U.S. 185 (1909).

37. *Henry v. Cherry & Webb,* 73 A. 97 (R.I. 1909); *Hillman v. Star Publishing Co.,* 117 P. 594 (Wash. 1911).

38. "The Right to Immunity from Wrongful Publicity," *Columbia Law Review* 11 (1911): 566; Roscoe Pound, "Interests of Personality," *Harvard Law Review* 28 (1915): 363; Clowry Chapman, *The Law of Advertising and Sales* (Denver: Clowry Chapman, 1908), 38; Louis D. Frolich and Charles Schwartz, *The Law of Motion Pictures* (New York: Baker, Voorhis and Co., 1918), 267–290; *Brents v. Morgan,* 299 S.W. 967 (Ky. 1927); *Bazemore v. Savannah Hospital,* 155 S.E. 194

(Ga. 1930); *Melvin v. Reid,* 297 P. 91 (Cal. 1931); "The Right to Privacy Today," *Harvard Law Review* 43 (1929): 297; L. S. Clemons, "The Right of Privacy in Relation to the Publication of Photographs," *Marquette Law Review* 14 (1930): 198; "The Right of Privacy," *Temple Law Quarterly* 4 (1930): 381; Roy Moreland, "The Right of Privacy To-Day," *Kentucky Law Journal* 19 (1931): 122; John R. Fitzpatrick, "The Unauthorized Publication of Photographs," *Georgetown Law Journal* 20 (1932): 158; Basil W. Kacedan, "The Right of Privacy," *Boston University Law Review* 12 (1932): 646; *Restatement of the Law of Torts* (St. Paul: American Law Institute Publishers, 1934–1939), 4:398; Leon Green, "The Right of Privacy," *Illinois Law Review* 27 (1932): 244; see also John B. Pew, "The Right of Privacy— Protector of Man's Personality," *Kansas City Law Review* 1 (1932): 4.

39. *Eliot v. Jones,* 120 N.Y.S. 989 (N.Y. Sup. 1910).

40. *New York Times,* 25 May 1925, 16; 22 Jan. 1936, 14; *Ellis v. Hurst,* 121 N.Y.S. 438 (N.Y. Sup. 1910); *D'Altomonte v. New York Herald Co.,* 139 N.Y.S. 200 (App. Div. 1913); *Loftus v. Greenwich Lithographing Co.,* 182 N.Y.S. 428 (App. Div. 1920); *Garden v. Parfumerie Rigaud,* 271 N.Y.S. 187 (N.Y. Sup. 1933); *Sinclair v. Postal Telegraph & Cable Co.,* 72 N.Y.S.2d 841 (N.Y. Sup. 1935); *Krieger v. Popular Publications, Inc.,* 3 N.Y.S.2d 480 (N.Y. Sup. 1938); *Redmond v. Columbia Pictures Corp.,* 14 N.E.2d 636 (N.Y. 1938); *Lane v. F. W. Woolworth Co.,* 11 N.Y.S.2d 199 (N.Y. Sup. 1939); *Fisher v. Murray M. Rosenberg, Inc.,* 23 N.Y.S.2d 677 (N.Y. Sup. 1940); *Sharkey v. National Broadcasting Co.,* 93 F. Supp. 986 (S.D.N.Y. 1950); "Is There a Common Law Right of Privacy?" *United States Law Review* 65 (1931): 64.

41. *Edison v. Edison Polyform Manufacturing Co.,* 67 A. 392 (N.J. Ch. 1907); "Right of Privacy," *Harvard Law Review* 21 (1907): 63; *Foster-Milburn Co. v. Chinn,* 120 S.W. 364 (Ky. 1909); *Flake v. Greensboro News Co.,* 195 S.E. 55 (N.C. 1938); Wilbur Larremore, "The Law of Privacy," *Columbia Law Review* 12 (1912): 701.

42. Charles Clark to Learned Hand and Robert Patterson, 21 June 1940, *RCA Manufacturing Co. v. Whiteman,* Learned Hand papers, box 202, folder 3, HLS; *Martin v. F.I.Y. Theatre Co.,* 1 Ohio Supp. 19 (1938); *Paramount Pictures, Inc., v. Leader Press, Inc.,* 24 F. Supp. 1004 (W. D. Okla. 1938); *Cohen v. Marx,* 211 P.2d 320 (Cal. App. 1949); *Vassar College v. Loose-Wiles Biscuit Co.,* 197 F. 982 (W.D. Mo. 1912).

43. *O'Brien v. Pabst Sales Co.,* 124 F.2d 167 (5th Cir. 1941).

44. John H. Wigmore, "A General Analysis of Tort-Relations," *Harvard Law Review* 8 (1895): 382n2; "An Actionable Right of Privacy?" *Yale Law Journal* 12 (1902): 37; George J. Leicht, "The Law Relating to a Right of Privacy," *Lawyer and Banker* 7 (1914): 347; "Moving Pictures and the Right of Privacy," *Yale Law Journal* 28 (1919): 270–271; "Possible Interests in One's Name or Picture," *Harvard Law Review* 28 (1915): 689–691; Wilfred Feinberg, "Recent Developments in the Law of Privacy," *Columbia Law Review* 48 (1948): 726–730; Leon R. Yankwich, "The Right of Privacy: Its Development, Scope and Limitations," *Notre Dame Lawyer* 27 (1952): 513–517.

45. Ty Cobb with Al Stump, *My Life in Baseball: The True Record* (Garden City, NY: Doubleday and Co., 1961), 89; Marlis Schweitzer, " 'The Mad Search for Beauty': Actresses' Testimonials, the Cosmetics Industry, and the 'Democratization of Beauty,' " *Journal of the Gilded Age and Progressive Era* 4 (2005): 255–292.

46. "Should a Name Be Protected as 'Property'?" *Michigan Law Review* 11 (1913): 393; Henry Brandis, Jr., "The Right of Privacy," *North Carolina Law Review* 7 (1929): 438.

47. "Bad Names," *Time,* 11 Mar. 1929; Kerry Segrave, *Endorsements in Advertising: A Social History* (Jefferson, NC: McFarland and Co., 2005), 34–80; "From Peruna to Piffle," *Nation* 128 (1929): 364; *New York Times,* 8 May 1930, 15; 7 Jan. 1932, 16; *Northam Warren Corp. v. Federal Trade Commission,* 59 F.2d 196 (2nd Cir. 1932).

48. Roland Marchand, *Advertising the American Dream: Making Way for Modernity, 1920–1940* (Berkeley: University of California Press, 1985), 96–98; Daniel Delis Hill, *Advertising to the American Woman 1900–1999* (Columbus: Ohio State University Press, 2002), 289–296; Eileen Bowser, *The Transformation of Cinema 1907–1915* (Berkeley: University of California Press, 1990), 114–117.

49. "*Pekas Co. v. Leslie,*" *New York Law Journal* 52 (1915): 1864.

50. *Hanna Manufacturing Co. v. Hillerich & Bradsby Co.,* 78 F.2d 763 (5th Cir. 1935).

51. "Assignability of Rights in a Person's Name as Property," *Yale Law Journal* 45 (1936): 522; "Unfair Competition—Rights Under Contract Granting Exclusive Advertising Use of Famous Name," *Harvard Law Review* 49 (1936): 497; "Trade-Marks and Trade Names," *Columbia Law Review* 36 (1936): 503.

52. J. Gordon Hylton, "Baseball Cards and the Birth of the Right of Publicity: The Curious Case of *Haelan Laboratories v. Topps Chewing Gum,*" *Marquette Sports Law Review* 12 (2001): 273–294; *Haelan Laboratories v. Topps Chewing Gum, Inc.,* 202 F.2d 866 (2nd Cir. 1953).

53. See, e.g., *State ex rel. Elvis Presley International Memorial Foundation v. Crowell,* 733 S.W.2d 89 (Tenn. App. 1987).

54. Melville B. Nimmer, "The Right of Publicity," *Law & Contemporary Problems* 19 (1954): 203; Joseph R. Grodin, "The Right of Publicity: A Doctrinal Innovation," *Yale Law Journal* 62 (1953): 1123; Green, "The Right of Privacy," 239; Gerald Dickler, "The Right of Privacy: A Proposed Redefinition," *United States Law Review* 70 (1936): 435; "Pictures and the Law of Torts," *Illinois Law Review* 33 (1938): 96–97.

55. Peter Guralnick, *Last Train to Memphis: The Rise of Elvis Presley* (Boston: Little, Brown, 1994), 354; *Wall Street Journal,* 31 Dec. 1956, 1.

56. "Action for Infringement of Right of Privacy Based upon Breach of Trust or Confidence," *Central Law Journal* 57 (1903): 363; "White v. PA Rolling Mill Co.," *Forum* 7 (1903): 82; St. Clair McKelway, "Journalism and Publicity,"

Journal of Social Science 41 (1903): 39; "Right of Privacy," *Virginia Law Register* 12 (1906): 91–92; Donald Baldwin, "If Your Photograph Were News," *Notre Dame Lawyer* 4 (1929): 386–387; *Colyer v. Richard K. Fox Pub. Co.,* 146 N.Y.S. 999 (App. Div. 1914); *Humiston v. Universal Film Mfg. Co.,* 178 N.Y.S. 752 (App. Div. 1919); *Themo v. New England Newspaper Pub. Co.,* 27 N.E.2d 753 (Mass. 1940).

57. *Sweenek v. Pathe News, Inc.,* 16 F. Supp. 746 (E.D.N.Y. 1936); *Barber v. Time, Inc.,* 159 S.W.2d 291 (Mo. 1942); *Berg v. Minneapolis Star & Tribune Co.,* 79 F. Supp. 957 (D. Minn. 1948); *Chaplin v. National Broadcasting Co.,* 15 F.R.D. 134 (S.D.N.Y. 1953).

58. *Binns v. Vitagraph Co. of America,* 103 N.E. 1108 (N.Y. 1913); *Toscani v. Hersey,* 65 N.Y.S.2d 814 (App. Div. 1946); *Spahn v. Julian Messner, Inc.,* 221 N.E.2d 543 (N.Y. 1966); *Donahue v. Warner Bros. Pictures Distributing Corp.,* 272 P.2d 177 (Utah 1954).

59. *Damron v. Doubleday, Doran & Co.,* 231 N.Y.S. 444 (N.Y. Sup. 1928); *Nebb v. Bell Syndicate, Inc.,* 41 F. Supp. 929 (S.D.N.Y. 1941); *People ex rel. Maggio v. Charles Scribner's Sons,* 130 N.Y.S.2d 514 (N.Y. Mag. 1954); *Cason v. Baskin,* 20 So.2d 243 (Fla. 1945); *Cason v. Baskin,* 30 So.2d 635 (Fla. 1947); Patricia Nassif Acton, *Invasion of Privacy: The Cross Creek Trial of Marjorie Kinnan Rawlings* (Gainesville: University of Florida Press, 1988).

60. *Smith v. Suratt,* 7 Alaska 416 (1926); *Metter v. Los Angeles Examiner,* 95 P.2d 491 (Cal. App. 1939).

61. *Wyatt v. Hall's Portrait Studio,* 128 N.Y.S. 247 (N.Y. Sup. 1911); Francis Finkelhor, *Legal Phases of Advertising* (New York: McGraw-Hill Book Co., 1938), 21; Louis Nizer, "The Right of Privacy: A Half Century's Developments," *Michigan Law Review* 39 (1941): 553–554; *New York Times,* 28 May 1926, 2; *Schumann v. Loew's Inc.,* 135 N.Y.S.2d 361 (N.Y. Sup. 1954); *Maritote v. Desilu Productions, Inc.,* 345 F.2d 418 (7th Cir. 1965).

62. *In re Hart's Estate,* 83 N.Y.S.2d 635 (N.Y. Sur. 1948); *Runyon v. United States,* 281 F.2d 590 (5th Cir. 1960); *Miller v. Commissioner of Internal Revenue,* 299 F.2d 706 (2nd Cir. 1962).

63. *Lugosi v. Universal Pictures,* 603 P.2d 425 (Cal. 1979); *Price v. Hal Roach Studios,* 400 F. Supp. 836 (S.D.N.Y. 1975); Stan Soocher, *They Fought the Law: Rock Music Goes to Court* (New York: Schirmer Books, 1999), 13–14.

64. *Lahr v. Adell Chemical Co.,* 300 F.2d 256 (1st Cir. 1962); *Davis v. Trans World Airlines,* 297 F. Supp. 1145 (C.D. Cal. 1969); *Midler v. Ford Motor Co.,* 849 F.2d 460 (9th Cir. 1988); *Waits v. Frito-Lay, Inc.,* 978 F.2d 1093 (9th Cir. 1992).

65. *White v. Samsung Electronics America, Inc.,* 971 F.2d 1395 (9th Cir. 1992); *Wendt v. Host International, Inc.,* 125 F.3d 806 (9th Cir. 1997).

66. *White v. Samsung Electronics America, Inc.,* 989 F.2d 1512, 1513 (9th Cir. 1993) (Kozinski, J., dissenting from the denial of rehearing en banc).

8. From the Tenement to the Condominium

1. Alexis de Tocqueville, *Democracy in America* (1835–1840), ed. Harvey C. Mansfield and Delba Winthrop (Chicago: University of Chicago Press, 2000), 553; Susan B. Carter et al., eds., *Historical Statistics of the United States, Millennial Edition On Line* (New York: Cambridge University Press, 2006), table Dc761–780; *American Housing Survey for the United States: 2005* (Washington, DC: U.S. Department of Housing and Urban Development, 2006), 42.

2. Joseph Story, *Commentaries on the Constitution of the United States* (Boston: Hillard, Gray, and Co., 1833), 1:159–160; J. Hector de St. John de Crèvecoeur, *Letters from an American Farmer* (1783), ed. Susan Manning (Oxford: Oxford University Press, 1997), 27, 56; Thomas Jefferson, *Notes on the State of Virginia* (Philadelphia: Richard and Hall, 1788), 174; Tocqueville, *Democracy in America*, 553.

3. Gregory A. Stiverson, *Poverty in a Land of Plenty: Tenancy in Eighteenth-Century Maryland* (Baltimore: Johns Hopkins University Press, 1977), 144–145; James T. Lemon, *The Best Poor Man's Country: A Geographical Study of Early Southeastern Pennsylvania* (Baltimore: Johns Hopkins University Press, 1972), 94–96; Sung Bok Kim, *Landlord and Tenant in Colonial New York: Manorial Society, 1664–1775* (Chapel Hill: University of North Carolina Press, 1978).

4. Mark Peel, "On the Margins: Lodgers and Boarders in Boston, 1860–1900," *Journal of American History* 72 (1986): 817; Louise E. Furniss, "New-York Boarding-Houses," *Appleton's Journal* 5 (1871): 259; Wendy Gamber, *The Boardinghouse in Nineteenth-Century America* (Baltimore: Johns Hopkins University Press, 2007); A. K. Sandoval-Strausz, *Hotel: An American History* (New Haven: Yale University Press, 2007), 263–283; Paul Groth, *Living Downtown: The History of Residential Hotels in the United States* (Berkeley: University of California Press, 1994), 26–89.

5. Sean Wilentz, *Chants Democratic: New York City and the Rise of the American Working Class, 1788–1850* (New York: Oxford University Press, 1984), 52; "New-York Daguerreotyped: Private Residences," *Putnam's Monthly Magazine* 3 (1854): 246–247; "The New Homes of New York," *Scribner's Monthly* 8 (1874): 64.

6. Elizabeth Blackmar, *Manhattan for Rent, 1785–1850* (Ithaca, NY: Cornell University Press, 1989), 271; John N. Taylor, *A Treatise on the Law of Landlord and Tenant* (New York: Charles Wells, 1840), 3.

7. Samuel Woodworth, *Quarter-Day, or The Horrors of the First of May* (New York: S. Woodworth and Co., 1812), 4, 6–7, 26–27. Woodworth is best known for his 1817 poem "The Old Oaken Bucket," which, set to music in 1826, became one of the most popular songs of the nineteenth century.

8. Blackmar, *Manhattan for Rent*, 183–212; *Poulson's American Daily Advertiser*, 25 Mar. 1815, 4; see also *City Gazette and Daily Advertiser* [Charleston, SC], 13 Aug. 1800, 4; *Carlisle Gazette*, 27 Dec. 1805, 4; *National Intelligencer* [Washington, DC], 16 May 1811, 3.

9. Stuart M. Blumin, *The Emergence of the Middle Class: Social Experience in the American City, 1760–1900* (Cambridge: Cambridge University Press, 1989), 147.

10. Anthony Jackson, *A Place Called Home: A History of Low-Cost Housing in Manhattan* (Cambridge: MIT Press, 1976), 4–19; *New York Daily Times,* 14 Mar. 1856, 2; 20 June 1856, 4; 14 Mar. 1856, 4.

11. Egbert P. Watson, "Houseless," *Harper's New Monthly Magazine* 26 (1863): 789–790; *New York Times,* 18 July 1869, 4; "The Man About Town: Hotel Morals," *Harper's Weekly,* 5 Sept. 1857, 563.

12. Elizabeth Collins Cromley, *Alone Together: A History of New York's Early Apartments* (Ithaca, NY: Cornell University Press, 1990); "Home and Foreign Gossip," *Harper's Weekly,* 7 May 1870, 295; "French Flats," *New York Times,* 26 Dec. 1876, 2; "Parisian 'Flats,'" *Appleton's Journal* 6 (1871): 561.

13. "Apartment Houses Practically Considered," *Putnam's Magazine* 6 (1870): 306; "Apartment-Houses," *Appleton's Journal* 5 (1878): 529; "Living on a Flat," *Christian Union* 5 (1872): 96; *New York Times,* 5 Mar. 1882, 6; *Musgrave v. Sherwood,* 54 How. Pr. 338 (N.Y. Sup. 1878).

14. Charlotte Perkins Gilman, "The Passing of the Home in Great American Cities," *Cosmopolitan* 38 (1904): 140.

15. R. Heber Newton, "The Progress of Co-operation in the United States," *Princeton Review* 2 (1882): 201–214; Carl J. Guarneri, *The Utopian Alternative: Fourierism in Nineteenth-Century America* (Ithaca, NY: Cornell University Press, 1991), 398; *Los Angeles Times,* 17 Nov. 1911, 17.

16. *New York Times,* 14 July 1880, 2; Christopher Gray, "Philip Gengembre Hubert: The 19th-Century Innovator Who Invented the Co-op," *New York Times,* 15 Aug. 2004; Charles Barnard, *Co-operation as a Business* (New York: G. P. Putnam's Sons, 1881), 63; Charles Ledyard Norton, "Home Clubs," *Christian Union* 23 (1881): 277.

17. Otis H. Castle, "Legal Phases of Co-operative Buildings," *Southern California Law Review* 2 (1928): 3.

18. Matthew Gordon Lasner, *No Lawn to Mow: Co-ops, Condominiums, and the Revolution in Collective Homeownership in Metropolitan America, 1881–1973* (Harvard University Ph.D. dissertation, 2007), 36–90; *New York Times,* 20 Nov. 1881, 14; 2 July 1883, 8; 11 Feb. 1884, 4; 8 Dec. 1888, 24; Everett N. Blanke, "The Cliff-Dwellers of New York," *Cosmopolitan* 15 (1893): 358; *American Architect and Building News,* 28 June 1902, 97.

19. Florence Finch Kelly, "Co-operative Apartment Houses in New York," *Independent* 64 (1908): 1139; *New York Times,* 10 Feb. 1907, 16; 25 Apr. 1909, RE2; *New York Times,* 1 May 1910, XX7; "Co-operative Apartments Prove Popular," *Chicago Commerce,* 29 Mar. 1924, 13; *Los Angeles Times,* 9 Apr. 1924, 11; Nathan William MacChesney, *The Principles of Real Estate Law* (New York: Macmillan, 1927), 368; *New York Times,* 11 Jan. 1925, RE2; Frank Parker Stockbridge, "Own Your Own Flat," *Saturday Evening Post,* 17 Oct. 1925, 18.

20. Herbert Emmerich, "The Problem of Low-Priced Cooperative Apartments: An Experiment at Sunnyside Gardens," *Journal of Land & Public Utility Economics* 4 (1928): 225–234; "Cooperative Home Ownership in the United States," *Monthly Labor Review* 23 (1926): 1–6; "Must the State Build Our Homes?" *Independent* 116 (1926): 675–676.

21. Chester C. McCullough, Jr., "Co-operative Apartments in Illinois," *Chicago-Kent Law Review* 26 (1948): 322; Cecil M. Self and H. Richard McGrath, *Florida's Fabulous Co-operative Apartment Boom* (Fort Lauderdale: Florida Publications, 1958); Seneca B. Anderson, "Cooperative Apartments in Florida: A Legal Analysis," *University of Miami Law Review* 12 (1957): 13; *Los Angeles Times*, 14 Apr. 1957, R10; 27 Dec. 1959, G3; "Federal Assistance in Financing Middle-Income Cooperative Apartments," *Yale Law Journal* 68 (1959): 542–613; United States Department of Labor, *Organization and Management of Cooperative and Mutual Housing Associations* (Washington, DC: Government Printing Office, 1946); U.S. Department of Housing and Urban Development, *HUD Condominium/Cooperative Study* (Washington, DC: Government Printing Office, 1975), III-2, III-17.

22. Elmer A. Claar, "Why the Cooperative Plan of Home-Ownership Is Popular," *National Real Estate Journal*, 18 May 1925, 46–48; Felix Isman, "The Accountings of a Real-Estate Man," *Saturday Evening Post*, 20 Oct. 1923, 105.

23. Imagine a taxpayer who could either (a) buy an apartment in a cooperative building or (b) rent an otherwise identical apartment, investing his money in income-producing assets instead. Option (a) has no income tax consequences, while in option (b), the taxpayer must pay income tax on his gains, without having any offsetting deduction for the rent he has paid. This tax benefit grew even greater in 1942, when cooperative homeowners were allowed a deduction for interest on their shares of the cooperative's mortgage. The best discussion of these issues is Henry Hansmann, "Condominium and Cooperative Housing; Transactional Efficiency, Tax Subsidies, and Tenure Choice," *Journal of Legal Studies* 20 (1991): 25–71.

24. Robert F. Bingham and Elmore L. Andrews, *Financing Real Estate* (Cleveland: Stanley McMichael Publishing Organization, 1924), 224.

25. Elmer A. Claar, *Co-operative Apartment Homes as an Investment* (Chicago: Northwestern University School of Commerce, 1924), 8.

26. Lawrence B. Elliman, "Cooperative Apartments," in Blake Snyder and Wilmot Lippincott, eds., *Real Estate Handbook* (New York: McGraw-Hill, 1925), 243; R. K. Packard, "Co-operative Ownership from the Owner's Point of View," in *Co-operative Apartments: Proceedings & Reports of the Co-operative Apartment Section* (Chicago: National Association of Real Estate Boards, 1925), 1, 5.

27. Gilbert H. Hennessey, Jr., "Co-operative Apartments and Town Houses," *University of Illinois Law Forum* 1956 (1956): 24; *American Housing: Problems and Prospects* (New York: Twentieth Century Fund, 1949), 234.

28. William K. Kerr, "Condominium . . . A New Term," *Lawyers Title News*, Aug. 1961, 2. On the persistent belief in the condominium's ostensible Roman

origins, see Robert G. Natelson, "Comments on the Historiography of Condominium: The Myth of Roman Origin," *Oklahoma City University Law Review* 12 (1987): 17–58.

29. *Los Angeles Times,* 29 Oct. 1961, 11.

30. William Sheppard, *The Touchstone of Common Assurances* (1648; New York: Isaac Riley, 1808–1810), 1:205; Walter Henry Burton, *An Elementary Compendium of the Law of Real Property* (1828; Philadelphia: John S. Littell, 1839), 81; S. M. Tolson, "'Land' without Earth: Freehold Flats in English Law," *Conveyancer and Property Lawyer* 14 (1950): 350; John Erskine, *An Institute of the Law of Scotland,* 4th ed. (1773; Edinburgh: Bell and Bradfute, 1805), 1:357; *The Code Napoleon* (London: Charles Hunter, 1824), 182 (§664); J. Leyser, "The Ownership of Flats—A Comparative Study," *International and Comparative Law Quarterly* 7 (1958): 33.

31. E. S. M., "Horizontal Divisions of Land," *American Law Register* 10 (1862): 578–580; *American Architect and Building News* 28 (1890): 125; Stuart S. Ball, "Division into Horizontal Strata of the Landspace Above the Surface," *Yale Law Journal* 39 (1930): 621–622; *Loring v. Bacon,* 4 Mass. 575 (1808); *McConnel v. Kibbe,* 33 Ill. 175 (1864); *Badger Lumber Co. v. Stepp,* 57 S.W. 1059 (Mo. 1900); *Madison v. Madison,* 69 N.E. 625 (Ill. 1903); *Rhodes, Pegram & Co. v. McCormack,* 4 Iowa 368 (1857).

32. Laird Bell, "Air Rights," *Illinois Law Review* 23 (1928): 250–264.

33. Charles E. Ramsey, *Condominium: The New Look in Co-ops* (Chicago: Chicago Title and Trust Co., 1961), 6–7; *Thisted v. Country Club Tower Corp.,* 405 P.2d 432 (Mont. 1965); *Housing Legislation of 1960: Hearings Before a Subcommittee of the Committee on Banking and Currency, United States Senate,* 86th Cong., 2nd Sess. (1960), 597.

34. *New York Times,* 10 Dec. 1961, 66; 12 May 1963, R1; David E. MacEllven, "Cooperative or Condominium," *Title News,* April 1962, 2–4; "Need Condominium Legislation," *Title News,* March 1962, 19; *Los Angeles Times,* 25 Mar. 1962, N1; Herbert J. Friedman and James K. Herbert, "Community Apartments: Condominium or Stock Cooperative?" *California Law Review* 50 (1962): 302–304; Boyce C. Outen, "May Draw Suburbanites Back to City," *Lawyers Title News,* Sept. 1962, 3.

35. William K. Kerr, *Condominium: A Preview* (s.l.: Association of Life Insurance Counsel, 1962), 234; *Housing Legislation of 1960,* 587; *New York Times,* 3 Apr. 1960, R1.

36. *General Housing Legislation: Hearings Before the Subcommittee on Housing of the Committee on Banking and Currency, House of Representatives,* 86th Cong., 2nd Sess. (1960), 257–259; *Housing Legislation of 1960,* 594.

37. 75 Stat. 160 (1961).

38. W. Robert Fokes, "Legal and Practical Aspects of Condominium," *Business Lawyer* 19 (1963): 233; "Co-ops and Condominiums," *Time,* 17 Apr. 1964.

39. "First FHA Condominium," *Title News,* June 1962, 20–21; *Los Angeles Times,* 3 June 1962, I27; 5 Aug. 1962, O6; 12 Aug. 1962, M11; *New York Times,* 1 Dec. 1963, R1; 8 Mar. 1964, R1; 8 Mar. 1964, R12; *Los Angeles Times,* 29 July 1962, L1; *New York Times,* 17 May 1964, F25; 12 Mar. 1964, 71.

40. *Los Angeles Times,* 10 Dec. 1961, 11; *New York Times,* 29 Mar. 1964, R1; John E. Cribbet, "Condominium—Home Ownership for Megalopolis?" *Michigan Law Review* 61 (1963): 1240; Curtis J. Berger, "Condominium: Shelter on a Statutory Foundation," *Columbia Law Review* 63 (1963): 998–999.

41. "Cashing in on Condominiums," *Time,* 7 Aug. 1972; *American Housing Survey,* 42.

42. Michael H. Schill, Ioan Voicu, and Jonathan Miller, "The Condominium Versus Cooperative Puzzle: An Empirical Analysis of Housing in New York City," *Journal of Legal Studies* 36 (2007): 275–324. An earlier study, using a national sample but with less-detailed information on each apartment, estimated the premium at approximately 12 percent. Allen C. Goodman and John L. Goodman, Jr., "The Co-op Discount," *Journal of Real Estate Finance and Economics* 14 (1997): 223–233.

43. *HUD Condominium/Cooperative Study,* III-2; *American Housing Survey,* 42; Mendes Hershman, "Operating Problems of the Condominium," in *Symposium: The Practical Problems of Condominium* (New York: Chicago Title Insurance Co., 1964), 35–36; Robert G. Natelson, *Law of Property Owners Associations* (Boston: Little, Brown, and Co., 1989), 593–600; Schill et al., "Condominium Versus Cooperative Puzzle," 312–314.

9. The Law of the Land

1. *Hurlbut v. McKone,* 10 A. 164 (Conn. 1887).

2. John F. Hart, "Colonial Land Use Law and Its Significance for Modern Takings Doctrine," *Harvard Law Review* 109 (1996): 1259–1281; John F. Hart, "Land Use Law in the Early Republic and the Original Meaning of the Takings Clause," *Northwestern University Law Review* 94 (2000): 1107–1131.

3. Christine Meisner Rosen, "Businessmen Against Pollution in Late Nineteenth Century Chicago," *Business History Review* 69 (1995): 351–397; Joseph Gordon Hylton, "Prelude to *Euclid:* The United States Supreme Court and the Constitutionality of Land Use Regulation, 1900–1920," *Washington University Journal of Law & Policy* 3 (2000): 1–37; Robert M. Fogelson, *Downtown: Its Rise and Fall, 1880–1950* (New Haven: Yale University Press, 2001), 112–182; *St. Louis v. Dorr,* 46 S.W. 976 (Mo. 1898).

4. Stanley K. Schultz, *Constructing Urban Culture: American Cities and City Planning, 1800–1920* (Philadelphia: Temple University Press, 1989); William H. Wilson, *The City Beautiful Movement* (Baltimore: Johns Hopkins University Press, 1989); Marc A. Weiss, *The Rise of the Community Builders: The American*

Real Estate Industry and Urban Land Planning (New York: Columbia University Press, 1987), 80–85 (ordinance quoted at 81); *Ex parte Quong Wo,* 118 P. 714 (Cal. 1911); *Hadacheck v. Sebastian,* 239 U.S. 394 (1915).

5. *Hadacheck,* 410.

6. Weiss, *Rise of the Community Builders,* 86; *State ex rel. Civello v. City of New Orleans,* 97 So. 440 (La. 1923); *Spann v. City of Dallas,* 235 S.W. 513 (Tex. 1921); Robert B. Fairbanks, "Rethinking Urban Problems: Planning, Zoning, and City Government in Dallas, 1900–1930," *Journal of Urban History* 25 (1999): 809–837.

7. Raphaël Fischler, "The Metropolitan Dimension of Early Zoning: Revisiting the 1916 New York City Ordinance," *Journal of the American Planning Association* 64 (1998): 170–188; Commission on Building Districts and Restrictions, *Final Report* (New York: Board of Estimate and Apportionment, 1916).

8. *State ex rel. Penrose Investment Company v. McKelvey,* 256 S.W. 474 (Mo. 1923); *State ex rel. Westminster Presbyterian Church v. Edgecomb,* 189 N.W. 617 (Neb. 1922); *State ex rel. Carter v. Harper,* 196 N.W. 451 (Wis. 1923); *Fourcade v. City and County of San Francisco,* 238 P. 934 (Cal. 1925); *Schait v. Senior,* 117 A. 517 (N.J. 1922); *Ware v. Wichita,* 214 P. 99 (Kan. 1923); *Morrow v. City of Atlanta,* 133 S.E. 345 (Ga. 1926); *Inspector of Buildings of Lowell v. Stoklosa,* 145 N.E. 262 (Mass. 1924); *City of Providence v. Stephens,* 133 A. 614 (R.I. 1923); *Kroner v. City of Portland,* 240 P. 536 (Ore. 1925); *Mayor and Council of Wilmington v. Turk,* 129 A. 512 (Del. Ch. 1925); *Goldman v. Crowther,* 128 A. 50, 55 (Md. Ct. App. 1925); *Deynzer v. City of Evanston,* 149 N.E. 790 (Ill. 1925); Alfred Bettman, "Constitutionality of Zoning," *Harvard Law Review* 37 (1924): 834–835.

9. Ruth Knack, Stuart Meck, and Israel Stollman, "The Real Story Behind the Standard Planning and Zoning Acts of the 1920s," *Land Use Law,* Feb. 1996, 3–9; *A Standard State Zoning Enabling Act,* rev. ed. (Washington, DC: Government Printing Office, 1926) (originally published in 1922); Brief on Behalf of the National Conference on City Planning et al., 5, *Village of Euclid v. Ambler Realty Company,* 272 U.S. 365 (1926).

10. *In re White,* 234 P. 396 (Cal. 1925); *State ex rel. Beery v. Houghton,* 204 N.W. 569, 570 (Minn. 1925).

11. Michael Allan Wolf, *The Zoning of America: Euclid v. Ambler* (Lawrence: University Press of Kansas, 2008); Brief for Appellee, 14–15, *Village of Euclid v. Ambler Realty Co.,* 272 U.S. 365 (1926).

12. *Village of Euclid v. Ambler Realty Co.,* 272 U.S. 365, 386–387 (1926).

13. *Village of Euclid,* 388.

14. Seymour I. Toll, *Zoned American* (New York: Grossman Publishers, 1969), 193; *Nectow v. City of Cambridge,* 277 U.S. 183 (1928).

15. Frank Backus Williams, *The Law of City Planning and Zoning* (New York: Macmillan, 1922), 200; Martha A. Lees, "Preserving Property Values? Preserving Proper Homes? Preserving Privilege?: The Pre-*Euclid* Debate Over Zoning for Exclusively Private Residential Areas, 1916–1926," *University of Pittsburgh*

Law Review 56 (1994): 367–439; William Bennett Munro, *Municipal Government and Administration* (New York: Macmillan, 1923), 2:92–93.

16. Roger L. Rice, "Racial Segregation by Law, 1910–1917," *Journal of Southern History* 34 (1968): 181–182; *Buchanan v. Warley*, 245 U.S. 60 (1917); David E. Bernstein, "Philip Sober Controlling Philip Drunk: *Buchanan v. Warley* in Historical Perspective," *Vanderbilt Law Review* 51 (1998): 797–879; Michael J. Klarman, *From Jim Crow to Civil Rights: The Supreme Court and the Struggle for Racial Equality* (New York: Oxford University Press, 2004), 90–93.

17. Lawrence Gene Sager, "Tight Little Islands: Exclusionary Zoning, Equal Protection, and the Indigent," *Stanford Law Review* 21 (1969): 767–800; *Stein v. City of Long Branch*, 2 N.J. Misc. 121 (1924); *County Commissioners of Queen Anne's County v. Miles*, 228 A.2d 450 (Md. Ct. App. 1967); *Board of County Supervisors of Fairfax County v. Carper*, 107 S.E.2d 390, 396 (Va. 1959).

18. *Southern Burlington County NAACP v. Township of Mount Laurel*, 336 A.2d 713, 723, 728 (N.J. 1975).

19. Edward L. Glaeser and Joseph Gyourko, "The Impact of Building Restrictions on Housing Affordability," *Federal Reserve Bank of New York Economic Policy Review*, June 2003, 21–39; William A. Fischel, "An Economic History of Zoning and a Cure for Its Exclusionary Effects," *Urban Studies* 41 (2004): 317–340.

20. *Parker v. Nightingale*, 88 Mass. 341, 347 (1863).

21. Robert M. Fogelson, *Bourgeois Nightmares: Suburbia, 1870–1930* (New Haven: Yale University Press, 2005), 25–81; Helen C. Monchow, *The Use of Deed Restrictions in Subdivision Development* (Chicago: Institute for Research in Land Economics and Public Utilities, 1928), 28–31, 8.

22. Monchow, *Deed Restrictions*, 50; *Koehler v. Rowland*, 205 S.W. 217 (Mo. 1918); Andrew A. Bruce, "Racial Zoning by Private Contract in the Light of the Constitutions and the Rule Against Restraints on Alienation," *Illinois Law Review* 21 (1927): 704.

23. *Corrigan v. Buckley*, 271 U.S. 323, 330 (1926); Bruce, "Racial Zoning," 711.

24. *Title Guarantee & Trust Company v. Garrott*, 183 P. 470, 473 (Cal. App. 1919); *Los Angeles Investment Company v. Gary*, 186 P. 596 (Cal. 1919).

25. Christopher Bonastia, *Knocking on the Door: The Federal Government's Attempt to Desegregate the Suburbs* (Princeton: Princeton University Press, 2006), 63; John P. Dean, "Only Caucasian: A Study of Race Covenants," *Journal of Land & Public Utility Economics* 23 (1947): 428–432.

26. Clement E. Vose, *Caucasians Only: The Supreme Court, the NAACP, and the Restrictive Covenant Cases* (Berkeley: University of California Press, 1959); *Shelley v. Kraemer*, 334 U.S. 1 (1948); Motoko Rich, "Restrictive Covenants Stubbornly Stay on Books," *New York Times*, 21 Apr. 2005; Colin Gordon, *Mapping Decline: St. Louis and the Fate of the American City* (Philadelphia: University of Pennsylvania Press, 2008), 83–111.

27. *Neponsit Property Owners' Association v. Emigrant Industrial Savings Bank,* 15 N.E.2d 793 (N.Y. 1938); Stewart E. Sterk, *"Neponsit Property Owners' Association v. Emigrant Industrial Savings Bank,"* in Gerald Korngold and Andrew P. Morriss, eds., *Property Stories,* 2nd ed. (New York: Foundation Press, 2009), 379–400.

28. Uriel Reichman, "Residential Private Governments: An Introductory Survey," *University of Chicago Law Review* 43 (1976): 256; Donald R. Stabile, *Community Associations: The Emergence and Acceptance of a Quiet Innovation in Housing* (Westport, CT: Greenwood Press, 2000), 1; Evan McKenzie, *Privatopia: Homeowner Associations and the Rise of Residential Private Government* (New Haven: Yale University Press, 1994).

29. *Los Angeles Times,* 21 June 1991, 6; *Nahrstedt v. Lakeside Village Condominium Association,* 878 P.2d 1275 (Cal. 1994).

30. Edward H. Rabin, "The Revolution in Residential Landlord-Tenant Law: Causes and Consequences," *Cornell Law Review* 69 (1984): 517–584; Roger A. Cunningham, "The New Implied and Statutory Warranties of Habitability in Residential Leases: From Contract to Status," *Urban Law Annual* 16 (1979): 51–59; Herbert Thorndike Tiffany, *A Treatise on the Law of Landlord and Tenant* (Chicago: Callaghan and Company, 1912), 1:557–558.

31. *Javins v. First National Realty Corporation,* 428 F.2d 1071, 1074 (D.C. Cir. 1970).

32. Lawrence M. Friedman, *Government and Slum Housing* (New York: Arno Press, 1978), 25–55.

33. Tiffany, *Landlord and Tenant,* 2:1513, 2:1985; *Berg v. Wiley,* 264 N.W.2d 145, 151 (Minn. 1978).

34. *Block v. Hirsh,* 256 U.S. 135, 162 (1921).

35. Richard Arnott, "Time for Revisionism on Rent Control?" *Journal of Economic Perspectives* 9 (1995): 101.

36. *Chicago Board of Realtors v. City of Chicago,* 819 F.2d 732, 741–742 (7th Cir. 1987) (Posner, J.).

10. Owning Wavelengths

1. Edwin S. Oakes, "The Caseless Law of Wireless Telegraphy," *Case and Comment,* Aug. 1911, 138–142; Susan J. Douglas, *Inventing American Broadcasting, 1899–1922* (Baltimore: Johns Hopkins University Press, 1987), 216–239.

2. 37 Stat. 302, 303 (1912); *Radio Communication—Issuance of Licenses,* 29 Op. Atty. Gen. 589 (1912).

3. *Hoover v. Intercity Radio Co.,* 286 F. 1003 (D.C. App. 1923).

4. Hearing Before the Federal Radio Commission, *In re Zenith Radio Corp.* (27 May 1927), RG 173, A1/6, box 1, docket 1a, 9–17 (quotation at 15), NA; *United States v. Zenith Radio Corp.,* 12 F.2d 614 (N.D. Ill. 1926).

5. William Donovan to Herbert Hoover, 8 July 1926, Herbert Hoover Papers, Commerce Period, box 501, HHL; Herbert Hoover to Everett Sanders,

27 July 1926, Herbert Hoover Papers, Commerce Period, box 501, HHL; Silas Bent, "Radio Squatters," *Independent* 117 (1926): 389; Minutes, 28 May 1926, RG 417, 34B, box 1, NA.

6. James Patrick Taugher, "The Law of Radio Communication with Particular Reference to a Property Right in a Radio Wave Length," *Marquette Law Review* 12 (1928): 182; Hearing, *In re Zenith Radio Corp.*, 19; "Radio Confusion," *Youth's Companion* 100 (1926): 1038; Ithiel de Sola Pool, *Technologies of Freedom* (Cambridge: Harvard University Press, 1983), 112–119; H.R. Doc. No. 483, 69th Cong., 2nd Sess. (1926), 10.

7. *WGN v. Oak Leaves Broadcasting Station*, decided 17 November 1926, in the Circuit Court of Cook County, Illinois, was not published in the official case reports, but it nevertheless circulated widely. It is reproduced at *Congressional Record* 68 (1926): 216–219.

8. "The Survival of the Loudest," *Independent* 117 (1926): 663; "Courts Aid in the Radio Tangle," *Radio Broadcast* 10 (1927): 358; Stephen Davis, *The Law of Radio Communication* (New York: McGraw-Hill, 1927), 131; Frank S. Rowley, "Problems in the Law of Radio Communication," *University of Cincinnati Law Review* 1 (1927): 31; Hiram L. Jome, "Public Policy Toward Radio Broadcasting," *Journal of Land & Public Utility Economics* 1 (1925): 203.

9. Hearing, *In re Zenith Radio Corp.*, 40; C. A. Seoane to Chief Signal Officer of the Army, 29 June 1923, Herbert Hoover Papers, Commerce Period, box 491, HHL; *Proceedings of the Fourth National Radio Conference* (Washington, DC: Government Printing Office, 1926), 35; Hearing Before the Federal Radio Commission, *In re Application of Station WMSG* (21 June 1927), RG 173, A1/6, box 3, docket 13a, 17, NA; "Interim Report on Radio Legislation," *American Bar Association Journal* 12 (1926): 848, 869.

10. Statement of the National Radio Coordinating Committee, 2 Dec. 1926, Herbert Hoover Papers, Commerce Period, Box 490, HHL.

11. Herbert Hoover to Frank Kellogg, 23 Apr. 1921, Herbert Hoover Papers, Commerce Period, box 501, HHL; "Minutes of Open Meetings of Department of Commerce Conference on Radio Telephony" (27 Feb. 1922), Herbert Hoover Papers, Commerce Period, box 496, HHL; "Radio Problems" (16 Aug. 1924), Herbert Hoover Papers, Commerce Period, box 490, HHL; Herbert Hoover to E. E. Plummer, 10 Mar. 1924, Herbert Hoover Papers, Commerce Period, box 489, HHL; Herbert Hoover to Norman Hapgood, 26 Mar. 1924, Herbert Hoover Papers, Commerce Period, box 489, HHL; "Statement by Secretary Hoover" (20 Apr. 1926), Herbert Hoover Papers, Commerce Period, box 502, HHL.

12. Clarence C. Dill, *Radio Law* (Washington, DC: National Law Book Co., 1938), 80; S. Rep. No. 311, 68th Cong., 1st Sess. (1924), 1.

13. *Congressional Record* 65 (1924): 5735; William Wallace Childs, "Problems in the Radio Industry," *American Economic Review* 14 (1924): 523; Walter S. Rogers, "Air as a Raw Material," *Annals of the American Academy of Political and*

Social Science 112 (1924): 254; "Unscrambling the Ether," *Literary Digest,* 5 Mar. 1927, 6.

14. David A. Moss and Michael R. Fein, "Radio Regulation Revisited: Coase, the FCC, and the Public Interest," *Journal of Policy History* 15 (2003): 389–416; "Statement by Secretary Hoover" (11 Mar. 1924), Herbert Hoover Papers, Commerce Period, box 501, HHL; Herbert Hoover, *The Memoirs of Herbert Hoover: The Cabinet and the Presidency, 1920–1933* (New York: Macmillan, 1952), 143.

15. Marvin R. Bensman, *The Beginning of Broadcast Regulation in the Twentieth Century* (Jefferson, NC: McFarland and Co., 2000), 121–122; "Drunken Sailors on the Air," *Independent* 117 (1926): 58; *To Regulate Radio Communication: Hearings Before the Committee on the Merchant Marine and Fisheries, House of Representatives, Sixty-Eighth Congress, First Session, on H.R. 7357* (Washington, DC: Government Printing Office, 1924), 36.

16. Robert W. McChesney, "Free Speech and Democracy! Louis G. Caldwell, the American Bar Association and the Debate Over the Free Speech Implications of Broadcast Regulation, 1928–1938," *American Journal of Legal History* 35 (1981): 365; Morris L. Ernst, "Who Shall Control the Air?" *Nation,* 21 Apr. 1926, 443; *New York Times,* 31 Mar. 1927, 16.

17. Thomas W. Hazlett, "The Rationality of U.S. Regulation of the Broadcast Spectrum," *Journal of Law & Economics* 33 (1990): 133–175; Charlotte Twight, "What Congressmen Knew and When They Knew It: Further Evidence on the Origins of U.S. Broadcasting Regulation," *Public Choice* 75 (1998): 247–276; Laurence F. Schmeckebier, *The Federal Radio Commission: Its History, Activities, and Organization* (Washington, DC: Brookings Institution, 1932), 55.

18. 44 Stat. 1162 (1927).

19. "Proceedings: Fifth Annual Convention of the National Association of Broadcasters" (Sept. 1927), Herbert Hoover Papers, Commerce Period, box 491, HHL; Benson Pratt to Walter Newton, 16 July 1929, Herbert Hoover Papers, Presidential Period, box 151, HHL.

20. Chicago Federation of Labor to "Dear Senator," 5 Jan. 1929, Herbert Hoover Papers, Presidential Period, box 151, HHL; Robert W. McChesney, "The Battle for the U.S. Airwaves, 1928–1935," *Journal of Communication* 40(4) (1990): 29–57.

21. *White v. Federal Radio Commission,* 29 F.2d 113, 114–115 (N.D. Ill. 1928); *United States v. American Bond & Mortgage Co.,* 31 F.2d 448, 456 (N.D. Ill. 1929); Carl Zollman, "Radio Act of 1927," *Marquette Law Review* 11 (1927): 124–125; "Federal Control of Radio Broadcasting," *Yale Law Journal* 39 (1929): 250–253; Richard D. Sturtevant, "The Law of Radio Broadcasting," *Dakota Law Review* 3 (1930): 72–74; Erik Barnouw, *A Tower in Babel: A History of Broadcasting in the United States* (New York: Oxford University Press, 1966): 1:174–175; *Radio Control: Hearings Before the Committee on Interstate Commerce, United States Senate, Sixty-*

Ninth Congress, First Session, on S. 1 and S. 1754 (Washington, DC: Government Printing Office, 1926), 39; Hugh G. J. Aitken, "Allocating the Spectrum: The Origins of Radio Regulation," *Technology and Culture* 35 (1994): 709; *Radio Control,* 127.

22. *Radio Control,* 88; *To Regulate Radio Communication: Hearings Before the Committee on the Merchant Marine and Fisheries, House of Representatives, Sixty-Ninth Congress, First Session, on H.R. 5589* (Washington, DC: Government Printing Office, 1926), 207; S. Rep. No. 772, 69th Cong., 1st Sess. (1926), 4; *Radio Control,* 167, 160.

23. *New York Times,* 24 July 1929, 29; Hearing Before the Federal Radio Commission, *In re Boston Broadcasting Co.* (27 Apr. 1931), RG 173, A1/6, box 3, docket 1157, 192, NA; Harry P. Warner, "Transfers of Broadcasting Licenses Under the Communications Act of 1934," *Boston University Law Review* 21 (1941): 601.

24. Warner, "Transfers," 607.

25. Robert Sears McMahon, *Federal Regulation of the Radio and Television Broadcast Industry in the United States 1927–1959* (New York: Arno Press, 1979), 267–285; Paul M. Segal and Harry P. Warner, " 'Ownership' of Broadcasting 'Frequencies': A Review," *Rocky Mountain Law Review* 19 (1947): 111–122.

26. Leo Herzel, " 'Public Interest' and the Market in Color Television Regulation," *University of Chicago Law Review* 18 (1951): 802–816; Dallas W. Smythe, "Facing Facts About the Broadcast Business," *University of Chicago Law Review* 20 (1952): 96–105; Leo Herzel, "Rejoinder," *University of Chicago Law Review* 20 (1952): 106–107.

27. R. H. Coase, "The Federal Communications Commission," *Journal of Law & Economics* 2 (1959): 1–40.

28. R. H. Coase, "Comment on Thomas W. Hazlett: Assigning Property Rights to Radio Spectrum Users: Why Did FCC License Auctions Take 67 Years?" *Journal of Law & Economics* 41 (1998): 577–580. The RAND report was eventually published as Ronald Coase, William H. Meckling, and Jora Minasian, *Problems of Frequency Allocation* (Santa Monica, CA: RAND, 1995) (written 1963).

29. Thomas W. Hazlett, "Assigning Property Rights to Radio Spectrum Users: Why Did FCC License Auctions Take 67 Years?" *Journal of Law & Economics* 41 (1998): 529–575; Krystilyn Corbett, "The Rise of Private Property Rights in the Broadcast Spectrum," *Duke Law Journal* 46 (1996): 611–650.

30. Harvey J. Levin, "Regulatory Efficiency, Reform and the FCC," *Georgetown Law Journal* 50 (1961): 1–45; Arthur S. De Vany et al., "A Property System for Market Allocation of the Electromagnetic Spectrum: A Legal-Economic-Engineering Study," *Stanford Law Review* 21 (1969): 1499–1561; Jora R. Minasian, "Property Rights in Radiation: An Alternative Approach to Radio Frequency Allocation," *Journal of Law & Economics* 18 (1975): 221–272; Milton

Friedman, "How to Free TV," *Newsweek*, 1 Dec. 1969, 82; George P. Schultz, "Memorandum for the President," 31 Aug. 1970, Nixon Presidential Materials, White House Central Files, UT 1–1, box 16, NA; John D. Ehrlichman to Peter Flanigan, 2 Dec. 1970, Nixon Presidential Materials, White House Central Files, UT 1–1, box 16, NA; Tod Hullin to Peter Flanigan, 4 Dec. 1970, Nixon Presidential Materials, White House Central Files, UT 1–1, box 16, National Archives; Jon Rose to Clay T. Whitehead, 29 Jan. 1971, Nixon Presidential Materials, UT 1–1, box 16, NA; Clay T. Whitehead to John Ehrlichman, 8 Feb. 1971, Nixon Presidential Materials, White House Central Files, FG 118, box 1, folder 7, NA.

31. Howard A. Shelanski and Peter W. Huber, "Administrative Creation of Property Rights to Radio Spectrum," *Journal of Law & Economics* 41 (1998): 581–607; Clay T. Whitehead to Dean Burch, 17 Aug. 1973, Nixon Presidential Materials, White House Central Files, UT 1–1, box 17, NA.

32. Auction results are summarized at http://wireless.fcc.gov/auctions.

33. *Spectrum Management: Auctions* (11 May 2005), Congressional Research Service, Order Code RL31764; Eli Noam, "Spectrum Auctions: Yesterday's Heresy, Today's Orthodoxy, Tomorrow's Anachronism," *Journal of Law & Economics* 41 (1988): 765–790.

34. Thomas W. Hazlett, "Optimal Abolition of FCC Spectrum Allocation," *Journal of Economic Perspectives* 22 (2008): 103–128.

11. The New Property

1. John Taylor, *An Inquiry into the Principles and Tendency of Certain Public Measures* (Philadelphia: T. Dobson, 1794), 56–57.

2. Karen M. Tani, "*Flemming v. Nestor:* Anticommunism, the Welfare State, and the Making of 'New Property,'" *Law and History Review* 26 (2008): 379–414.

3. *Nestor v. Folsom,* 169 F. Supp. 922, 934 (D.D.C. 1959).

4. *Flemming v. Nestor,* 363 U.S. 603, 610, 624 (1960); Conference notes, *Flemming v. Nestor,* William O. Douglas Papers, box 1223, LC.

5. *Cafeteria & Restaurant Workers Union v. McElroy,* 367 U.S. 886, 896 (1961).

6. Lawrence M. Friedman, *Total Justice* (New York: Russell Sage Foundation, 1985).

7. Henry Paul Monaghan, "Of 'Liberty' and 'Property,'" *Cornell Law Review* 62 (1977): 409; *Flemming,* 610; *Slochower v. Board of Education,* 350 U.S. 551 (1956).

8. Charles Reich, *The Sorcerer of Bolinas Reef* (New York: Random House, 1976); Roger D. Citron, "Charles Reich's Journey from the *Yale Law Journal* to the *New York Times* Best-Seller List: The Personal History of *The Greening of America,*" *New York Law School Law Review* 52 (2007–2008): 387–416.

9. Charles A. Reich, "The New Property after 25 Years," *University of San Francisco Law Review* 24 (1990): 236.

10. Charles A. Reich, "The New Property," *Yale Law Journal* 73 (1964): 737, 768, 770, 783.

11. Gregory S. Alexander, *Commodity & Propriety: Competing Visions of Property in American Legal Thought 1776–1970* (Chicago: University of Chicago Press, 1997), 368–377; Joel F. Handler, "Controlling Official Behavior in Welfare Administration," *California Law Review* 54 (1966): 483.

12. Fred R. Shapiro, "The Most-Cited Law Review Articles Revisited," *Chicago-Kent Law Review* 71 (1996): 767; Susan B. Carter et al., eds., *Historical Statistics of the United States, Millennial Edition On Line* (New York: Cambridge University Press, 2006), tables Bf188, Aa6, Ca10; Felicia Kornbluh, *The Battle for Welfare Rights: Politics and Poverty in Modern America* (Philadelphia: University of Pennsylvania Press, 2007).

13. Earl Johnson, Jr., *Justice and Reform: The Formative Years of the OEO Legal Services Program* (New York: Russell Sage Foundation, 1974), 6, 188; Martha F. Davis, *Brutal Need: Lawyers and the Welfare Rights Movement, 1960–1973* (New Haven: Yale University Press, 1993), 86; Charles R. Epp, *The Rights Revolution: Lawyers, Activists, and Supreme Courts in Comparative Perspective* (Chicago: University of Chicago Press, 1998); Susan E. Lawrence, *The Poor in Court: The Legal Services Program and Supreme Court Decision Making* (Princeton: Princeton University Press, 1990).

14. Davis, *Brutal Need*, 27–39, 86.

15. Plaintiffs' stories are taken from the appendix to Brief for Appellees, *Goldberg v. Kelly*, 397 U.S. 254 (1970).

16. *Kelly v. Wyman*, 294 F. Supp. 893, 898 (S.D.N.Y. 1968); *Goldberg v. Kelly*, 397 U.S. 254, 261–262 (1970); Brief for Appellees, 7, *Wheeler v. Montgomery*, 397 U.S. 280 (1970); Brief for the United States as Amicus Curiae, 19–20, *Wheeler v. Montgomery*, 397 U.S. 280 (1970); Brief for Appellees, 25n25, *Goldberg v. Kelly*, 397 U.S. 254 (1970); Brief for Appellants, *Wheeler v. Montgomery*, 397 U.S. 280 (1970); Oral Argument Transcript, 12, *Wheeler v. Montgomery*, 397 U.S. 280 (1970).

17. W. Taylor Reveley III, Richard M. Cooper, and Douglas A. Poe, "Opinions of William J. Brennan, Jr.: October Term 1969," 1–2, William J. Brennan, Jr., Papers, box II:6, folder 12, LC; William J. Brennan, Jr., "Reason, Passion, and 'The Progress of the Law,'" *Cardozo Law Review* 10 (1988): 20–22.

18. *Goldberg v. Kelly*, 397 U.S. 254, 262 and n8 (1970) (internal quotation marks omitted). The quotation was from a short article Reich wrote a year after "The New Property" that focused more sharply on welfare, "Individual Rights and Social Welfare: The Emerging Legal Issues," *Yale Law Journal* 74 (1965): 1245–1257. Brennan also cited "The New Property."

19. Hugo L. Black and Elizabeth Black, *Mr. Justice and Mrs. Black* (New York: Random House, 1986), 234; "2/20 Conference," undated and unsigned memorandum (apparently by one of Justice Brennan's law clerks), William J. Brennan, Jr., Papers, box I:209, folder 5, LC; *Goldberg*, 275, 279 (Black, J., dissenting).

20. *New York Times,* 24 Mar. 1970, 23, 81.

21. Letter and unidentified newspaper clippings from William J. Brennan, Jr., Papers, box I:209, folder 2, LC.

22. *New York Times,* 14 Aug. 1972, 1; 11 May 1990, B7.

23. William Van Alstyne, "Cracks in 'The New Property': Adjudicative Due Process in the Administrative State," *Cornell Law Review* 62 (1977): 456.

24. *Perry v. Sindermann,* 408 U.S. 593 (1972); *Board of Regents of State Colleges v. Roth,* 408 U.S. 564 (1972).

25. Potter Stewart, "Memorandum to the Conference" (21 June 1972), William J. Brennan, Jr., Papers, box I:260, folder 1, LC.

26. *Roth,* 588–589 (Marshall, J., dissenting); Conference notes, *Board of Regents v. Roth,* William O. Douglas papers, box 1562, LC; Warren Burger, "Memorandum to the Conference" (21 June 1972), William J. Brennan, Jr., Papers, Box I:260, folder 1, LC.

27. *Roth,* 408 U.S. at 577; *Perry,* 408 U.S. at 599–600. Strictly speaking, Sindermann only *alleged* the informal practice of permanent tenure, but because the trial court had granted the defendants' motion for summary judgment, that was enough.

28. *Arnett v. Kennedy,* 416 U.S. 134, 153–154 (1974); *Cleveland Board of Education v. Loudermill,* 470 U.S. 532, 541 (1985).

29. *Bell v. Burson,* 402 U.S. 535 (1971); *Barry v. Barchi,* 443 U.S. 55 (1979); *Memphis Light, Gas and Water Division v. Craft,* 436 U.S. 1 (1978); *Goss v. Lopez,* 419 U.S. 565 (1975); *Bishop v. Wood,* 426 U.S. 341 (1976); *Logan v. Zimmerman Brush Company,* 455 U.S. 422 (1982); *Town of Castle Rock v. Gonzales,* 545 U.S. 748 (2005); *Mathews v. Eldridge,* 424 U.S. 319 (1976).

30. Owen Fiss, *The Law as It Could Be* (New York: New York University Press, 2003), 220; Charles A. Reich, "Property Law and the New Economic Order: A Betrayal of Middle Americans and the Poor," *Chicago-Kent Law Review* 71 (1996): 819; Sylvia A. Law, "Some Reflections on *Goldberg v. Kelly* at Twenty Years," *Brooklyn Law Review* 56 (1990): 805, 828–829.

31. *New York Times,* 26 Nov. 1995, BR7.

32. Jerry L. Mashaw, "The Management Side of Due Process: Some Theoretical and Litigation Notes on the Assurance of Accuracy, Fairness, and Timeliness in the Adjudication of Social Welfare Claims," *Cornell Law Review* 59 (1974): 811–815; William H. Simon, "Legality, Bureaucracy, and Class in the Welfare System," *Yale Law Journal* 92 (1983): 1220–1221.

12. Owning Life

1. Michael Sappol, *A Traffic of Dead Bodies: Anatomy and Embodied Social Identity in Nineteenth-Century America* (Princeton: Princeton University Press, 2002).

2. *Griffith v. Charlotte, Columbia & Augusta R.R. Co.*, 23 S.C. 25, 39–40 (1885); Francis L. Wellman, "Law of Burial," *American Law Review* 14 (1880): 59–60; Marshall D. Ewell, "Recent English Decisions," *American Law Register* 30 (1882): 512; John F. Baker, "Legal Custodian of Deceased Bodies—Who Is?" *Albany Law Journal* 10 (1874): 71; Francis King Carey, "The Disposition of the Body After Death," *American Law Review* 19 (1885): 264–265; "Property in Human Bodies," *Albany Law Journal* 4 (1871): 57; *Bogert v. City of Indianapolis*, 13 Ind. 120, 123 (1859).

3. "The Ownership of a Corpse Before Burial," *Central Law Journal* 10 (1880): 327; *Griffith*, 38.

4. John Howard Corwin, *Burial Law* (New York: Diossy and Co., 1889), 4; *Larson v. Chase*, 50 N.W. 238, 239 (Minn. 1891).

5. *Pierce v. Proprietors of Swan Point Cemetery*, 10 R.I. 227, 238 (1872); *Louisville & Nashville Railroad Co. v. Wilson*, 51 S.E. 24, 26–27 (Ga. 1905).

6. W. C. Rodgers, "Property Rights in Human Bodies," *Central Law Journal* 73 (1911): 39–44.

7. "Human Hair—A Trade and its Tricks," *Phrenological Journal* 56 (1873): 393–395; "The Trade in Locks," *London Society* 15 (1869): 547–552; Samuel Smiles, *Self-Help* (London: John Murray, 1876), 33; "Human Hair," 394; *Law Times*, 22 Jan. 1875, 52; *New York Times*, 27 Mar. 1904, 12; Louisa M. Alcott, *Little Women* (Cambridge: University Press, 1880), 201–203; Victor Hugo, *Les Misérables* (New York: George Routledge and Sons, 1893), 236; O. Henry, "The Gift of the Magi," in *The Four Million* (New York: Doubleday, Page and Co., 1909), 16–25.

8. *Los Angeles Times*, 17 Aug. 1910, II9; *New York Times*, 6 Oct. 1907, 10.

9. Janet Golden, *A Social History of Wet Nursing in America: From Breast to Bottle* (Cambridge: Cambridge University Press, 1996), 179–200, 121–127.

10. Susan E. Lederer, *Flesh and Blood: Organ Transplantation and Blood Transfusion in Twentieth-Century America* (New York: Oxford University Press, 2008), 68–106; *New York Times*, 27 Jan. 1931, 18; 15 Sept. 1938, 27; *Los Angeles Times*, 10 Jan. 1927, A1; Richard M. Titmuss, *The Gift Relationship: From Human Blood to Social Policy* (London: George Allen and Unwin, 1970), 94.

11. *Los Angeles Times*, 13 Aug. 1911, III27; 12 Sept. 1926, B11; Charles V. Nemo, "I Sell Blood," *American Mercury* 31 (1934): 194.

12. *Perlmutter v. Beth David Hospital*, 123 N.E.2d 792, 794, 797–798 (N.Y. 1954); *Green v. Commissioner of Internal Revenue*, 74 T.C. 1229, 1233–1234 (1980).

13. Cynthia R. Daniels and Janet Golden, "Procreative Compounds: Popular Eugenics, Artificial Insemination and the Rise of the American Sperm Banking Industry," *Journal of Social History* 38 (2004): 5–27; "Proxy Fathers," *Time*, 26 Sept. 1938; *New York Times*, 18 Aug. 1971, 19; *Hecht v. Superior Court*, 16 Cal. App. 4th 836, 846 (1993); *Hecht v. Superior Court*, 50 Cal. App. 4th 1289, 1295–1296 (1996).

14. Debora L. Spar, *The Baby Business: How Money, Science, and Politics Drive the Commerce of Conception* (Boston: Harvard Business School Press, 2006), 41–46; *New York Times*, 8 Jan. 1996, 10; *York v. York*, 717 F. Supp. 421 (E.D. Va. 1989); *Davis v. Davis*, 842 S.W.2d 588, 597 (Tenn. 1992).

15. Keith J. Mueller, "The National Organ Transplant Act of 1984: Congressional Response to Changing Biotechnology," *Policy Studies Review* 8 (1989): 346–356.

16. Cécile Fabre, *Whose Body Is It Anyway? Justice and the Integrity of the Person* (Oxford: Clarendon Press, 2006), 135–149; Stephen R. Munzer, "Human Dignity and Property Rights in Body Parts," in J. W. Harris, ed., *Property Problems from Genes to Pension Funds* (London: Kluwer Law International, 1997), 25–38; Thomas H. Murray, "On the Human Body as Property: The Meaning of Embodiment, Markets, and the Meaning of Strangers," *University of Michigan Journal of Law Reform* 20 (1987): 1088; *National Organ Transplant Act: Hearings Before the Subcommittee on Health of the Committee on Ways and Means, House of Representatives*, 98th Cong., 2nd Sess. (1984), 26; Donald Joralemon and Phil Cox, "Body Values: The Case Against Compensating for Transplant Organs," *Hastings Center Report* 33(1) (2003): 27–33.

17. *Procurement and Allocation of Human Organs for Transplantation: Hearings Before the Subcommittee on Investigations and Oversight of the Committee on Science and Technology, U.S. House of Representatives*, 98th Cong., 1st Sess. (1983), 42; David W. Meyers, *The Human Body and the Law*, 2nd ed. (Stanford, CA: Stanford University Press, 1990), 207.

18. Julia D. Mahoney, "The Market for Human Tissue," *Virginia Law Review* 86 (2000): 163–223; Mark J. Cherry, *Kidney for Sale by Owner: Human Organs, Transplantation, and the Market* (Washington, DC: Georgetown University Press, 2005); Annie Cheney, *Body Brokers: Inside America's Underground Trade in Human Remains* (New York: Broadway Books, 2006); Renée C. Fox and Judith P. Swazey, *Spare Parts: Organ Replacement in American Society* (New York: Oxford University Press, 1992), 43–72.

19. *New York Times*, 16 Apr. 2006, E38; *Moore v. Regents of the University of California*, 793 P.2d 479 (Cal. 1990).

20. *Newman v. Sathyavaglswaran*, 287 F.3d 786, 796 (9th Cir. 2002).

21. Jack Ralph Kloppenburg, Jr., *First the Seed: The Political Economy of Plant Biotechnology*, 2nd ed. (Madison: University of Wisconsin Press, 2004); Glenn E. Bugos, "Intellectual Property Protection in the American Chicken-Breeding Industry," *Business History Review* 66 (1992): 127–168.

22. L. H. Bailey, *Annals of Horticulture in North America for the Year 1890* (New York: Rural Publishing Co., 1891), 112–129; "Protection to the Originator of Varieties," *American Garden* 11 (1890): 481; *Reports of the Missouri State Horticultural Society, for the Years 1880 and 1881* (Jefferson City: Tribune Printing Co., 1881), 135.

23. "Protection for the Originators of New Plants," *Journal of Horticulture* 21 (1890): 279; David Fairchild, "The Fascination of Making a Plant Hybrid," *Journal of Heredity* 18 (1927): 62; S. Folsom, "Deterioration of Varieties," *Seventh Annual Report of the Secretary of the State Pomological Society of Michigan* (Lansing: W. S. George and Co., 1878), 375.

24. W. M. Hays, "Distributing Valuable New Varieties and Breeds," *American Breeders' Association* 1 (1905): 60; Joseph Rossman, "Plant Patents," *Journal of the Patent Office Society* 13 (1931): 10.

25. "Our New Fruits," *Magazine of Horticulture* 34 (1868): 293; Jacob Stauffer, "The Plant Patent," *Gardener's Monthly* 17 (1875): 12; "Those Plant Patents," *Gardener's Monthly* 22 (1880): 62.

26. *Congressional Record* 72 (1930): 7201; Cary Fowler, "The Plant Patent Act of 1930: A Sociological History of Its Creation," *Journal of the Patent and Trademark Office Society* 82 (2000): 621–644; Robert S. Allyn, *The First Plant Patents* (Brooklyn: Educational Foundations, Inc., 1934), 84–85.

27. Glenn E. Bugos and Daniel J. Kevles, "Plants as Intellectual Property: American Practice, Law, and Policy in World Context," *Osiris* 7 (1992): 88–95; Cary Fowler, *Unnatural Selection: Technology, Politics, and Plant Evolution* (Yverdon, Switzerland: Gordon and Breach, 1994), 99–123; *Patent Law Revision: Hearings Before the Subcommittee on Patents, Trademarks, and Copyrights of the Committee on the Judiciary, United States Senate*, 90th Cong., 2nd Sess. (1968), 643.

28. A. M. Chakrabarty, "Patenting of Life-Forms: From a Concept to Reality," in David Magnus et al., eds., *Who Owns Life?* (Amherst, NY: Prometheus Books, 2002), 18–20.

29. Brief for the Petitioner, 1, 27, Brief on Behalf of the Peoples Business Commission, 27–28, 30, *Diamond v. Chakrabarty*, 447 U.S. 303 (1980).

30. Bench memorandum, *Diamond v. Chakrabarty*, 41–42, Harry Blackmun papers, box 312, folder 7, LC.

31. *Diamond v. Chakrabarty*, 447 U.S. 303, 309 (1980).

32. *Ex parte Hibberd*, 227 U.S.P.Q. 443 (1985); *Ex parte Allen*, 2 U.S.P.Q.2d 1425 (1987); "Animals—Patentability," *Official Gazette of the U.S. Patent and Trademark Office* 1077 (1987): 24; Daniel J. Kevles, "Of Mice & Money: The Story of the World's First Animal Patent," *Daedalus* 131 (2002): 78–88.

33. Susan Wright, *Molecular Politics: Developing American and British Regulatory Policy for Genetic Engineering, 1972–1982* (Chicago: University of Chicago Press, 1994), 78–109; Leon R. Kass, "Patenting Life," *Journal of the Patent Office Society* 63 (1981): 596–597; *Transgenic Animal Patent Reform Act of 1989: Hearings Before the Subcommittee on Courts, Intellectual Property, and the Administration of Justice of the Committee on the Judiciary, House of Representatives*, 101st Cong., 1st Sess. (1989).

34. *Parke-Davis & Co. v. H. K. Mulford & Co.*, 189 F. 95 (C.C.S.D.N.Y. 1911); Gary Stix, "Owning the Stuff of Life," *Scientific American*, Feb. 2006, 76–83;

Michael Crowley, "Outrageous! They Own Your Body," *Reader's Digest,* Aug. 2006; Michael Crichton, "Patenting Life," *New York Times,* 13 Feb. 2007; Michael A. Heller and Rebecca S. Eisenberg, "Can Patents Deter Innovation? The Anticommons in Biomedical Research," *Science* 280 (1998): 698–701.

35. Michael F. Brown, *Who Owns Native Culture?* (Cambridge: Harvard University Press, 2003), 95–143; Ikechi Mgbeoji, *Global Biopiracy: Patents, Plants, and Indigenous Knowledge* (Vancouver: UBC Press, 2006).

13. Property Resurgent

1. Roger J. Marzulla, "Opening Remarks," *Santa Clara Law Review* 46 (2006): 781.

2. Richard J. Lazarus, *The Making of Environmental Law* (Chicago: University of Chicago Press, 2004), 47–97.

3. Errol Meidinger, "On Explaining the Development of 'Emissions Trading' in U.S. Air Pollution Regulation," *Law & Policy* 7 (1985): 447–479; Jan-Peter Voß, "Innovation Processes in Governance: The Development of 'Emissions Trading' as a New Policy Instrument," *Science and Public Policy* 34 (2007): 329–343.

4. Richard McKeon, ed., *The Basic Works of Aristotle* (New York: Random House, 1941), 1148 (*Politics* II:3); Garrett Hardin, "The Tragedy of the Commons," *Science* 162 (1968): 1245.

5. H. Scott Gordon, "The Economic Theory of a Common-Property Resource: The Fishery," *Journal of Political Economy* 62 (1954): 135.

6. A. C. Pigou, *The Economics of Welfare* (London: Macmillan, 1920), 159–162, 168.

7. R. H. Coase, "The Problem of Social Cost," *Journal of Law and Economics* 3 (1960): 1–44.

8. Thomas D. Crocker, "The Structuring of Atmospheric Pollution Control Systems," in Harold Wolozin, ed., *The Economics of Air Pollution* (New York: W. W. Norton, 1966), 83; J. H. Dales, *Pollution, Property & Prices* (Toronto: University of Toronto Press, 1968), 93–100; W. David Montgomery, "Markets in Licenses and Efficient Pollution Control Programs," *Journal of Economic Theory* 5 (1972): 395–418.

9. *Economic Report of the President* (Washington, DC: Government Printing Office, 1971), 118.

10. Robert W. Hahn, "Economic Prescriptions for Environmental Problems: How the Patient Followed the Doctor's Orders," *Journal of Economic Perspectives* 3 (1989): 95–114; T. H. Tietenberg, *Emissions Trading: An Exercise in Reforming Pollution Policy* (Washington, DC: Resources for the Future, 1985), 7–10; Richard Schmalensee et al., "An Interim Evaluation of Sulfur Dioxide Emissions Trading," *Journal of Economic Perspectives* 12 (1998): 53–68; A. Denny Ell-

erman, "Are Cap-and-Trade Programs More Environmentally Effective than Conventional Regulation?" in Jody Freeman and Charles D. Kolstad, eds., *Moving to Markets in Environmental Regulation: Lessons from Twenty Years of Experience* (Oxford: Oxford University Press, 2007), 48–62; Jim Skea, "Flexibility, Emissions Trading and the Kyoto Protocol," in Steve Sorrell and Jim Skea, eds., *Pollution for Sale: Emissions Trading and Joint Implementation* (Cheltenham, U.K.: Edward Elgar, 1999), 354–379.

11. Todd Gitlin, "Buying the Right to Pollute? What's Next?" *New York Times,* 28 July 1989; Steven Kelman, *What Price Incentives? Economists and the Environment* (Boston: Auburn House, 1981), 27–28.

12. Samuel P. Hays, *A History of Environmental Politics Since 1945* (Pittsburgh: University of Pittsburgh Press, 2000), 163–165.

13. U.S. Environmental Protection Agency, *Tools of the Trade: A Guide to Designing and Operating a Cap and Trade Program for Pollution Control* (Washington, DC: U.S. Environmental Protection Agency, 2003), 3–23.

14. Kurt Stephenson, Patricia Norris, and Leonard Shabman, "Watershed-Based Effluent Trading: The Nonpoint Source Challenge," *Contemporary Economic Policy* 16 (1998): 412–421; Daniel Huppert and Gunnar Knapp, "Technology and Property Rights in Fisheries Management," in Terry L. Anderson and Peter J. Hill, eds., *The Technology of Property Rights* (Lanham, MD: Rowman and Littlefield, 2001), 79–100; Robert J. Smith, "Resolving the Tragedy of the Commons by Creating Private Property Rights in Wildlife," *Cato Journal* 1 (1981): 439–468; Terry L. Anderson and Donald R. Leal, *Free Market Environmentalism* (Boulder, CO: Westview Press, 1991), 165.

15. Joseph L. Sax, "Why America Has a Property Rights Movement," *University of Illinois Law Review* 2005 (2005): 513–520; Nancie G. Marzulla, "The Property Rights Movement: How It Began and Where It Is Headed," in Bruce Yandle, ed., *Land Rights: The 1990s' Property Rights Rebellion* (Lanham, MD: Rowman and Littlefield, 1995), 1–30; William French Smith, *Law and Justice in the Reagan Administration: The Memoirs of an Attorney General* (Stanford, CA: Hoover Institution Press, 1991), 46–47; James G. Watt, "Commentary," *Bulletin of the Ecological Society of America* 62 (1981): 235; "The Legacy of James Watt," *Time,* 24 Oct. 1983.

16. *Major Policy Statements of the Attorney General: Edwin Meese III, 1985–1988* (Washington, DC: U.S. Department of Justice, 1989), 141; Douglas W. Kmiec, *The Attorney General's Lawyer: Inside the Meese Justice Department* (New York: Praeger, 1992), 118–126; Charles Fried, *Order and Law: Arguing the Reagan Revolution—A Firsthand Account* (New York: Simon and Schuster, 1991), 183.

17. Brief for the United States, *Nollan v. California Coastal Commission,* 483 U.S. 825 (1987); Brief for the United States, *Lucas v. South Carolina Coastal Council,* 505 U.S. 1003 (1992).

18. *Nomination of Sandra Day O'Connor* (Washington, DC: Government Printing Office, 1982); *Nomination of Judge Antonin Scalia* (Washington, DC:

Government Printing Office, 1987); *Nomination of Anthony M. Kennedy to Be Associate Justice of the Supreme Court of the United States* (Washington, DC: Government Printing Office, 1989); *Nomination of David H. Souter to be Associate Justice of the Supreme Court of the United States* (Washington, DC: Government Printing Office, 1991); Antonin Scalia, "Economic Affairs as Human Affairs," *Cato Journal* 4 (1985): 704.

19. Scott Douglas Gerber, *First Principles: The Jurisprudence of Clarence Thomas* (New York: New York University Press, 1999), 54; *Nomination of Judge Clarence Thomas to be Associate Justice of the Supreme Court of the United States* (Washington, DC: Government Printing Office, 1993), 111.

20. Steven M. Teles, *The Rise of the Conservative Legal Movement: The Battle for Control of the Law* (Princeton: Princeton University Press, 2008), 87, 241–243; Ann Southworth, *Lawyers of the Right: Professionalizing the Conservative Coalition* (Chicago: University of Chicago Press, 2008), 72–73.

21. *Pennsylvania Coal v. Mahon*, 260 U.S. 393 (1922); *Penn Central Transportation Co. v. New York City*, 438 U.S. 104 (1978).

22. *Loretto v. Teleprompter Manhattan CATV Corp.*, 458 U.S. 419 (1982).

23. *Nollan v. California Coastal Commission*, 483 U.S. 825, 837 (1987).

24. *First English Evangelical Lutheran Church of Glendale v. County of Los Angeles*, 482 U.S. 304 (1987); *Hodel v. Irving*, 481 U.S. 704 (1987); Ronald Reagan, "Remarks Announcing America's Economic Bill of Rights" (3 July 1987), www .reagan.utexas.edu/archives/speeches/1987/070387a.htm.

25. *Lucas v. South Carolina Coastal Council*, 505 U.S. 1003 (1992).

26. Richard J. Lazarus, "The Measure of a Justice: Justice Scalia and the Faltering of the Property Rights Movement Within the Supreme Court," *Hastings Law Journal* 57 (2006): 759–825.

27. *Federal Register* 53 (1988): 8859.

28. Mark W. Cordes, "Leapfrogging the Constitution: The Rise of State Takings Legislation," *Ecology Law Quarterly* 24 (1997): 187–242.

29. *International Paper Co. v. United States*, 282 U.S. 399, 408 (1931).

30. *Berman v. Parker*, 348 U.S. 26, 33–34 (1954); *Hawaii Housing Authority v. Midkiff*, 467 U.S. 229, 244 (1984).

31. *Midkiff*, 241.

32. Dana Berliner, *Public Power, Private Gain: A Five-Year, State-by-State Report Examining the Abuse of Eminent Domain* (Washington, DC: Institute for Justice, 2003), 4.

33. *Kelo v. City of New London*, 545 U.S. 469, 503 (2005).

34. Ilya Somin, "The Limits of Backlash: Assessing the Political Response to *Kelo*," *Minnesota Law Review* 93 (2009): 2100–2178.

14. The End of Property?

1. The quotation originated as conference remarks in 1984. It appears in Stewart Brand, *The Media Lab: Inventing the Future at MIT* (New York: Penguin Books, 1988), 202.

2. Dorothy E. Denning, "Concerning Hackers Who Break into Computer Systems," *Proceedings of the 13th National Computer Security Conference* (1990), http://www.cs.georgetown.edu/~denning/hackers/Hackers-NCSC.txt; John Perry Barlow, "The Next Economy of Ideas," *Wired,* Oct. 2000.

3. Robert J. Kost, "The End of Copyright," in Sigrid G. Harriman, ed., *Intellectual Property Rights in an Electronic Age* (Washington, DC: Library of Congress, 1987), 22; Raymond T. Nimmer and Patricia Ann Krauthaus, "Copyright on the Information Superhighway: Requiem for a Middleweight," *Stanford Law and Policy Review* 6 (1994): 25.

4. Mark Katz, *Capturing Sound: How Technology Has Changed Music* (Berkeley: University of California Press, 2004), 153, 137; http://www.the-breaks .com/perl/full.pl?genre=1&page=B; Eric Steuer, "The Remix Masters," *Wired,* Nov. 2004.

5. *Los Angeles Times,* 6 Aug. 1989, 61.

6. *New York Times,* 21 Apr. 1992, C13.

7. "Internet Encyclopaedias Go Head to Head," *Nature* 438 (2005): 900–901.

8. Yochai Benkler, *The Wealth of Networks: How Social Production Transforms Markets and Freedom* (New Haven: Yale University Press, 2006), 62, 63.

9. "Poll: Young Say File Sharing OK," http://www.cbsnews.com/stories/ 2003/09/18/opinion/polls/main573990.shtml.

10. John Perry Barlow, "A Declaration of the Independence of Cyberspace," http://homes.eff.org/~barlow/Declaration-Final.html; John Perry Barlow, "The Economy of Ideas," *Wired,* Mar. 1994; Debora J. Halbert, *Intellectual Property in the Information Age: The Politics of Expanding Ownership Rights* (Westport, CT: Quorum Books, 1999), 154–155.

11. M. Ethan Katsh, *Law in a Digital World* (New York: Oxford University Press, 1995), 218–219, 224; Ithiel de Sola Pool, *Technologies of Freedom* (Cambridge: Harvard University Press, 1983), 214.

12. Richard Stallman, *Free Software, Free Society: Selected Essays of Richard M. Stallman,* 2nd ed. (Boston: GNU Press, 2004), 47; Esther Dyson, *Release 2.0: A Design for Living in the Digital Age* (New York: Broadway Books, 1997), 139, 142.

13. Benkler, *Wealth of Networks,* 4; Kevin Kelly, *New Rules for the New Economy: 10 Radical Strategies for a Connected World* (New York: Penguin Books, 1999), 41; Robert N. Wright, "Rock 'n' Roll Heaven," *Slate,* 31 July 2000.

14. Fred Turner, *From Counterculture to Cyberculture: Stewart Brand, the Whole Earth Network, and the Rise of Digital Utopianism* (Chicago: University of Chicago Press, 2006).

15. Frank H. Easterbrook, "Cyberspace Versus Property Law?" *Texas Review of Law & Politics* 4 (1999): 112; Eugene Volokh, "Technology and the Future of Law," *Stanford Law Review* 47 (1995): 1395; *Intellectual Property and the National Information Infrastructure: The Report of the Working Group on Intellectual Property Rights* (Washington, DC: Information Infrastructure Task Force, 1995), 17; Peter Huber, "Tangled Wires," *Slate,* 19 Oct. 1996.

16. Carol M. Rose, "The Several Futures of Property: Of Cyberspace and Folk Tales, Emission Trades and Ecosystems," *Minnesota Law Review* 83 (1998): 129–182; William W. Fisher III, "Property and Contract on the Internet," *Chicago-Kent Law Review* 73 (1998): 1203–1256; Lawrence Lessig, *Code: and Other Laws of Cyberspace* (New York: Basic Books, 1999), 122–141.

17. *Grand Upright Music Limited v. Warner Brothers Records, Inc.,* 780 F. Supp. 182 (S.D.N.Y. 1991).

18. *Bridgeport Music, Inc. v. Dimension Films,* 410 F.3d 792 (6th Cir. 2005); Said Vaidhyanathan, *Copyrights and Copywrongs: The Rise of Intellectual Property and How It Threatens Creativity* (New York: New York University Press, 2001), 132–145.

19. *A&M Records, Inc. v. Napster, Inc.,* 239 F.3d 1004 (9th Cir. 2001); *Sony Corporation of America v. Universal City Studios, Inc.,* 464 U.S. 417 (1984); *Metro-Goldwyn-Mayer Studios, Inc. v. Grokster, Ltd.,* 545 U.S. 913 (2005); *New York Times,* 10 Aug. 2009, A11; Jack Goldsmith and Tim Wu, *Who Controls the Internet?* (New York: Oxford University Press, 2006), 105–125.

20. *Eldred v. Ashcroft,* 537 U.S. 186 (2003); Lawrence Lessig, *Free Culture: How Big Media Uses Technology and the Law to Lock Down Culture and Control Creativity* (New York: Penguin Press, 2004), 213–246.

21. *eBay, Inc. v. Bidder's Edge, Inc.,* 100 F. Supp. 2d 1058 (N.D. Cal. 2000); *Intel Corporation v. Hamidi,* 71 P.3d 296 (Cal. 2003); *Kremen v. Cohen,* 337 F.3d 1024 (9th Cir. 2003).

22. Pamela Samuelson, "Google Book Search and the Future of Books in Cyberspace" (2010), http://ssrn.com/abstract=1535067; Pamela Samuelson, "Google Book Settlement 1.0 Is History," *Huffington Post,* 24 Sept. 2009.

23. Brand, *Media Lab,* 202.

24. Debora L. Spar, *Ruling the Waves: Cycles of Discovery, Chaos, and Wealth from the Compass to the Internet* (New York: Harcourt, 2001).

25. Cheryl I. Harris, "Whiteness as Property," *Harvard Law Review* 106 (1993): 1707–1791; Kristen A. Carpenter, Sonia K. Katyal, and Angela R. Riley, "In Defense of Property," *Yale Law Journal* 118 (2009): 1024–1125; Allen M. Parkman, "The Recognition of Human Capital as Property in Divorce Settlements," *Arkansas Law Review* 40 (1987): 439–467; Goutam U. Jois, "Marital Status as Property: Toward a New Jurisprudence for Gay Rights," *Harvard Civil Rights–Civil Liberties Law Review* 41 (2006): 509–551; William B. Gould IV, "The Idea of the Job as Property in Contemporary America: The Legal and Collective

Bargaining Framework," *Brigham Young University Law Review* 1986 (1986): 885–918; Joseph William Singer, "The Reliance Interest in Property," *Stanford Law Review* 40 (1988): 611–751; Gary L. Francione, "Animals as Property," *Animal Law* 2 (1996): i–vi.

26. Harold Demsetz, "Toward a Theory of Property Rights," *American Economic Review Papers and Proceedings* 57 (1967): 347–359.

Acknowledgments

For financial assistance, I am grateful to Mike Schill and the UCLA School of Law, the UCLA Faculty Senate, and the National Endowment for the Humanities. For help with the research, thanks to Abe Zuckerman; to June Kim, Gabe Juarez, and their colleagues at UCLA's Darling Law Library; to Lesley Schoenfeld at the Harvard Law School Library; to Steven Wheeler at the New York Stock Exchange; and to the archivists at the Herbert Hoover Presidential Library, the Library of Congress, the National Archives, the Newberry Library, and the New York Public Library. For helpful comments on early drafts of chapters, thanks to the many colleagues who attended workshops at UCLA and Tel Aviv University. And thanks to John Witt, Greg Alexander, and Joyce Seltzer for extremely valuable suggestions about the book as a whole.

Index